GUIDE TO

Photographic Collections

AT THE SMITHSONIAN INSTITUTION

Cooper-Hewitt Museum • Freer Gallery of Art
Hirshhorn Museum and Sculpture Garden
National Museum of African Art
National Museum of American Art
National Portrait Gallery • Arthur M. Sackler Gallery
Office of Horticulture

VOLUME III

Diane Vogt O'Connor

Smithsonian Institution Press

Washington and London

© 1992 by the Smithsonian Institution
All rights reserved

Library of Congress Cataloging-in-Publication Data

Smithsonian Institution
  Guide to photographic collections at the Smithsonian
Institution

  Includes indexes
  Contents: v. 1. National Museum of American History —
v. 2. National Museum of Natural History, National
Zoological Park, Smithsonian Astrophysical Observatory,
Smithsonian Tropical Research Institute — v. 3.
Cooper-Hewitt Museum, Freer Gallery of Art, Hirshhorn
Museum and Sculpture Garden, National Museum of African
Art, National Museum of American Art, National Portrait
Gallery, Arthur M. Sackler Gallery, and the Office of
Horticulture.
  1. National Museum of American History (U.S.)—
Photograph collections. I. O'Connor, Diane Vogt. II. Title
Q11.S79 1989   026′.779′074753
89-600116
ISBN 0-87474-927-1 (v. 1 : alk. paper)
ISBN 1-56098-033-8 (v. 2 : alk. paper)
ISBN 1-56098-188-1 (v. 3 : alk. paper)

British Library Cataloguing-in-Publication Data is available

Cover photo: Man Ray. "Gertrude Stein, 1874–1946, and
Jo Davidson, 1883–1952." 1922. Silver gelatin photoprint.
Curatorial Department National Portrait Gallery
Photography Collection (*PG.3*). Accession #NPG.90.35.
Copyright Gregory Browner, Man Ray Trust.

Manufactured in the United States of America
99 98 97 96 95 94 93 92   5 4 3 2 1

∞ The paper used in this publication meets the minimum
requirements of the American national Standard for
Permanence of Paper for Printed Library Materials
Z39.48-1984

Contents

FREER GALLERY OF ART

(FG) Introduction   140

Freer Gallery of Art and Arthur M. Sackler Gallery Archives   141

Acknowledgments

Many people helped with the production of this volume. First, the administrators, curators, art historians, and collections managers of the Cooper-Hewitt Museum, the Freer Gallery of Art, the Hirshhorn Museum and Sculpture Garden, the National Museum of African Art, the National Museum of American Art, the National Portrait Gallery, the Sackler Gallery of Art, and the Office of Horticulture offered assistance and advice to the project staff. Their cooperative spirit and informed assistance made this volume possible. Particular thanks are due to Maricia Battle and Joan Stahl at NMAA; David Black and Linda Dunne at CH; Chris Geary and Janet Stanley at NMAfA; Colleen Hennessey and Lily Kecskes at the FGA and ASG; Ann Shumard at NPG; and Phyllis Rosenzweig and Judith Zilczer at HMSG.

Second, the editors wish to thank the staff and management of the Smithsonian Archives, Smithsonian Institution Libraries, and the Smithsonian Institution Press, and our indexer Trudi Olivetti. SI Press staff editors Amy Pastan and Duke Johns and designer Linda McKnight merit a special thank you. Volunteer editor Anne Rollins assisted with this volume as she did with volume II of the series. Volunteer Richie McGuire assisted with preparing the index.

The hard-working project staff of the Photographic Survey Project, including editor Michael Frost, program assistant Deborah Kapper, and surveyor Joan Redding, helped survey, write, fact-check, edit, and index this volume. They deserve praise for their dedication, skills, and grace under pressure.

Finally, a special thanks to Dorothy and Joseph Vogt for offering the best possible introduction to the arts and to Hugh O'Connor for once again serving as a one-man support system.

Introduction

The *Guide to Photographic Collections at the Smithsonian Institution: The Cooper-Hewitt Museum, the Freer Gallery of Art, the Hirshhorn Museum and Sculpture Garden, the National Museum of African Art, the National Museum of American Art, the National Portrait Gallery, the Sackler Gallery of Art, and the Office of Horticulture* is the third volume of a five-part set documenting the Smithsonian's vast holdings of photographs. This volume provides a comprehensive overview of over 3.5 million photographs found in 180 photographic collections within 7 Smithsonian art bureaus and one office. Many of the collections previously were unknown outside of their own divisions.

These collections serve many purposes. They document museum artifacts, activities, exhibits, and staff. They illustrate the lives, works, and studios of artists and craftsmen from around the globe. The images represent the work of both professional and amateur photographers using a wide range of photographic processes and formats.

Scope of the *Guide*

This *Guide* focuses on still photographs, defined here as images captured by the action of radiation (usually light) on a photosensitive surface, often by means of a camera, lens, mirror, or other optical device. The term "photography" thus includes photonegatives, photoprints, phototransparencies, and direct positive processes. Architectural plans, audiotapes, drawings, graphic prints, manuscripts, motion-picture film footage, photomechanical prints, videotapes, and xerographic copies are mentioned only when they were found in collections that also contained photographs.

Both organic and assembled collections are represented in this volume. Organic collections include photographs by a single photographer or studio, or photographs created to further the work of a particular corporate entity. Assembled collections are photographs gathered from disparate sources around a central purpose or theme.

Preparation of the *Guide*

To develop the collection descriptions in this volume, the project staff visited each art bureau office. With the assistance of the art bureau staff, they identified, located, and examined all collections that contained photographs. Using a collection-level survey form based on the MARC-VM (Machine Readable Cataloging-Visual Materials) format, the project staff gathered data on access policies, copyright, location, origins, ownership, physical characteristics, subject contents, and other pertinent data for each collection.

Descriptive subject terms are taken directly from collection captions and finding aids, from art bureau style guides and reference sources (see the Subject Index for a listing), or from the Library of Congress Prints and Photographs Division subject heading list, *Topical Terms for Subject Access*. Photographers' and other creators' names were checked in a variety of name authority files listed in the introduction to the Creators Index.

During the preparation of this guide, a hierarchical authority file of photographic process and format terminology was created to facilitate consistent image identification and description. This authority file forms the basis for the Forms and Processes Index found at the end of the guide.

From the completed survey forms, a survey report was drafted for each collection. Following review by the division curators and custodians, these reports were abstracted for use in this volume. The original survey reports may be found in the respective curatorial divisions, or in a master database at the Smithsonian Institution Archives.

Organization and Use of the *Guide*

This volume describes the photographic holdings of seven art museums and one office at the Smithsonian Institution: the Arthur M. Sackler Gallery; the Cooper-Hewitt Museum; the Freer Gallery of Art; the Hirshhorn Museum and Sculpture Garden; the National Museum of African Art; the National Museum of American Art; the National Portrait Gallery; and the Office of Horticulture. Each museum or office is introduced by a brief history and an overview of its collecting interests.

Most chapters include an introduction to each curatorial division or support office, describing its research objectives and collecting policies within the overall bureau framework. Each introduction also provides policies for reference use of the collections including restrictions; access information including the address, telephone number, a contact person's name or title, and hours of operation; the number of collections; the total number of images; major subjects documented in the holdings; photographic processes represented; and other kinds of materials included, such as manuscripts and objects.

The heart of this *Guide* is a collection-level description or "entry" for each collection found within the curatorial divisions or support offices. Each collection is identified by a collection title and by an alphanumeric code assigned by the writers of the *Guide*. The code consists of a two-letter abbreviation for the bureau in which the collection may be found; for example, FG stands for the Freer Gallery of Art. The number following the two-letter code indicates the sequence of that collection within the bureau. The table of contents outlines the arrangement of divisions/offices and collection titles, and refers readers to them by this alphanumeric code.

The *Guide* is extensively indexed, providing precise access to specific photographic collections. There are three separate indexes: a Creators Index; a Forms and Processes Index; and a Subject Index. The indexer relied on the Library of Congress Prints and Photographs Division's *Topical Terms for Subject Access* and several fine arts reference books (for specific titles, please see the Subject Index) as authority files for the subject terms; the Photo Survey Project's "Draft Photographic Thesaurus" for the form and process terms; and the International Museum of Photography's *Photographers Name Authority File* and other publications (see the Creators Index for specific titles) for creator names. Terms in each index are keyed to the alphanumeric collection codes. Strategies for index searches may be found at the beginning of each index.

Collection Level Descriptions

Collection descriptions vary in length, reflecting the size, coherence, and complexity of the collections described. More diverse and eclectic collections demand longer descriptions to provide appropriate descriptive detail.

Each collection-level description is itself a complex arrangement of information organized as follows:

Collection Code.   The unique alphanumeric code assigned to this collection. For more information on this, see "Abbreviations."

Collection Name.   The full title by which the collection is known in the museum. The phrase "*A.K.A.*" (meaning "also known as") following a collection name indicates an alternative name by which staff may refer to the collection.

Dates of Photographs.   The dates used are inclusive, describing the period during which the images in the collection were produced. These dates do not describe the period during which the non-photographic materials were produced, nor do they describe the dates of other generations of images which may exist in other repositories, for example, original photonegatives in other museums. Researchers wishing to determine the dates of original negatives which were used to create copy images in Smithsonian collections should look at the dates listed in the subject description.

Collection Origins.   This section gives the name, dates, and a capsule biography of the collection creator or assembler. It explains when, by whom, and for what purpose a collection was created. If a single photographer, studio, or other corporate creator produced these materials as an organic collection, he (or it) will be identified as the collection creator.

If the collection is assembled or artificial, the collection origins field will list names of specific photographers, studios, or other creators (such as correspondents or authors) whose work is included in the collection. When "Unknown" appears in the field, it means no information exists on the collection origins, either within the division's records, or as clear internal evidence within the collection itself.

Physical Description.   The total number of photographs in the collection is given first. This number may change over time as a collection continues to grow or is weeded down. Next, all photographic processes and formats are listed. Unusual photograph sizes and support materials are noted, as are the presence of photo albums, scrapbooks, and notebooks. Other materials found with the photographs, such as archival document types or specimens, also are listed.

Subjects.   This field opens with a broad summary of the range of subject dates, geographic areas, and major subject emphases in the collection. This summary may be followed by more specific descriptions of cultural groups, genres (such as landscapes and portraits), geographic locales, individuals and their occupations or disciplines, and topical information (such as activities, animals, events, objects, and themes) represented in the collection.

Arrangement.   This section identifies the major series into which a collection may be arranged. If the series are few, they will be listed by name. If the series are many, their number and organizing principle will be identified, for example, "Into 25 series by year of creation." Suborganization within series may be noted if it aids in locating photographs (for example, "Series 2, photographic portraits, arranged chronologically by subjects' dates of birth"). When a collection consists mainly of other types of materials (non-photographic), all the series that contain photographs are indicated.

Captions. All information accompanying photographs will be described in this field, including cutlines and album labels. When similar descriptive categories are used in most captions, the categories used will be noted, for example, "With location, date, and culture group name."

Finding Aids. This includes descriptions of the registers, indexes, and other guides used by the division staff to search the collection. When a finding aid has a title, a full citation is given. When a finding aid uses standard categories of data to describe photographs, those data elements and any cross-referencing will be noted, for example, "A card catalog that lists subject, negative number, and on occasion, the source of the image."

When they are consistent, the filing rules for card catalogs are noted, for example, "The cards are filed by: 1) last name of subject; 2) negative number; and 3) object name." If several finding aids exist to a collection, they are described in sequence, for example, "1) card catalog; 2) index." Where another form of document (such as an object inventory sheet) may serve as a finding aid, it will be described here.

Some major forms of finding aids, and their definitions as used in this *Guide,* include the following:

Authority file: A list of approved names and terms to be used in describing a collection.

Card catalog: An item-level index on cards that may include cross-references and broader and narrower terms.

Container list: A box-by-box or drawer-by-drawer list of materials to be found in each container, often further divided into folder-by-folder listings.

Guide entry: A brief summary description of a collection as it would appear in a published guide to a repository's holdings or a database.

Index: An alphabetical list of terms used to identify and locate all items relating to that term. An index is often in card form, with one term used per card.

Inventory: A list organized by document types (forms of material) or occasionally by subject or creator.

List: An item-level enumeration in sequential order.

Log book: An item-level list of photographs created by a photographer as he or she works, sometimes called a "shot log." It can include an image number; date; technical information, such as light conditions, filters used, camera settings, and film used; a brief summary of the subject in the photographer's own words; and the purpose of the shot.

Register: An inventory of all collection document types, usually in a book or ledger format.

Restrictions. The last section of the collection-level entry lists any special restrictions that limit access to, or use of, a collection, for example, "For reference only. No copying allowed." Restrictions also may appear in the "Collection Origins" field, if the creator, in the process of creating the images, caused the restrictions, for example, "This copyrighted collection was created for a planned publication." Restrictions may be due to copyright status, donor wishes, preservation issues, privacy legislation concerns, patent or trademark status of the subject matter, or security concerns, for example, insurance photographs of high value items.

Abbreviations

The Guide is divided into sections by museum, then by division, department, or support office. The museums appear in alphabetical order by collection code. Each museum is assigned an abbreviation and each photograph collection is assigned a number. For example, the Freer Gallery of Art is FG; the John M. Crawford, Jr., Picture Set collection is FG-8. The following abbreviations are used in this book's alphanumeric codes.

AA	National Museum of American Art.
AF	National Museum of African Art.
CH	Cooper-Hewitt Museum of Decorative Arts and Design.
FG	Freer Gallery of Art.
HM	Hirshhorn Museum and Sculpture Garden.
HO	Office of Horticulture.
PG	National Portrait Gallery.
SG	Arthur M. Sackler Gallery of Art.

Within the body of the book, museums (as opposed to their photographic collections) are referred to by acronyms. These, as well as other abbreviations and acronyms used throughout the book, are as follows:

A.K.A.	Also Known As. This phrase is used to indicate alternate titles of collections, or alternate names (pseudonyms) of collection creators or photographers.
Anon.	Anonymous. The creator of the images or the collection is unknown.
CH	Cooper-Hewitt Museum of Decorative Arts and Design.
FGA	Freer Gallery of Art.
HMSG	Hirshhorn Museum and Sculpture Garden.
NMAfA	National Museum of African Art.
NMAA	National Museum of American Art.
NMAH	National Museum of American History.
NMNH	National Museum of Natural History.
NPG	National Portrait Gallery.
OPPS	Office of Printing and Photographic Services.
POP	Printing-Out Paper (photoprints).
SEM	Scanning Electron Microscope.
SGA	Arthur M. Sackler Gallery of Art.
SI	Smithsonian Institution.

Public Access

Appointments are required for any collections not on public exhibition. The accuracy of the information in the *Guide* will change over time, as collections grow and divisions reorganize. Calling ahead will save researchers time and trouble searching for collections and staff that have moved. With the exception of the Archives of the Freer and Arthur M. Sackler Galleries of Art, the Eliot Elisofon Archives at the National Museum of African Art, and the Research and Scholars Center at the National Museum of American Art, museum departments, divisions, or offices do not have full-time reference staff. Researchers should allow ample time for scheduling appointments, locating collections, and creating copy images.

Recommended times for research appointments are stated in the division introductions, as are appropriate addresses and phone numbers. Written requests for appointments should explain the purpose and scope of the research project, and any publication or exhibition plans. Most Smithsonian offices are open to the public from 10 a.m. to 5 p.m., Monday through Friday, except federal holidays.

Handling Photographs

Researchers must respect the requests of staff members to ensure preservation of Smithsonian photographic collections. Gloves may be required while working with these collections. Since photographs are fragile, researchers must not bend or touch photographic emulsions. Only pencil should be used for note-taking near photographs. Researchers may not eat, drink, or smoke while working near photographs. Following completion of research, individual photographs must be returned to their original position in the collection. Future availability of these collections depends upon the care with which they are treated today.

Photoduplication Service

Unless restricted, xerographic or photographic copies of images in Smithsonian collections are available to researchers once written permission has been obtained from the appropriate division. Restricted materials may require additional clearance. If the copyright is held outside the Smithsonian, the researcher is responsible for obtaining necessary permissions. For example, to reproduce images from the *Time* Collection *(PG·5)*, the National Portrait Gallery requires prior written permission from Time, Inc.

Photographs may not be used to show or imply Smithsonian endorsement of any commercial product or enterprise, or to indicate that the Smithsonian concurs with, or confirms the accuracy of, any text accompanying these images. No photographs may be cropped, overprinted, or altered without prior permission, and each must be accompanied by the division's preferred caption and credit line.

Photographs held by the Horticulture Services Division must be requested through the Smithsonian's Office of Printing and Photographic Services (OPPS). Each art museum has its own photography laboratory and procedures for ordering reproductions. OPPS, the Cooper-Hewitt Museum, the Freer Gallery of Art, and the Arthur M. Sackler Gallery provide permission request forms (which must be completed and returned first) and photograph order forms. The Hirshhorn Museum and Sculpture Garden, National Museum of American Art, and National Portrait Gallery require written requests. The National Museum of African Art accepts telephone as well as written requests.

For each museum, researchers must describe the subject of the image desired along with any additional known information such as photographer and date; the format, size, and number of images desired; and the projected use of the image including title and bibliographic information for publications. OPPS must also have the image's negative number, which can be obtained from the custodial division. The Hirshhorn Musuem and Sculpture Garden requires a detailed description of the proposed publication and requests that images be used only in works focusing on art or the particular artist, rather than for other illustration purposes.

Each museum determines the cost of reproductions and provides current price lists on request. OPPS and the National Museum of African Art require prepayment for images; the other museums will send bills with the photographs. The Freer Gallery of Art, Arthur M. Sackler Gallery, and National Museum of African Art require a copy of each publication printing their photographs; the Cooper-Hewitt Museum requires two copies. Additional restrictions or requirements may be imposed by the museums. Requests should be sent to the following addresses:

Cooper-Hewitt Museum: Cooper Hewitt Museum, 2 East 91st Street, New York, New York, 10128, Attention: Photographic Services; (212) 860-6868

Freer Gallery of Art and Arthur M. Sackler Gallery: Rights and Reproductions Office, Freer Gallery of Art, Smithsonian Institution, Washington, D.C., 20560; (202) 786-2088

Hirshhorn Museum and Sculpture Garden: Photographic Services, Hirshhorn Museum and Sculpture Garden, Room G24, Smithsonian Institution, Washington, D.C., 20560, Attention: Mary O'Neill; (202) 357-3098

National Museum of African Art: Eliot Elisofon Photographic Archives, National Museum of African Art, Smithsonian Institution, Washington, D.C., 20560; (202) 357-4600

National Museum of American Art: Rights and Reproductions, Office of Registration & Collections Management, National Museum of American Art, Smithsonian Institution, Washington, D.C., 20560; (202) 357-1381

National Portrait Gallery: National Portrait Gallery, Office of Rights and Reproductions, Room 185, Smithsonian Institution, Washington, D.C., 20560; (202) 357-2791

OPPS: Customer Services Branch, Office of Printing and Photographic Services, Smithsonian Institution, Washington, D.C., 20560; (202) 357-1933. Researchers can request permission request forms (SI-2940), photographic policies and charges explanation sheets (SI-318a), and photo order forms (SI-318)

Other Related Publications

This volume follows two photographic guides, the *Guide to Photographic Collections at the Smithsonian Institution: National Museum of American History* (1989, ISBN number 0-87474-927-1) and *Guide to Photographic Collections at the Smithsonian Institution: National Museum of Natural History, National Zoological Park, Smithsonian Astrophysical Observatory, and Smithsonian Tropical Research Institute* (1991, ISBN number 1-56098-033-8). There are also two nonphotographic guides: the *Finders' Guide to Prints and Drawings in the Smithsonian Instutution* (1981, ISBN number 0-87474-317-6) and the *Finders' Guide to Decorative Arts in the Smithsonian Institution* (1985, ISBN 0-87474-636-1). All these publications can be purchased by contacting the Smithsonian Press at Department 900, Blue Ridge Summit, Pennsylvania 17294-0900; or call (717) 794-2148. Refer to the book's ISBN number when ordering.

Subsequent volumes in this series of *Guides to Photographic Collections* will cover photographic collections in other Smithsonian museums, research bureaus, public service bureaus, and administrative offices. The fourth photographic guide volume will be the *Guide to Photographic Collections at the Smithsonian Institution: The National Air and Space Museum*. These 350 collections contain almost two million photographs, primarily focusing on the history of aviation and space exploration.

The Mechanical Eye: Photography and the Arts

There is no such thing as art photography. In photography, as in everything else, there are people who know how to see and others who don't even know how to look.
— Felix Tournachon A.K.A. Nadar[1]

I photograph what I do not wish to paint and I paint what I cannot photograph . . .
— Man Ray[2]

Introduction

This volume reveals the breadth of the photographic collections in the Smithsonian Institution's seven art museums. Scanning the creator and subject indexes to this volume provides an idea of the extent of coverage found including advertising, anthropological, documentary, fashion, fine art, and historical photographs. Smithsonian photographs also serve as curatorial research files, exhibit components, public education tools, and registrar's holdings documentation. The diversity of the collections has as much to do with the history of photography as it does with the history of these museums. Since the Smithsonian Institution's founding in 1846, its photographic holdings have grown each year, just as the Smithsonian itself has expanded into the world's largest museum complex and research center. The Smithsonian's art museums have photographs from all eras of the medium's history, reflecting the first 150 years of photographic activity in the arts.

Photography Defined

Photographs are images formed by the action of radiation (usually light) upon a sensitized surface. While often thought of as a single technique, photography actually is many hundreds of related chemical processes on a variety of supports such as paper, plastic film, or glass. Although produced by the objective mechanism of the camera, photographs are composed by a subjective mind. Since the advent of photography in 1839, photographers' visions have grown out of the traditions of the visual arts and popular culture, making the medium one that can accomodate the subjective as well as the objective and the abstract as well as the representational.

Photographs serve three primary functions. First, as durable visual records of transient moments and things, photographs operate as administrative, evidential, historical, scientific, or souvenir documents. Second, photographs can be used for persuasive communication, engaging the emotions for purposes of advertising, fashion sales, propaganda, or reform. Finally, photographs are physical objects, functioning as material culture or fine art artifacts. Photographs also may acquire value as expressions of their creator's viewpoint; as objects capable of poetic or symbolic interpretation by the viewer; and as objects associated with a particular photographer, subject, or owner. Often, a single photograph fufills more than one of these functions. To serve successfully as a record or a form of persuasive communication, a photograph requires a context, such as a caption explaining the subject matter or brand name. Without a caption the viewer can supply variant meanings to a single image.

While most people study photographs' subject matter, art historians and artists also are interested in photographs as physical artifacts to be evaluated according to the conventions of picture-making. Over the last 150 years, art museums have exhibited, researched, and collected photographs from all three functional categories. In many museums, curators routinely treat documentary and persuasive photographs as art objects. To shift the focus from the subject or original purpose of the photographic image to the image's aesthetic content, one need only place the photograph in the context of a recognized body of fine art photographs, remove the original caption, and provide information only on the photographer, the process, the composition, and the genre, such as portraiture or still life. When the original caption and context is removed, the photograph is understood as an artifact in which aesthetic issues such as composition, light, shadow, color, tone, form, line, texture, and focus predominate.

Documentary Photographs and the Arts

Since 1839 artists have used photographs as a primary source material (substitutes for models); as secondary sources of inspiration (reminders of how things look); and as tertiary sources (stylistic inspirations for paintings that emulate photographic vision, such as the snapshot aesthetic or photorealism). Artists also use photography as a tool for seeing otherwise unviewable parts of the visual world, such as distant nebulae; as a way of documenting their own work; and as an expressive medium.

Museums initially created photographs as documentary tools. For example, the Smithsonian Institution first commissioned photographers Alexander Gardner and Antonio Zeno Shindler to photograph North American Indians for an exhibit in 1867. In 1868 the Smithsonian hired its first staff photographer, Thomas W. Smillie (1843–1917), to record museum collections. Smillie and later staff photographers documented museum accessions, events, exhibitions, expeditions, staff, and visitors, and recorded specialized topics for curatorial research files.[3] Photographic documentation became an essential part of museum life.

In the 19th century photography rapidly became the medium of choice for recording portraits, war scenes, and travel images, once the exclusive domain of painters and graphic printmakers. Some early portrait photographers originally painted miniatures, switching to photography to follow the demand for the new medium. Pierre Auguste Renoir observed, "[Photography] freed painting from a lot of tiresome chores, starting with family portraits. Now the shopkeeper who wants his portrait has only to go to the photographer. So much the worse for us, but so much the better for the art of painting."[4] The work of war photographers, from Roger Fenton and the Mathew Brady Studio in the 19th century to Robert Capa and Larry Burrows in the 20th century, frequently functions both as visual records, informing the public of the milestones of the war, and as advocates for soldiers and civilians caught in the conflict.

In Victorian times, travel and expeditionary photography served as both entertainment and education. Traveling photographers—such as Auguste-Rosalie Bisson, Samuel Bourne, and Maxim Du Camp—created images that later were marketed as stereographs, cabinet cards, or illustrations published in books.[5] Some of these documentary photographs also served a persuasive purpose. In both the United States and the United Kingdom, travel photography functioned as a way to link remote areas and make them less threatening. For example, photographic books of India were sent home to England, enhancing support for the Empire.[6] After the American Civil War, photographers such as John Carbutt, Alexander Gardener, William Henry Jackson, Timothy O'Sullivan, Andrew J. Russell, and Carleton E. Watkins created images of the American West. These documentary photographs helped convince the government to fund land and mineral surveys and studies of American Indians, resulting ultimately in the opening of the West to the railroads and other businesses and the disenfranchisment of Native Americans.[7]

Some American and European travel photographers created photographs as souvenirs, recording cultures that they considered curiosities sure to vanish.[8] By reducing other cultures to the same familiar viewing format as animals, artifacts, and other objects, non-European peoples could be viewed as specimens "captured" by the lens. The tendency to use the camera to categorize and objectify people was also turned towards peoples of other classes by some 19th century photographers. E. Alice Austen documented New York street people; Charles Nègre made similar informal portraits in France.[9] Few photographers, other than Germany's August Sander, systematically studied daily life at all levels in their own society.[10]

In some cases photographic surveys, such as the Parisian Historical Documents Commission, were undertaken to record the vanishing 19th century world. Thomas Annan, Eugène Atget, Charles Marville, and Charles Nègre recorded the physical changes taking place in England and France as old buildings vanished, making way for the 20th century.

Moving directly counter to historical documentation photography, which is often eligiac in tone, is documentary reform imagery, which speaks of the need for change. Among the earliest social reform images are the photographs made by Richard Beard for wood engravings in Henry Mayhew's 1851 publication *London Labour and London Poor*[11] and John Thomson's photographs, which served as the basis for illustrations in his 1877 publication *Street Life in London*.[12] Photographs of the plight of slaves raised support for emancipation. Sojourner Truth sold her own portrait to the public imprinted with her motto "I sell the shadow to support the substance."[13] Photographs also were used to raise funds for the relief of peoples suffering the effects of poverty, disaster, and war. Reformer Jacob Riis used his photographs of American tenements in his multi-media reform lectures, which incorporated lights, music, and lantern slides,[14] later publishing many of the images in his books *How the Other Half Lives*[15] and *The Children of the Poor*.[16] Lewis Hine's widely published 1905 photographs of children at work helped persuade U.S. lawmakers to prohibit child labor.[17]

Victorian horizons were broadened by photographic visions of foreign art, cityscapes, landscapes, and peoples, as well as other classes within their own society. The arts were enriched and enlivened by the wealth of new imagery. Artists previously unable to travel or to see the specialized worlds of the anthropologist, archaeologist, astronomer, and biologist began to have access to the visual records of these fields. Expeditionary photography by Carleton E. Watkins[18] and Eadweard Muybridge[19] provided artists like Frederic Remington with their first views of the American West, just as travel images of Egypt taken by Maxim Du Camp, Francis Frith, and Paul Vernet introduced artists to the East. Alternate systems of aesthetics, such as those reflected in Japanese and Chinese architecture and ancient Egyptian sculpture, became more commonly known in the West through photographs. Many photographs serve as historical records of lost art works which vanished, victims of war, modern tastes, or neglect. While the record-keeping and persuasive roles of photography are essential to understanding its place in the arts, photography's function as an artifact with distinctive characteristics would play an increasingly large part in redefining the arts.

Artists and Photography

First recorded in medieval Arab literature, the camera's predecessor, the *camera obscura,* was developed as an aid to drawing.[20] Illustrious 17th and 18th century artists such as Canaletto, Guardi, and Jan Vermeer are thought to have used the *camera obscura* in planning their paintings.[21] In 1839, when it became possible to chemically fix and keep the camera image, many artists created photographs as visual aids rather than art works. Working from photographs allowed artists to follow the camera's lead in details, modifying only the aspects of the image they found displeasing. Unlike landscapes, photographs were portable. Unlike models, photographs didn't move. Many portrait painters (including Thomas Eakins, Henri Fantin-Latour, Paul Gauguin, George P. Healy, David Octavius Hill, Edouart Manet, William Page, and Thomas Sully) occasionally used photographs as substitutes for impatient or unavailable sitters.[22]

Many other artists—including Americans Frederick Edwin Church, Thomas Eakins, and Thomas Moran and Europeans Georges Braque, Gustave Courbet, Paul Cézanne, Edgar Degas, Eugene Delacroix, Andre Derain, James Ensor, and Jean Auguste Ingres—used photographs as source material for specific paintings. Atget's elegant photographic studies of Paris inspired French painters Maurice Utrillo and, later, Marcel Duchamp.[23] Jean Baptiste Corot used photographic landscapes as source material for some landscape paintings.[24] Painter-illustrators such as Winslow Homer drew on photographic imagery for magazines including *Ballou's Weekly, Harper's Weekly,* and *Leslie's Illustrated Monthly.*[25] In the 1850s artists used photographs of current events such as disasters and wars as sources for etchings, mezzotints, steel engravings, and wood engravings for the popular press. Photographically-inspired images were identified as such in captions to encourage belief in their veracity.

Between 1875 and the early 1890s, photographic technology evolved from bulky cameras with glass plates to hand-held cameras with sheet film, greatly simplifying the work of the photographer. On March 4, 1880, the first halftone photomechanical was printed in a New York newspaper; by 1895 widespread publication of halftones had become financially feasible. This led to an explosion in the demand for news photographs.[26] Blatantly unrealistic paintings and graphics became unacceptable, and a new class of reporter, the photojournalist, emerged.

Although photography's influence initially led to a new realism in painting, camera-vision—based upon lens, shutter, and film capabilities—suffers its own distortions. Cameras and humans see the world differently. The eye is necessarily more selective, capable of recognizing a single item in the visual field and ignoring the rest.[27] Early British photographer Peter Henry Emerson built the aesthetic of photographic naturalism, an attempt to make photographs resemble human vision, by producing low contrast images with only the main subject of the picture in sharp focus.[28]

The distortions in many early photographs were not due to the photographer's intent, but rather to the limits of the cameras that produced them. Movement, strong contrast, wide panoramas, great depth of field, deep shadows, or bright light each could defeat the camera's ability to take an accurate photograph. Art works derived from photographs echoed the camera's visual distortions including foreshortening (due to the focal length), selective focus, condensed or distorted perspective, and an expanded picture plane.[29]

In some cases, photographic vision changed the way artists looked at the world. Amateur photographers, who created spontaneous, lively, and uncomposed images for documentary and souvenir purposes, inspired the "snapshot" aesthetic. French impressionist and intimist painters Pierre Bonnard and Édouard Vuillard used the casual views provided by their snapshots as source material for their paintings of families in light-filled rooms.[30]

Although Eadweard Muybridge and Etienne Jules Marey were more intent on improving photography's abilities to record motion than on producing fine art images, their work had a significant impact on the arts. Muybridge pioneered motion photography in 1872, when he photographed the position of a galloping horse's legs to settle a bet. His later stop-action images of humans and animals in motion provided source imagery to generations of artists including Edgar Degas, Thomas Eakins, and Francis Bacon.[31] After meeting Muybridge in Paris in 1881, French physiologist Etienne Jules Marey invented the repeating-shutter camera to record sequential images on the same plate. Marey's motion work later inspired Marcel Duchamp to produce his famous *Nude Descending a Staircase*.[32] Muybridge and Marey's work eventually led to the invention of motion pictures, another medium that profoundly changed the way we look at the world.

Other pioneers of photography experimented with recording images at faster speeds, with less light, and in color. Technical experiments, from Titian Ramsey Peale's early work with the collodion process[33] to the the innovative stop-action images of Harold Edgerton,[34] brought photographers a fuller understanding of their medium's capabilities and a corresponding expansion of visual imagery.

Photographers and the Fine Arts

Understanding the nature of the new medium was not an easy task for photography's early critics and practitioners. Like painting, photography provides a two-dimensional representation of a three-dimensional world, essentially an illusion incorporating time-honored principles of composition, lighting, and subject matter. When faced with determining the status of photography, many artists were forced to rethink their definition of art. Since the Renaissance, artists had attempted to provide detailed, life-like works that, if successful, could be confused with reality. In the 19th century, this tendency towards illusionistic detail was coupled with an interest in providing beautiful images illustrating themes supporting conservative moral beliefs.[35] With little training, photographers could create images faster and with greater detail; they also could produce multiples of the finished work. Indeed the ability to easily reproduce images of great visual complexity led both to photography's public popularity and its lack of acceptance as a fine art.

To the romantic late-19th century viewpoint, the photograph was the product of a machine, not of human craftsmanship. Many artists and critics felt that photography lacked the spice of originality, creativity, and imagination essential to a fine art. Photography was too easy to master and seemingly too objective. Taken together, these concerns caused great difficulties for photographers aspiring to the status of artist. In the 1850s photographers Oscar G. Rejlander and Henry Peach Robinson imitated the subject matter of the fine arts in their work. Rejlander, an academically trained painter and sculptor, often sketched out his compositions first. Printing his images from many pieced-together negatives, he blended the staged picture elements together to make a single work through the use of painterly retouching. Robinson photographed many staged scenes to obtain all pieces of a composition, pieced bits of the prints together, and rephotographed the final image to produce a master negative. Both Rejlander and Robinson wanted to produce photographs equal to the work of graphic printmakers and painters, thus bringing stature to their medium.[36]

Pictorialist Photography

Between 1875 and the early 1890s, the number of photographers grew with the availability of hand-held cameras and the silver gelatin dry plate process, followed by the faster film-based photonegatives. As the number of amateur practitioners proliferated, serious photographers began to question the value of much of the work being produced. To help set up standards and identify an elite within the field, photographers turned to the fine arts.

Photographers such as J. Craig Annan, Alvin Langdon Coburn, F. Holland Day, Rudolf Eickemeyer, Frederick Evans, and Gertrude Käsebier openly emulated painting by adopting fine arts subject matter such as landscapes, portraits, still lifes, and waterscapes, emphasizing beauty and nature.[37] Influenced by the the work of such painters as J.M.W. Turner and James Abbott McNeill Whistler, pictorialist photographers pioneered the use of non-traditional processes such as gum bichromate to produce soft-focus, often heavily manipulated images. Since these processes allowed the photographer substantial tonal control, the pictorialist photographer claimed an equal measure of originality, creativity, and imagination as his colleagues in painting and printmaking.

However, changing the status of photography seemed an impossible task to isolated artists working alone. Photographers interested in the arts joined together in exclusive camera clubs such as the Brotherhood of the Linked Ring, the Photo-Club de Paris, and the Vienna Camera Club. In these clubs photographers compared work; developed aesthetic criteria for selecting members and jurying exhibits; published exhibit catalogs and reports; reviewed new processes and techniques; and staged international exhibits. They also accumulated the wealth and prestige necessary to undertake these activities.[38] As these photographic fraternities redefined the status of photographs, museums began accessioning pictorialist photography into their collections as fine art objects. The Smithsonian's first purchase of uncommissioned photographs consisted of 50 pictorialist images from the 1896 Capital Camera Club exhibit, a local camera club modeled after the larger international groups.[39]

Perhaps the best known of these clubs, the Brotherhood of the Linked Ring, was founded in London in 1892. Created as a reaction to the Royal Photographic Society's policy of exhibiting the works of hobbyists and scientists beside those of professional photographers, the Linked Ring was the first organization created to further the cause of photography as an independent fine art medium. Between 1893 and 1908 the Link's annual "Photographic Salon" exhibit showcased the finest international photographic work, juried by art photographers.[40] Many Link members also joined the primarily American Photo-Secession movement, Alfred Stieglitz's informal group of fine art photographers, which grew out of the Camera Club of New York. The Photo-Secession's primary vehicles were the magazine *Camera Work* and Stieglitz's New York art gallery, the Little Galleries of the Photo-Secession, later called 291. When the Smithsonian opened its "Hall of Photography" in 1913 to illustrate the history and development of photography, the gallery included 27 photographs by Photo-Secession members purchased from Alfred Stieglitz.[41]

The early efforts of these groups and the photographers who belonged to them, such as Alvin Langdon Coburn, Frank Eugene, Frederick Evans, Gertrude Käsebier, Edward Steichen, and Clarence H. White, helped develop pictorialism as an international fine art style that stressed the emotive and subjective over the factual.[42] In changing the photograph's role from historical or persuasive document to that of an original physical artifact with expressive content, pictorialism placed the photographer in the same creative role as a painter or graphic printmaker.

Photography and the Avant Garde

The later efforts of Stieglitz and his circle moved photography from pictorialism to the modern avant-garde. Around 1908, five years before the ground-breaking Armory Show of modern art, Stieglitz's 291 gallery introduced international modern art to America. By 1910 Stieglitz's *Camera Work* had begun printing reproductions of avant-garde paintings as well as photographs. His publication and exhibition of photographs in the 1910s and 1920s helped shape a new photographic aesthetic, which concentrated the medium's expressive capabilities by simplifying form and technique.[43]

Photography took a prominent role in the changing ideas about art emerging during World War I. In 1916 a group of Swiss artists, angered by the war, created the dada art movement to satirize conventional culture. Dadaists such as Francis Picabia and Marcel Duchamp appropriated photographs for use in collages, montages, and journals as if the images were the visual equivalent of automatic writing, a dada speciality. Photographs were readily reproduced, swiftly manipulated, and easily disassociated from their function and context. Dadaists rediscovered alternative photographic processes and manipulative techniques that had slid into oblivion after the decline of pictorialism. When Man Ray began making commercial portrait and fashion photographs in Paris in the 1920s, he discovered the photographs of Eugène Atget and rediscovered William Henry Fox Talbot's photogram process (exposing objects to light directly on sensitized paper).[44] Atget's work influenced the surrealist painters and such later photographers as Berenice Abbott, much as it had influenced French painter Maurice Utrillo during an earlier age.[45]

In the early 1920s the influence of the Bauhaus and constructivism, as well as cubism, dadaism, precisionism, surrealism, and vorticism, began to be felt in American photography. As the decade progressed, the precisionist aesthetic predominated in the United States. Abstraction, unconventional viewpoints, close-ups, powerful tonal contrasts, unusual subject matter, and a strong interest in form and geometry appeared in the work of such photographers as Manuel Alvarez Bravo, André Kertész, and Paul Outerbridge.[46] The "new" photography was heavily influenced by modern art and by the city itself, the skyscraper, modern bridges, and the technology of modern life. Advertising and corporate public relations firms hired professional photographers such as Margaret Bourke-White to produce idealized abstractions of industial subjects in the precisionist style. Photography became a popular sales tool during the economic boom of the twenties, idealizing and promoting the most prosaic products. During this period, photography's persuasive functions included advertising, fashion promotion, public relations, and Hollywood movie publicity.

Later dubbed "straight photography," this photographic movement focused on the direct, objective, and documentary capabilities of the camera.[47] On the West Coast, photographers Ansel Adams, Imogen Cunningham, and Edward Weston adopted this new aesthetic, placing emphasis on abstraction, form, and the landscape, as well as on industrialization and the close-up. By 1930 a number of photographers, including Ansel Adams, Imogen Cunningham, John Paul Edwards, Sonya Noskowiak, Henry Swift, Willard Van Dyke, and Edward Weston, banded together to form the f/64 group—named after the smallest camera aperture, hence the sharpest focus available. Many major photographers not actually part of the f/64 group, including Alvin Langdon Coburn, Dorothea Lange, Paul Strand, Edward Steichen, Charles Sheeler, and Karl Struss, felt their influence.[48]

Documentary Photography

When America's boom turned to bust in the 1930s, many photographers turned their attention to documenting America's needy. The aesthetics of straight photography were joined to a larger concern with social content. By 1935 even some of the f/64 group had moved from photographing forms and patterns in nature to documenting contemporary life. In some cases the social comment was solidly rooted in a sense of place, as with Laura Gilpin's images of Arizona's Navajo, Doris Ulmann's portraits of the Appalachian peoples and African-American life in South Carolina, and Berenice Abbott's photographs of New Yorkers.[49]

Politically committed documentary projects, such as the New York Photo League's Harlem Document led by Aaron Siskind and the federally funded Farm Security Administration (FSA) photographic project run by Roy Stryker, produced comprehensive bodies of work. FSA photographers initially documented unemployed farmhands, later broadening their focus to include many aspects of rural and urban life between 1935 and 1943. The resulting photographs serve as a cross-section of an era, illustrating America's rural and urban underclasses, small-town life during the recovery period, and, finally, the nation's preparations for World War II.[50] Ultimately, FSA photographers—such as Jack Delano, Walker Evans, Dorothea Lange, Russell Lee, Carl Mydans, Gordon Parks, Arthur Rothstein, Ben Shahn, and Marion Post Wolcott—helped sway public opinion in favor of humanitarian government action, in the tradition of Jacob Riis and Lewis Hine.[51]

Outside the government, documentary photography flourished under the guidance of the Photo League, founded in 1936 to promote social reform through photography and improve the quality of documentary photography. Under the guidance of Sid Grossman and Aaron Siskind, Photo League members such as Robert Disraeli, Eliot Elisofon, and Paul Strand produced memorable street photography for three projects titled the Chelsea Document, the Harlem Document, and the Pitt Street Document.[52]

In the late 1930s and early 1940s documentary photography became an industry whose products were increasingly visible. The new picture magazines such as *Life* and *Look* featured work by Margaret Bourke-White, Alfred Eisenstaedt, Carl Mydans, and W. Eugene Smith, arranged in narrative sequence next to carefully edited prose. Publications such as Walker Evans and James Agee's *Let Us Now Praise Famous Men*[53] and Richard Wright's *Twelve Million Black Voices,*[54] as well as exhibits such as the Museum of Modern Art's 1937 history of photography show, helped broaden photography's audience.

In the 1930s and 1940s photographers once more banded together, as the pictorialists had done before them, to achieve a shared goal. Photojournalists formed picture agencies such as Black Star and Magnum to gain autonomy from the pressures of publishers and editors. Founded by Robert Chim, Henri Cartier-Bresson, George Rodger, and David Seymour in Paris in 1946 as the first cooperative photo agency, Magnum selected its own editors and controlled the way its members's photographs were shown and sold.[55]

The American military quickly recognized that photographs could serve effectively as both documentary and persuasive images. When the FSA was transferred to the Office of War Information during World War II, photographers began to produce morale-building images in support of war preparations. As the U.S. Navy's director of photography, Edward Steichen also produced images with multiple functions. When Steichen joined the staff of the Museum of Modern Art (MOMA) as director of the Department of Photography in 1947, he accessioned commercial photojournalistic images into the MOMA collections.[56] With the acceptance of documentary and persuasive images as fine art photographs, the lines previously drawn between fine arts and other types of photography began to blur.

After the war, the demand for photography in advertising, fashion, journalism, publicity, teaching, and publishing proliferated. Photographers Alexey Brodovitch, Louise Dahl-Wolfe, André Kertész, and Irving Penn were preeminent commercial photographers of this period, strongly influenced by current trends in the fine arts and the new color photographic materials available.[57]

At the same time, the demand for social documentary photography diminished. Commercial documentary photographers such as W. Eugene Smith and Henri Cartier-Bresson fought an ongoing battle to maintain control of their commissions for the struggling picture magazines.[58] Many long-lived documentary photographic projects disappeared in the the 1940s and 1950s: the FSA project ended in 1943 and the Photo League, placed upon the attorney general's "subversive list" in 1947, disbanded in 1951.[59] Influential works of social documentation that dealt with the underside of the American dream became scarce, with the exception of works such as Robert Frank's *The Americans*[60] and William Klein's *Life is Good and Good for You in New York: Trance Witness Reveals.*[61]

Social content in photography, when visible, tended toward the affirmative, such as the images in Steichen's 1955 Museum of Modern Art exhibition "The Family of Man," which resulted in a best-selling exhibition catalog.[62] The public taste was for hobby, family, and fashion magazines or television, rather than documentary news magazines or picture journals. The work of photographers Richard Avedon, Alfred Eisenstaedt, Philippe Halsman, Yousuf Karsh, Gjon Mili, and Irving Penn reflected the demand for stylish new images.[63]

Photography and Academia

As documentary photography declined in favor of persuasive commercial work, many photographers left the marketplace in favor of academia. On the East Coast, Berenice Abbott and Lisette Model taught at the New School for Social Research in New York, and Nathan Lyons founded the Visual Studies Workshop in Rochester, New York. In the Midwest, Harry Callahan and Aaron Siskind taught at the Chicago Institute of Design. A West Coast school formed around Ansel Adams, who taught workshops at Yosemite and published through the Sierra Club. Other West Coast teachers included Wynn Bullock and Jack Welpott, founder of the Visual Dialogue Foundation, both of whom taught at the San Franciso State College. Particularly influential was author, photographer, publisher, and teacher Minor White, who taught at the California School of Fine Arts and later at M.I.T. and the Rochester Institute of Technology.[64]

These photographer/teachers were influenced by abstract expressionism, mysticism, psychological theory, surrealism, and Zen, as well as by the work of f/64 photographers Ansel Adams and Edward Weston. Bullock, Callahan, Paul Caponigro, Aaron Siskind, and White worked with experimental techniques, producing photographs as expressive poetic objects rather than as documents or persuasive images. Photograper/teachers active in the 1960s, such as Robert Heinecken, Henry Holmes Smith, Jerry Uelsmann, and Todd Walker,[65] experimented with manipulative techniques such as combination printing, retouching, and assemblage. As documentary realism became the jurisdiction of commercial photography, non-commercial photographers moved into the world of imagination, metaphor, and increasing abstraction.[66]

The meaning of photographs came increasingly under discussion as art historians, critics, and philosophers such as Nathan Lyons and Henry Holmes Smith joined Beaumont Newhall, John Szarkowski, and Minor White in the debate over how to comprehend, describe, and judge photographs. An increasing number of photographic journals, including *Afterimage, The Archive, Camera, Camera Arts, Center Quarterly,* and *History of Photography,* joined the already established *Aperture* in examining the photograph as a contemporary and historical art medium. In the 1950s and 1960s, museums that collected and exhibited photographs, such as the Center for Creative Photography, Chicago Art Institute, George Eastman House, International Center for Photography, J. Paul Getty Museum, and the University of California's Museum of Photography, either opened their doors or greatly expanded their facilties and holdings.[67]

Recent Photography

In the 1970s documentary photography again emerged as a major influence on fine art photographers. Influenced by the 1950s published photographs of William Klein and Robert Frank, free-lance photographers Ralph Gibson, Duane Michaels, and Lucas Samaras published autobiographical books of photography.[68] Other major 1970s photo books published in the documentary tradition include Larry Clark's *Tulsa*,[69] Danny Lyon's *Conversations with the Dead*,[70] Bill Owen's *Suburbia*,[71] and Garry Winogrand's *The Animals*.[72]

In the 1980s digitization and computer-imaging systems offered photographers greater control over the creative possibilities of picture-making, while "still" or freeze-frame video cameras offered freedom from darkrooms. Since digitally stored photographs can be manipulated and retouched without leaving a trace, some historians speculate that these new imaging systems may diminish public faith in the value of photographs as records. Consequently digital images may become almost purely persuasive or expressive artifacts.[73] The importance of maintaining records on the image's creation is even greater with these images than it is with standard photographs, since they can seamlessly incorporate segments of documentary images alongside artificial imagery.

Imaging technologies offer new opportunities to photographers as well as challenges to archivists and curators. Museums, such as those at the Smithsonian Institution, must develop new ways to collect, document, preserve, exhibit, interpret, and provide access to these new types of images, as they have with the more traditional images described in this volume.

Diane Vogt O'Connor, Associate Archivist

Notes

1. Roger Greaves, *Nadar ou le Paradoxe Vitale* (Paris: Flammarion, 1980).
2. Susan Sontag, *On Photography* (New York: Farrar, Straus and Giroux, 1977).
3. David Haberstitch, "Photographs at the Smithsonian Institution: A History," *Picture Scope* 32(1): pp. 4–20.
4. Jean Renoir, *Renoir, My Father* (Boston: Little, Brown, 1962).
5. Maxim Du Camp, *Egypte, Nubie, Palestine et Syrie: Dessins Photographiques Recueillis Pendant Les Années 1849, 1850 et 1851* (Paris: Gide et J. Baudry, 1852).
6. A good example of the use of photography for purposes of linking an empire is the Freer Gallery of Art's *The People of India Collection (FG·37)*, created and published by the (British) India Office's India Museum staff. An example of linking a different sort of empire is the *Pères Blancs (White Fathers) Mission Photograph Collection (AF·56)* in the Eliot Elisofon Archives at the National Museum of African Art.
7. Jean-Claude Lemagny and André Rouilleé, eds., *A History of Photography: Social and Cultural Perspectives* (Cambridge, Massachussetts: Cambridge University Press, 1986), pp. 58–59. See also the Cooper-Hewitt Museum's *The CH Drawings and Prints Carleton Eugene Watkins Yosemite Photograph Collection, (CH·13)* for an overview of the work of a major photographer involved in the geographical and geological surveys of the American West. Watkins's photographs also can be found in the National Museum of American Art's collection *AM·1*; the National Museum of American History's collection *AC·60*; and the National Portrait Gallery's *PG·13*.
8. While the work of Edward Sheriff Curtis immediately occurs as an obvious example of this phenomenon, perhaps the best example in this volume is *The Casimir d'Ostoja Zagourski Photograph Collection (AF·74)* in the National Museum of African Art's Eliot Elisofon Archives. This collection includes postcards published under the title *L'Afrique qui Disparait (Vanishing Africa)*.
9. For a description of the work of Charles Nègre, who photographed French street people and tradesmen in Paris, France, around 1860, see Diane Vogt-O'Connor, *Guide to Photographic Collections at the Smithsonian Institution: National Museum of American History, Volume I* (Washington, D.C.: Smithsonian Institution Press, 1989), p. 237.
10. August Sander, *August Sander, Citizens of the Twentieth Century, Portrait Photographs, 1892–1952* (Cambridge, Massachussetts: MIT Press, 1980). Sander's photographs can also be found in the National Portrait Gallery's collection *PG·3*.
11. Henry Mayhew, *London Labour and London Poor* (London: Griffin, 1862).
12. John Thomson, *Street Life in London* (London: S. Low, Marston, Searle & Rivington, 1877–1878).

13. Portraits of Sojourner Truth may be found in the National Portrait Gallery collections *PG·3, PG·8,* and *PG·9.* One such portrait appears in the illustrations section of this volume.

14. Maren Stange, "Gotham's Crime and Misery. Ideology and Entertainment in Jacob Riis's Lantern Slide Exhibition," *Views* 8 (Spring 1987).

15. Jacob Riis, *How the Other Half Lives* (New York: Scribner's Sons, 1890).

16. Jacob Riis, *Children of the Poor* (New York: Scribner's Sons, 1892).

17. Judith Mara Gutman, *Lewis W. Hine and the American Social Conscience* (New York: Walker, 1967). Hine's photographs can be found in the National Museum of American Art's collection *AM·1,* in the National Museum of American History's collection *PH·33* (see Volume I of this series), and in the Hirshhorn Museum and Sculpture Garden's collection *HM·11.*

18. See collection *CH·13* in this volume for a description of Watkins photographs at the Cooper-Hewitt. See also the National Museum of American Art's collection *AM·1;* the National Museum of American History's collection *AC·60;* and the National Portrait Gallery's *PG·3.*

19. Vogt-O'Connor, op. cit., pp. 236–237, describes the *Eadweard Muybridge Collection (PH·36)* at the National Museum of American History, which incorporates 48,600 Muybridge photographs; other collections in the same museum which incorporate Muybridge's work are *PH·41* and PH·42. Muybridge's work may also be found in the National Museum of American Art in collection *AM·1* and at the National Portrait Gallery in collection *PG·3.*

20. Helmut Gernsheim, *The Origins of Photography* (Oxford: Oxford University Press, 1982).

21. Van Deren Coke, *The Painter and the Photograph from Delacroix to Warhol* (Albuquerque: University of New Mexico Press, 1964), pp. 1–5.

22. Aaron Scharf, *Art and Photography* (London: Allen Lane, 1968), pp. 47–56.

23. Atget's photographs may be found at the Smithsonian's National Museum of American History (see Volume I of this series) in collection *PH·33.*

24. Coke, op. cit., 193–196.

25. Ibid., p. 45.

26. Edward W. Earle, *Halftone Effects: A Cultural Study of Photographs in Reproduction, 1895–1905* (Riverside, California: California Museum of Photography, 1989), pp. 4–5.

27. Lemagny and Rouilleé, op. cit., pp. 84–85.

28. Peter Henry Emerson, *Naturalistic Photography for Students of the Art* (London: S. Low, Marston, Serle & Rivington, 1889).

29. Coke, op. cit., pp. 3–5.

30. Sara Greenough, Joel Snyder, David Travis, and Colin Westerbeck, *On the Art of Fixing a Shadow: One Hundred and Fifty Years of Photography* (Washington, D.C.: National Gallery of Art, 1989), pp. 132–135.

31. The *Eadweard Muybridge Collection (PH·36)* at the National Museum of American History (see Volume I of this series), incorporates 48,600 Muybridge photographs; other NMAH collections which contain Muybridge's work are *PH·41* and PH·42. Muybridge's work may also be found in the National Museum of American Art's collection *AM·1* and in the National Portrait Gallery's collection *PG·3.* Also see the Hirshhorn Museum and Sculpture Garden's collection *HM·17* in this volume for a discussion of Eakins's work, which is also included in collections *HM·11* and *HM·15* and in the National Portrait Gallery's collection *PG·3.*

32. Coke, op. cit., p. 165

33. Vogt-O'Connor, op. cit., pp. 238–239, describes Titian Ramsey Peale's experimental work with the collodion wet plate process and his later work as principal examiner in the Division of Fine Arts and Photography in the U.S. Patent Office in the collection description for the National Museum of American History's *Titian Ramsay Peale Collection (PH·39).*

34. Ibid., p. 224, describes the National Museum of American History's *Harold Eugene Edgerton Collection (PH·16),* including Edgerton's experimental development of stroboscopic high speed motion and still photography equipment, which later became the basis for all subsequent electronic flash units.

35. Many popular genre photographs, like academic paintings, were captioned so as to stress the dignity of work; the joys of motherhood and family; and the perils of stepping outside social conventions.

36. Lemagny and Rouilleé, op. cit., pp. 82–84. H.P. Robinson's photographs may be found in the National Museum of American History in collections *PH·33* and *PH·53.*

37. Ibid., pp. 82–84. See also Vogt-O'Connor, op. cit., pp. 234–235. Alvin Langdon Coburn's photographs at the Smithsonian are in the National Museum of American History's collection *PH·33,* in the Freer Gallery of Art in collections *FG·19* and *FG·59,*

and at the National Portrait Gallery in collection *PG·3*. The photographs of F. Holland Day and of Frederick Evans appear in the National Museum of American History's collection *PH·33;* those by Rudolf Eickmeyer appear in collection *PH·17*. Gertrude Käsebier's work is featured in two collections at the National Museum of American History, *PH·29* and *PH·41*, as well as in *PG·3* at the National Portrait Gallery.

38. David Haberstitch, op. cit., pp. 4–20. See also the *Paris Salon of Women Photographers, 1900, Collection, (PH·38),* in the National Museum of American History, Vogt-O'Connor, op. cit., pp. 237–238.

39. International Center of Photography, *International Center of Photography Encyclopedia of Photography* (New York: Crown Publishers, 1984), p. 307.

40. William Inness Homer, *Alfred Stieglitz and the American Avant-Garde* (Boston: New York Graphics Society, 1977).

41. Haberstitch, op. cit., pp. 4–20. The Smithsonian also contains photographs by Stieglitz in the Freer Gallery of Art's collection *FG·19*, in the Hirshhorn Museum and Sculpture Garden's collection *HM·11*, in the National Museum of American History's collection *PH·33*, and in the National Portrait Gallery's collection *PG·3*.

42. Alvin Langdon Coburn's photographs may be found in the National Museum of American History's collection *PH·33*, in the Freer Gallery of Art's collections *FG·19* and *FG·59*, and in the National Portrait Gallery's collection *PG·3*. The photographs of F. Holland Day, Frank Eugene, and Frederick Evans appear in the National Museum of American History's collection *PH·33*, and those of Clarence H. White appear in *PH·33* and in the National Portrait Gallery's collection *PG·3*. Steichen's work appears in the Freer Gallery of Art's collections *FG·19* and *FG·59*, in the National Museum of American Art's collection *AM·1*, in the National Museum of American History's collection *PH·33* (see Volume I of this series), and in the National Portrait Gallery *PG·3*.

43. National Museum of American Art, *Perpetual Motif, The Art of Man Ray* (Washington, D.C.: Smithsonian Institution, 1988). Man Ray's photographs can be found in the National Museum of African Art's collection *AF·57*, National Museum of American Art's collection *AM·1*, and in the National Portrait Gallery's collection *PG·3*. Several National Museum of American History collections (see Volume I of this series) contain photographs by Talbot, such as collection *EI·149, PH·42*, and *PH·49*, while there are photographs of Atget in collection *PH·33*.

44. Greenough, Snyder, Travis, and Westerbeck, op. cit., pp. 225–256.

45. Abbott's work is contained in the Hirshhorn Museum and Sculpture Garden's collection *HM·11*, in the National Museum of American Art's collection *AM·1*, in the National Museum of American History's collection *PH·33* (see Volume I of this series), and in the National Portrait Gallery's collection *PG·3*.

46. The work of both Outerbridge and Kertész may be found in collection *PH·33* at the National Museum of American History, while Kertész's work is also in collection *PH·11*, as well as at the National Portrait Gallery's collection *PG·3*.

47. James Enyeart, ed., *Decade by Decade: Twentieth Century American Photography* (Boston: Bullfinch Press, 1988), pp. 35–46.

48. Arnold Gassan, *A Chronology of Photography: A Critical Survey of the History of Photography as a Medium of Art.* (Athens, Ohio: Handbook Company, 1972). The work of Ansel Adams is found in the National Museum of American Art's collection *AM·1*, in the National Museum of American History's collection *PH·33* (see Volume I of this series), in the National Museum of Natural History's collection *NH·104*, and in the National Portrait Gallery's collection *PG·3*. The work of Imogen Cunningham is found in the National Museum of American History's collection *PH·33* (see Volume I of this series) and in the National Portrait Gallery's collection *PG·3*. The work of Dorothea Lange is found in the National Museum of American Art's collection *AM·1* and in the National Museum of American History's collection *PH·33* (see Volume I of this series). The work of Sonya Noskowiak and of Paul Strand is found in the National Museum of American Art's collection *AM·1* and in the National Portrait Gallery's collection *PG·3*. The work of Edward Weston is found in the National Museum of American Art's collection *AM·1;* in the National Museum of American History's collections *PH·7, PH·33,* and *PH·58* (see Volume I of this series); and in the National Portrait Gallery's collections *PG·3* and *PG·5*.

49. Laura Gilpin's work appears in the National Museum of American Art's collections *AM·1* and *AM·11*, in the National Museum of American History's collection *PH·33* (see Volume I of this series), and in the National Portrait Gallery's collection *PG·3*. Doris Ulmann's work appears in the National Portrait Gallery's collection *PG·3*.

50. F. Jack Hurley, *Portrait of a Decade: Roy Stryker and the Development of Documentary Photography in the Thirties* (Baton Rouge: Louisiana State University Press, 1972). Aaron Siskind's work appears in the National Museum of American Art's collection *AM·1* and in the National Museum of American History's collection *PH·33*.

51. International Center of Photography, op. cit., pp. 188–189. Walker Evans's photographs are located at the National Museum of African Art's collections *AF·22* and *AF·57*, National Museum of American History's collection *PH·33* (see Volume I of this series), and in the National Portrait Gallery's collection *PG·3*. Carl Mydans's photographs are located in the National Portrait Gallery's collection *PG·5*. Arthur Rothstein's photographs are located at the National Museum of American History (see Volume I of this series) in collection *PH·45*.

52. James Enyeart, op. cit., pp. 50–52. Robert Disraeli's photographs are located in the National Portrait Gallery's collection *PG·3*. Eliot Elisofon's photographs are located in the National Museum of African Art's collections *AF·7, AF·8, AF·19, AF·20, AF·21, AF·45, AF·47, AF·50,* and *AF·57,* and in the National Museum of Natural History's collections *NH·90* and *NH·95*. Sid Grossman's photographs are located in the National Museum of American Art's collection *AM·1* and in the National Portrait Gallery's collection *PG·3*.

53. Walker Evans and James Agee, *Let Us Now Praise Famous Men* (Boston, Massachusetts: Houghton Mifflin Company, 1941). Margaret Bourke-White's photographs are located in the National Museum of American History's collection *PH·33* (see Volume I of this series). Alfred Eisenstaedt's photographs are located in the National Museum of American History's collection *PH·33* (see Volume I of this series), in the National Museum of American Art's collection *AM·11*, and in the National Portrait Gallery's collection *PG·5*. W. Eugene Smith's photographs are located in the National Museum of American Art collection *AM·1* and in the National Museum of American History's collection *PH·33* (see Volume I of this series).

54. Richard Wright, *Twelve Million Black Voices* (New York: Viking Press, 1941).

55. International Center of Photography, op. cit., p. 318. The photographs of Henri Cartier-Bresson are in the National Portrait Gallery's collection *PG·3*.

56. Lemagny and Rouilleé, op. cit., pp. 160–162. Steichen's photographs are located in the National Museum of American History's collection *PH·33* (see Volume I of this series), in the National Museum of American Art's collection *AM·1*, in the Freer Gallery of Art's collection *FG·59*, and in the National Portrait Gallery's collection *PG·3*.

57. Louise Dahl-Wolfe's photographs are located in the Freer Gallery of Art's collection *FG·45* and in the National Portrait Gallery's collection *PG·3*. Irving Penn's photographs are located in the National Museum of American Art's collection *AM·1*, in the National Museum of American History's collection *PH·33* (see Volume I of this series), and in the National Portrait Gallery's collections *PG·3* and *PG·5*.

58. Enyeart, op. cit., 103–106.

59. International Center of Photography, op. cit., pp. 195–196.

60. Robert Frank, *The Americans* (New York: Grove Press, 1959).

61. William Klein, *Life is Good and Good for You in New York: Trance Witness Reveals.* (London: Photography Magazine, 1956).

62. Lemagny and Rouilleé, op. cit., pp. 184–185

63. Richard Avedon's photographs are located in the National Museum of American History's collection *PH·4* (see Volume I of this series) and in the National Portrait Gallery's collections *PG·3* and *PG·5*. Philippe Halsman's photographs are located in the National Museum of American Art's collection *AM·11* and in the National Portrait Gallery's collections *PG·3* and *PG·5*. Yousuf Karsh's photographs are located in the Freer Gallery of Art's collections *FG·17, FG·19,* and *FG·59* and in the National Portrait Gallery collection *PG·3*.

64. Enyeart, op. cit., pp. 103–106. Wynn Bullock and Harry Callahan's photographs are located in the National Museum of American History's collection *PH·33* (see Volume I of this series) and in the National Museum of American Art's collection *AM·1*. Lisette Model's photographs are located in the National Museum of American History's collection *PH·33* (see Volume I of this series), in the National Museum of American Art's collection *AM·1*, and in the National Portrait Gallery's collection *PG·3*. Aaron Siskind's photographs are located in the National Museum of American History's collection *PH·33* (see Volume I of this series) and in the National Museum of American Art's collection *AM·1*. Minor White's work appears in the National Museum of American History's collection *PH·33* (see Volume I of this series).

65. Jerry Uelsmann's photographs are located in the National Museum of American History's collection *PH·33* (see Volume I of this series) and in the National Museum of American Art's collection *AM·1*. Todd Walker's photographs are located in the National Museum of American Art's collection *AM·1*.

66. Enyeart, op. cit., pp. 62–71.

67. Ibid., pp. 103–106.

68. Larry Clark, *Tulsa* (New York: Lustrum Press, 1971).

69. Robert Frank's photographs are located in the National Museum of American Art's collection *AM·1*, in the National Museum of American History's collection *PH·33* (see

Volume I of this series), and in the National Portrait Gallery's collection *PG·3*. Ralph Gibson's photographs appear in the National Museum of American Art's collection *AM·1*. William Klein's photographs are in the National Museum of American Art's collection *AM·1*. Duane Michaels's photographs are located in the National Museum of American History's collection *PH·33* (see Volume I of this series). Lucas Samaras's photographs are in the Hirshhorn Museum and Sculpture Garden's collection *HM·11*, in the National Museum of American Art's collection *AM·1,* and in the National Portrait Gallery's collection *PG·3*.

70. Danny Lyon, *Conversations with the Dead* (New York: Holt, Rinehart, Winston, 1971).
71. Bill Owen, *Suburbia* (San Francisco: Straight Arrow Books, 1972).
72. Garry Winogrand, *The Animals* (New York: Museum of Modern Art, 1969).
73. Peter Turner, *History of Photography* (New York: Exeter Books, 1987), 189–203.

NATIONAL MUSEUM OF AFRICAN ART

Sylvia H. Williams, Director

The National Museum of African Art (NMAfA) is the only museum in the United States dedicated solely to the collection, display, and study of the visual traditions of Africa. Founded by a small group of interested citizens under the leadership of Warren M. Robbins (1923–   ), a U.S. government official and African art collector, the Museum of African Art opened to the public in 1964. It was located in the Capitol Hill area of Washington, D.C., in the first Washington residence of African-American abolitionist, government official, orator, and publisher Frederick Douglass. The museum became part of the Smithsonian Institution in 1979, and its name changed to the National Museum of African Art in 1981. In December 1986 the museum moved from its original location to new facilities on the Mall, adjoining the Arthur M. Sackler Gallery, Freer Gallery of Art, and S. Dillon Ripley International Center. The museum opened to the public in its new building in September 1987.

Through collections, exhibitions, public programs, and research, the NMAfA encourages interest in and understanding of the diverse peoples of sub-Saharan Africa by examining their aesthetic achievements in the visual arts. The museum accepts into its holdings sub-Saharan and North African arts, as well as contemporary arts from the entire continent. The museum's holdings of over 7,000 objects include sculptures, textiles, and paintings, as well as architectural elements, decorative arts, and household objects such as basketry and ceramics.

NMAfA sponsors many research activities such as symposia and hosts visiting research fellows, supporting in-depth examination of scholarly topics. Its Education Department oversees public programs such as art classes, film series, museum tours, and performances. NMAfA's library contains over 20,000 volumes on African art and culture. The library also receives 200 periodicals and maintains vertical files.

There are 77 photographic collections at the NMAfA, containing nearly 251,000 images. Approximately 80,000 images were bequeathed to the museum by photographer Eliot Elisofon. His pictures, like most of the other NMAfA photographic collections, are part of the Eliot Elisofon Photographic Archives. In addition, the Archives holds 120,000 feet of unedited motion-picture footage on African art and peoples, also bequeathed by Elisofon, as well as engravings and maps.

AF

Conservation Laboratory

Conservation Laboratory
National Museum of African Art
Smithsonian Institution
Washington, D.C. 20560
Stephen Mellor, Conservator
(202) 357-4600, ext. 271
Hours: Monday–Friday, 10 a.m.–5 p.m.

Scope of the Collection

There is one photographic collection with approximately 19,000 images.

Focus of the Collection

The photographs document the conservation of National Museum of African Art (NMAfA) objects including images taken before, during, and after treatment.

Photographic Processes and Formats Represented

There are color dye coupler slides, dye diffusion transfer photoprints (Polaroid), and silver gelatin photonegatives, photoprints (mostly contact prints), and radiographs.

Other Materials Represented

None.

Access and Usage Policies

Available by appointment only to Smithsonian Institution staff. No reproductions may be made.

Publication Policies

Photographs are not available for publication.

AF·1

NMAfA Conservation Laboratory Photograph Files

Dates of Photographs: 1960s–Present

Collection Origins

National Museum of African Art (NMAfA) Conservation Laboratory staff created the collection to document their conservation of NMAfA holdings.

Physical Description

There are 19,000 photographs including color dye coupler slides, dye diffusion transfer photoprints (Polaroid), and silver gelatin photonegatives, photoprints (mostly contact prints), and radiographs.

Subjects

The photographs document NMAfA holdings and objects loaned to the museum that have undergone conservation treatment. Images show items before, during, and after conservation. Objects illustrated include ceramic pottery, costume, figures, masks, ornaments, and textiles from Africa.

Arranged: In three series. 1) Slides, by object's accession number. 2) Silver gelatin photonegatives and contact prints, by roll number. 3) Miscellaneous photographs, by object's accession number.

Captioned: Photonegatives and contact prints with image and roll number; other photographs and slides with date and object's accession number.

Finding Aid: Condition reports for each object treated, while not true finding aids, include information on the object, its condition, and its treatment, as well as roll numbers of photographs taken.

Restrictions: Restricted collection. Available by appointment only. No reproductions may be made.

AF

Curatorial Department

Curatorial Department
National Museum of African Art
Smithsonian Institution
Washington, D.C. 20560
Philip Ravenhill, Chief Curator
(202) 357-4600, ext. 230
Hours: Monday–Friday, 10 a.m.–5 p.m.

Scope of the Collections
There are two photographic collections with approximately 2,300 images.

Focus of the Collections
The photographs document African art objects in European and North American collections, especially sub-Saharan sculpture.

Photographic Processes and Formats Represented
There are color dye coupler photonegatives, photoprints, and phototransparencies and silver gelatin photoprints.

Other Materials Represented
None.

Access and Usage Policies
The collections are available to NMAfA curatorial staff only.

Publication Policies
The collections are restricted.

AF·2

NMAfA Curatorial Department Research Collection

Dates of Photographs: 1950s–1980s

Collection Origins

National Museum of African Art (NMAfA) Curatorial Department staff assembled the collection to document sub-Saharan African sculpture in European and North American art collections. Approximately half the images were purchased or borrowed from outside sources; the other half were photographed by Curatorial Department staff. Outside photographers and studios represented include the British Museum, London; Dallas Museum of Fine Arts; Detroit Institute of Art; Donald Morris Gallery; Field Museum of Natural History, Chicago; Indiana University Art Museum, Bloomington; Linden Museum, Stuttgart; Metropolitan Museum of Art, New York City; Museum für Völkerkunde, Berlin; Museum of Mankind, London; Rietberg Museum, Zürich; Royal Ontario Museum; University Museum, Philadelphia; University of Iowa Art Museum, Iowa City; and Walker Art Center, Minneapolis.

Physical Description

There are 2,240 photographs including color dye coupler photonegatives, photoprints, and phototransparencies and silver gelatin photoprints.

Subjects

The photographs document figurative sculpture from sub-Saharan Africa found in public and private collections throughout North America and Europe.

Arranged: Some by medium of the sculpture.

Captioned: With object's accession number, description, size, country of origin, and collection name.

Finding Aid: No.

Restrictions: Available to NMAfA curatorial staff only. No reproductions may be made.

AF·3

NMAfA Curatorial Department Study Collection

Dates of Photographs: 1949–Present

Collection Origins

National Museum of African Art (NMAfA) Curatorial Department staff assembled the collection while conducting research on African art and culture. Photographers and studios represented include Etnografiska Museet, Stockholm; Musée de L'Homme, Paris; Rijksmuseum voor Volkenkunde, Leiden, the Netherlands; and Staatliches Museum für Völkerkunde, Munich.

Physical Description

There are 65 silver gelatin photoprints.

Subjects

The photographs document African art objects located in European and North American museums.

Arranged: By stylistic category.

Captioned: With negative number and object's catalog number, description, museum, and size.

Finding Aid: No.

Restrictions: Available to NMAfA curatorial staff only. No reproductions may be made.

AF

Eliot Elisofon Archives

Eliot Elisofon Archives
National Museum of African Art
Smithsonian Institution
Washington, D.C. 20560
Christraud M. Geary, Curator
(202) 357-4600, ext. 280
Hours: Monday–Friday 10 a.m.–5 p.m.

Scope of the Collections

There are 71 photographic collections with approximately 220,350 images.

Focus of the Collections

The photographs primarily document African art, as well as the built environment, landscape, and peoples of Africa. Art objects documented include examples from every country in Africa, dating from prehistory to the present. Field photographs of African culture, dating from the 19th century to the present, show architecture, body art and costume, celebrations and rituals, and economic activity such as agriculture and trade. For a biography of Eliot Elisofon, after whom the Archives is named, see *Collection Origins* in *AF·19*.

Photographic Processes and Formats Represented

There are albumen photoprints; collodion gelatin photoprints (POP); color dye bleach photoprints (Cibachrome); color dye coupler photonegatives, photoprints, phototransparencies, and slides (including Agfachrome, Ektachrome, Fujichrome, and Kodachrome); dye diffusion transfer photoprints (some Polaroid); silver gelatin dry plate lantern slides and photonegatives; and silver gelatin photonegatives (some on nitrate) and photoprints. Other formats represented include cabinet cards, cartes-de-visite, contact sheets, postcards, and stereographs.

Other Materials Represented

The Archives also contains audiotape cassettes, books, brochures, correspondence, diaries, exhibit catalogs, manuals, manuscripts, maps, motion-picture film footage, museum guides, newsletters, newspaper clippings, notebooks, notes, pamphlets, photomechanical postcards, reports, and xerographic copies.

Access and Usage Policies

Many collections are open to the public by appointment. Some photonegative and photoprint collections may be available to Smithsonian Institution staff only. Researchers should call or write in advance for an appointment, describing their research topic, the type of material that interests them, and their research aim. Requests for slides or photographs should include the following information about the desired image: 1) subject or object; 2) geographic region or specific people; 3) format, including size (such as 35mm color slide); 4) number of views or image sequences desired; 5) number of copies; and 6) total number of images. There is a charge for photographic and xerographic copies of unrestricted photographs, based on rates set by the National Museum of African Art. Prepayment is required on all orders.

Publication Policies

Researchers must obtain permission from the Smithsonian Institution's National Museum of African Art to reproduce a photograph and may also have to obtain permission from the copyright holder, which is not necessarily the Smithsonian Institution. The preferred credit line is "[Photographer's name,] Courtesy of National Museum of African Art, Eliot Elisofon Archives, Smithsonian Institution."

AF·4

Philip M. Abrams Collection

Dates of Photographs: 1957–1973

Collection Origins

Philip M. Abrams, a U.S. foreign service official, created the collection and donated it to the National Museum of African Art (NMAfA) in 1986. Segments of the collection have been transferred to the NMAfA Postcard Collection *(AF·51)* and to the museum's Warren M. Robbins Library. NMAfA assigned the collection accession number A1986-02.

Physical Description

There are 390 color dye coupler slides. Other materials include maps, the *Official Standard Names Gazetteer* for Liberia (transferred to NMAfA's Warren Robbins Library), and postcards (transferred to the NMAfA Postcard Collection, *AF·51*).

Subjects

The photographs document architecture and people in Ghana, Liberia, Nigeria, Mali, Senegal, and Upper Volta (now Burkina Faso). Peoples portrayed include Bassa, Bundu, Dogon, Grebo, and Vai. Images of the built environment include traditional African architecture such as Dogon villages, the Mopti mosque in Mali, and Vai villages in Liberia, as well as modern architecture in such cities as Kumasi, Ghana, and Dakar, Senegal.

Activities documented include a Bundu *sande* women's society performance with Sowei (female guardian spirit) masks in Liberia; a Dogon *dama* (festival) masquerade staged for tourists in Sangha, Mali; a Grebo war dance in Krutown, Monrovia, Liberia; young Vai boys during initiation into the *poro* male secret society; and masked Vai dancers performing on Providence Island, Monrovia.

Arranged: By caption number.

Captioned: With date, location, photographer, and subject.

Finding Aid: No.

Restrictions: No.

AF·5

Agbenyega Adedze Slide Collection

Dates of Photographs: 1989

Collection Origins

Agbenyega Adedze, a graduate student in archaeology at the University of California at Los Angeles, created the collection while he was a Smithsonian Institution fellow. The photographs were commissioned jointly by the National Museum of Natural History and the National Museum of African Art (NMAfA). NMAfA received the photographs in 1990 and assigned them accession number A1990-06.

Physical Description

There are 375 color dye coupler slides.

Subjects

The photographs document textile marketing and production among the Ewe people in southeastern Ghana and Togo, as well as an Ewe festival in Togo. Images of a cloth market in Agbozume, Ghana, show activities such as buying and selling thread and all stages of weaving on a narrow strip loom including laying the warp, sewing strips together on a sewing machine, and assembling the finished garment.

Objects depicted include beaters, cloth such as *batakali*, dyed thread samples, heddle straps, iron pegs, loom foot pedals, reels, shuttles, shuttle bobbins, tool boxes, and weights. People portrayed include children weaving, cloth sellers, a family of dyers, and weavers. There are also images of cloth stalls in a market and storefronts. Festival images, taken in Notse, Togo, show people dressed in Ewe strip-woven cloth. A photograph from this collection is reproduced in the illustrations section of this volume.

Arranged: By assigned number.

Captioned: With assigned number, date, photographer, place, and subject.

Finding Aid: Caption list.

Restrictions: No.

AF·6

Africa and Brazil Photograph Album

Dates of Photographs: 19th Century

Collection Origins

Unknown. The National Museum of African Art purchased the collection in 1988 and assigned it accession number A1988-08.

Physical Description

There are 24 albumen photoprints.

Subjects

The photographs document 19th century built environments in Africa and Brazil including buildings, cities, docks, and ships. The African photographs document Cape Town, South Africa, including Adderley Street, the docks, and the Parliament; Dakar, Senegal, including the harbor and street scenes; and Libreville, Gabon, including government buildings and ships. Images of Brazil show government buildings and ships in Rio de Janeiro.

Arranged: No.

Captioned: With location and subject in French.

Finding Aid: No.

Restrictions: No.

AF·7

African Art in American Collections Photograph File

Dates of Photographs: Pre-1966

Collection Origins

Warren M. Robbins (1923–), founding director emeritus of the National Museum of African Art (NMAfA), assembled the collection as source material for his book: *African Art in American Collections.* New York: Praeger, 1966. (Many of the photographs from this collection appear in the book.) Robbins received a B.A. from the University of New Hampshire in 1945 and an M.A. from the University of Michigan in 1949. Professional positions Robbins held included the following: instructor in the American school system in Germany (1948–1950); educational advisor to the U.S. High Command in Austria (1951–1955); consul for cultural and public affairs in Stuttgart, Germany (1955–1957); attaché to the chief in charge of American cultural programs in Bonn, Germany (1958–1960); assistant staff director of the U.S. State Department's Advisory Commission on Educational and Cultural Relations (1960–1961); and course chairman of the U.S. State Department's Foreign Service Institute (1962–1963). In 1962 Robbins founded and became director of the Center for Cross Cultural Communication in Washington, D.C. Two years later he established the Museum of African Art, which became NMAfA in 1981.

Photographers and studios represented include the American Museum of Natural History, Brooklyn Museum, Eliot Elisofon, Joya Hairs, Elisabeth Little, Arnold Newman, Charles Uht, and the University of Pennsylvania. NMAfA assigned the collection accession number A1991-06.

Physical Description

There are 330 silver gelatin photoprints.

Subjects

The photographs document African art in American collections including museums and private holdings. African peoples whose works are represented include the Asante, Baga, Bamum, Baule, Bembe, Bobo, Dan, Dogon, Fante, Fon, Grebo, Guro, Ibibio, Igbo, Kissi, Luba, Mangbetu, Mende, Mpongwe, Pende, Songye, Teke, Yaka, Yoruba, and Zulu. Items shown include architectural details such as doors, furniture such as headrests and stools, household objects such as utensils and vessels, personal adornments such as headpieces, ritual objects such as masks and power figures, sculptures such as anthropomorphic and zoomorphic figures, textiles, and tools such as gold weights and heddle pulleys.

Arranged: Sequentially according to arrangement in the book.

Captioned: With country, figure number, material, people, size, source, and type of object.

Finding Aid: No.

Restrictions: Available for reference only. No reproductions may be made.

AF·8

African Art Objects (Non-Holdings) Study Photograph Collection

Dates of Photographs: 1950s–Present

Collection Origins

Staff at the National Museum of African Art (NMAfA) and its predecessor, the Museum of African Art, assembled the collection to document African art objects not held by the museum. Some of the images show objects that have been offered to the museum as donations or for purchase. Photographs show selected objects from the collections of the British Museum; Brooklyn Museum; Metropolitan Museum of Art; and the Musée Royal de l'Afrique Centrale, Tervuren, Belgium.

Photographers and studios represented include the British Museum, Ina Bundy, Brooklyn Museum, A.C. Cooper Ltd., Eliot Elisofon, W. Bernard Fagg, Delmar Lipp, Elisabeth Little, Musée du Congo Belge, Museum of Primitive Art, Lydia Puccinelli, Sanders Media, Seattle Art Museum, Emmanuel Sougez, Taylor & Dull, Charles Uht, and the Wallace Collection. NMAfA assigned the collection accession number A1973-04.

Physical Description

There are 850 photographs including color dye coupler photoprints, phototransparencies, and slides; dye diffusion transfer photoprints; and silver gelatin photoprints.

Subjects

The photographs document African art objects owned by individuals and private and public institutions other than NMAfA. Objects depicted include anthropomorphic figures, beadwork, gold weights, headdresses, jewelry, masks, murals, musical instruments, ornaments, stools, staffs, textiles, and vessels created by the following peoples: Abua, Anyi, Asante, Baga, Bamana, Bamileke, Bangwa, Baule, Bembe, Bobo, Bozo, Chamba, Chokwe, Dan, Dogon, Ejagham, Ewe, Fang (Pahouin), Fon, Guro, Gurunsi, Ibibio, Igbo, Ijo, Kota, Kuba, Lega, Lele, Lobi, Loma, Lozi, Luba, Lulua, Makonde, Malinke, Mambila, Mende, Mossi, Ndaka, Ndebele, Ndengese, Pende, Senufo, Shona, Songye, Teke, Temne, Wee, Woyo, Yaka, Yoruba, Zande, and Zulu. Other objects shown come from African kingdoms such as Benin, Ife, and Rwanda.

Arranged: By geographical region of Africa, then by people or kingdom and country, then by type of object.

Captioned: Some with people or kingdom, region, and subject.

Finding Aid: Partial inventory.

Restrictions: Available to Smithsonian Institution staff only. No reproductions may be made.

AF·9

David Wason Ames Slide Collection

Dates of Photographs: 1950

Collection Origins

Anthropologist David Wason Ames (1922–) created the collection to document his work among the Wolof people of the Gambia. Ames, who received a Ph.D. in anthropology from Northwestern University in 1953, taught at California State University at San Francisco, the Illinois Institute of Technology, and the University of Wisconsin. His research interests include acculturation in West Africa, economic anthropology, ethnography of the Hausa and Wolof peoples, and ethnomusicology. Ames co-wrote the following book with Anthony V. King: *Glossary of Hausa Music and Its Social Contexts.* Evanston, Illinois: Northwestern University Press, 1971. In 1987 the collection was donated to the National Museum of African Art, which assigned it accession number A1987-04.

Physical Description

There are 165 color dye coupler slides.

Subjects

The photographs document the Wolof peoples and their villages in the Gambia, West Africa. Activities illustrated include celebrating a wedding, planting crops, tending livestock, and weaving. There are images of the built environment, including shelters, and textiles, including clothes and fabrics.

Arranged: No.

Captioned: A few with photographer, slide number, and subject.

Finding Aid: No.

Restrictions: No.

AF·10

Burton E. Ashley Photograph Collection

Dates of Photographs: 1930–1933, 1950–1952

Collection Origins

Geologist Burton E. Ashley (1908–) created the collection to document his travels in Africa in the 1930s. Ashley worked for the British South Africa Company from 1930 to 1933. He received an M.A. from the University of Minnesota in 1936 and later worked for the Texas Company (1936–1943), Phillips Petroleum Company (1943–1950), U.S. Geological Survey (1950–1957), and U.S. Bureau of Mines (1957–1960). In 1961, he became minerals officer for the U.S. Department of State, serving in Australia. After retiring, Ashley served as a volunteer in the Mineral Sciences Department of the National Museum of Natural History. Photographers represented include Burton E. Ashley and Sydney Schafer. The collection was assigned National Museum of African Art accession number 1979-01.

Physical Description

There are 1,150 photographs including color dye coupler phototransparencies and silver gelatin photonegatives (some on nitrate) and photoprints. Other materials include postcards, which have been transferred to the NMAfA Postcard Collection *(AF·51)*.

Subjects

The photographs are cityscapes and landscapes taken in Egypt, South Africa, Tanzania, and Zambia during the early 1930s and early 1950s. The images illustrate architecture such as Islamic buildings in Tanzania, a mission in Zambia, and the Mohamed Ali Mosque in Cairo, Egypt; cityscapes of Cape Town, South Africa, and Port Said, Egypt; market scenes in Cairo and Mozambique; and ships, structures, and waterscapes in the Suez Canal, Egypt. There are also images of animals, geological features, and vegetation, including landscapes of the Kalahari Desert in Botswana and waterscapes of rivers (such as the Luangwa River, Nile River, and Zambezi River) and waterfalls (such as Victoria Falls).

Arranged: By figure number.

Captioned: With figure number and subject.

Finding Aid: Caption list.

Restrictions: No.

AF·11

Herbert Baker Slide Collection

Dates of Photographs: 1966–1975

Collection Origins

Art dealer Herbert Baker (1924–) assembled the collection for personal reference purposes. Baker studied art in Chicago and, after serving in the South Pacific during World War II, worked for Raymond Loewy Associates, Burton Browne Advertising, and Wetzel Brothers. In 1950 he founded Herbert Baker Advertising. That same year he began collecting African art. A member of the Committee on Primitive Art at the Art Institute of Chicago between 1960 and 1970, Baker is an authority on African and Oceanic art. His art holdings have been shown at Lake Forest College in Illinois, the Museum of African Art (now the National Museum of African Art [NMAfA]), and the Nelson-Atkins Museum of Art in Kansas City. In 1978 Baker donated this photograph collection to NMAfA, which assigned it accession number A1978-01.

Physical Description

There are 225 color dye coupler slides.

Subjects

The photographs document African anthropomorphic and zoomorphic figures, ceremonial containers, masks, and weapons. African masks documented are from the following peoples: Bamana, Dogon, Fang (Pahouin), Igbo, Lega, Senufo, and Yaka. Sculptures shown include an Asante *akuaba* (wooden child figure), Jukun figures, a Kongo power figure, a Luba figure, a Mumuye figure, and Senufo figures. Other objects depicted include an Asante state sword, a Bamana *chiwara* (antelope headdress), a beaded gourd from the Cameroon Grassfields, and a Dogon door and stool.

Arranged: No.

Captioned: With subject.

Finding Aid: No.

Restrictions: Available for reference only. No reproductions may be made.

AF·12

William W. Brill Collection

Dates of Photographs: ND

Collection Origins

William W. Brill (1918–) created the collection to document his holdings of African art objects. Brill, who received a B.A. from Yale University, works in real estate. He has donated some of his art objects to museums. Photographers represented include Tony Fitsch, Al Mozell, and Bernard Pierre Wolff. The collection is National Museum of African Art accession number A1985-01.

Physical Description

There are 420 silver gelatin photoprints. Other materials include correspondence and xerographic copies.

Subjects

The photographs document African art objects from William Brill's personal collection, which primarily contains masks, sculpted figures, and tools. Masks documented are from the following peoples: Hemba, Lulua, Makonde, and Mbagani. Sculptural figures shown were created by the following groups: Bassa, Dogon, Kulango, Kuyu, Loma, Luba, Lunda, Punu, and Tabwa. Other objects shown include an Asante comb, Asante royal staff, Baule animal head, Bete heddle pulley, Chokwe comb, Ijo staff, Kuba headrest, Lele staff, Ndengese axe handle, Senufo ceremonial container, Senufo wine strainer, Yela staff, Yoruba house post, Zulu comb, and Zulu hunter's staff. There are also images of musical instruments including bells, flutes, and rhythm pounders from Cameroon, Mali, Nigeria, and Zaire.

Arranged: No.

Captioned: With description and dimensions.

Finding Aid: No.

Restrictions: Available for reference only. No reproductions may be made.

AF·13

Bronson Catalog Collection

Dates of Photographs: 1970s

Collection Origins

Staff of the North Carolina Museum of Art in Raleigh created the collection to document art objects from Zaire owned by Lee Bronson, Dona Bronson (his wife), and Robert Bronson (his brother) for publication in the following exhibit catalog: Joseph Cornet. *A Survey of Zairian Art: The Bronson Collection.* Raleigh: North Carolina Museum of Art, 1978. Studios represented include the North Carolina Museum of Art. The National Museum of African Art assigned the collection accession number A1986-11.

Physical Description

There are 185 silver gelatin photoprints. Other materials include a typed manuscript version of the exhibit catalog.

Subjects

The photographs document Zairian art objects owned by the Lee Bronson family. There are images of figures from the Bembe, Hemba, Songye, and Yombe peoples. Other objects shown include a Kongo power object, Lele cup, Lwena comb, Teke chief's collar, and Yaka mask.

Arranged: By geographic region within Zaire, then by people of origin.

Captioned: With people of origin as well as description, medium, size, and type of object.

Finding Aid: Index to the catalog.

Restrictions: Available for reference only. No reproductions may be made.

AF·14

Augustus Browning Photograph Collection

Dates of Photographs: 1982–1984

Collection Origins

Augustus Browning created the collection during his frequent travels in Nigeria. Browning, who studied under Ansel Adams, resides in California and works as a free-lance photographer. The National Museum of African Art assigned the collection accession number A1986-13.

Physical Description

There are 25 silver gelatin photoprints.

Subjects

The photographs show the land and peoples of Nigeria. Informal portraits include a horseman announcing the arrival of the emir at a *sallah* (Islamic festival) celebration in Zaria; a Fulbe cattleman and children crossing a road during the harmattan (dry wind) season; and a Hausa weaver working on a loom in Katsina. Other Nigerians shown include Fulbe women, a Hausa girl in Kaduna, a Kanuri man from Bornu, and a Tuareg man. Other images show the Nigerian landscape during the harmattan season and lightning in

Kaduna. A photograph from this collection is reproduced in the illustrations section of this volume.

Arranged: By negative number in a portfolio box.

Captioned: With location, negative number, photographer, subject, and year.

Finding Aid: No.

Restrictions: Available for reference only. No reproductions may be made.

AF·15

Frank Christol Photograph Collection

Dates of Photographs: Circa 1920–1930

Collection Origins

Missionary Frank Christol created the collection during his stay in the Cameroon Grassfields. The National Museum of African Art (NMAfA) bought the photoprints in 1989. The Photothèque of the Musée de l'Homme in Paris owns some of the original photonegatives and photoprints. The NMAfA assigned the collection accession number A1989-04.

Physical Description

There are 215 silver gelatin photoprints.

Subjects

The photographs document the peoples of the Cameroon Grassfields, particularly the Bamileke. Activities documented included dancing and playing musical instruments. Objects depicted include figures, masks, textiles, and vessels. There are images of chiefs' palaces and architectural details such as carved doors, house posts, and window frames. Portraits document costume, hairstyles, jewelry, and scarification, often with people posed in groups with objects. People portrayed include carvers with their work and chiefs with their palaces.

Arranged: No.

Captioned: With subject in French.

Finding Aid: No.

Restrictions: Reproductions of some images may be made only with the permission of the Photothèque, Musée de l'Homme, Musée National d'Histoire Naturelle, 17 Place de Trocadéro, Paris, France, 75116, telephone 011-45-53-70-60.

AF·16

Patricia C. Coronel Slide Collection

Dates of Photographs: 1972–1974

Collection Origins

Patricia C. Coronel created the collection to document the art and culture of the Aowin of western Ghana for research purposes. Coronel, a professor of art history at Colorado State University, received a Ph.D. in African Art History from the University of California, Santa Barbara, in 1978. The photographs have appeared in the following article: Patricia C. Coronel. "Aowin Terracotta Sculpture." *African Arts* 13(1) (1979): 28–35. In 1990 Coronel donated the images to the National Museum of African Art, where they were assigned accession number A1990-02.

Physical Description

There are 20 color dye coupler slides, all of which are duplicates of original slides.

Subjects

The photographs document the Aowin, a group of Akan people in western Ghana, and their art. People portrayed include chiefs, the king, masqueraders, musicians, and priestesses. Activities shown include a festival and a festival procession. Objects documented include jewelry, a linguist's staff, a sword, and terracotta funerary sculptures.

Arranged: No.

Captioned: With subject.

Finding Aid: Caption list.

Restrictions: Available for reference only. No reproductions may be made.

AF·17

David and Mary Kay Davies Slide Collection

Dates of Photographs: 1966, 1967, 1973

Collection Origins

Mary Kay Davies, anthropology librarian at the National Museum of Natural History, and David Davies, her husband, created the collection during their vacation trips to Africa in 1966, 1967, and 1973. In 1972 and 1987 the Davies donated the collection to the National Museum of African Art, where it received accession number A1972-01.

Physical Description

There are 75 color dye coupler slides (Kodachrome).

Subjects

The photographs document the animals, landscapes, peoples, and towns of Kenya and Nigeria in the 1960s and 1970s. Animals depicted include camels and a baby eland. Images of Kenya show the architecture of the Rendille and Samburu peoples, clothing and adornment of the Samburu, and the harbor at Lamu. The Nigerian images depict dye pits for indigo cloth production and the market in Kaduna.

Arranged: No.

Captioned: Some with subject.

Finding Aid: No.

Restrictions: No.

AF·18

Guy Ederheimer, Jr., Photograph Collection

Dates of Photographs: Circa 1930–1931, 1970s–1980s

Collection Origins

Guy Ederheimer, Jr., created the collection to document South Africa in the 1930s. In 1985 he donated the collection to the National Museum of African Art, where it received accession number A1986-15.

Physical Description

There are 70 photographs including color dye bleach photoprints (Cibachrome) and silver gelatin photoprints.

Subjects

The photographs are cityscapes and waterscapes of Egypt and portraits of South Africans, including a Zulu wedding dance. There are portraits of the best man, the bride, dancers, the groom, mothers with children, and other women. The Egyptian images show Cairo and the Nile River.

Arranged: No.

Captioned: With subject.

Finding Aid: No.

Restrictions: Available for reference only. No reproductions may be made.

AF·19

Eliot Elisofon Art Object Photograph Collection

Dates of Photographs: 1942–1972

Collection Origins

Eliot Elisofon (1911–1973), a photographer best known for his work in *Life* magazine, was the primary creator of the collection. After studying at Fordham University, Elisofon worked as a free-lance magazine photographer from 1933 to 1937. From 1937 to 1942, he worked as a staff photographer for *Life,* traveling extensively in Africa, Asia, Europe, and South America. Between 1942 and 1962, Elisofon went on photographic assignments for many publications including *Smithsonian* magazine. He specialized in documenting the diverse peoples of Africa, Europe, Japan, the Pacific Islands, and South America, as well as their arts and environments. A founding member and curatorial

associate at the Museum of African Art, which in 1981 became the National Museum of African Art (NMAfA), Elisofon bequeathed his collection of African photographs to the museum when he died in 1973. To honor Elisofon's contributions to the understanding of African art and culture, NMAfA named its archives after him.

Elisofon's work appears in many books and articles on Africa. Photographs from this collection have appeared in issues of *Life* magazine and in the following publications: 1) William Fagg. *The Sculpture of Africa.* London: Thames & Hudson, 1958. 2) Paul Radin. *African Folktales and Sculpture.* New York: Pantheon Books, 1952. NMAfA assigned the collection accession number A1973-02.

Physical Description

There are 20,000 photographs including color dye coupler photoprints, phototransparencies, and slides (Ektachrome and Kodachrome) and silver gelatin photonegatives and photoprints.

Subjects

The photographs document African art works including objects in bronze, clay, copper, fiber, ivory, and wood. The collection contains photographs of architectural ornaments such as carved doors and plaques; costume and personal adornments such as hair ornaments, headdresses, jewelry, pectorals, and staffs; furniture and vessels such as bowls, boxes, chairs, cups, divination bowls, headrests, pipes and pipe bowls, and stools; sculptures such as carved tusks, funerary figures, masks, memorial figures, and power figures; and other objects such as cloth, combs, game boards, gold weights, and musical instruments.

African kingdoms and peoples represented include Afo, Anyi, Asante, Atie, Baga, Bamana, Bamum, Baule, Bembe, Benin, Bobo, Boki, Bozo, Chamba, Chokwe, Dan, Dinka, Dogon, Ebrie, Efik, Ejagham, Hausa, Ibibio, Idoma, Ife, Igbo-Ukwu, Ijo, Jenne, Jukun, Kamba, Kissi, Kom, Kongo, Kono, Kota, Kpelle, Kuba, Kuyu, Kwele, Lega, Lobi, Loma, Lozi, Luba, Lulua, Lunda, Mambila, Mende, Mossi, Nalu, Ndebele, Ngbaka, Ngoni, Nok, Nupe, Nyamwezi, Pende, Salampasu, Senufo, Sherbro, Shilluk, Shona, Songye, Suku, Susu, Tabwa, Teke, Temne, Tetela, Tiv, Tuareg, Urhobo, Vai, Woyo, Yaka, Yoruba, and Zande.

Specific objects shown include an Afo stool from Nigeria; an Anyi terra-cotta funerary figure from the Ivory Coast; an Asante state sword, stool, and terra-cotta funerary head from Ghana; an Atie animal figure made of gold from the Ivory Coast; a Bamana *chiwara* (antelope headdress) and puppet from Mali; a Baule mother and child figure from the Ivory Coast; a Bembe male figure from Congo; a Benin bronze head of a queen mother and plaque from Nigeria; a Chokwe mask from Angola; a Dan mask from Liberia; a Dogon figure of a horse and rider from Mali, a primordial couple figure, and wooden house posts from several *toguna* (male meeting houses) in Mali; an Ife bronze head from Nigeria; an Igbo mask from Nigeria; an Igbo-Ukwu bronze bowl from Nigeria; a Jukun head-dress from Nigeria; a Kom throne figure from Cameroon; and a Kongo *ntadi* (guardian figure) and staff from Zaire.

There also are images of a Kuba *ndop* (royal statue) from Zaire; a Kwele mask from Gabon; a Luba male figure and stool from Zaire; a Lulua warrior figure from Zaire; a Mambila figure from Nigeria; a Mende mask from Sierra Leone; a Mossi mask from Burkina Faso; a Nok terra-cotta figure (fragment) from Nigeria; a Pende ceremonial adze from Zaire; a Senufo staff finial in the shape of a bird and a female figure from the Ivory Coast; a Songye power figure from the Ivory Coast; a Yaka mask from Zaire; a Yoruba *gelede* (men's society) mask and *ibeji* (twin figures) from Nigeria; and a Zulu doll from South Africa.

Institutions whose works of art are documented include the American Museum of Natural History; Art Institute of Chicago; British Museum; Brooklyn Museum; Buffalo Museum of Science; Dallas Museum of Fine Arts; Denver Art Museum; Ghana National Museum, Accra; Hampton Institute (now Hampton University); Horniman Museum; Ife Museum, Nigeria; Jos Museum, Nigeria; Linden Museum, Stuttgart, Germany; Los Angeles County Museum; Metropolitan Museum of Art; Musée Royal de l'Afrique Centrale, Tervuren, Belgium; Musées Nationaux, Kinshasa, Zaire; Museum für Völkerkunde, Berlin; Museum für Völkerkunde, Vienna; National Museum, Lagos, Nigeria; Peabody Museum, Harvard University; Peabody Museum, Salem, Massachusetts; Philadelphia Museum of Art; and University Museum, Philadelphia.

There also are photographic reproductions of objects from the collections of Ernst Anspach, Robert and William Arnett, Gaston de Havenon, Jacob Epstein, Harry Franklin, Mark and Denyse Ginzberg, Chaim Gross, Ben Heller, Irwin Hersey, J.J. Klejman, Gertrude Mellon, Werner Muensterberger, Arnold Newman, Robert and Nancy Nooter, Charles Ratton, Milton Rosenthal, James J. Sweeney, Tristan Tzara, Katherine C. White, and Lester Wunderman.

Arranged: By format in five series. 1) Silver gelatin contact sheets. 2) Filing cards with silver gelatin contact prints. 3) Slides. 4) Silver gelatin photonegatives housed in negative files. 5) Oversize photoprints. Series 1 and 4 are arranged in the sequence they were taken. Series 2, 3, and 5 are arranged according to the Archives Classification System for photographs of art in collections, which organizes images by geographic region, people of origin, country of origin or artist,

object type, photographer, date, series number, and collector or collection.

Captioned: Photonegatives with classification number (according to date) and negative number. Slides with country, date, geographical region, object type, people of origin or individual artist, and photographer.

Finding Aid: "Guide to the Classification System: Art in Collections," which reviews the size and scope of the collection, explains the organization of the art photographs, and provides maps. The guide lists owners, special categories, and subject headings.

Restrictions: Available for reference only. No reproductions may be made without permission from the owner of the object illustrated.

AF·20

Eliot Elisofon Field Photograph Collection

Dates of Photographs: 1942–1972

Collection Origins

Photographer Eliot Elisofon (1911–1973) created most of the photographs in the collection to document his travels and work. For a biography of Elisofon, see the *Collection Origins* field in *AF·19*. Photographs from this collection appeared in *Life* magazine and the following publications: 1) Eliot Elisofon. *Colour Photography*. London: Thames & Hudson, 1962. 2) Eliot Elisofon. *The Nile*. New York: Viking Press, 1964. 3) Eliot Elisofon. *Zaire: A Week in Joseph's World*. New York: Crowell-Collier Press, 1973. 4) Tom Maloney, ed. "Africa by Eliot Elisofon." *U.S. Camera Annual*. New York, 1953. 5) Edward Steichen. *Memorable Life Photographs*. New York: Museum of Modern Art, 1951.

At present, the collection contains the work of several other photographers; however, these images will be removed from *AF·20* and given independent collection status in the near future. Other photographers represented include Frank and Georgette Ballance, Ruth Barnes, Laurel Cooper, John Dean, Amina Dickerson, Mark A. Hukill, Brigitta Mitchell, Roy Mitchell, Carl Purcell, Amy Richwine, Warren M. Robbins, Susan Ryan, Peter Schub, Janet Stanley, Philips Stevens, Albert Votaw, Richard Wechsler, Volkmar Wentzel, and Michael Yoffe. In 1973 Elisofon bequeathed these images to the Museum of African Art (now the National

Museum of African Art [NMAfA]), where it received accession number A1973-01.

Physical Description

There are 80,000 photographs including color dye coupler photoprints, phototransparencies, and slides (Ektachrome and Kodachrome) and silver gelatin photonegatives and photoprints.

Subjects

The photographs document many aspects of African life and culture including agriculture, animals, archaeology, architecture, art and artisans, children, cityscapes, dance and music, domestic scenes, education, flora, hunting and fishing, industry, landscapes, leaders, markets, medicine, recreation, rituals and celebrations, and transportation.

Artisans shown include an Asante weaver making *kente* cloth in Ghana; a Dogon carver in Mali making a *kanaga* mask; an Ebrie goldsmith in the Ivory Coast; Hausa dyers in Kano, Nigeria; and Nupe beadmakers in Nigeria; as well as contemporary artists at the École des Beaux Arts in Kinshasa, Zaire. Portraits of leaders include the Asante court at Kumase in Ghana; Ebrie chiefs and notables in the Ivory Coast; the *timi* (king) of Ede, a town in Yoruba, Nigeria; the emir of Katsina, Nigeria; and the Kuba king and his court in Zaire. There are informal portraits showing children of the Kuba royal court dancing, Fulbe women with gold earrings in Mali, Mangbetu women in Zaire (including one receiving an elaborate coiffure), Maasai elders, and a Mbuti girl in Zaire with a painted face and torso.

Masked dances documented include a Dogon *dama* festival celebration in Mali, an Igbo festival in Nigeria, and Kuba and Pende masked dancers in Zaire. There are also images of Yoruba *gelede* (men's association) masks in Nigeria. Non-masked dancers shown include Dan professional acrobatic dancers in the Ivory Coast, Irigwe dancers in Nigeria, Mangbetu dancers in Zaire, Mbuti dancers in Zaire, and Wodaabe men dancing in Nigeria. Events shown include Hausa riders in chain mail during the Independence Day celebration in Katsina, Nigeria.

Images of art in situ include ancestral altars in the King of Benin's palace in Nigeria; Dogon rock paintings in Mali; and Yoruba Shango (religious sect) shrine sculptures in the palace courtyard of the *timi* (king) of Ede in Nigeria. Traditional architecture in Ghana shown includes Asante shrine houses with raised wall decorations, Dogon villages in Mali, and mosques in Mopti. Landscapes include views of Mount Kilimanjaro, Tanzania. Animals shown include birds, buffalos, elephants, and giraffes. Several photographs from this collection are reproduced in the illustrations section of this volume.

Arranged: By format in six series. 1) Silver gelatin contact sheets. 2) Filing cards with silver gelatin contact prints. 3) Vintage field photographs. 4) Slides. 5) Silver gelatin photonegatives housed in negative files. 6) Oversize photoprints. Series 1 and 5 are arranged according to the sequence of Eliot Elisofon's trips. Series 2, 3, 4, and 6 are arranged by the Archives Classification System, which organizes images by subject, art producing area, people of origin, photographer, photographic series, and year and indicates whether an image is an original or a copy.

Captioned: Photonegatives with classification number indicating date, negative number, and trip. Slides with country or people of origin, date, geographical region, photographer, series number, and subject.

Finding Aid: "Guide to the Collection (Field)," which reviews the size and scope of the collection, explains the organization of the photographs, provides maps, and explains the procedure for ordering photographs. It also lists other photographers whose images still are interfiled with the collection, special categories, and subject headings.

Restrictions: No.

AF·21

Eliot Elisofon Kress Photograph Collection *A.K.A.* Kress Collection

Dates of Photographs: Circa 1965

Collection Origins

Eliot Elisofon (1911–1973) created the collection to document African art objects in private and public collections in the United States and other countries. For a biography of Elisofon, see *Collection Origins* in *AF-19*. The photographs were distributed by the Kress Foundation and can be found in the following repositories: Indiana University, the Metropolitan Museum of Art in New York, and the Peabody Museum at Harvard University. The National Museum of African Art assigned the collection accession number A1973-03.

Physical Description

There are 7,500 photographs including silver gelatin photonegatives and photoprints.

Subjects

The photographs document African art works, primarily wooden sculptures from western and central Africa as well as bronze, clay, copper, fiber, and ivory objects. Objects illustrated include bowls (such as divination bowls), boxes, carved tusks, chairs, cloth, combs, cups, doors, figures (such as funerary, memorial, and power figures), game boards, gold weights, hair ornaments, headdresses, headrests, masks (some miniature), pectorals, pipe bowls, pipes, plaques, portraits, staffs of office, stools, and window shutters.

Peoples and kingdoms represented include the Asante, Baga, Baule, Bembe, Benin, Bini, Bobo, Chokwe, Dan, Dogon, Ejagham, Esie, Ewe, Fang (Pahouin), Fon, Guro, Huana, Ibibio, Ife, Igala, Igbo, Ishan, Jenne, Kete, Kissi, Kongo, Kota, Kuba, Kwele, Lega, Lobi, Loma, Lozi, Luba, Lulua, Lumbu, Makonde, Mangbetu, Marka, Mbata, Mende, Mossi, Ngbaka, Nok, Pende, Sao, Senufo, Sherbro, Shilluk, Songye, Sorongo, Susu, Teke, Tetela, Urhobo, Vai, Wee, Yaka, Yoruba, Zande, and Zulu.

Sculpted figures shown include a Baga female figure from Guinea; a Baule male wooden figure with beard from the Ivory Coast; a Bembe ivory figure from Congo; a Dogon wooden ancestral figure from Mali; a Fang (Pahouin) male figure from Gabon; a Kissi stone figure from Guinea; a Kota funerary figure from Gabon; a Lega animal figure and wooden two-sided figure from Zaire; Mossi wooden female and male figures from Burkina Faso; a Senufo female figure, male figure rhythm-pounder, wooden horse and rider figure, and wooden seated mother and child figures from the Ivory Coast; a Songye power figure from Zaire; a Teke male figure from Congo; a Yaka figure with cowry shells from Zaire; and Yoruba *ibeji* (twin figures) from Nigeria.

Masks illustrated include a Baga shoulder mask from Guinea, a Dan wooden mask from the Ivory Coast, a Kwele four-faced mask from Congo, a Lega wooden mask from Zaire, a Loma wooden mask from Guinea, a Pende miniature ivory mask from Zaire, a Senufo double fire spitter mask from the Ivory Coast, a Vai *sande* society wooden mask from Liberia, and a Wee mask with shotgun shells from the Ivory Coast.

Other objects shown include architectural elements such as a Dogon granary door from Mali and a Senufo wooden door from the Ivory Coast; dishes and utensils such as a Fang (Pahouin) ceremonial spoon with figure from Gabon, a Guro wood spoon from the Ivory Coast, a Kuba drinking horn and wooden cup from Zaire; musical instruments such as an Asante drum from Ghana; and ornaments such as a Huana ivory pendant from Zaire. There are also images of an Asante *akuaba* (wooden child figure) from Ghana, Benin bronze idiophone from Nigeria, Kuba box made of jukula wood from Zaire, Shilluk comb cutout from the Sudan, Songye plaque from Zaire, Yoruba wooden staff from Nigeria,

Zande throwing knife from the Sudan, and Zulu headrest from South Africa.

The African sculptures documented in this collection are in the holdings of the British Museum, London; Brooklyn Museum, New York; Commercial Museum, Philadelphia; Ghana National Museum, Accra; Howard University, Washington, D.C.; Metropolitan Museum of Art, New York; Musée de l'Homme, Paris; Musée Ethnographie de Porto Novo, Benin; Musée Royale de Congo Belge, Tervuren, Belgium; Museum für Völkerkunde, Berlin; Museum für Völkerkunde, Vienna, Austria; National Museum, Jos, Nigeria; National Museum, Lagos, Nigeria; NMAfA; Peabody Museum, Harvard University; Philadelphia Museum of Art; Prempeh II Jubilee Museum, Kumasi, Ghana; and the University Museum, Philadelphia.

There also images of objects from the holdings of Herbert Baker, Mr. and Mrs. Gordon Bunshaft, Julian Carlebach, Paul Chadourne, Mr. and Mrs. Arthur Cohen, Miguel Covarrubias, David Crownover, Donald Deskey, Eliot Elisofon, Jacob Epstein, Chaim Gross, Laurence Gussman, Pascal James Imperato, Carl Kyersmeier, Ralph Linton, Arnold Newman, Mrs. Franz Olbrecht, Mrs. Sherman Parsons, Roland Penrose, Margaret Plass, Webster Plass, Claude Puglkonsi, Charles Ratton, Harold Rome, Samuel Rubin, Helena Rubinstein, Merton Simpson, Paul Tishman, Tristan Tzara, and Suzanne Verite.

Arranged: In three series by format. 1) Photoprints arranged by region, then by people of origin, object type, and negative number. 2) Photoprints arranged by original negative number. 3) Photonegatives arranged by original negative number.

Captioned: With archives number, collection source, country, dimensions, people of origin, and subject.

Finding Aid: Catalog.

Restrictions: Available for reference only. No reproductions may be made without permission from the owner of the object illustrated.

AF·22

Walker Evans Photograph Collection *A.K.A.* Samuel Stern Photograph Collection

Dates of Photographs: 1935

Collection Origins

Photographer, educator, and author Walker Evans (1903–1975) created this portfolio titled "African Negro Art: Photographs by Walker Evans" in conjunction with the exhibit "African Negro Art," held at the Museum of Modern Art (MOMA) in New York in 1935. Evans, who studied at Williams College in 1923 and the Sorbonne in Paris in 1926, worked as a photographer for the Farm Security Administration from 1935 to 1937. From 1943 to 1945 he was a contributing editor to *Time* magazine, and from 1946 to 1965 he served as an associate editor and staff photographer at *Fortune* magazine. Evans also taught graphic arts at Yale University and served as artist-in-residence at Dartmouth College.

The images have been published in the following books: 1) Paul Radin. *African Folktales & Sculpture.* New York: Pantheon Books, 1952. 2) James Johnson Sweeney. *African Negro Art.* New York: Museum of Modern Art, 1935. 3) James Johnson Sweeney. *African Sculpture.* Princeton, New Jersey: Princeton University Press, 1970. The collection duplicates part of a set of 475 photographs available for study at MOMA. Samuel Stern, a New York physician, donated the photographs to the National Museum of African Art (NMAfA), where it received accession number A1985-10.

Physical Description

There are 225 silver gelatin photoprints.

Subjects

The collection documents African art works shown in the 1935 MOMA exhibit "African Negro Art." Objects depicted include costume, doors, fly whisks, gold weights, headrests, jewelry, masks, musical instruments such as bells and rhythm pounders, power figures, pipes, staff finials, stools, and wood sculptures of men and women. Peoples and kingdoms whose art works are shown include the Asante, Baule, Benin, Boki, Dogon, Fang (Pahouin), Ijo, Kuba, Lumbu, Mama, Mende, Mpongwe, Punu, and Yoruba.

Arranged: By assigned number.

Captioned: With negative number.

Finding Aid: List of captions.

Restrictions: Available for reference only. No reproductions may be made without permission from the owner of the object illustrated.

AF·23

William B. Fagg Photograph Collection

Dates of Photographs: 1949–1959

Collection Origins

William B. Fagg (1914–) created the collection to document his fieldwork in Nigeria and trips to Benin, Congo, Senegal, Sierra Leone, and Zaire. Fagg received an M.A. in archaeology and anthropology from Magdalen College at Cambridge University. From 1938 to 1974, except during World War II, he worked for the Department of Ethnography at the British Museum in London, where he became deputy keeper (1955–1969) and keeper (1969–1974). In addition to his fieldwork in Africa, Fagg served as a consulting fellow in African art at the Museum of Primitive Art in New York (now part of the Metropolitan Museum of Art); as chairman of the African Fine Art Gallery Trust, organizing international loan exhibits; and as a consultant to Christie's auction house. He has lectured extensively on the arts of Nigeria. Fagg's publications include the following: *The Sculpture of Africa.* London: Thames & Hudson, 1958. Paul and Ruth Tishman of New York donated the collection of photographs to the National Museum of African Art (NMAfA), where it received accession number A1986-14.

Physical Description

There are 2,450 silver gelatin photoprints.

Subjects

The photographs document William Fagg's extensive survey work in Nigeria and his trips to Benin, Congo, Senegal, Sierra Leone, and Zaire. The photographs illustrate African cultures and works of art, especially those of the Yoruba in Nigeria. Nigerian artisans portrayed include a blacksmith in the town of Jebba, a craftsman casting brass at Ijebu-Ode, and a potter at work in Nok. Celebrations and ceremonies documented include the *igue oba* and *itue* ceremonies and the festival of leaves in Benin. There are also images of dances of the Bargesh in northern Nigeria and a masked dance at Nok. Architecture documented includes altars and shrines in Benin and in Oyo, Nigeria; a Birom settlement; Brazilian-style houses in Porto Novo, Benin; an emir's house in Nigeria; a Jarawa village in Nigeria; the mosque in Keffi, Nigeria; and palaces of Yoruba kings.

Most of the photographs show sculpture including Benin bronze plaques and hip masks; Esie stone sculpture; Ife divination boards, drums, and figures; a Kuba *ndop* (royal statue) in the Kinshasa Museum; Nok terra-cotta and wooden figures; and Tada bronze figures. There also are images of *epa* (masquerade) masks; *gelede* (men's society) masks; a head of Olokun (a male Yoruba divinity) from Ibadan, Nigeria; and Yoruba *edan ogboni* (bronze staffs) and *ibeji* (twin figures) from Nigeria. Images of objects by identifiable artists include a palace pillar, post, and sculpture by Agbonbiofe; a door and *epa* mask by Areogun; and a house post and lidded bowl by Olowe of Ise. There are also images of other bronzes, ceramics, crowns, drums, jewelry, staffs, and textiles. Many of the pieces shown are from the British Museum in London; the Musée de l'I.F.A.N. (Institut Fondamental d'Afrique Noire) in Dakar, Senegal; the National Museum at Jos, Nigeria; and the National Museum at Lagos, Nigeria.

Arranged: Chronologically by year, roll number, and frame number.

Captioned: Most with date, description, location, and roll and frame numbers.

Finding Aid: Catalogs, compiled by William B. Fagg, Deborah Stokes Hammer, and Jeffrey S. Hammer, arranged by location, negative number, and subject.

Restrictions: Available for reference only. Permission to publish or reproduce these images must be obtained in writing from the Royal Anthropological Institute of Great Britain and Ireland, 50 Fitzroy Street, London, W1P 5HS, England, telephone 011-44-71-387-0455.

AF·24

Richard Flach Photograph Album *A.K.A.* Firestone Rubber Plantation Photograph Album

Dates of Photographs: 1936–1938

Collection Origins

Richard Flach created the collection, a photograph album titled "A Pictorial Story of Two Years Service on the Firestone Rubber Plantations, Monrovia, Liberia, West Africa; Jan. 5, 1936–Mar. 4, 1938," to document his experiences working for Firestone in Africa during the 1930s. In 1984 he donated the collection to the National Museum of African Art, where it received accession number A1984-01.

Physical Description

There are 240 photographs including silver gelatin photonegatives and photoprints. Other material includes a xerographic copy of the album that held the original photographs.

Subjects

The photographs document the Firestone Rubber Plantation near Monrovia, Liberia. There are pictures of Africans, many of them Firestone workers; the plantation; and the surrounding landscape. Images of Africans portray Bassa, Kpelle, Mende, and Vai peoples, including a women's *sande* society masked dance and market scenes near the plantation. Plantation facilities illustrated include the African laborers' camp, the brick plant, and the gasoline storage area. Plantation activities shown include clearing the land and planting and caring for rubber trees. There are also portraits of Americans hunting, traveling by boat to West Africa, traveling to the interior, and visiting African cities such as Monrovia, Liberia; Dakar, Senegal; and Freetown, Sierra Leone.

Arranged: By assigned number.

Captioned: With location or photographer's description.

Finding Aid: A captioned xerographic copy of the original album.

Restrictions: No.

AF·25

Joel S. Fogel Collection

Dates of Photographs: 1973

Collection Origins

Joel S. Fogel created the collection to document his 1973 expedition in Ethiopia. Fogel traveled mainly by raft 500 miles along the Omo River, studying the peoples who live near the river. In 1986 Fogel donated the collection to the National Museum of African Art, where it received accession number A1986-03.

Physical Description

There are 400 color dye coupler slides. Other materials include an audiotape cassette and motion-picture film footage.

Subjects

The photographs document Fogel's trip on Ethiopia's Omo River and the peoples he encountered, including the Karo and Mursi. The photographs primarily show Fogel and his traveling companions, including images of fishing, hunting, and rafting. There are a few portraits of Africans showing costume and adornment. Events documented include the *maskal* festival and a military parade in Addis Ababa. Karo objects depicted include a bow and arrows, bracelets, gourds, sandals, a shield, a stool, walking sticks, and a wooden headrest. Mursi art work shown include arm rings, body decoration, ear plugs, fishing poles, lip ornaments, and a tobacco pouch. Animals shown include African fish hawks, crocodiles, gazelles, tree snakes, water buffalo, and white herons.

Arranged: By slide number.

Captioned: With date and slide number.

Finding Aid: Caption list.

Restrictions: No.

AF·26

L. Gabriel Photograph Collection

Dates of Photographs: Circa 1914–1940

Collection Origins

National Museum of African Art (NMAfA) staff assembled the collection from donations and purchases of photographs by L. Gabriel, a commercial photographer who worked in the Belgian Congo (now Zaire), the French Congo (now the People's Republic of Congo), Mozambique, and Zambia from the 1910s to 1940. The NMAfA assigned the collection accession number A1989-01.

Physical Description

There are 370 silver gelatin postcards, some in panorama sets.

Subjects

The photographs document African cityscapes, landscapes, and peoples, mainly in the French and Belgian Congo during the first half of the 20th century. Cities documented include Elisabethville (now Lubumbashi), Kansenia, Likasi, and Panda in Zaire. Peoples portrayed include Luba, Ngala, Songye, and Tutsi. Activities documented include men weaving baskets; prisoners in chains carrying wood and working in fields; soldiers performing military exercises and playing in a band; women making pots; and workers building a railroad. There also are portraits of the *mwami* (king) of Ruanda and his wife in Western dress, as well as people with different clothing, hair styles, and scarification. Objects depicted include baskets, gourds, and pots. Buildings shown include a church, a hospital, houses in villages, a prison, and a school. There are several images of a copper mine at Likasi, showing the buildings, pits, and workers' quarters. Modes of transportation illustrated include canoes, cars, and railroad tracks. Landscapes and waterscapes include images of palm trees, rivers, and waterfalls. Animals shown include camels and elephants.

Arranged: By subject.

Captioned: Some with subject in French.

Finding Aid: No.

Restrictions: Until the location of the original negatives has been established, the collection is available for reference only.

AF·27

Christraud M. Geary Senegal Slide Collection

Dates of Photographs: 1990

Collection Origins

Christraud M. Geary (1946–), curator of the Eliot Elisofon Archives at National Museum of African Art (NMAfA) since 1990, created the collection during a 1990 trip to Dakar and Gorée Island, Senegal. Geary received a doctorate in cultural anthropology from the University of Frankfurt, Germany, in 1973. She has conducted fieldwork in Cameroon for several years and written on the arts of the Cameroon Grassfields. Geary also specializes in the history of photography in Africa. Among her publications are the following: 1) *Things of the Palace. A Catalogue of the Bamum Palace Museum in Foumban, Cameroon.* Wiesbaden, Germany: Steiner Verlag, 1983. 2) *Images from Bamum: German Colonial Photography at the Court of King Njoya, Cameroon, West Africa, 1902–1915.* Washington, D.C.: Smithsonian Institution Press, 1988. The NMAfA assigned the collection accession number A1991-02.

Physical Description

There are 155 color dye coupler slides.

Subjects

The photographs primarily document archives and museums in Dakar and Gorée Island, Senegal, showing cataloging, exhibits, records, storage, and workrooms. Institutions documented include the historical museum on Gorée Island, Library of I.F.A.N. (Institut Fondamental de l'Afrique Noire), Museum of Dakar, National Archives in Dakar, and Slave House Museum on Gorée. There are also images of architecture on Gorée, including a Christian church, a fort (now the historical museum), and a mosque, as well as souvenir shops. Other images of Dakar show the harbor and a market with stores displaying tourist art. Activities documented include glass painting in Dakar and on Gorée, as well as producing paintings for tourists and sandpaintings on Gorée.

Arranged: By image number.

Captioned: With date, image number, location, and subject.

Finding Aid: No.

Restrictions: No.

AF·28

Veronique Goblet-Vanormelingen Photograph Collection

Dates of Photographs: 1985–1986

Collection Origins

Veronique Goblet-Vanormelingen created the collection to document her stay among the Luba people of Zaire. In 1987 she donated the collection to the National Museum of African Art, where it received accession number A1987-03.

Physical Description

There are 390 photographs including color dye coupler photoprints and slides.

Subjects

The photographs document the life of the Luba people in Kaniama and surrounding towns in Zaire. Activities documented include building houses, hairdressing, hunting, making pottery, metal smithing, performing an ancestor ritual at the royal court, playing music, and weaving baskets. Occupations portrayed include diviners, leaders such as the king, musicians, potters, and weavers. Some of the portraits show body art, costume, and hairstyles. There are also images of Luba architecture.

Arranged: By subject.

Captioned: With subject.

Finding Aid: No.

Restrictions: No.

AF·29

Emile E.O. Gorlia Photograph Collection *A.K.A.* Sanford M. and Nancy H. Harris Photograph Collection

Dates of Photographs: 1910–1927, 1988

Collection Origins

Emile E.O. Gorlia, a circuit court judge for the Congo Administration of the Belgian government and later secretary general of the Belgian Ministry of Colonies, created the collection. Between 1910 and 1927 Gorlia toured extensively through the southern Belgian Congo (now Zaire) and nearby areas in Angola, the French Congo (now the People's Republic of Congo), and Rhodesia (now Zimbabwe). Most of the photographs are attributed to his last two trips, which took place after World War I. Sanford M. Harris inherited the collection and donated it in 1981 to the National Museum of African Art, where it received accession number A1981-01.

Physical Description

There are 2,285 photographs including silver gelatin dry plate lantern slides (some stereograph) and photonegatives and silver gelatin photoprints.

Subjects

The photographs document several of Gorlia's voyages to Zaire, showing the sights on common travelers' routes on the African coasts such as Dar es Salaam and Zanzibar, Tanzania; Port Said, Egypt; and Teneriffe, Canary Islands. Most of the photographs document city life, primarily in the Belgian Congo (now Zaire) and the French Congo (now the People's Republic of Congo), focusing on the experience of colonials in the first part of the 20th century and on Gorlia's family. Most of them were taken in Kassai and Katanga (now Shaba) provinces in the Belgian Congo. Cities documented include Albertville (now Kalémié), Leopoldville (now Kinshasa), Lusambo, and Matadi in the Belgian Congo and Brazzaville in the French Congo. There are images of Chokwe and Luba villages. There are portraits of Africans such as chiefs from the Chokwe, Luba, and Lunda peoples. Images of the built environment include markets and other city scenes. Images of the natural environment show Lake Tanganyika and a savannah in what is now southwestern Zaire.

Arranged: By voyage and image number.

Captioned: Some with date, image number, location, and people of origin.

Finding Aid: Caption list.

Restrictions: No.

AF·30

Melville J. Herskovits Photograph Collection

Dates of Photographs: 1931

Collection Origins

American anthropologist Melville J. Herskovits (1895–1963) created the collection during his fieldwork in Dahomey, a former kingdom located in what is now the Republic of Benin. After receiving a Ph.D. from Columbia University in 1923, Herskovits began teaching at Northwestern University in 1927 and served as chairman of the Department of Anthropology from 1938 to 1956. Conducting research on cultural dynamics and African-American ethnology, he went on a number of expeditions to South America and Africa. In Benin, he and his wife, Frances Shapiro Herskovits, studied the arts and culture of the kingdom of Dahomey. Herskovits belonged to the American Anthropological Association and the Association of Physical Anthropologists. He published several books including the following: 1) *Economic Anthropology: A Study in Comparative Economics*. New York: Alfred A. Knopf, 1952. 2) *The Human Factor in Changing Africa*. New York: Alfred A. Knopf, 1962. 3) *Man and His Works: The Science of Cultural Anthropology*. New York: Alfred A. Knopf, 1948. Some of these photographs were published in the book: Melville J. Herskovits. *Dahomey: An Ancient West African Kingdom*. New York: J.J. Augustin, 1938. The photographs were transferred for preservation from the Northwestern University Library to the Eliot Elisofon Archives, where they received National Museum of African Art accession number A1986-29.

Physical Description

There are 270 photographs including silver gelatin photonegatives and photoprints.

Subjects

The photographs document art and culture in the cities of Abomey, Allada, and Whydah in the Dahomey kingdom, now the Republic of Benin. Activities documented include dancing, glorifying the kings at the palace in Abomey, making pottery, metal smithing, and thatching the roof of the palace. There are portraits of chiefs and palace inhabitants, many in prestige attire, and villagers. Structures shown include a farming village outside Abomey, markets in Abomey and Whydah, the palace in Abomey, and shrines. Art works reproduced include relief sculptures on the palace wall and royal regalia.

Arranged: By image number.

Captioned: No.

Finding Aid: No.

Restrictions: Available for reference only. No reproductions may be made without permission from the Herskovits family.

AF·31

Bennett Higbee Photograph Collection

Dates of Photographs: 1929, 1990

Collection Origins

Bennett Higbee created the collection to document a tour he took through Africa in 1929. The tour began with a cruise from New York to Senegal, continuing by train through Sierra Leone, then by boat again to South Africa; Madagascar; British East Africa (now Kenya, Tanzania, and Uganda); and Egypt. At each stop passengers went ashore and occasionally took train rides. In 1989, Trew Bennett, Bennett Higbee's daughter, donated the collection to the National Museum of African Art, which created copy prints and assigned the collection accession number A1989-11.

Physical Description

There are 410 photographs including silver gelatin photonegatives and photoprints (half are copies).

Subjects

The photographs document a 1929 tour of Africa taken by Bennett Higbee and other Americans. Africans are portrayed building houses, carrying firewood and water, dancing in masks, gathering plants, pulling rickshaws, rowing boats, working on docks, and working with crops. There are portraits of tourists in cars, rickshaws, and tourist camps. Structures shown include a dam, the pyramids, the Sphinx in Egypt, and unidentified buildings throughout Africa. There are cityscapes with trucks and waterscapes with boats, as well as images of body adornment, ceremonial weapons, and masks.

Arranged: No.

Captioned: No.

Finding Aid: No.

Restrictions: No.

AF·32

Bryce P. Holcombe Photograph Collection

Dates of Photographs: 1977–1978

Collection Origins

Bryce P. Holcombe, an art history instructor at the University of California at Davis, created the collection. It was used as a teaching collection for the study of African art objects in various California institutions. In 1985, after Holcombe died, his mother, Mrs. Bryce Holcombe, donated the collection to the National Museum of African Art, where it received accession number A1986-01.

Physical Description

There are 950 color dye coupler slides (Agfachrome and Ektachrome).

Subjects

The photographs document African art objects that were located in California institutions and collections in the 1970s. Costume and masks shown include a Baga Nimba (goddess of fertility) mask from Guinea, a Bamana *chiwara* (antelope headdress) from Mali, a Baule antelope mask from the Ivory Coast, a Dan mask from Liberia, an Ibibio mask from Nigeria, an Igbo mask from Nigeria, a Kuba mask from Zaire, a Mende mask from Sierra Leone, a Mossi mask from Burkina Faso, a Senufo mask from the Ivory Coast, a Songye mask from Zaire, a Yaka mask from Zaire, and a Yoruba beaded chief's apron and a *gelede* (men's society) mask from Nigeria.

Sculptures depicted include human figures by the following peoples: Bamana, Baule, Benin, Fang (Pahouin), Hemba, Kom, Kongo, Kota, Lega, Mossi, Senufo, Songye, and Yoruba. There are also images of dishes and utensils such as a Dan spoon from Liberia and a Kuba cup from Zaire; furniture such as an Asante stool from Ghana, a Chokwe chair from Angola, and a Dan chair from Liberia; jewelry such as a Benin ivory pendant from Nigeria; and staffs and staff finials made by the Sangu of Gabon, the Senufo of the Ivory Coast, and the Yoruba of Nigeria. Other objects depicted include a Bamana door lock from Mali, a Kongo ivory knife and tusk from Zaire, and a Yoruba divination board from Nigeria.

Arranged: By negative number.

Captioned: With negative number and subject.

Finding Aid: 1) Catalog titled "Masterpieces of African, Oceanic & Pre-Columbian Art from Los Angeles Collections," listing negative number and object's country, description, and people of origin. 2) Handwritten log listing collection date, copy number, duplicate number, location, negative number, photograph number, people of origin, references, series, and type of object.

Restrictions: Available for reference only. No reproductions may be made.

AF·33

Keystone-Underwood Stereograph Collection

Dates of Photographs: 19th Century–1930s

Collection Origins

National Museum of African Art (NMAfA) staff assembled the collection from various donors. The stereographs were produced commercially by the Keystone View Company and the Underwood and Underwood Company, mass publishers and distributors of stereographic views. In 1882 the Underwood and Underwood Company began operations in Kansas. Founded by brothers Bert Elias (1862–1943) and Elmer (1860–1947) Underwood, the company pioneered the technique of selling stereographs door-to-door. By 1884, Underwood and Underwood's operations had expanded to the West Coast, and the company soon opened offices throughout the world. In the 1890s, the firm began selling images to publications such as *Illustrated London News* and *Harper's Weekly*. At its peak in the early 20th century, the company produced 25,000 images per day. In the late 1910s, Underwood and Underwood was purchased by a competing stereograph company, the Keystone View Company.

The University of California at Riverside acquired the Keystone View Company's archive—Keystone-Mast Collection, made up of 250,000 photonegative and stereocards—and later sold some of the stereographs. The collection's NMAfA accession number is A1985-13. Note: Two related collections are described in Volume I of this *Guide* series, the Underwood and Underwood Glass Sterograph Collection *(AC·58)* and the Underwood and Underwood News Collection *(PH·54)*.

Physical Description

There are 240 photographs including albumen stereographs and silver gelatin stereographs.

Subjects

The photographs document African businesses, cities, industry, landscapes, peoples, and resources. Places documented include Moshi Province, Mount Kilimanjaro, Mount Meru, the Serengeti Plain, and Zanzibar in German East Africa (now Tanzania); Victoria Falls and the Zambezi River in Rhodesia (now Zimbabwe); Cape Town, Devil's Peak, Johannesburg, Kimberly, Natal Province, and Port Elizabeth in South Africa; the waterfront of Dar es Salaam, Tanzania; and Basoko, Boma, Leopoldville (now Kinshasa), Stanley Falls (now Boyoma Falls), and Yakusu in Zaire. There are also photographs of the Nile during a flood.

People portrayed include a Kikuyu man paying brideprice for a wife; Kikuyu women carrying water vessels and planting beans; Maasai women building houses; Swahili people dancing; Swahili women using a power figure to ward off evil; and Zulu men training for war. Other peoples portrayed include Bangala, Bangi,

Chagga, Kongo, Ndombe, and Poto. Other activities documented include buying ivory, carrying rubber, clearing the ground for a coffee plantation, fishing, gambling, grinding corn, hunting zebra, making pottery, mining diamonds and gold, peeling bark for bark cloth, picking coffee, preparing food, smoking meat, threshing beans, and tying house poles. There are also images of church services at a Catholic mission, a gathering of chiefs at a court, a lion-killing ceremony, and war dances.

Businesses and industries shown include coffee plantations in Rhodesia; the DeBeers Diamond Mine in South Africa; a diamond mine compound and crushing mill; fishing boats off Cape Town; a hemp plantation in Uganda; ivory trade in Mombasa, Kenya; a market; and the stock market in Johannesburg. A photograph from this collection is reproduced in the illustrations section of this volume.

Arranged: By image number.

Captioned: With subject.

Finding Aid: No.

Restrictions: Available for reference only. No reproductions may be made.

AF·34

Otto Lang
Slide Collection

Dates of Photographs: Circa 1950

Collection Origins

Otto Lang created the collection to document the peoples of Zaire. The National Museum of African Art received the collection from the Seattle Art Museum in 1989 and assigned it accession number A1989-13.

Physical Description

There are 55 color dye coupler slides.

Subjects

The photographs document the arts, cultures, and peoples of Zaire, especially the Kuba and Mangbetu peoples. Kuba activities documented include building a house, carving, dancing, performing a ceremony, and weaving. Kuba art works and structures depicted include decorated boxes (the royal treasures), a house post, and houses in a village. There are portraits of a Kuba drummer, king, and warriors. Mangbetu people portrayed include dancers, musicians, and a princess. There is also an image of a funeral procession.

Arranged: No.

Captioned: Most with peoples and subject.

Finding Aid: No.

Restrictions: Available for reference only. No reproductions may be made.

AF·35

James W. Lankton
Slide Collection

Dates of Photographs: 1989

Collection Origins

Art gallery owner James W. Lankton created the collection to document Kuba art and culture in Zaire. In 1990 he donated the collection to the National Museum of African Art, where it received accession number A1990-04.

Physical Description

There are 340 color dye coupler slides.

Subjects

The photographs document activities, architecture, and arts of the Kuba people in Zaire, primarily in Mushenge, the Kuba capital. Activities documented include building a house, carrying baskets, carving wood, drying coffee, embroidering, making hats, playing drums, styling hair, and weaving baskets. Objects depicted include a loom, a mask, musical instruments, royal costumes, road signs, and textiles. There are images of buildings such as an art school; houses in villages; the king's palace and reception area; a mission church including altar, doors, and interior; shops in a market; and a weaver's house. Portraits include the Kuba king, his guards, his sons, and a weaver.

Arranged: By image number.

Captioned: With date, image number, photographer, place, and subject.

Finding Aid: Caption list.

Restrictions: No.

AF·36

Constance Stuart Larrabee Photograph Collection

Dates of Photographs: 1941–1949, 1985

Collection Origins

Photographer Constance Stuart Larrabee (1914–) created the collection during her career as a photographer in South Africa. Born in England, Larrabee grew up in Pretoria, South Africa. She studied photography in London (1933–1935) and at the Bavarian State Institute for Photography in Munich (1935–1936), where she was influenced by the avant-garde work of the Bauhaus school. Returning to South Africa, Larrabee set up a studio and photographed many leading cultural and political figures of the period. During World War II she served as South Africa's first woman war correspondent, and in 1950 she married an American and moved to the United States.

Larrabee began photographing the peoples of South Africa in the late 1930s. She published extensively, including a portfolio produced for the following book: Alan Paton. *Cry, the Beloved Country.* New York: C. Scribner's Sons, 1948. Her work appeared in exhibits throughout the world, including the following: "The Lovedu" in Pretoria, 1947; "The Family of Man" at the Museum of Modern Art, 1955; "Tribal Photographs" at the Corcoran Gallery, 1984; and "Go Well, My Child" at the National Museum of African Art (NMAfA), 1986. Larrabee donated the collection to NMAfA for the latter exhibit, and it received NMAfA accession number A1986-16.

Physical Description

There are 135 silver gelatin photoprints. Other materials include exhibit catalogs.

Subjects

The photographs document peoples of South Africa. People are portrayed in Basutoland (now Lesotho); Bechuanaland (now Botswana); Johannesburg; Natal province (including an Anglican mission school, the town of Ixopo, and the south coast); Soweto; Swaziland; Transkei; eastern Transvaal; the Umzimkulu Valley; and Zululand.

Arranged: No.

Captioned: No.

Finding Aid: No.

Restrictions: Available for reference only. No reproductions may be made.

AF·37

James Lee Slide Collection

Dates of Photographs: 1963–1965

Collection Origins

James Lee created the slides as a personal collection and donated them to the National Museum of African Art, where they received accession number A1985-06.

Physical Description

There are 315 color dye coupler slides (Kodachrome).

Subjects

The photographs document cultures, landscapes, and peoples of the African countries of Burkina Faso, Cameroon, Ghana, the Ivory Coast, Kenya, Mali, Nigeria, and Zambia. Nigerian cities and villages illustrated include Asaba, Calabar, Enugu, Funtua, Ibadan, Kano, Katsina, Lagos, Okigwi, Onitsha, Opobo, Oshogbo, Uyo, Wudil, and Zaria. People portrayed include the emir of Katsina, leopard society members at Uyo, and a weaver. Activities documented include a Bobo masquerade in Burkina Faso; a celebration at the court of the emir of Kano; a contest of traditional dance groups in Enugu stadium, Nigeria; and a Mossi dance in Burkina Faso. Architectural images show government colleges and schools, a house under construction outside Uyo, a mosque in Kano, a painted house in Wudil, ruins of a wall at Zaria, and a shrine to a river god in Oshogbo. Art works reproduced include funerary sculpture and sculptures made of concrete in southeastern Nigeria, mostly at Oshogbo. Images of the natural environment show cattle, egrets, the Niger river crossing in the town of Jebba, the riverside at Opobo, and Victoria Falls.

Arranged: No.

Captioned: With date and subject.

Finding Aid: No.

Restrictions: No.

AF·38

John Lomas Slide Collection

Dates of Photographs: 1960s–Early 1970s

Collection Origins

John Lomas, a contract photographer for *National Geographic* magazine who worked in the Sudan in the 1960s and early 1970s, created the collection. He took most of the photographs during his non-working hours while in the Sudan. Some of the photographs may have been used in *National Geographic* publications or exhibits at the magazine's national headquarters. The collection was assigned National Museum of African Art accession number A1985-05.

Physical Description

There are 905 color dye coupler slides (Ektachrome and Kodachrome).

Subjects

The photographs document the art and culture of village peoples of the Sudan, such as the Dinka, Murle, and Shilluk, in the 1960s and early 1970s. Most are portraits showing body painting and scarification. Activities documented include buying and selling in markets, doing domestic chores, hunting, and metal smithing among the Dinka. There are also images of modern and traditional architecture.

Arranged: By subject.

Captioned: Some with country, date, and photographer.

Finding Aid: No.

Restrictions: Available for reference only. No reproductions may be made.

AF·39

C.B. MacCloskey Photograph Collection

Dates of Photographs: 1943

Collection Origins

Captain C.B. MacCloskey, who served as a public relations officer with Colonel A.B. McMullen at the Air Transport Command Base in Accra, created the collection. Mrs. Douglas Griffith Lindsey, a relative of McMullen, donated it to the National Museum of African Art, where it received accession number A1991-04.

Physical Description

There are 35 silver gelatin photoprints.

Subjects

The photographs document Africans in the Akan chiefdom of Akim near Accra, Ghana, in 1943. Activities shown include dancing and drum playing, as well as the funeral of the king of Akim and funerary dances. There is also an image of an effigy of the deceased king. People portrayed include Africans in Western clothes and uniforms and U.S. soldiers.

Arranged: By image number.

Captioned: With image number.

Finding Aid: No.

Restrictions: No.

AF·40

Beverly Mack Slide Collection

Dates of Photographs: 1979–1984

Collection Origins

Beverly Mack, a Washington, D.C., photographer, created the collection during a 1979 to 1984 sojourn in Africa. In 1984 she donated the collection to the National Museum of African Art, where it received accession number A1984-02.

Physical Description

There are 740 color dye coupler slides (Agfachrome, Fujichrome, and Kodachrome).

Subjects

The photographs document the cultures of northern Nigeria and Sierra Leone, including the Hausa people. Locations illustrated include Fourah Bay College in Freetown and Port Loko, Sierra Leone, and Kano and Zaria, Nigeria. Africans are shown buying and selling in markets, holding an Islamic celebration at the palace in Kano, and riding horses. Architecture shown includes exteriors and interiors of buildings such as houses and Islamic structures, as well as street scenes.

Arranged: By subject.

Captioned: A few with subject.

Finding Aid: No.

Restrictions: Available by special permission only. No reproductions may be made.

AF·41

Eva L.R. Meyerowitz Photograph Collection

Dates of Photographs: 1930s, 1970s

Collection Origins

Eva L.R. Meyerowitz and Herbert V. Meyerowitz, her husband, created the collection to document their travels in Africa in the 1930s, including visits to Burkina Faso, northern Ghana, Mali, and Nigeria. Born in Germany, Eva Meyerowitz became a sculptor in South Africa and later attended the University of London for advanced study in anthropology. She conducted anthropological research in Africa, concentrating on the Akan of Ghana and other peoples in northern Ghana. Meyerowitz published several articles and books including the following: 1) *At the Court of an African King.* London: Faber and Faber Limited, 1962. 2) *The Early History of the Akan States of Ghana.* London: Red Candle Press, 1974. 3) "The Museums in the Royal Palaces at Abomey, Dahomey." *Burlington Fine Arts Magazine* (June 1944). 4) "Our Mothers: The Amazons of Dahomey." *Geographical Magazine* 15(9) (1943). The collection was assigned National Museum of African Art accession number A1986-18.

Physical Description

There are 510 photographs including silver gelatin photonegatives and photoprints.

Subjects

The photographs document several regions of Africa, including Burkina Faso, Ghana, Mali, Nigeria, and Togo. Activities shown include a man making a wax model for brass casting, Tallensi people buying and selling in a market, a woman shaping a clay pot, and workers harvesting beans. Portraits include a Frafra girl with Eva Meyerowitz; a Konkomba farmer; Nabdam children at mines; a Tallensi blacksmith; Tallensi elders; and the *ya na* (king of Dagomba), Abdulai II; as well as a Koran scholar at Yendi, Ghana. Other peoples portrayed include the Asante and the Mamprusi. Art works shown include brass figures, clay toys and pots, and wall paintings. Images of the built environment include a market in Bawku, Ghana; a gold mining settlement; a mosque at Walewale, Ghana; the palace of the king of Dahomey, Benin; and a poultry market at Kumasi, Ghana.

Arranged: No.

Captioned: No.

Finding Aid: 1) Partial caption list. 2) Catalog by Timothy F. Garrard to northern Ghana photographs.

Restrictions: No.

AF·42

Mozambique Trading Company Photograph Collection

Dates of Photographs: Circa 1888, 1990

Collection Origins

The Portuguese Mozambique Trading Company created the collection to document its activities and conditions in Mozambique. Photographers represented include d'Andrade e Serrano, Freire, and Soura Machado. The collection was assigned National Museum of African Art accession number A1988-09.

Physical Description

There are 70 photographs including albumen photoprints and silver gelatin copy photoprints.

Subjects

The photographs document the environment and people, both African and European, in Mozambique in the 1880s. Images of the built environment show forts, government buildings, markets, and villages. Activities documented include constructing the roof of a house, cutting vegetation, and using a mortar and pestle. There are also portraits of agricultural workers shown with cattle and a wagon; a cook with his helpers; and government officials.

Arranged: By photographer.

Captioned: With photographer and subject.

Finding Aid: No.

Restrictions: No.

AF·43

Abdin-Rahim Muhammad Photograph Collection

Dates of Photographs: 1987

Collection Origins

Abdin-Rahim Muhammad created the collection to document aspects of royal court life in Foumban, Cameroon. In 1988 he donated the collection to the National Museum of African Art, where it received accession number A1988-02.

Physical Description

There are 30 photographs including color dye coupler photoprints and phototransparencies.

Subjects

The photographs show the sultan of Foumban, El Hadj Seidouh Njimoluh Njoya, and his surroundings. The sultan is shown attending a Friday prayer at a mosque and greeting pilgrims returning from Mecca. Objects and structures shown include a brass statue of King Njoya, the courtyard of the sultan's palace, the entrance to the sultan's residence, items now in the Palace Museum such as the skull of a defeated enemy, and the sultan's beaded two-figure throne.

Arranged: No.

Captioned: With subject.

Finding Aid: Caption list.

Restrictions: No.

AF·44

Museum of African Art Exhibits and Installations Photograph Collection

Dates of Photographs: 1970s and Early 1980s

Collection Origins

Staff of the Museum of African Art assembled the collection from photographs documenting exhibits at the museum, which was housed in several Capitol Hill town houses before it moved to the Mall and became the National Museum of African Art (NMAfA). Photographs of NMAfA exhibits are contained in *AF·48*. The collection was assigned NMAfA accession number A1973-06.

Physical Description

There are 490 silver gelatin photoprints.

Subjects

The photographs document several exhibit installations and openings at NMAfA's former site on Capitol Hill, where it was called the Museum of African Art. Exhibits shown include "Appliquéd Cloths of the Dahomey Kingdom" (1980), "Traditional Costume and Jewelry of Africa" (1981), and "The Useful Arts of Kenya" (1979). There are also photographs of several galleries in the old facility.

Arranged: No.

Captioned: With subject.

Finding Aid: No.

Restrictions: Available for reference only. No reproductions may be made.

AF·45

NMAfA Activities Collection

Dates of Photographs: 1960s–Present

Collection Origins

National Museum of African Art (NMAfA) staff created the collection to document museum events, programs, staff, and visitors. Photographers represented include Mark Avino, Georgette Ballance, Barry Blackman, Walter J. Booze, Ed Brennan, S. Carmichael, Libby Cullen, Winnie Day, Eliot Elisofon, Ramiro Fernandez, Patricia Gordon, R.A. Gumbs, Andy Hanson, Ken Heinen, Mary Hurlbut, Gretchen Jennings, Patty Kaffer, Delmar Lipp, Elisabeth Little, William Long,

Roy Lustig, Al Mozell, Kim Nielsen, Robert Lawrence Pastner, Paul Perrot, Jeffrey Ploskonka, Carol Rosen, Philip D. Rush, Pete Turner, Rick Vargas, Michael Watson, Jim Wells, and Bob Zucker. Studios represented include City News Bureau; Hickey & Robertson; Leorke; Malstrom; Martuk; NMAfA; Rich's Studio; U.S. Information Agency; U.S. State Department; and the *Washington Post*. The collection was assigned NMAfA accession number A1973-07.

Physical Description

There are 10,000 photographs including color dye coupler photonegatives, photoprints, and slides and silver gelatin photonegatives and photoprints. Other materials include brochures, correspondence, and postcards.

Subjects

The collection documents NMAfA activities such as docent training, exhibit openings, festivals, performances, receptions, tours, and workshops; building construction, plans, and renovations; object holdings; and staff and visitors.

Architectural images show the former Capitol Hill town house buildings of the Museum of African Art, construction of the current NMAfA facility on the Mall in Washington, D.C., and a model of the current museum building. Events documented include an African Islam Workshop, an appliqué workshop, fashion shows, a festival of African games, Georgetown University class tours, an International Year of the Child reception, the opening of the Anacostia Neighborhood Museum exhibit "Phil Ratner's Washington," and a Smithsonian folklife festival. Exhibit openings shown include "African Masterpieces from the Musée de L'Homme" (1985), "Images from Bamum: German Colonial Photography at the Court of King Njoya, Cameroon, West Africa, 1902–1915" (1988), and "Yoruba: Nine Centuries of African Art and Thought" (1990). People portrayed include Muhammad Ali; William Fagg; Henry Kissinger; Robert McNamara; Senator Frank Moss; Gregory Peck; Warren M. Robbins; President Leopold S. Senghor of Senegal; and Sylvia Williams, director of NMAfA.

Arranged: By subject and date.

Captioned: Some with catalog name, catalog number, and object's accession number.

Finding Aid: List of images on contact sheets.

Restrictions: Available to Smithsonian Institution staff only. No reproductions may be made.

AF·46

NMAfA Cartes-de-Visite Collection

Dates of Photographs: 19th Century

Collection Origins

National Museum of African Art (NMAfA) staff assembled the collection from donations and purchases of cartes-de-visite. Cartes-de-visite are photographic calling cards produced between the 1860s and 1900s, most popular during their first decade of production. The card-mounted photographs were generally either portraits of private individuals produced by a commercial studio or mass-produced portraits of public figures (less commonly group portraits), comic images, or travel scenes. They are usually 2 1/2″ × 3 1/2″ albumen, collodion, or silver gelatin photoprints mounted on 2 1/2″ × 4 1/2″ cards, often embossed with the studio name and address. Some photomechanical images were also used for cartes-de-visite. Photographers and studios represented include M. Beaumont, Bonnevide Photographic Studio, J. Lascoumettes, and Noel Frères. The collection is NMAfA accession number A1986-31.

Physical Description

There are 45 albumen cartes-de-visite.

Subjects

The photographs document African peoples and their culture. Countries illustrated include the Gold Coast (now Ghana) and Senegal. People portrayed include children, a priest, warriors, and a Wolof man with gold jewelry. There are also photographs of camel caravans, ports, and villages. A photograph from this collection is reproduced in the illustrations section of this volume.

Arranged: By assigned number.

Captioned: Some with location or subject.

Finding Aid: No.

Restrictions: No.

AF·47

NMAfA Copy, Internegative, and Color Conversion Photograph Collection

Dates of Photographs: 1970s–Present

Collection Origins

National Museum of African Art (NMAfA) staff created these duplicate and copy images for internal record and publication purposes. The materials are drawn from Eliot Elisofon Archives collections. Photographers and studios represented include Arthur P. Bourgeois, William Clark, F. Clement, Diane Cooke, C. Egerton, Eliot Elisofon, Ramiro Fernandez, Valerie Franklin, Mattiebelle Gittinger, Emile E.O. Gorlia, Robin Jagoe, Bunyan Knight, Robert Lautman, Delmar Lipp, M. Michel, Peter Nelson, Kim Nielsen, Robert Nooter, D. Pieters, Jeffrey Ploskonka, Richard Saunders, Roy Sieber, Robert F. Thompson, Paul Tishman, the University of Washington, and Robert Wallace. NMAfA assigned the collection accession number A1973-05.

Physical Description

There are 1,000 photographs including color dye coupler photonegatives, photoprints, and phototransparencies and silver gelatin photonegatives and photoprints.

Subjects

The photographs document African art works including NMAfA holdings, African landscapes, and the cultures of African peoples from the late 19th century to the present. There are also images of NMAfA events and staff members. Items depicted include furniture, masks, metalwork, musical instruments, ritual objects, sculptures, staffs, and textiles. Images of African life include architecture; artists and artisans at work; body art and costume; celebrations, dances and rituals; and economic activity such as agriculture and trade.

Arranged: By format or type of material; part also by order of production and laboratory number.

Captioned: With date, material, photographer, and subject.

Finding Aid: No.

Restrictions: Some materials are restricted and may not be reproduced.

AF·48

NMAfA Exhibits Photograph Collection

Dates of Photographs: Circa 1979–Present

Collection Origins

National Museum of African Art (NMAfA) staff created the collection to document the exhibits held at the museum since it became part of the Smithsonian Institution in 1979. Some of the photographs were used to illustrate exhibit catalogs. Photographers represented include Henry Eastwood, Joanne Eicher, Franko Khoury, and Jeffrey Ploskonka. The collection's NMAfA accession number is A1979-02.

Physical Description

There are 3,000 photographs including color dye coupler photoprints, phototransparencies, and slides and silver gelatin photonegatives and photoprints.

Subjects

The photographs document exhibits held at NMAfA since 1979, including field photographs, images of individual objects, and exhibit installation photographs. Exhibits documented include "African Art in the Cycle of Life" (1988), "The African Desert" (1990), "Echoes of the Kalabari: Sculpture of Sokari Douglas Camp" (1988–1989), "The Essential Gourd" (1990), "Gold of Africa: Jewelry and Ornaments from Ghana, Côte d'Ivoire, Mali, and Senegal" (1989), "Icons: Ideals and Power in the Art of Africa" (1989–1990), "Images from Bamum: German Colonial Photography at the Court of King Njoya, Cameroon, West Africa, 1902–1915" (1988), "Kalabari Ancestral Screens: Levels of Meaning" (1988–1989), "Objects of Use" (1987), "Patterns of Life: West African Strip-Weaving Traditions" (1988), "Shoowa Design: Raffia Textiles from Zaire" (1988), "Sounding Forms: African Musical Instruments" (1989), and "Yoruba: Nine Centuries of African Art and Thought" (1990). Objects depicted include clothing, icons, jewelry, knives, masks, sculpture, and textiles. Field photographs show architecture, craftspeople at work, and festivals.

Arranged: By exhibit.

Captioned: Most with exhibit and subject.

Finding Aid: Some exhibit slides are arranged in binders, which have content lists.

Restrictions: Available for reference only. No reproductions may be made.

AF·49

NMAfA Miscellaneous Vintage Photograph Collection

Dates of Photographs: Circa 1880–1930s

Collection Origins

National Museum of African Art (NMAfA) staff assembled the collection from several different sources. Photographers represented include Charles M. Cronin and J. Jascoumittes. Most of the images' origins are unidentified. The collection's NMAfA accession number is A1973-09.

Physical Description

There are 30 photographs including albumen photoprints and silver gelatin photoprints.

Subjects

The photographs document the people and regions of Africa, as well as Americans traveling in Africa. Most of the images are portraits, including an image of Ovonramwen, the king of Benin, on his way to exile in 1897; a woman from Sierra Leone; South African men at a mining camp; west African peoples; and the Zulu people including an elder with his family, a man with a head ring, and warriors. Activities illustrated include buying and selling in markets, dancing, and dressing hair with beads. A photograph from this collection is reproduced in the illustrations section of this volume.

Arranged: No.

Captioned: Some with subject.

Finding Aid: No.

Restrictions: Some images are restricted and may not be reproduced.

AF·50

NMAfA Permanent Collection Objects Photograph Collection

Dates of Photographs: 1960s–Present

Collection Origins

National Museum of African Art (NMAfA) staff and contract photographers created the collection to document art objects in the museum's permanent holdings. Photographers and studios represented include African Art Center, Inc., Richard Beatty, Arthur P. Bourgeois, Richard M. Cohen, Sheldon Collins, D'Arcey Gallery, Henry Eastwood, Eliot Elisofon, Raymond Fortt, Galerie Kamer, Gimpel Fils Gallery, Ken Heinen, Hirshhorn Museum and Sculpture Garden, Franko Khoury, Delmar Lipp, Marcus Lipp, O.E. Nelson, Arnold Newman, Kim Nielsen, Robert Nooter, OPPS, Jeffrey Ploskonka, Jann & John Thomson, Katherine White, and Ernie Wolfe. The collection was assigned NMAfA accession number A1973-08.

Physical Description

There are 30,000 photographs including color dye coupler photoprints, phototransparencies, and slides; dye diffusion transfer photoprints (Polaroid); and silver gelatin photonegatives and photoprints. Other materials include correspondence, exhibit catalogs, and postcards.

Subjects

The photographs document art works in the museum's holdings, including household objects, masks, prestige paraphernalia, sculpted figures, and textiles from all over Africa. Peoples and kingdoms whose art is shown include Asante, Baga, Bamana, Bamum, Baule, Bembe, Benin, Bobo, Chewa, Chokwe, Dan, Dogon, Ejagham, Fante, Fulbe, Hausa, Hemba, Igbo, Jenne, Kongo, Koro, Kota, Kran, Kuba, Lega, Ligbi, Loma, Luba, Lunda, Mambila, Mangbetu, Mbembe, Mende, Ndebele, Nupe, Pende, Samburu, Shilluk, Songye, Swahili, Tetela, Vili, Yombe, Yoruba, and Zande.

Costume, jewelry, and masks shown include a Baga wood Nimba (goddess of fertility) mask, a Bamana *chiwara* (antelope headdress), a Baule pendant mask, a Chokwe mask, a Dan mask, Dogon masks, Fulbe gold earrings, a Hausa embroidered gown, a Koro headdress, Kran wooden masks, Kuba masks, a Loma mask, a Mangbetu back apron, a Mende Sowei (female guardian spirit) helmet mask, an Ndebele beaded bridal apron, and a Pende mask and mask costume. Furniture, tools, and utensils shown include a Chewa vessel, a Chokwe divination basket and stool, a Dan ladle, Lega carved spoons, a Luba axe, a Yoruba bowl and divination board, and a Yoruba door carved by Olowe of Ise. Musical instruments depicted include a Baga figurative drum and a Zande harp. Sculpted objects shown include an Asante *akuaba* (wooden child figure), Bamum memorial figure, Baule male figure and staff, Benin bronze memorial head and plaque, Dogon ceremonial staff, Kongo elephant tusk and figure of a woman and child, Kuba box, Mambila figure, Mbembe figure of a woman and child, Songye figure, Vili ivory staff finial, and a Yombe figure of a woman and child and staff finial. Textiles shown include *adinkra* and *kente* cloth.

Arranged: By object's accession number.

Captioned: With object's accession number, date, description, location, and people of origin, as well as negative number and photographer.

Finding Aid: The guide to the Eliot Elisofon Art Object Photograph Collection *(AF·19)* also serves as a guide to this collection.

Restrictions: Some photographs are for reference only, and no reproductions may be made of them.

AF·51

NMAfA Postcard Collection

Dates of Photographs: 19th Century–Circa 1950s

Collection Origins

National Museum of African Art (NMAfA) Archives staff assembled the collection from many sources, including book dealers. Photographers and studios represented include Joy Adamson, Bason, Bonnin, Hoa-Qui, Imperial Institute, Karakashian Brothers, G. Lerat, G.N. Morhig, C.D. Patel, Photo-Home, Sapra, and S. Skulina. The collection was assigned NMAfA accession number A1985-14.

Physical Description

There are 120 silver gelatin postcards. Other materials include several thousand photomechanical postcards.

Subjects

The photographs document the peoples and the built and natural environments of Africa. Places documented include Belgian Congo (now Zaire), Kenya, Nigeria, Ruanda, Tunisia, and Uganda. Peoples portrayed include the Dinka, Maasai, Shilluk, Yoruba, and Zulu. Activities documented include carrying elephant tusks, dancing, drying and harvesting sisal fiber, eating, fishing with traps, hoeing, hunting, making baskets, playing instruments, and styling hair. Portraits, including Islamic chiefs and their families and rickshaw pullers in Durban, illustrate costume, hairstyles, jewelry, lip plates, and scarification. Many of the portraits are posed. Images of the built environment include hotels, missionary churches, and street scenes. Animals shown include camels, gorillas, and leopards.

Arranged: Alphabetically by photographer or publisher.

Captioned: Most with subject.

Finding Aid: List of postcards.

Restrictions: Available for reference only. No reproductions may be made.

AF·52

NMAfA Teaching Slide Collection

Dates of Photographs: Circa 1960s–Present

Collection Origins

National Museum of African Art (NMAfA) curatorial and educational staff assembled the collection for lectures and seminars on African art and culture. The photographs reproduce illustrations in books, magazines, and other sources. The collection was assigned NMAfA accession number A1973-10.

Physical Description

There are 4,000 color dye coupler slides (mostly Ektachrome).

Subjects

The photographs document African culture, including activities (such as divination and initiation ceremonies), architecture, art works, and body art. Art works shown include containers, furniture (such as stools), gold weights, jewelry, masks (such as helmet masks), musical instruments (such as drums), heddle pulleys, rock art, sculpture (such as terra-cotta figures and wooden figures), and textiles.

Arranged: In two series. 1) Photographs of art. 2) Field photographs, which are further divided by subject.

Captioned: With region and subject.

Finding Aid: One for each series. The field index lists country or people of origin, date, photographer, region, series number, and subject and indicates whether a duplicate or copy of an image is available.

Restrictions: Available to NMAfA staff only.

AF·53

Northern Nigeria Photograph Album

Dates of Photographs: Circa 1905–1907

Collection Origins

The collection was created to document the peoples of north-central Nigeria. The National Museum of African Art bought the collection in 1979 from McBlain Books of Hamden, Connecticut, and assigned it accession number A1979-01.

Physical Description

There are 90 silver gelatin photoprints, mounted in an album.

Subjects

The photographs document the Fulbe, Tiv, and Wurkun peoples of north-central Nigeria. Informal portraits include Fulbe people on horseback in Hausa-style attire, Tiv women and children, a Wurkun headman, and Wurkun people in traditional costume. Activities illustrated include dancing and playing musical instruments such as drums, horns with gourd resonators, and string bows.

Arranged: No.

Captioned: With people; some also with activity, person's name, or other subject.

Finding Aid: No.

Restrictions: No.

AF·54

M. Marvin Breckinridge Patterson Collection

Dates of Photographs: 1932

Collection Origins

M. Marvin Breckinridge Patterson created the collection to document her 1932 trip with Olivia Stokes Hatch from Capetown, South Africa, to Cairo, Egypt. A filmmaker, photographer, and photojournalist, Patterson graduated from Vassar College in 1927. The following year she traveled to Europe and joined the Frontier Nursing Service. During World War II she broadcast news from Europe for the Columbia Broadcasting System. Photographs from the collection were published in the *Boston Herald* on July 30, 1933, and in the *Crown Colonist* in August 1933. Patterson donated the collection to the National Museum of African Art, where it received accession number A1985-09.

Physical Description

There are 415 silver gelatin photoprints. Other materials include an excerpt from a report, maps, motion-picture film footage, museum exhibit materials and guides, pamphlets, and photomechanical postcards.

Subjects

The photographs document the peoples of Africa between Cairo and Cape Town—particularly in Egypt, Kenya, South Africa, Sudan, Tanganyika (now Tanzania), Uganda, Zaire, and Zanzibar—such as the Baila, San, Shona, Xhosa, and Zulu. Africans portrayed include a bride and groom at Lovedale, South Africa; dancers at the Crown Mine near Johannesburg; flower sellers in Cape Town; two leading elders at Amanzimtoti, South Africa; a man making spears; a man

tanning leather in Sudan; miners with their wives in Katanga (now Shaba), Zaire; schoolboys in Sudan; a Shona man; women lining up for rations in the Belgian Congo (now Zaire); workers pouring out gold at the Crown Mine near Johannesburg; and a Zulu woman at a market in Durban, Natal, South Africa. There are also portraits of M. Marvin Breckinridge Patterson using a movie camera and Olivia Stokes Hatch with a tripod.

Structures shown include Queen Hatshepsut's room at Karnak, Luxor, Egypt; Outspan Hotel in Nyeri, Kenya; and the ruins of Great Zimbabwe. There are also images of cloves drying in Zanzibar and drawings by San people. Landscapes and waterscapes include a mountain at Cape Town, South Africa; a park in Port Elizabeth, South Africa; and Victoria Falls, Rhodesia (now Zimbabwe). Animals shown include egrets, ostriches, and wildebeests.

Arranged: In four series by region, then chronologically. 1) Tanganyika and Zanzibar. 2) Kenya. 3) Uganda. 4) The Sudan and Egypt.

Captioned: With location and subject.

Finding Aid: Index listing captions.

Restrictions: No.

AF·55

James E. Payne Slide Collection

Dates of Photographs: 1973–1977

Collection Origins

James E. Payne (1941–) created the collection to document Coptic Christians in Lalibela, Ethiopia, and the Nuba people in Sudan between 1973 and 1977. Payne received a B.S. in 1963 from Jackson State College and held several positions in the personnel management field. Since 1990 he has been a personnel manager at the Liberty Science Museum in Jersey City, New Jersey. Payne took the photographs while on vacation in East Africa and lent the National Museum of African Art (NMAfA) his slides to make copies. NMAfA subsequently assigned the copies accession number A1988-06.

Physical Description

There are 325 copy color dye coupler slides.

Subjects

The photographs document the churches and religious ceremonies of Coptic Christians in Ethiopia and daily life of the Nuba people in the Sudan. Images of Coptic Christians, mostly taken in the village of Lalibela, show activities such as celebrating the *timkat* festival, cooking, studying the Bible, and washing; art works such as crosses and illuminated manuscripts; and structures such as churches, houses, and tents. Images of the Nuba in Sudan, many from the Kordofan region, illustrate activities such as boat building in Omdurman, celebrating an Islamic festival in Omdurman, buying and selling in markets, and wrestling; portraits showing body art and costumes; and structures such as burial mounds and decorated houses.

Arranged: By image number.

Captioned: With image number and subject.

Finding Aid: No.

Restrictions: Researchers must receive permission from James E. Payne to publish the photographs.

AF·56

Pères Blancs (White Fathers) Mission Photograph Collection

Dates of Photographs: Circa 1903–1924

Collection Origins

Members of the Pères Blancs (White Fathers) Society created the collection to document their missions and the Africans living near them in the East African kingdoms of Rwanda and Burundi (now the state of Ruanda-Urundi). Cardinal Charles M. Lavigerie, the Catholic Archbishop of Algiers, founded the Society of Missionaries of Africa (which became known as Pères Blancs) in 1869. Beginning a plan of expansion in 1878, Lavigerie sent a group of missionaries across the Sahara to establish a mission in Timbuktu, but the effort failed when the accompanying Africans revolted. Over 23

missionaries died before the mission was completed in the 1890s.

The Pères Blancs also established themselves in Uganda, Tanganyika (now Tanzania), and the Upper Congo by the 1880s, as well as in Burundi (1879) and Rwanda (1900), the last two of which are documented in this collection. Despite resistance from local chiefs and governments, the society continued to expand in the first part of the 20th century, setting up hospitals; elementary, normal, and technical schools; and seminaries in Africa, as well as training schools in several European countries. After World War II the society's influence declined, although it still operates today. The collection was assigned National Museum of African Art accession number A1987-10.

Physical Description

There are 215 photographs including collodion gelatin photoprints (POP) and silver gelatin photoprints, some mounted in albums.

Subjects

The photographs document the Africans living near the Pères Blancs (or White Fathers) Mission stations at Rwanda and Burundi. Most photographs are individual and group portraits of Africans, especially members of the Tutsi royal family and Tutsi elite of Rwanda and Burundi. Other portraits include Christian families of Hutu origin, the missionaries and Western visitors, and Twa people on an elephant hunt. Activities documented include attending a mission class, building grass and brick structures, carrying royalty on palanquins, carrying visitors, dancing, digging, getting water, and weaving baskets. Objects depicted include baskets, combs, costumes, jewelry, lances, and shields. There are images of African village and mission buildings, as well as landscapes of mountains and volcanoes. A photograph from this collection appears in this volume's illustration section.

Arranged: Some in original albums; some by assigned number in binders.

Captioned: With names and subjects.

Finding Aid: Caption list.

Restrictions: No.

AF·57

Princeton University Press Photograph Collection

Dates of Photographs: 1950–1960

Collection Origins

Princeton University Press staff assembled the collection to illustrate the following book: Paul Radin, ed. *African Folktales & Sculpture*. New York: Pantheon Books, 1952. Photographers represented include Ina Bundy, Eliot Elisofon, Walker Evans, and Man Ray. The collection was assigned National Museum of African Art accession number A1985-02.

Physical Description

There are 285 silver gelatin photoprints.

Subjects

The photographs document a variety of art works created by Africans. Objects depicted include boxes, bracelets, figures, gold weights, headrests, heads, masks, pendants, stools, and trumpets. Peoples and kingdoms represented include Anyi, Asante, Bamum, Bangwa, Baule, Benin, Chokwe, Fang (Pahouin), Fon, Ife, Lega, Luba, Mende, Nok, Pende, and Yoruba.

Arranged: By plate number.

Captioned: With plate number; most also with people of origin, place, and subject.

Finding Aid: Caption list.

Restrictions: Available for reference only. No reproductions may be made.

AF·58

Jacob A. and Eleanor N. Reis Photograph Collection *A.K.A.* Eleanor R. Henry Collection

Dates of Photographs: 1910–1920

Collection Origins

Jacob A. Reis (1883–1945) created the collection to document his experiences while serving with his wife as a Presbyterian missionary in southern Cameroon. After graduating from Wooster College, Reis attended Bloomfield Theological Seminary and was ordained in 1908. He joined the Presbyterian Church's mission in Cameroon in 1909, returned to the United States to complete his studies at the Western Theological Seminary in Pittsburgh in 1912, then went back to Africa where he served until his death. In 1985 Eleanor R. Henry, Reis's daughter, donated the collection to the National Museum of African Art, where it received accession number A1985-04.

Physical Description

There are 360 photographs including silver gelatin dry plate lantern slides and silver gelatin photonegatives and photoprints.

Subjects

The photographs document the life and people at Jacob A. Reis's mission stations, especially in and near Efulen, Cameroon. African peoples pictured include Bassa, Bulu, and Ntum. Informal portraits show African boys learning to read and making furniture in a workshop of the missionary school, Africans building houses, African women carrying cargo and firewood, armed soldiers standing at attention, and Westerners riding bicycles and motorcycles. Structures documented include churches, a dispensary, a fishing hut, a saw mill, school buildings such as a Baptist girls' school in Douala, and thatched roof buildings. There are images of African ritual objects confiscated by the mission and a photographic reproduction of a handwritten statistical list of bible readers, communicants, preachers, and students.

Arranged: Photonegatives by negative number.

Captioned: Some with subject.

Finding Aid: Index to photonegatives listing sleeve number and subject.

Restrictions: No.

AF·59

Andrew H. and Martha W. Ruch Collection

Dates of Photographs: 1922–1925

Collection Origins

Andrew H. Ruch (1899–1966) and Martha W. Ruch (1898–1989), his wife, created the collection to document their experience as missionaries in Africa in the 1920s. Andrew graduated from Moody Bible Institute in 1921 and received a Th.D. from Webster University in 1930. In 1922, after Martha graduated from Moody, they married and left for Africa. They set up a mission in a Kikuyu Reserve in Ruiru, Kenya, and worked there until 1925, when they returned to the United States. Andrew spent most of his life as pastor in Philadelphia. In 1991 Cynthia Cassey, the Ruches' granddaughter, donated the collection to the National Museum of African Art, where it received accession number A1991-13.

Physical Description

There are 325 photographs including silver gelatin dry plate lantern slides (some tinted) and silver gelatin photoprints, most mounted in an album. Other materials include books, correspondence, diaries, a lantern slide projector, manuscripts, notebooks, and travel pamphlets.

Subjects

The photographs document Andrew H. and Martha W. Ruch's missionary work and the activities of the local Kikuyu people. Places shown include Cairo, Egypt; the Mediterranean Sea; a Mombasa, Kenya, beach; Mount Kenya; Mount Kilimanjaro; Port Said, Egypt; and the Suez Canal.

Activities illustrated include building huts; carrying loads such as grass (for thatching), luggage, water, and wood; cooking; drying skins; grinding millet; pounding sugar cane; and selling items from boats to passengers on a ship; as well as ceremonies such as baptisms,

church services, classes, and medical treatments. People portrayed include African Christians; chiefs; children; families; Muhia, the Ruches' assistant; the Ruches; and warriors. Many of the portraits document African clothing, ornaments, scarification, and weapons.

Architectural images include building materials, grain bins, houses (including the Ruches' home), mosques, museums (in Cairo), pyramids (in Cairo), railroads, temples (in Egypt), and villages. Transportation vehicles illustrated include boats, motorcycles, and ships. There are landscapes showing mountains, paths, rivers, vegetation, and waterfalls. Animals depicted include birds, camels, cattle, donkeys, a lion, and lizards.

Arranged: By image number.

Captioned: Lantern slides with image number; photoprints with subject.

Finding aid: Index cards.

Restrictions: No.

AF·60

Wilhelm Schneider Collection

Dates of Photographs: 1930–1940

Collection Origins

Wilhelm Schneider (1902–1990) created the collection to document his experiences as a missionary for the Swiss Basel Mission in Cameroon. After being trained at the Basel Mission, he was stationed in Bali and in Weh. He later worked as a pastor in Baden-Württemberg, Germany. In 1991 Maria Petzold (Schneider's daughter) of Reutlingen, Germany, and Walter Schneider (Schneider's son) of York, Pennsylvania, donated the collection to the National Museum of African Art, where it received accession number A1991-11.

Physical Description

There are 150 silver gelatin photoprints. Other materials include copies of Schneider's notes and official reports from Cameroon.

Subjects

The photographs document the culture of the Weh people and their neighbors in the Cameroon Grassfields in the 1930s. Activities documented include attending a funeral, braiding hair, building houses, carrying loads such as corn and wood, cleaning groundnuts, crossing bridges, holding celebrations, listening to a missionary preach, playing drums, preparing a pig for cooking, selling items in the market, sharpening knives, spinning cotton, weaving baskets, and working in the fields. Architecture shown includes chiefs' palaces, houses, a mission school house, shrines, and villages. There are portraits of chiefs, kings, members of the secret society *kweifo* with their paraphernalia, and other people, showing costume, masks, ornaments, and scarification. A photograph from this collection is reproduced in the illustrations section of this volume.

Arranged: By image number.

Captioned: With image number and subject (some in German); some also with date.

Finding Aid: No.

Restrictions: No.

AF·61

Victoria Scott Slide Collection

Dates of Photographs: 1960s–1970s

Collection Origins

Artist and teacher Victoria Scott (1943–) created the collection to document contemporary Nigerian art, in particular the Oshogbo school. Scott received a B.A. in art history from Smith College in 1965 and subsequently studied with Frank Willet and Robert Plant Armstrong. From 1969 to 1979 she lived in Nigeria, where she taught at the Jebba Technical College and worked as a visual artist. She used these images in courses on Nigerian art she taught at the college. In 1984 Scott donated the collection to the National Museum of African Art, where it received accession number A1984-03.

Physical Description

There are 435 color dye coupler slides (Ektachrome and Kodachrome).

Subjects

The photographs document drawings, graphic prints, paintings, and textiles of the Oshogbo school of artists. There are photographic reproductions of the following works: *Elephant* by Nike; *Elmina Castle* by Kwe Ade Odus; *Free Yourself and See Yourself* by Twins Seven-Seven; *Mamiwata Voyibo II* by Bruce Onobrakpeya; *Obatala and his Wife* by Joseph Olu-Billy; *Ogun, God of Iron* by Sam Babarinsa; *Reindeer* by Jimoh Buraimoh; *The Secret Life of the Twins of Nigeria* by Asiru Olatunde; and *Yam Festival Masquerade* by Adebisi Fabunmi.

There are also images of artists at work and the towns in which they live. People portrayed include artist Adebisi Fabunmi; a blacksmith at work in Kaduna, Nigeria; and potters in Ghana. Images of the built environment include a market in Abeokuta, Nigeria; a Portuguese fort in Cape Coast, Ghana; and an Osun (deity) shrine in Oshogbo.

Arranged: No.

Captioned: Most with artist, medium, and title.

Finding Aid: No.

Restrictions: Available for reference only. No reproductions may be made.

AF·62

Larry Scully Photograph Collection

Dates of Photographs: 1971–1978

Collection Origins

South African painter and photographer Larry Scully created the collection to document wall paintings he discovered in an abandoned hostel. Belonging to the Crown Mine of South Africa, the hostel housed miners of the Sotho peoples of South Africa and neighboring Mozambique, who may have created the paintings. Scully exhibited the photographs and then donated them in 1989 to the National Museum of African Art, where they received accession number A1989-09.

Physical Description

There are 21 photographs including color dye coupler photoprints and slides.

Subjects

The photographs document wall paintings in the rooms of an abandoned, partly destroyed hostel owned by the Crown Mine of South Africa. The paintings shown incorporate abstract designs, photographic images, and words. There are also images of paintings by Larry Scully.

Arranged: By image number.

Captioned: With date, location, photographer, and subject.

Finding Aid: No.

Restrictions: Available for reference only. No reproductions may be made.

AF·63

Segy Art Gallery Collection

Dates of Photographs: 1949–1985

Collection Origins

Artist and gallery director Ladislas Segy (1904–1988) created the collection to document African art objects for his publications. Segy studied at the Collège de France and exhibited his own work in the 1930s and 1940s. Later he began collecting African art and opened the Segy Art Gallery in New York City. The photographs appeared in the following books by Segy: 1) *African Art: The Segy Gallery.* Bolton, Massachusetts: Skinner, 1988. 2) *African Sculpture.* New York: Dover Publications, 1958. 3) *African Sculpture Speaks.* Fourth edition. New York: Da Capo Press, 1975. 4) *Masks of Black Africa.* New York: Dover Publications, 1976. 5) *Traditional Sculpture of Western Africa.* New York: L. Segy, 1976. The collection was assigned National Museum of African Art accession number A1988-07.

Physical Description

There are 40,000 photographs including color dye coupler photonegatives, photoprints, and slides and silver gelatin photonegatives and photoprints. Other materials include books, manuscripts, newspaper clippings, and notebooks.

Subjects

The photographs document African art objects including marionettes, masks, sculpted figures, stools, and vessels, primarily from museums. Peoples and kingdoms whose art is shown include Baule, Benin, Bundu, Chamba, Ibibio, Ijo, Kota, Mbala, Mpongwe, Songye, Yaka, and Yoruba. There are portraits of Africans including artists at work and dancers, illustrating body art and costume. There are also travel photographs of Segy's trips, showing architecture, art objects, cityscapes, landscapes, and museums in Colombia, Egypt, Germany, India, Japan, Mexico, Peru, Russia, and Spain.

Arranged: No.

Captioned: Most with location, people, and subject.

Finding Aid: No.

Restrictions: Available for reference only. No reproductions may be made.

AF·64

Senegal Photograph Collection

Dates of Photographs: 1880s–1913

Collection Origins

National Museum of African Art (NMAfA) staff assembled the collection from vintage photographs and cabinet cards of Senegal purchased from several sources. Popular from the mid-1860s to the 1900s, cabinet cards were commercially produced 4″ × 5 1/2″ photoprints mounted on card stock measuring 4 1/4″ × 6 1/2″—often with an embossed studio name in the corner. Frequently sold as collectors' items, these cards often contained images of attractive women or royalty of various nationalities. Photographers and studios represented include J. Barbier and Bonnevide Photographic Studio. The collection received NMAfA accession number A1989-03.

Physical Description

There are 40 photographs including albumen photoprints (some cabinet cards) and silver gelatin photoprints.

Subjects

The photographs document the environment and people of Senegal including the city of St. Louis. People portrayed include African soldiers, shown marching, on horses, and with cannons, as well as villagers, some with camels. Structures depicted include a bridge, docks, a fort, houses, monuments, and a train station. There are also images of ships on a river.

Arranged: By image number.

Captioned: Some with date and subject.

Finding Aid: No.

Restrictions: No.

AF·65

Roy Sieber Textile Slide Collection

Dates of Photographs: 1960s

Collection Origins

Roy Sieber (1923–), associate director for collections and research at the National Museum of African Art (NMAfA), created the collection for a 1972 exhibit at the Museum of Modern Art in New York City. Sieber received a Ph.D. in 1957 from Iowa State University, where he taught art history from 1950 to 1962. In 1962 he became a professor at Indiana University and curator of primitive art at the university's Fine Arts Museum. Throughout his career he served as lecturer and visiting professor at several universities in Africa as well as the United States. Sieber was a member of the American Council of Learned Societies/Social Science Research Council Joint Committee on Africa between 1963 and 1971. He is also a member of the African Studies Association and the primitive art advisory committee at the Metropolitan Museum of Art. The photographs were published in the following exhibit catalog: Roy Sieber. *African Textiles and Decorative Arts.* New York: Museum of Modern Art, 1972. Photographers include Herbert Cole, Melville J. Herskovitz, Arnold Rubin, and Roy Sieber. The collection received NMAfA accession number A1985-11.

Physical Description

There are 65 color dye coupler slides (Ektachrome and Kodachrome).

Subjects

The photographs document African textiles and the dyeing and weaving processes. Objects depicted include Asante *kente* cloth, Hausa embroidered pants, Jukun tie-dye waist cloth, a Kuba hat, Yoruba indigo dye, and a Zulu cloak, as well as *akwete* cloth from Nigeria, an appliqué dress from Cameroon, an appliqué robe from Ghana, cloth from Dahomey (now Benin), and dye pots from Ede. People portrayed include a Dogon dancer, Kajiado warriors with spears and shields, a weaver making cloth, and women dyeing cloth with indigo. There is also an image of a mosque at Jenne, Mali.

Arranged: No.

Captioned: With subject and photographer.

Finding Aid: No.

Restrictions: Available for reference only. No reproductions may be made.

AF·66

Anni Siranne-Coplan Photograph Collection

Dates of Photographs: 1973

Collection Origins

Anni Siranne-Coplan, a Washington, D.C., photographer, created the collection and donated it in 1975 and 1976 to the National Museum of African Art, where it received accession number A1975-01.

Physical Description

There are 455 silver gelatin contact photoprints and photonegatives.

Subjects

The photographs document daily life in Benin, Ghana, Nigeria, and Togo. Locations in Benin illustrated include Cotonou, Natitingou, and Porto Novo. Images show architecture, markets, and street scenes in African cities, coastal towns (with houses on stilts), and villages. People and activities shown include an artist working with wood, a baptism in the sea, bus travel to Nigeria, a midwife in Cotonou, and a nurse in Benin.

Arranged: Numerically by film roll.

Captioned: No.

Finding Aid: Index listing entry number, location, and subject including activity and name of the people.

Restrictions: No.

AF·67

H.G.L. Smith Photograph Album

Dates of Photographs: 1905–1907

Collection Origins

H.G.L. Smith created the collection to document his hunting trips in Africa between 1905 and 1907. Deborah Cooney, a former staff member at the Museum of African Art, purchased the album from Joe and Carol Lehman of Claymont, Delaware, to add to the Eliot Elisofon Archives. The collection received National Museum of African Art accession number A1980-01.

Physical Description

There are 90 photographs including albumen and silver gelatin photoprints, mounted in an album.

Subjects

The photographs document H.G.L. Smith's hunting party in Rhodesia (now Zimbabwe) and the accompanying African workers. There are also images of local animals and landscapes. Smith and the other hunters are portrayed in a boat on the Zambezi River, in camps, and posing with rifles and dead animals. The African workers are portrayed carrying loads and posing with or retrieving dead animals. Other Rhodesians portrayed include policemen shown both on camels and outside a building with an official of European descent on "court day," Tonga people, and a "pioneer" of European descent shown in front of his house. Animals illustrated include cape buffalos, crocodiles, elands, hippopotamuses, impalas, leopards, lions, sable

antelopes, wart hogs, wildebeests, and zebras. There is also an image of Victoria Falls.

Arranged: No.

Captioned: Some with subject.

Finding Aid: No.

Restrictions: No.

AF·68

Stanley Collection Slides

Dates of Photographs: 1984

Collection Origins

Christopher D. Roy created the collection to illustrate a catalog for a 1985 exhibit at the University of Iowa Art Museum in Iowa City, titled "Art and Life in Africa: Selections from the Stanley Collection." The exhibit featured African art works owned by Iowa businessman and philanthropist C. Maxwell Stanley (1904–1984) and Betty Stanley, his wife. The Stanleys purchased their first piece of African art in 1960, during a business trip to West Africa, and eventually acquired nearly 600 objects. The pieces in the exhibit now belong to the University of Iowa Art Museum.

Roy, who received a Ph.D. from Indiana University, is an associate professor at the University of Iowa, where he also works at the Museum of Art. The photographs appeared in the following publication: Christopher D. Roy. *Art and Life in Africa: Selections from the Stanley Collection.* Iowa City: University of Iowa Museum of Art, 1985. In 1987 Roy donated the photographs to the National Museum of African Art, where they received accession number A1987-02.

Physical Description

There are 205 color dye coupler slides.

Subjects

The photographs document African art objects exhibited in 1985 at the University of Iowa Art Museum, which were formerly owned by C. Maxwell and Betty Stanley and now belong to the museum. Art works shown include figures, masks, musical instruments, sculptures, and staffs from the following peoples and kingdoms: Baga, Benin, Bwa, Dan, Dogon, Fang (Pahouin), Ibibio, Idoma, Jenne, Kongo, Lega, Punu, Senufo, Songye, and Yoruba. Countries represented include Gabon, Guinea, Ivory Coast, Liberia, Mali, Mozambique, Nigeria, and Zaire.

Arranged: By people of origin.

Captioned: With dimensions, medium, people of origin, and type of object.

Finding Aid: Caption list.

Restrictions: Available for reference only. No reproductions may be made.

AF·69

Jerry Taddeo
Slide Collection

Dates of Photographs: 1971–1973

Collection Origins

Jerry Taddeo (1944–   ) created the collection to document his travels in Ethiopia in the 1970s. Taddeo received a B.A. from the City University of New York (1969) and an M.A. from Long Island University (1974). He served as a Peace Corps volunteer in Africa from 1971 to 1973, when these photographs were taken. In 1988 Taddeo donated the photographs to the National Museum of African Art, where they received accession number A1988-03.

Physical Description

There are 60 color dye coupler slides.

Subjects

The photographs document Ethiopian art works, cityscapes, landscapes, and people in the 1970s. There are images of traditional architecture, crosses, and 17th and 18th century diptychs (two-part painted or sculpted relief panels). There are individual and group portraits of Ethiopians, some showing activities such as house building.

Arranged: No.

Captioned: No.

Finding Aid: No.

Restrictions: No.

AF·70

David L. and Hazel B.
Watts Collection

Dates of Photographs: 1922–1938

Collection Origins

David L. and Hazel B. Watts created the collection during their work as missionaries with the Disciples of Christ Congo Mission among the Kundu people in Zaire during the 1920s and 1930s. In 1984 the Watts donated the collection to the National Museum of African Art, where it received accession number A1984-04.

Physical Description

There are 17 silver gelatin photoprints. Other materials include newsletters and photomechanical postcards.

Subjects

The photographs document the Disciples of Christ Congo Mission in Zaire, the Kundu people, and surrounding cityscapes and landscapes. Portraits include boys cutting grass at the mission, an old chief, Christian women, and David L. Watts with workmen. Images of the built environment include a train station and a train en route from Matadi to Leopoldville (now Kinshasa). Images of the natural environment include waterscapes of the Congo River and pictures of a dead leopard.

Arranged: No.

Captioned: With subject.

Finding Aid: No.

Restrictions: No.

AF·71

Thomas Weir Collection

Dates of Photographs: 1960–1966

Collection Origins

Thomas Weir, a U.S. government official in Liberia, created the collection to document Liberian culture. The National Museum of African Art assigned the collection accession number A1987-01.

Physical Description

There are 2,330 photographs including color dye coupler slides (Kodachrome) and silver gelatin photonegatives and photoprints. Other materials include audiotape cassettes.

Subjects

The photographs document the architecture, arts, events, and people of Liberia, particularly the Bassa, Kru, and Vai. Activities documented include blacksmithing, carving ivory, making a dugout canoe, making a pot, selling food in the market, and weaving baskets and cloth. Architectural images include government ministries, hospitals, schools, and numerous street scenes in Monrovia, as well as Bassa houses and villages. Art works depicted include paintings on houses and signs, as well as paintings, sculptures, and textiles created as tourist art. Events documented include official government ceremonies with staged indigenous dances; rituals in villages such as young members of the female *sande* society returning from the initiation camp; and visits by foreign heads of state such as Queen Elizabeth II and Josip Broz Tito of Yugoslavia. Liberians portrayed include President William V.S. Tubman and the people of Monrovia and other towns.

Arranged: Photonegatives and photoprints by roll number; slides by topic.

Captioned: Some with subject.

Finding Aid: No.

Restrictions: No.

AF·72

World History Slide Set

Dates of Photographs: 1980s

Collection Origins

Instructional Resources Corporation (IRC), a producer of educational material based in Annapolis, Maryland,

created the collection to sell to schools and other institutions. IRC donated a set called "Slides on the History of Africa" from its series "The World History Slide Collection" to the National Museum of African Art (NMAfA), which contributed original slides to the series. The museum received the collection in 1988 and assigned it accession number A1988-05.

Physical Description

There are 680 color dye coupler slides. Other materials include manuals.

Subjects

The photographs document aspects of African history and culture, from prehistory to the present, including agricultural labor, festivals, handcrafts, industrial labor, political events, protests, and religious practices. There are images of archaeological artifacts, architecture, and art objects. There are also portraits of political figures and photographic reproductions of drawings, maps, and prints.

Arranged: By historical period.

Captioned: With date and subject.

Finding Aid: Guide book with caption list.

Restrictions: Only NMAfA photographs may be reproduced. All others are available for reference only.

AF·73

Wosene Kosrof Slide Collection

Dates of Photographs: 1985–1986

Collection Origins

Ethiopian artist Wosene Kosrof (1950–) created the collection to document his art work. Wosene received a B.A. in fine arts in 1972 from the School of Fine Arts in Addis Ababa, where he taught for several years. He came to the United States in 1978 and received an M.A. from Howard University in 1980. His work has been exhibited in Africa, the Caribbean, Europe, and the United States, including a 1987 show at Howard University, "Graffiti Magic: Recent Paintings and Sculptures by Wosene." The collection was assigned National Museum of African Art accession number A1986-06.

Physical Description

There are 20 color dye coupler slides.

Subjects

The photographs reproduce art works by Wosene Kosrof, including paintings and sculptures. Many of the pieces have American themes but incorporate African imagery. Titles of works reproduced include *The Ancestor, Ancient Gossip, Brooklyn Bridge, John Coltrane, Primitive America, Self Portrait, Talisman,* and *Television City.*

Arranged: No.

Captioned: With date, dimensions, medium, and title of work.

Finding Aid: No.

Restrictions: Available for reference only. No reproductions may be made.

AF·74

Casimir d'Ostoja Zagourski Photograph Collection

Dates of Photographs: 1926, 1980s

Collection Origins

The National Museum of African Art (NMAfA) assembled the collection for research purposes from commercial images created by Casimir d'Ostoja Zagourski (1880–1941), a Polish photographer who worked in Leopoldville (now Kinshasa), Zaire, during the 1920s and 1930s. Zagourski photographed African animals, landscapes, and peoples for commercial purposes, including postcards. NMAfA purchased a group of his postcards from a series published under the title *L'Afrique qui Disparait (Vanishing Africa).* NMAfA also made copy photoprints of the complete series from original photonegatives lent by Indiana University. The collection was assigned NMAfA accession number A1987-24.

Physical Description

There are 1,535 photographs including silver gelatin photonegatives and photoprints (some postcards). Some of the photoprints are copies.

Subjects

The photographs document the cultures, built and natural environments, and peoples of the Central African Republic, the Belgian Congo (now Zaire), the French Congo (now the People's Republic of Congo), Kenya, Rwanda and Burundi (now Ruanda-Urundi), Tanganyika (now part of Tanzania), and Uganda in the 1920s. There are numerous photographs showing body art (such as body paint, hairstyles, and scarification) and costume. Historical personalities portrayed include the Kuba king, the king of Rwanda, and the queen mother of Rwanda. Activities illustrated include dances, masquerades, and rituals. There are also images of African architecture, such as Mangbetu villages, and landscapes.

Arranged: By original number and series.

Captioned: With subject.

Finding Aid: List of postcards.

Restrictions: Available for reference only. No reproductions may be made until the location of the original photonegatives has been established.

AF

Registrar's Office

Registrar's Office
National Museum of African Art
Smithsonian Institution
Washington, D.C. 20560
(202) 357-4600, ext. 240
Hours: Monday–Friday, 10 a.m.–5 p.m.

Scope of the Collections

There are three photographic collections with approximately 9,300 images.

Focus of the Collections

The photographs document objects in the holdings of the National Museum of African Art (NMAfA) and objects borrowed for exhibits. Items shown are from most of the countries in Africa, particularly the central and western regions, and date from the 16th century to the present.

Photographic Processes and Formats Represented

There are color dye coupler photoprints, dye diffusion transfer photoprints (Polaroid), and silver gelatin photoprints.

Other Materials Represented

The office also contains accession records, catalog cards, donor lists, exhibit lists, loan records, pamphlets, shipping lists, shipping orders, and xerographic copies.

Access and Usage Policies

The collections are open for research by appointment only. Researchers should call or write in advance, describing their research topic, the type of material that interests them, and their research aim.

Publication Policies

Copies for publication may be purchased by contacting Christraud M. Geary, Curator of the Eliot Elisofon Archives, NMAfA, Room 2140, Smithsonian Institution, Washington, D.C., 20560, (202), 357-4600, ext. 280.

AF·75

NMAfA Registrar's Office Accession Card Catalog

Dates of Photographs: 1979–Present

Collection Origins

Staff at the National Museum of African Art (NMAfA) Office of the Registrar created the collection to document the museum's holdings. The card catalog will eventually include images of all NMAfA accessioned objects.

Physical Description

There are 5,250 dye diffusion transfer photoprints (Polaroid). Other materials include 9,000 catalog cards, one each for the museum's 7,000 objects and 2,000 cross-reference cards.

Subjects

The photographs document about 75 percent of the roughly 7,000 African art objects in NMAfA's holdings. Objects illustrated are from most countries in Africa, particularly the central and western regions of the continent, and date from the 16th century to the present. Ceremonial, decorative, and functional objects documented include baskets, blankets, ceramic pots for cooking and storage, costumes, crosses, crowns, drums, fishing traps, fly whisks, fowl carriers, granary doors, harps, headdresses, headrests, horns, incense burners, jewelry, locks, masks, staffs, stools, textiles, whistles, window frames, and zithers, as well as other brass, clay, ivory, and wooden items.

Arranged: By object's accession number.

Captioned: With object's accession number; condition; format, medium, and shape; donor and donation date; exhibit number; and geographical area and people of origin.

Finding Aid: No.

Restrictions: Available by appointment only. No reproductions may be made.

AF·76

NMAfA Registrar's Office Accession Files

Dates of Photographs: 1983–Present

Collection Origins

Staff at the National Museum of African Art (NMAfA) Office of the Registrar created the collection to document the museum's holdings.

Physical Description

There are 540 photographs including color dye coupler photoprints, dye diffusion transfer photoprints (Polaroid), and silver gelatin photoprints. Other materials include accession records.

Subjects

The photographs document some of the objects held by NMAfA, including baskets, beadwork, bowls, headrests, masks, pipes, pottery, staffs, stools, and utensils.

Arranged: By object's accession number.

Captioned: With object's accession number and accompanied by accession records

Finding Aid: No.

Restrictions: Available by appointment only.

AF·77

NMAfA Registrar's Office Loan Records Files

Dates of Photographs: 1979–Present

Collection Origins

Staff at the National Museum of African Art (NMAfA) Office of the Registrar created the collection as a record of loan activity. Photographs document art objects that have been borrowed from or lent to other museums or institutions.

Physical Description

There are 3,500 dye diffusion transfer photoprints (Polaroid). Other materials include donor lists, loan records, pamphlets, shipping lists, shipping orders, and xerographic copies.

Subjects

The photographs document the condition and packaging of African art objects borrowed from or lent to NMAfA for exhibits. Items shown include ceramics, furniture, jewelry, paintings, sculptures, textiles, and various functional and ceremonial objects such as crowns, drums, fly whisks, and staffs. Objects illustrated have appeared in the following exhibits: "African Art in Color"; "African Emblems of Status"; "African Islam"; "Bakanki Tungo"; "From the Earth: African Ceramic Art"; "Praise Poems: The Katharine White Collection"; "The Stranger Among Us"; and "Thinking with Animals: African Images and Perceptions"; as well as a Smithsonian Institution Traveling Exhibition Service (SITES) exhibit on Ethiopia.

Arranged: By exhibit title, then date, then object's accession number.

Captioned: With loan number; name of the lender; and object's accession number, condition, description, material, size, and value.

Finding Aid: No.

Restrictions: Available to NMAfA curatorial staff only. No reproductions may be made.

NATIONAL MUSEUM OF AMERICAN ART

Elizabeth Broun, Director

The origins of the National Museum of American Art (NMAA) predate the founding of the Smithsonian. In 1829 John Varden, an art collector living in Washington, D.C., opened a gallery of art works in the nation's capital. In 1842 Varden's holdings were combined with the collections of the National Institution for the Promotion of Science to form a new museum called the National Institute. When the National Institute ceased operations in 1862, its holdings became part of the Smithsonian Institution. An 1865 fire in the Smithsonian Institution Building destroyed many of the pieces from Varden's collection. Subsequently, many government-owned art works were sent to the Corcoran Gallery of Art, a Washington, D.C., museum not affiliated with the Smithsonian.

Following a 1906 court order, the National Gallery of Art, composed of the remaining objects from the National Institute collection, began serving as the central repository for all Smithsonian-owned paintings, sculpture, and decorative arts. The Gallery occupied space at the Smithsonian's Arts and Industries building until 1910, when the holdings were moved to what is now the Smithsonian's National Museum of Natural History building. The museum became a separate bureau in 1920. In 1937 Andrew Mellon left his art holdings to the government, with the stipulation that the new collection be called the National Gallery of Art, after the museum in England. To accommodate Mellon's wishes, the Smithsonian changed the name of its collection to the National Collection of Fine Arts (NCFA). In 1968 the NCFA relocated in the restored Patent Office Building. (For a description of the building's history, see *PG·6*.) In 1980 the NCFA became the National Museum of American Art, a name that more precisely reflects the scope of the museum's holdings and activities.

Besides sponsoring exhibits, lectures, and public programs, the NMAA supports research through its fellowship and internship programs, as well as its scholarly journal, *American Art*. Along with a 50,000-volume library and a 416,000-item slide and photograph archives, the NMAA Research and Scholars Center maintains seven research databases that describe over 500,000 American art objects located throughout the country.

In addition to its operations in the old Patent Office Building, the NMAA maintains two other public facilities in Washington, D.C. The Renwick Gallery, housed in the original Corcoran Gallery of Art building designed by James Renwick, functions as a curatorial department within the NMAA. The Renwick collects and exhibits American crafts, decorative arts, and design objects. The second facility is the Alice Pike Barney Studio House, built in the early 20th century for socialite and painter Alice Pike Barney, based on the design of a Paris salon. Donated in 1960 to the Smithsonian by Barney's daughters, the house is used for musical and literary events as well as small exhibits.

The NMAA's 16 photographic collections contain 600,530 photographs that document American artists and art objects including crafts, decorative arts, design objects, folk arts, graphic arts, paintings, photographs, and sculptures, as well as NMAA activities, exhibits, facilities, programs, and staff.

AM

Curatorial Office

Curatorial Office
Photography Division
National Museum of American Art
Smithsonian Institution
Washington, D.C. 20560
Merry Foresta, Curator
Maricia Battle, Assistant Curator
(202) 357-2593
Hours: By appointment.

Scope of the Collection

There is one photographic collection with approximately 2,500 photographs.

Focus of the Collection

The collection primarily consists of contemporary American fine art photography including abstract works, cityscapes, landscapes, portraits, still lifes, and waterscapes. The collection also includes examples of historical American photographs.

Photographic Processes and Formats Represented

There are color dye bleach photoprints (Cibachrome), color dye coupler photoprints, color dye transfer photoprints, cyanotypes, gum bichromate photoprints, platinum photoprints, and silver gelatin photoprints.

Other Materials Represented

The department also contains photomechanicals (photogravures).

Access and Usage Policies

Available by appointment for scholarly research and exhibit planning purposes only. Researchers should call or write in advance for an appointment, describing their research topic, the type of material that interests them, and their research aim.

Publication Policies

No photographic or xerographic copies may be made of images in this collection.

AM·1

American Art Photograph Collection

Dates of Photographs: 19th Century–Present

Collection Origins

Curator of photography Merry Foresta, assistant curator Maricia Battle, and other National Museum of American Art (NMAA) staff assembled these photographs by contemporary and historical American photographers from individual purchases and donations. Most of the images were created after 1940, although some earlier photographs are included in the collection.

Many of the photographs were received from the National Endowment for the Arts (NEA) in 1983. These images originally were submitted to the NEA by individual artists as part of their grant applications. The permanent collection also includes photographs of the 1984 Olympics by Walter Iooss, Jr., donated by Fuji Photo Film U.S.A.; an accession of contemporary landscape photographs donated by the Consolidated Natural Gas Company Foundation; a large accession of Irving Penn photographs; and a sizeable representation of work by Photo League photographers; as well as photographs by contemporary artists.

Photographers represented include Berenice Abbott, Adal, Ansel Adams, Lynn Adams, Rod Amberg, Diane Arbus, Dick Arentz, Lawrence Babis, Grace M. Ballentine, Lewis Baltz, C.P. Barber, George N. Barnard, Ricardo T. Barros, Herbert Bayer, Michael Becotte, Bell & Bro., Jim Bengston, Richard Benson, Dan Biferie, Michael Bishop, Jeffrey Blankfort, Howard Bond, Charles H. Breed, Dennis Brokaw, Ellen Brooks, Romaine Brooks, Wynn Bullock, Jerry Burchard, Bill Burke, Marsha Burns, Rebecca Busselle, Edward Pierre Buyck, Harry Callahan, Paul Caponigro, Bobbi Carrey, Sarah Charlesworth, V. Checa, Carl Chiarenza, William Christenberry, Larry Clark, William Clift, Alan Cohen, Lois Conner, Linda Connor, Mac Cosgrove-Davies, Eileen Cowin, Barbara Crane, David T. Culverwell, Robert Cumming, William Current, Edward S. Curtis, Robert D'Alessandro, Edward F. D'Arms, Bill Dane, Joseph Dankowski, Avery Danzinger, Bruce Davidson, Robert Dawnson, Agnes Denes, Irwin Dermer, Paul Diamond, John Divola, Jay S. Dunitz, William Eggleston, James Enyeart, Reed Estabrook, and Terry Evans.

There are also photographs by Larry Fink, Judy Fiskin, Steve Fitch, Christine B. Fletcher, Harris Fogel, Robert Frank, Godfrey Frankel, Jill Freedman, Roland Freeman, Lee Friedlander, Benno Friedman, George Fry, Oliver Gagliani, George W. Gardner, William Gedney, Ingeborg Gerdes, Ralph Gibson, Laura Gilpin, Mark Goodman, John R. Gossage, Emmet Gowin, Ken Graves, Gray, Ed Grazda, Jan Groover, Sid Grossman, John Gruen, Gary Hallman, John Harding, Chauncey Hare, Anthony Hernandez, Frank Herrera, Paul Herzoff, Marc Hessel, Paul Hester, Ed Hill, Lewis W. Hine, Tana Hoban, Bruce Horowitz, Bob Hower, Crystal K.D. Huie, Sandy Hume, Scott Hyde, Walter Iooss, Jr., Joseph D. Jachna, William Henry Jackson, Jay Jaffee, Allan Janus, L.R. John, Kenneth Josephson, Paul Juley, Peter A. Juley, Art Kane, Barbara Kasten, Gyorgy Kepes, Robert Glenn Ketchum, R.P. Kingston, William Klein, Paul Kohl, Arnold Kramer, Burton Kramer, George Krause, Les Krims, Yasuo Kuniyoshi, W. Kurtz, and Ted Kuykendall.

Other photographers represented include Ellen Land-Weber, Landreth, Dorothea Lange, William Larson, Clarence John Laughlin, John H. Lawrence, Wayne R. Lazorik, Minette Lehmann, Erica Lennard, Perry Letson, Robert Levin, Helen Levitt, Alvin Lieberman, Jerome Liebling, Ben Lifson, Leonard Lionni, Richard Loftis, Danny Lyon, Nathan Lyons, Man Ray, Mike Mandel, Blanche McManus Mansfield, Robert Mapplethorpe, Reginald Marsh, Grayson Mathews, Herbert Matter, Elaine Mayes, Duncan McCosker, Kenneth McGowan, John McWilliams, Roger Mertin, Gary Metz, Ray K. Metzker, David M. Miller, Roger Minick, Richard Misrach, Lisette Model, Andrea Modica, Benson Bond Moore, Barbara Morgan, Joseph S. Murray, Eadweard Muybridge, Joan Clark Netherwood, Bea Nettles, H.F. Nielson, Nicholas Nixon, Anne Noggle, Ira Norminsky, Kenda North, Sonya Noskowiak, Arthur L. Ollman, Timothy H. O'Sullivan, Bill Owens, Tod Papageorge, Horace Paul, Irving Penn, Charles L. Phillips, Stephen John Phillips, Paulus Potter, Charles Pratt, Douglas Prince, Joe B. Ramos, Edward Ranney, Lilo Raymond, Nancy Rexroth, Leland Rice, Eugene Richards, Frederick Richardson, Alvin Rosenbaum, Mary Roth, and Scott Rucker.

There also are photographs by Lucas Samaras, Doug L. Sandhage, Henry Sandham, Napoleon Sarony, Naomi Savage, Willie Schaff, Xanti Schawinsky, Larry W. Schwarm, David Semen, Charles Sheeler, Aaron Siskind, Gail Skoff, Neal Slavin, Michael P. Smith, William Eugene Smith, Rosalind Solomon, Frederick Sommer, Eva Sonneman, Wayne Sorce, Gregory Spaid, Edward Steichen, Louis Stettner, Jim Stone, Paul Strand, William Suttle, Steve Szabo, George A. Tice, Arthur Tress, Sarah Tuft, Alwyn Scott Turner, James W. Twitty, Jerry Uelsmann, Burk Uzzle, Sarah Van Keuren, Catherine Wagner, Max Waldman, Todd Walker, Robert Walsh, Ted Wathen, Carleton E. Watkins, Alex Webb, Todd Webb, Weegee, William Wegman, Brett Weston, Edward Weston, Geoff Winningham, Garry Winogrand, Joel-Peter Witkin, Alison Woolpert, Bill Woolston, John Yang,

Max Yanvo, Ronald Zegart, Armando Jerry Zelada, Tom Zetterstrom, and William Zorach.

Physical Description

There are 2,500 photographs including color dye bleach photoprints (Cibachrome), color dye coupler photoprints, color dye transfer photoprints, cyanotypes, gum bichromate prints, platinum photoprints, and silver gelatin photoprints. Other materials include photomechanicals (photogravures).

Subjects

The images are accessioned fine art photographs including abstracts, advertising images, allegorical and mythological images, animal studies, architectural studies, cityscapes, fashion photographs, landscapes, portraits, sequence photographs, travel photographs, still lifes, and waterscapes.

Cityscapes depict built environments including alleys; bridges (such as the Brooklyn Bridge, George Washington Bridge, and Golden Gate Bridge); churches (such as the China Grove Church, Grand Pre Church, Owings Presbyterian Church, St. Batholomew's Church, and St. Mark's Church); courthouses; factories; gasoline stations; grocery stores; gymnasiums; homes (such as log cabins); hospitals; hotels; markets; monumental sculpture (such as the Statue of Liberty); museums and galleries (such as the Limelight Gallery, Metropolitan Museum of Art, and Pompidou Center); office buildings (such as the Empire State Building and Rockefeller Center); railroad stations and yards (such as Grand Central Station); restaurants and taverns; stadiums; subways; and theaters (such as the RKO Palace in New York).

There are images of cities, regions, and towns in Arkansas (such as Fayetteville and Pine Bluff); California (such as Berkeley, Los Angeles, San Francisco, and Santa Cruz); Colorado (such as Colorado Springs and Pueblo); Delaware (such as Bethany Beach); Hawaii (such as Honolulu and Waikiki); Illinois (such as Chicago); Iowa (such as Cedar Rapids); Kansas (such as Concordia); Kentucky (such as Bowling Green, the Cumberland Gap, and Louisville); Louisiana (such as Baton Rouge); Maryland (such as Baltimore and Rockville); Massachusetts (such as Cape Cod, Martha's Vineyard, and Springfield); Michigan (such as Detroit); Missouri (such as Springfield and St. Joseph); Nebraska (such as David City, Lincoln, and North Platte); Nevada (such as Las Vegas); New Jersey (such as Hoboken); New Mexico (such as Albuquerque, Llanito, Santa Fe, and Taos); New York (such as Ellis Island, New York City, Oneonta, and Treadwell); Ohio (such as Dayton); Oklahoma (such as Muskogee and Tulsa); Pennsylvania (such as Philadelphia and Pittsburgh); Rhode Island (such as Newport and Providence); South Carolina (such as Charleston); Tennessee (such as Chattanooga and Memphis); Texas (such as Austin, Dallas, and Houston); Utah (such as Monument Valley); Virginia (such as Falls Church); and Washington (such as Seattle); as well as Washington, D.C.

Cities in countries such as Canada, England, France, Germany, Haiti, India, Mexico, Morocco, New Guinea, Pakistan, Peru, Spain, and Tibet (now Xizang) also are documented. Landscapes, including aerial views, show beaches, deserts, forests, gardens, mountains, parks, valleys, and volcanoes around the world. There are images of national parks in the United States, such as Big Bend National Park, Everglades National Park, Glacier National Park, and Great Basin National Park.

There are portraits of artists (such as Jean Cocteau, Salvador Dali, Alberto Giacometti, Charles Le Corbusier, John Marin, Reginald Marsh, Joan Miró, Georgia O'Keeffe, Pablo Picasso, and Raphael Soyer); athletes (such as Evander Holyfield, Carl Lewis, and Mary Lou Retton); dancers (such as Martha Graham); entertainers (such as Elvis Presley and Priscilla Presley); photographers (such as Man Ray and Alfred Stieglitz); presidents (such as George Bush, Jimmy Carter, Gerald R. Ford, John F. Kennedy, Richard M. Nixon, and Ronald Reagan); and writers (such as Eugene Ionesco).

Other occupations portrayed include architects; barbers; beauty contestants; bootblacks; chimney sweeps; circus performers (such as animal trainers, fortune tellers, and snake charmers); clergymen; composers; construction workers; cowboys; custodians; dancers; doormen; educators; farmers; fishermen; industrial workers; judges; lawyers; lifeguards; miners; models; policemen; sailors; salesmen (including coal, food, gasoline, and newspaper vendors); sign painters; street sweepers; strippers; truck drivers; upholsterers; veterinarians; and waiters.

The collection contains portraits of North American Indians, including members of the Arapaho, Cheyenne, Navajo, Oto, Wichita, and Zuni peoples. Other culture groups represented include African Americans, the Amish, gypsies, and Hispanic Americans.

There are images of art works, including figurines, paintings, and sculptures, as well as the studios of artists John Marin and Georgia O'Keeffe. Objects shown include clothes, food, furniture, musical instruments, tools, toys, vessels, and weapons. Modes of transportation shown include airplanes; automobiles; bicycles; boats (such as ferries, rowboats, schooners, steamboats, tugboats, and yachts); buses; carts; jeeps; motorcycles; recreational vehicles; tanks; trucks; and wagons.

Events documented include dances; disasters (such as airplane crashes, explosions, and volcanic eruptions); expositions; festivals (such as Mardi Gras and the Olympics); holidays (such as Christmas and Halloween); parades; and religious ceremonies (such as Communion). Activities shown include bathing, blowing bubbles, brushing hair, cheerleading, combing hair, conversing, dressing up, drinking, eating, playing with dolls, racing, reading, riding horses, shooting, sitting, smoking tobacco, and teaching. The collection includes images of sports, many from the 1984 Summer Olympics in Los Angeles, such as archery, baseball, basketball, bicycling, boxing, fencing, field hockey, fishing, gymnastics, judo, soccer, swimming, track and field, volleyball, weight lifting, wrestling, and yachting.

Animals shown include birds (such as chickens, geese, gulls, and turkeys); fish (such as manta rays, sea horses, sharks, and spearfish); invertebrates (such as insects and snails); mammals (such as bats, bears, buffaloes, cats, dogs, horses, lions, monkeys, muskrats, porpoises, seals, sheep, and zebras); and reptiles and amphibians (such as alligators and snakes). There are also photographs of equestrians and of animal locomotion. Several photographs from this collection are reproduced in the illustrations section of this volume.

Arranged: Alphabetically by photographer.

Captioned: Many with date, signature, and title.

Finding Aid: 1) Accession book, arranged by accession number, cross-referenced to database. 2) Database, arranged alphabetically by photographer, listing accession number, date, dimensions, genre, inscription, medium, source, subject, and title.

Restrictions: Available for scholarly research and exhibition only. Copies of photographs for research use only may be available. Contact Merry Foresta, Curator of Photography, or Maricia Battle, Assistant Curator, Department of Graphic Arts, NMAA, Room 153, Smithsonian Institution, Washington, D.C., 20560, (202) 357-2593.

AM

Office of Registration and Collections Management

Office of Registration and Collections Management
National Museum of American Art
Smithsonian Institution
Washington, D.C. 20560
Lenore Fein, Museum Registration Specialist
Kimberly Cody, Rights and Reproductions
(202) 357-1381
Hours: Monday–Friday, 10 a.m.–5 p.m.

Scope of the Collections

There are two photographic collections with approximately 142,650 images.

Focus of the Collections

The photographs reproduce the holdings of the National Museum of American Art (NMAA), both accessioned and on long-term loan, including graphic prints, paintings, photographs, and sculptures made in the United States from colonial times to the present.

Photographic Processes and Formats Represented

There are color dye coupler phototransparencies and slides and silver gelatin photonegatives and photoprints.

Other Materials Represented

The office also contains accession records, information forms, and xerographic copies.

Access and Usage Policies

To use the NMAA Accession Files *(AM·2)*, researchers should call or write the address above for an appointment, describing their research topic, the type of material that interests them, and their research aim. Images in the Rights and Reproductions Files *(AM·3)* are restricted; duplicates may be viewed in the Slide Library *(AM·14)* in the Research and Scholars Center. Contact Joan Stahl, Coordinator of Image Collections, Slide and Photograph Archives, NMAA, Room 331, Washington, D.C., 20560, (202) 357-1348.

Publication Policies

Researchers must obtain permission from the Smithsonian Institution's National Museum of American Art to reproduce a photograph and may also have to obtain permission from the copyright holder, which is not necessarily the Smithsonian Institution. Permission to reproduce images must be obtained in writing from Rights and Reproductions, Office of Registration and Collections Management, National Museum of American Art, Smithsonian Institution, Washington, D.C., 20560. The preferred credit line is "Courtesy of the National Museum of American Art, Smithsonian Institution." The photographer's name, if known, also should appear.

AM·2

NMAA Accession Files

Dates of Photographs: 1960s–Present

Collection Origins

National Museum of American Art (NMAA) staff created the collection to document the museum's accessions for collection management purposes.

Physical Description

There are 34,000 silver gelatin photoprints. Other materials include accession records.

Subjects

The photographs reproduce the NMAA's accessioned holdings including graphic prints, paintings, photographs, and sculptures made in America from colonial times to the present. Artists whose work is reproduced include Josef Albers, Ivan Albright, Alexander Archipenko, Milton Avery, Peggy Bacon, Edward M. Bannister, Alice Pike Barney, William Baziotes, George W. Bellows, Thomas Hart Benton, Ilya Bolotowsky, Rexford E. Brandt, Romaine Brooks, Paul Cadmus, Alexander Calder, Mary Cassatt, George Catlin, Frederic Edwin Church, Howard N. Cook, Joseph Cornell, Kenyon Cox, Stuart Davis, Willem de Kooning, Thomas W. Dewing, Werner Drewes, Robert Scott Duncanson, Thomas Eakins, Ralph Earl, Alvan Fisher, Walter Gay, Sam Gilliam, Adolph Gottlieb, Christian Gullager, Philip Guston, James Hampton, Childe Hassam, Hans Hofmann, Winslow Homer, Edward Hopper, George Inness, Joshua Johnson, William H. Johnson, Jacob Kainen, Morris Kantor, Rockwell Kent, Franz Kline, John LaFarge, Jacob Lawrence, Edmonia Lewis, Louis Lozowick, Paul Manship, Reginald Marsh, Thomas Moran, Kenneth Noland, Georgia O'Keeffe, Irving Penn, Hiram Powers, William Rimmer, Albert Pinkham Ryder, John Singer Sargent, Raphael Soyer, Henry Ossawa Tanner, Abbott H. Thayer, Alma W. Thomas, John Henry Twatchman, Elihu Vedder, Julian A. Weir, Benjamin West, and William Zorach.

Arranged: Chronologically by object's accession number.

Captioned: On accompanying records with object's accession number, artist, country of origin, execution date, medium, dimensions, source, subject, and title.

Finding Aid: Printout for Rights and Reproductions files, arranged alphabetically by artist, lists the object's accession number, execution date, medium, and title.

Restrictions: Xerographic copies may be made upon request, but photographic copies must be ordered through the Office of Rights and Reproductions. Contact Lenore Fein, Museum Registration Specialist, Office of Registration and Collections Management, National Museum of American Art, Smithsonian Institution, Washington, D.C., 20560, (202) 357-1381.

AM·3

NMAA Rights and Reproductions Files

Dates of Photographs: 1960s–Present

Collection Origins

National Museum of American Art (NMAA) staff created the collection to document the museum's holdings, including accessioned and long-term loan items, for research and publication purposes. Many of the slides were created by Rosenthal Art Slide Company.

Physical Description

There are 108,650 photographs including color dye coupler phototransparencies and slides and silver gelatin photonegatives and photoprints. Other materials include information forms and xerographic copies.

Subjects

The photographs reproduce NMAA holdings, both accessioned and on long-term loan, including graphic prints, paintings, photographs, and sculptures made in America from colonial times through the 20th century. Artists whose work is reproduced include Josef Albers, Ivan Albright, Alexander Archipenko, Milton Avery, Peggy Bacon, Edward M. Bannister, Alice Pike Barney, William Baziotes, George W. Bellows, Thomas Hart Benton, Ilya Bolotowsky, Rexford E. Brandt, Romaine Brooks, Paul Cadmus, Alexander Calder, Mary Cassatt, George Catlin, Frederic Edwin Church, Howard N. Cook, Joseph Cornell, Kenyon Cox, Stuart Davis, Willem de Kooning, Thomas W. Dewing, Werner Drewes, Robert Scott Duncanson, Thomas Eakins, Ralph Earl, Alvan Fisher, Walter Gay, Sam Gilliam, Adolph Gottlieb, Christian Gullager, Philip Guston, James Hampton, Childe Hassam, Hans Hofmann, Winslow Homer, Edward Hopper, George Inness, Joshua Johnson, William H. Johnson, Jacob Kainen, Morris Kantor, Rockwell Kent, Franz Kline, John LaFarge, Jacob Lawrence, Edmonia Lewis, Louis Lozowick, Paul Manship, Reginald Marsh, Thomas Moran, Kenneth Noland, Georgia O'Keeffe, Irving Penn, Hiram Powers, William Rimmer, Albert Pinkham Ryder, John Singer Sargent, Raphael Soyer, Henry Ossawa Tanner, Abbott Handerson Thayer, Alma W. Thomas, John Henry Twatchman, Elihu Vedder, Julian A. Weir, Benjamin West, and William Zorach.

Arranged: In two series by format, then alphabetically by artist, then by object's accession number. 1) Photoprints and phototransparencies. 2) Slides.

Captioned: With object's accession number, artist, date, dimensions, medium, and title; some also with exhibit.

Finding Aid: 1) Computer database with printout arranged alphabetically by artist and listing object's accession or long-term loan number, execution date, medium, and title. 2) List of art works reproduced on slides by the Rosenthal Art Slide Company, arranged alphabetically by artist and including date and title.

Restrictions: Researchers should view duplicate images in the Slide Library *(AM·14)* in the Research and Scholars Center. Requests for copies must be submitted in writing to Rights and Reproductions, Office of Registration and Collections Management, National Museum of American Art, Smithsonian Institution, Washington, D.C., 20560, (202) 357-1381.

AM

Research and Scholars Center

Research and Scholars Center
National Museum of American Art
Smithsonian Institution
Washington, D.C. 20560
Rachel M. Allen, Acting Chief
(202) 357-1626
Hours: Monday–Friday, 10 a.m.–5 p.m.

Scope of the Collections

There are 12 photographic collections with approximately 455,200 images.

Focus of the Collections

The Research and Scholars Center of the National Museum of American Art (NMAA) consists of the Inventory of American Painting, the Inventory of American Sculpture, the National Museum of Art and National Portrait Gallery Library, and the Slide and Photograph Archives. Photographs document contemporary and historical American art works with emphases on paintings, photographs, sculptures, and, to a lesser extent, architecture and graphic arts. There are also photographs of American artists and NMAA accessions, exhibits, facilities, programs, and staff.

Photographic Processes and Formats Represented

There are albumen photoprints; color dye coupler photonegatives, photoprints, phototransparencies, and slides; color screen plate phototransparencies; dye diffusion transfer photoprints; platinum photoprints; silver gelatin dry plate lantern slides and photonegatives; and silver gelatin photonegatives, photoprints, and slides.

Other Materials Represented

The Center also contains architectural drawings, articles, awards, catalogs, certificates, correspondence, diaries, exhibit catalogs, exhibit lists, field notes, inventories, invitations, magazines, maps, newspaper clippings, photomechanicals (some photogravures), programs, sketches, watercolors, and xerographic copies.

Access and Usage Policies

For non-restricted collections, researchers should call or write for an appointment, describing their research topic, the type of material that interests them, and their research aim.

Publication Policies

Researchers must obtain permission from the Smithsonian Institution's National Museum of American Art to reproduce a photograph and may also have to obtain permission from the copyright holder, which is not necessarily the Smithsonian Institution. No photographic or xerographic copies may be made of images in collections *AM·5* and *AM·6*. Requests for permission to reproduce objects in the museum's permanent collection should be directed to the Office of Registration and Collections Management, NMAA, Room 248, Smithsonian Institution, Washington, D.C., 20560, (202) 357-1381. The preferred credit line is "[Collection name], Courtesy of the National Museum of American Art, Smithsonian Institution." The photographer's name, if known, also should appear.

AM·4

Bourges-Bruehl Collection

Dates of Photographs: 1938–1953

Collection Origins

Photographers and color technicians Fernand A. Bourges and Anton Bruehl of the Bourges-Bruehl Studio (active 1930s to 1950s) created the collection as part of their commissions to reproduce art work for publication in magazines, particularly *Life* and *Time*. In the late 1920s Bourges, who began his career as a photo-engraver, became one of the first to produce color images for use in advertising. Bruehl controlled the arrangement and lighting of the subjects. Their photograph of fruit and silver, which appeared in the May 1, 1932, issue of *Vogue*, marked an advance in color reproduction with its composition, color values, and use of lighting.

When Bourges retired in 1953, he gave this collection to Louis Sipley's American Museum of Photography in Philadelphia. After Sipley's death in 1968, the 3M Company of St. Paul, Minnesota, bought the museum's entire holdings. In 1977 3M donated the holdings to the George Eastman House International Museum of Photography, which gave the art images to the National Museum of American Art (NMAA) in 1981. Note: The original phototransparencies are in the possession of OPPS, the Smithsonian Institution's central photography laboratory, which is in the process of making a copy photoprint of each image for the NMAA.

The images have appeared in many publications including *Art Treasures*, *Fortune*, *Harper's*, *Life*, *New York World*, *Time*, and *Vanity Fair*.

Physical Description

There are 1,500 copy color dye coupler phototransparencies.

Subjects

The photographs reproduce paintings that were used as magazine illustrations, mainly in *Life*, between 1936 and 1953. Artists whose work is reproduced include Ivan Albright, Fra Angelico, John J. Audubon, Giovanni Bellini, George W. Bellows, Pierre Bonnard, Hieronymous Bosch, Sandro Botticelli, Georges Braque, Paul Cézanne, Marc Chagall, Salvador Dali, Edgar Degas, Thomas Eakins, El Greco, Paul Gauguin, Marsden Hartley, Winslow Homer, Edward Hopper, Olaf Jordan, Reginald Marsh, Anna Mary Robertson (A.K.A. Grandma) Moses, Pablo Picasso, Henry Varnum Poor, Raphael, Rembrandt van Rijn, Pierre Auguste Renoir, Albert Pinkham Ryder, John Singer Sargent, Charles Sheeler, John Sloan, Walter Stuempfig, Jr., Titian, Henri de Toulouse-Lautrec, John Trumbull, Anthony Van Dyck, Vincent Van Gogh, Jan Vermeer, Benjamin West, James Abbott McNeill Whistler, and Andrew Wyeth.

Arranged: Alphabetically by artist.

Captioned: With negative number.

Finding Aid: 1) Index cards with artist, negative number, publication name, publication date, and title. 2) Computer database with printout arranged alphabetically by artist, listing negative number, publication name and date, and title of painting.

Restrictions: The collection is at OPPS, the Smithsonian's central photography laboratory, and is inaccessible until copies are received by the NMAA. Contact Joan Stahl, Coordinator of Image Collections, Slide and Photograph Archives, National Museum of American Art, Room 331, Washington, D.C., 20560, (202) 357-1348. Publication of images must acknowledge Eastman House as the donor.

AM·5

Inventory of American Paintings Executed Before 1914

Dates of Photographs: 1950–Present

Collection Origins

National Museum of American Art (NMAA) staff created the collection to document American paintings for exhibits and research purposes. Established in 1971, the Inventory of American Paintings (IAP) works with historical societies, museums, and volunteer organizations (such as the American Association of University Women, National Association of Retired Teachers, and the National Society of Colonial Dames) to describe, identify, and locate American paintings. The IAP documents paintings created before 1914 by artists born or working in the United States. If the artist was born before 1880, all post-1914 works are included as well.

The IAP computer database documents over 258,000 paintings, complemented by a 90,000-item photographic reference file. The Inventory is used for comparative analysis of related art works, for exhibit planning and research, and for thematic studies by museum professionals, private collectors, and scholars.

Physical Description

There are 90,000 photographs including color dye coupler photonegatives and slides, dye diffusion transfer photoprints, and silver gelatin photoprints and slides. Other materials include newspaper clippings and xerographic copies.

Subjects

The photographs document American paintings that were created prior to 1914 or made by artists who were born before 1880. Paintings shown are in traditional media such as oil, pastel, and watercolor, and include animal studies, architectural studies, genre scenes, landscapes, nudes, portraits, still lifes, and waterscapes.

Painters whose work is reproduced include Ezra Ames, Albert Bierstadt, George Caleb Bingham, Ralph A. Blakelock, James E. Buttersworth, Mary Cassatt, George Catlin, William Merritt Chase, John Singleton Copley, Jasper F. Cropsey, Arthur B. Davies, Guy Pène Du Bois, Asher B. Durand, Frank Duveneck, Jacob Eichholtz, Childe Hassam, Martin J. Heade, George P.A. Healy, Robert Henri, Winslow Homer, George Inness, William Keith, John F. Kensett, Charles B. King, John LaFarge, John Marin, Gari Melchers, Thomas Moran, Elizabeth Nourse, Charles Willson Peale, Rembrandt Peale, Ammi Phillips, Maurice B. Prendergast, William T. Richards, Charles M. Russell, John Singer Sargent, Gilbert Stuart, Thomas Sully, John Trumbull, Elihu Vedder, Benjamin West, and James Abbott McNeill Whistler.

Arranged: By image size, then by artist and title.

Captioned: With the artist, in-house classification number, owner, and title of the painting reproduced.

Finding Aid: An item-level database to the 262,000 paintings listing artist's name and life dates; the painting's date, dimensions, medium, owner or last-known location, subject, and title; bibliographic citations; and the source of the information. There are printouts of the database sorted by artist, location, medium, subject, and title. There is also a separate printout of all works that have photographic documentation, arranged first by catalog number of the work and then by artist, which also lists the work's owner and title and the source of the photograph.

Restrictions: Available for reference only. No reproductions may be made. For access to the database and

photographs, contact Christine Hennessey, Research Databases Coordinator, Research and Scholars Center, Inventory of American Paintings, Room 250, National Museum of American Art, Washington, D.C., 20560, (202) 357-2941.

AM·6

Inventory of American Sculpture

Dates of Photographs: Circa 1970–Present

Collection Origins

National Museum of American Art (NMAA) staff assembled the collection to document sculpture created since the colonial era by artists who either were born or worked in the United States. Begun in 1985, the Inventory of American Sculpture (IAS) includes records from the University of Delaware's manual Index of American Sculpture files, which represented holdings of approximately 800 institutions nationwide. To supplement this basic core of data, over 12,000 museums and historical societies have been contacted; introductory mailings also have been sent to selected corporate and individual owners. In addition, the Inventory is collaborating with the National Institute for the Conservation of Cultural Property to survey and assess the condition of America's outdoor public sculpture. As this book went to press, the IAS was scheduled to open to researchers in late 1992. The IAS will serve as a resource for comparative analyses of related art works; for conservation treatment studies; for exhibit planning and research; and for studies by museum professionals, private collectors, and scholars.

Physical Description

Presently, there are 2,000 photographs including color dye coupler photonegatives and slides, dye diffusion transfer photoprints, and silver gelatin photoprints and slides. The number of images increases constantly. Other materials include newspaper clippings, photomechanicals, and xerographic copies.

Subjects

The photographs document American abstract, monumental, and portrait sculpture created using either traditional media and methods (such as carving, casting, construction, or modeling) or more recent techniques (such as assemblage and site construction) and materials (such as neon or plastic). Minor architectural ornament, coins, decorative art objects, and tombstones generally are not included.

Sculptors whose work is reproduced include Samuel Herbert Adams, Carl Andre, Thomas Ball, Paul Wayland Bartlett, Harry Bertoia, John Gutzon Borglum, Louise Bourgeois, Henry Kirke Bush-Brown, Alexander Calder, Alexander Milne Calder, Alexander Stirling Calder, Christo, Joseph Cornell, Thomas Crawford, José de Creeft, Mark di Suvero, Jacob Epstein, Daniel Chester French, Nancy Graves, Horatio Greenough, Duane Hanson, Malvina Hoffman, Harriet Goodhue Hosmer, Vinnie Ream Hoxie, Anna Hyatt Huntington, Gaston Lachaise, Frederick MacMonnies, Elie Nadelman, Louise Nevelson, Isamu Noguchi, Claes Oldenburg, Beverly Pepper, William Rush, Charles M. Russell, Augustus Saint-Gaudens, George Segal, Richard Serra, Robert Smithson, Lorado Taft, Bessie Potter Vonnoh, John Quincy Adams Ward, Olin Levi Warner, Gertrude Vanderbilt Whitney, and William Zorach.

Arranged: By image size, then by artist and title.

Captioned: With artist, classification number, owner, and title.

Finding Aid: An item-level database to the 42,000 sculptures listing artist's name and life dates; sculpture's dimensions, execution date, founder's marks and other inscriptions, medium, owner and location, subject or theme, and title; bibliography and major exhibit history of the work; and condition assessment and conservation treatment for outdoor sculpture. There are printouts of the database sorted by artist, location, and subject.

Restrictions: Available for reference only. No reproductions may be made. For access to database and photographs, contact Christine Hennessey, Research Databases Coordinator, Research and Scholars Center, Inventory of American Paintings, Room 250, National Museum of American Art, Washington, D.C., 20560, (202) 357-2941.

AM·7

Peter A. Juley & Son Collection

Dates of Photographs: 1896–1975

Collection Origins

Peter A. Juley (1862–1937) and his son, Paul P. Juley (1890–1975), created the collection during their careers as professional photographers specializing in American fine arts. Born in Germany, Peter Juley graduated from the University of Coblentz in 1882 and emigrated to the United States in 1888. He opened his first office (a combination photographic studio and barber shop) in 1896 in Cold Spring, New York, where he also worked as a staff news photographer for *Harper's Weekly* between 1901 and 1906. His assignments included photographing the funeral of President William McKinley and President Theodore Roosevelt's national tours. In 1907 Juley moved the business to New York City, where his son Paul joined him the following year. A few years later they hired an assistant, Carlton Thorpe, who remained for the life of the firm.

Peter A. Juley & Son became the largest photography studio catering to the fine arts community in New York, serving art dealers, conservators, corporations, galleries, museums, private collectors, and many prominent American artists. Peter Juley developed techniques for accurately reproducing paintings in black-and-white photographs. The Juleys photographed the work of turn-of-the-century painters such as Childe Hassam, Thomas Eakins, and Albert Pinkham Ryder; ash can school artists such as Robert Henri and John Sloan; the avant-garde group associated with Alfred Stieglitz; regionalists of the 1930s and 1940s such as Thomas Hart Benton and Grant Wood; abstract expressionists such as Hans Hofmann and Robert Motherwell; and sculptors such as Daniel Chester French and William Zorach.

The Juleys also traveled widely, visiting San Francisco and artists colonies in New England and New Mexico. Photographing artists as well as art work, the Juleys became close friends with many of their clients. Members of New York's Salmagundi Club of artists and patrons, the Juleys served as official photographers for the National Academy of Design, the New York Public Library, and the Society of American Artists. They also acquired work by other American photographers. After Peter Juley's death, Paul moved the studio to West 57th Street, near the Art Students League and the artists' studios at Carnegie Hall. Paul continued photographing in the 1950s and 1960s, especially the work of the Art Students League and the National Academy of Design.

Following his retirement in 1975, the National Museum of American Art (NMAA) received the entire collection of Juley negatives. The museum is in the process of printing all the negatives, one-third of which are on unstable nitrate film (nearly 1,000 pieces already have deteriorated). Photographs in the collection are used by researchers wishing to view damaged or destroyed art works; conservators needing guidance in restoration projects; and collectors and scholars trying to locate missing art works. Images of artists at work and works-in-progress also provide information on artists' techniques. Photographers represented include Myra Albert, Bogart, George C. Cox, Paul P. Juley, Peter A. Juley, Walter Russell, A.E. Sproul, and DeWitt Ward.

Physical Description

There are 200,000 photographs including color dye coupler phototransparencies, silver gelatin dry plate photonegatives, and silver gelatin photonegatives and photoprints. Note: There are 126,442 original Juley negatives. Other images are silver gelatin photonegative direct copies of original nitrate-based silver gelatin photonegatives. The museum plans to make prints of all the Juley negatives.

Subjects

The photographs document primarily 20th century American art works—architecture, graphic prints, paintings, and sculptures—created by over 11,000 artists. The collection also contains formal and informal portraits of American artists and collectors, including images of activities such as judging exhibits, teaching classes, and working in studios.

Artists whose work is reproduced include Margaret Abell, Wayman Adams, Robert Aitken, Louise Altson, F. Julia Bach, Theodore Barbarossa, Paul Bartlett, Kenneth Bates, Gifford Beal, Cecilia Beaux, George W. Bellows, Frank C. Bensing, Rudolf Bernatschke, Elizabeth L. Bernstein, George Biddle, Robert Brackman, Harold M. Brett, Charles E. Burchfield, Alexander Calder, Alexander Stirling Calder, John Carroll, Charles S. Chapman, Joseph C. Chase, Howard C. Christy, Thomas C. Cole, Peter G. Cook, Salvador Dali, Arthur B. Davies, Sidney E. Dickinson, Stephen M. Etnier, Ralph Fabri, Ernest Fiene, C.J. Fox, James E. Fraser, Kahlil Gibran, William J. Glackens, Daniel E. Greene, Emile A. Gruppe, Molly Guion, Natalie H. Hammond, Channing Hare, Childe Hassam, Erik G. Haupt, Charles W. Hawthorne, Robert Henri, Winslow Homer, Joseph Kiselewski, Susan R. Knox, John Koch, Mario J. Korbel, Leon Kroll, Adrian Lamb, Jacob Lawrence, Jessie V. Lewis, DeWitt M. Lockman, George B. Luks, Oranzio Maldarelli, Paul Manship, Conrad Marca-Rêlli, John Marin, Reginald Marsh, Betsy F. Melcher, Eleanor M. Mellon, Ralph J. Menconi, Jo Mielziner, Robert Motherwell, Albert Murray, Raymond P.R. Neilson, Arturo Noci, A. Henry Nordhausen, Ivan Olinsky, Jane Peterson, Eleanor Platt, Ogden M. Pleissner, John Russell Pope, Ellen G.E. Rand, Stanislav Rembski, Diego Rivera, Ari Roussimoff, Onorio Ruotolo, Augustus Saint-Gaudens, Frank Salisbury, Nikol Schattenstein, Gertrude Schweitzer, Elizabeth Shoumatoff, John Sloan, Eugene E. Speicher, Albert Sterner, William Van

Dresser, Franklin B. Voss, Julian A. Weir, and William Zorach.

Artists portrayed include painters such as Wayman Adams, Chalmers Agnew, Charles A. Aiken, Victor Anderson, Thomas Hart Benton, Arnold Blanch, Herbert Bonhert, John Carlson, Alexander Clayton, Salvador Dali, Harry Gottlieb, Mary Gray, Ben Ali Haggin, Childe Hassam, Hans Hofmann, Edward Hopper, Ernest L. Ipsen, Frida Kahlo, Theodore Kautzy, Adrian Lamb, Edward A. Laning, Jacob Lawrence, William Robinson Leigh, Gari Melchers, Georgia O'Keeffe, Ivan Olinsky, Diego Rivera, Albert Pinkham Ryder, David A. Siqueiros, John Sloan, Eugene E. Speicher, Max Weber, and Grant Wood; as well as sculptors such as Richmond Barthe, Alexander Stirling Calder, Margaret Cresson, José de Creeft, Jacob Epstein, Leo Friedlander, Chaim Gross, Joseph Kiselewski, Paul Manship, Augustus Saint-Gaudens, Robert Scriver, and Wheeler Williams. There are also portraits of playwright Eugene O'Neill, actor Paul Robeson, and members of the Art Students League. Several photographs from this collection are reproduced in this volume's illustrations section.

Arranged: In three series. 1) Art works, alphabetically by artist, then by assigned number. 2) Photographic portraits, alphabetically by sitter. 3) Gallery shows and works belonging to dealers, alphabetically by show or dealer.

Captioned: With artist, assigned number, date, dimensions, location, medium, and title.

Finding Aid: An item-level database that describes photographs of paintings. Each database entry lists the artist's name, country, and life dates, and, when known, the art work's date of execution, location, medium, object class, period, source, subject, and title. The database can be searched by artist; title; assigned number; gallery or owner; name of portrait subject; and title.

Restrictions: Researchers should call or write for an appointment, describing their research topic, the type of material that interests them, and their research aim. Contact Joan Stahl, Coordinator of Image Collections, Slide and Photograph Archives, National Museum of American Art, Room 331, Washington, D.C., 20560, (202) 357-1348.

AM·8

Library of Congress Copyright Collection

Dates of Photographs: 1880–1930

Collection Origins

Library of Congress (LC) staff assembled the collection from some of the photographs received by the LC Copyright Office as part of the copyright registration process for art objects. The LC Prints and Photographs Division transferred the collection to the National Museum of American Art (NMAA) in 1987, although the LC retained other copyright materials. Studios and publishers represented include Braun, Clement & Cie; Detroit Publishing Co.; and Evans & Cameron, Inc.

Physical Description

There are 440 silver gelatin photoprints. Other materials include 9,500 photomechanicals (some photogravures).

Subjects

The photographs document drawings, graphic prints, paintings, and other works of art by late 19th and early 20th century American and European artists such as J. Millspaugh, E. Rost, Elliott B. Torrey, Constant Troyon, John Trumbull, and Dwight William Tryon.

Arranged: Alphabetically by artist and then by title.

Captioned: With artist, date of copyright, and title.

Finding Aid: Printed list arranged alphabetically by artist.

Restrictions: Available for reference only. Since the collection is stored off-site, researchers must call or write in advance for an appointment, describing their research topic, the type of material that interests them, and their research aim. Contact Joan Stahl, Coordinator of Image Collections, Slide and Photograph Archives, National Museum of American Art, Room 331, Washington, D.C., 20560, (202) 357-1348.

AM·9

Miscellaneous NMAA Lantern Slide and Glass Photonegative Collection

Dates of Photographs: Circa 1900–Circa 1945

Collection Origins

National Museum of American Art (NMAA) staff assembled the collection from donations made by Forbes Watson, from earlier documentation of the museum's collections, and from transfers of art works from New Deal projects such as the Works Progress Administration. Watson (1879–1960), an art collector and critic based in New York City, wrote several books including the following: 1) *American Painting Today*. Washington, D.C.: American Federation of the Arts, 1939. 2) *Art in Federal Buildings: An Illustrated Record of the Treasury Department's New Program in Painting and Sculpture*. Washington, D.C.: Art in Federal Buildings, Inc., 1936.

Physical Description

There are 1,500 photographs including color dye coupler slides, color screen plate phototransparencies, silver gelatin dry plate lantern slides and photonegatives (some tinted), and silver gelatin copy photonegatives and photoprints.

Subjects

The photographs reproduce American and European architecture, paintings, and sculptures. Architecture shown includes the Smithsonian Institution Building (the Castle). Art works reproduced include public murals and sculptures from New Deal art projects, originally displayed in post offices and other government buildings; paintings depicting World War II scenes; paintings by prominent early 20th century painters; and works by members of the Art Students League.

Artists whose work is reproduced include Roy V. Arnautoff, Antoine L. Barye, Gifford Beal, George Biddle, Edgar Britton, Mary Cassatt, Howard N. Cook, Woodrow Crumbo, John S. Curry, Emma L. Davis, Thomas W. Dewing, Thomas Donnelly, Helen Forbes, F.E. French, Robert Fuchs, Childe Hassam, Peter Hurd, William Hurt, Avery F. Johnson, Leon Kroll, Tom LaFarge, Tom Lea, Edmund C. Messett, Ben Shahn, Niles Spencer, Gideon T. Stanton, Lucia Wiley, Remington R. Wilson, Julius Wolz, Marguerite Thompson Zorach, and William Zorach.

Arranged: In three series by source. 1) Forbes Watson collection and New Deal art projects material. 2) Museum collections. 3) Miscellaneous donations.

Captioned: Half with artist, collection, date, and title.

Finding Aid: Draft box list (inventory).

Restrictions: No. Contact Joan Stahl, Coordinator of Image Collections, Slide and Photograph Archives, Research and Scholars Center, National Museum of American Art, Room 331, Washington, D.C., 20560, (202) 357-1348.

AM·10

NMAA Exhibitions, Installations, and Events Collection

Dates of Photographs: 1960s–Present

Collection Origins

Staff photographers from the National Museum of American Art (NMAA) and OPPS created the collection to document the activities of the NMAA, including the Renwick Gallery.

Physical Description

There are 7,200 photographs including color dye coupler slides and silver gelatin photonegatives, photoprints, and slides.

Subjects

The photographs document art works in exhibits, exhibit designs, exhibit openings, and events at the NMAA and the Renwick Gallery since 1968. Exhibits documented include "Academy"; "Albert Pinkham Ryder"; "America as Art"; "American Art Deco"; "American Art in the Barbizon Mood"; "American Landscape: A Changing Frontier"; "Animal Image"; "Art of the Pacific Northwest"; "Artist & the Indian"; "The Capital Image"; "Collages by Irwin Kremen"; "David Blythe"; "Edward Colonna"; "Eleven Pop Artists"; "Exposed and Developed"; "A Future for Our Past: Conservation of Art"; "Gene Davis"; "High School Graphics

VI"; "The Incisive Eye of Romaine Brooks"; "Inedible Birthday Cakes"; "James Rosenquist"; "Jan Matulka"; "José de Creeft"; "Joseph Cornell Symposium"; "Made in Chicago"; "Made with Passion: The Hemphill Folk Art Collection in the National Museum of American Art"; "New Glass"; "Painted Weavings"; "Past & Present"; "The Patricia and Philip Frost Collection: American Abstraction 1930–1945"; "Perpetual Motif: The Art of Man Ray"; "Quilts from the Indiana Amish"; "Robert Rauschenberg"; "Roots of Abstract Art"; "Russell Wright"; "Russia, the Land, the People"; "Santos"; "Sara Roby Collection"; "Stanley Hayter"; "Swedish Touch"; "Threads"; "To Be Alive"; "Venice Biennial"; "Werner Drewes"; "William H. Johnson"; "William Zorach"; and "Wooden Works." Events documented include Children's Day (1980 and 1981), a docent workshop, Kaleidoscope Day (1978 and 1979), and the Print Media Tour (1973).

Arranged: Alphabetically by artist or exhibit title.

Captioned: With artist's name and exhibit title.

Finding Aid: 1) List of exhibits arranged alphabetically by title. 2) Computer index to some individually cataloged slides.

Restrictions: Open to Smithsonian Institution staff and public for research; only staff may borrow photographs. Contact Joan Stahl, Coordinator of Image Collections, Slide and Photograph Archives, National Museum of American Art, Room 331, Washington, D.C., 20560, (202) 357-1348.

AM·11

NMAA General Photograph Collection

Dates of Photographs: 1960s–1980s

Collection Origins

National Museum of American Art (NMAA) staff assembled the collection from donations by staff and visiting artists. Other items in the collection were created for curatorial research, doctoral dissertations, in-house exhibits, and museum programs such as the Fellows Program and the International Art Program (see *AM·12*). Photographers and studios represented include Bernie Cliff, Alfred Eisenstaedt, Laura Gilpin, Philippe Halsman, S.A. Holmes, Paul H. Manship,

William McKillep, OPPS, Peter A. Juley & Son, and Adam Clark Vroman.

Physical Description

There are 46,000 photographs including color dye coupler photoprints and silver gelatin photonegatives and photoprints. Other materials include architectural drawings, catalogs, correspondence, inventories, magazines, newspaper clippings, photomechanicals, and xerographic copies.

Subjects

The photographs primarily document American artists and art works. Artists whose work is reproduced include Lucien Adrion, Josef Albers, Ivan L. Albright, Guy I. Anderson, Saul Baizerman, Paul W. Bartlett, Antoine L. Barye, George W. Bellows, William Blake, Robert F. Blum, François Boucher, Peter Brueghel the Elder, Alexander Calder, Gustave Courbet, Edgar Degas, Albrecht Dürer, Kahlil Gibran, Edward Hopper, John LaFarge, Henri Matisse, Michelangelo, Claude Monet, and George Segal.

Arranged: By artist.

Captioned: Most with artist.

Finding Aid: No.

Restrictions: Available for reference only. No reproductions may be made. Contact Joan Stahl, Coordinator of Image Collection, Slide and Photograph Archives, Research and Scholars Center, National Museum of American Art, Room 331, Washington, D.C., 20560, (202) 357-1348.

AM·12

NMAA International Art Program Collection

Dates of Photographs: 1965–1976

Collection Origins

International Art Program (IAP) staff created the collection to document the art work featured in IAP exhibits, as well as to portray contributing artists. The IAP was formed by the U.S. Information Agency (USIA) to arrange U.S. participation in overseas art exhibits, a responsibility first held in the mid-1940s by the State Department and transferred to the USIA in 1954. In 1965 the USIA shifted the IAP to the Smithsonian Institution's National Collection of Fine Arts, now the National Museum of American Art. The Smithsonian retained the USIA's staff including its chief, Lois A. Bingham.

Under the Smithsonian, the IAP organized exhibits for worldwide circulation and managed American participation in international exhibits such as the Venice and São Paulo biennials. The IAP ceased operations in 1976, when the privately sponsored International Exhibitions Committee, under the chairmanship of Guggenheim museum director Thomas M. Messer, took over its functions.

Photographers and studios represented include the Brooklyn Museum, Helga Photo Studio, the Metropolitan Museum of Art, the Newark Museum, Arnold Newman, Phillips Studio, Frank Thomas, and the Whitney Museum of Art.

Physical Description

There are 4,565 photographs including silver gelatin photonegatives and photoprints. Other materials include exhibit catalogs, exhibit lists, and photomechanical reproductions.

Subjects

The photographs reproduce drawings, graphic prints, paintings, and sculptures featured in IAP exhibits. There are also portraits of participating artists. Artists whose work is reproduced include Shirley V. Anger, William Baziotes, Arnold Blanch, Charles E. Burchfield, Frederic Edwin Church, Charles Culver, Juan Downey, John H. Eames, Philip Evergood, Erastus Field, Adolph Gottlieb, George Grosz, Philip Guston, Grace Hartigan, George Harvey, George P.A. Healy, Winslow Homer, Walt Kuhn, Jacob Lawrence, Morris Louis, Louis Lozowick, George B. Luks, Samuel F.B. Morse, Louise Nevelson, Kenneth Noland, Charles Willson Peale, Jackson Pollock, Abraham Rattner, Katherine Nash Rhoades, Theodore Roszak, Mark Rothko, Albert Pinkham Ryder, John Singer Sargent, Ben Shahn, John Sloan, Joseph Stella, Gilbert Stuart, Abraham Walkowitz, and William Zorach.

Artists portrayed include painters such as Charles Demuth, Jack Levine, John Marin, Reginald Marsh, Robert Motherwell, Gabor Peterdi, Maurice B. Prendergast, Hugo Robus, John Von Wicht, Max Weber, Grant Wood, and Andrew Wyeth; printers and illustrators such as Naoko Matsubara; and sculptors such as Jo Davidson, Kosso Eloul, Robert Laurent, Elie Nadelman, Reuben Nakian, and Niles Spencer. Exhibits documented include "The New Vein—Europe," "The New Vein—Latin America," the 8th and 9th São

Paulo Biennial exhibits, and the 32nd, 33rd, and 34th Venice Biennial exhibits.

Arranged: In two series. 1) By artist. 2) By exhibit.

Captioned: With artist, artist's life dates, IAP project, medium, and title of the art work reproduced.

Finding Aid: No.

Restrictions: No. Contact Joan Stahl, Coordinator of Image Collections, Slide and Photograph Archives, Research and Scholars Center, National Museum of American Art, Room 331, Washington, D.C., 20560, (202) 357-1348.

AM·13

"Random Records of a Lifetime Devoted to Science and Art, 1846–1931" by W.H. Holmes

Dates of Photographs: 1871–1931

Collection Origins

Anthropologist, archaeologist, artist, geologist, and museum administrator William Henry Holmes (1846–1933) created the collection to document his life and career. Holmes, who received a doctorate in science from George Washington University in 1918, began his association with the Smithsonian Institution as an illustrator of natural history specimens. Appointed artist/topographer to the U.S. Geological Survey of the Territories under Ferdinand V. Hayden in 1872, Holmes joined the U.S. Geological Survey (USGS) as an assistant geologist in 1874.

Holmes's later survey work in Yellowstone (1872 and 1878), the Colorado River in Arizona and New Mexico (1873–1876 and 1887), and Mexico (1887) led to his interest in archaeology and his transfer in 1889 from the USGS to the Bureau of American Ethnology (BAE). From 1894 to 1897 he served as head curator of anthropology at the Field Columbian Museum (now Field Museum of Natural History) in Chicago and as a professor at the University of Chicago.

Holmes returned to the Smithsonian to become head curator of the Department of Anthropology, U.S. Na-

tional Museum (1897–1902). He also served as chief of the BAE (1902–1909), curator of the first National Gallery of Art (1907–1920), and head curator of the Smithsonian's Department of Anthropology (1910–1920). When the National Gallery of Art (now the National Museum of American Art) became a separate bureau of the Smithsonian, Holmes served as its director from 1920 until his retirement in 1932.

Holmes organized his memorabilia, original papers, and recollections in 16 volumes, had them bound and indexed, and gave them as a gift to the National Gallery of Art two years before he died. Photographers represented include William Henry Jackson, Thomas Smillie, Julius Ulke, and photographers of the U.S. Geological and Geographical Survey of the Territories.

Physical Description

There are 415 photographs including albumen photoprints, platinum photoprints, and silver gelatin photoprints. Other materials include articles, awards, certificates, correspondence, diaries, field notes, invitations, maps, newspaper clippings, photomechanicals, programs, sketches, and watercolors.

Subjects

The photographs document William Henry Holmes's career, with emphasis on his archaeological and geological surveys, as well as his colleagues and friends. Surveys documented were conducted in Chile, Colombia, Cuba, Guatemala, Jamaica, Mexico, and the United States.

Mexican locales shown include an architectural ruin in the Yucatán and a cruciform tomb near Mitla, Mexico. U.S. sites and structures illustrated include the Canyon de Chelly, Arizona; a cliff palace in Mesa Verde, Colorado; Hopi mesas in Utah; Salt Lake City, Utah; fisheries on the Potomac near Washington, D.C. (ca. 1878); Piney Branch Indian quarries in Washington, D.C.; a pueblo in Walpi, Arizona; and Yellowstone National Park, Wyoming. There are also images of objects made of gold and gold alloy in Colombia.

People portrayed include E.A. Barber, Paul Bartsch, David G. Fairchild, Charles Lang Freer, Ferdinand V. Hayden, F. Webb Hodge, William Henry Jackson, Ella Leary, Harry Lee, Fielding B. Meek, Bob Mitchell, Mrs. Frances S. Nichols, Jesse Nussbaum, Theodore Roosevelt, Thomas Smillie, the Crown Prince of Sweden, and A.H. Thompson.

Arranged: In 16 volumes by type of material or subject.

Captioned: With subject; some also with dates.

Finding Aid: 1) Chronology for each volume. 2) Item-level indexes to documents, illustrations (including photographs), and text.

Restrictions: Available for scholarly use only. Contact Cecilia Chin, Librarian, Research and Scholars Center, National Museum of American Art, Room 331, Washington, D.C., 20560, (202) 357-1886.

AM·14

Research and Scholars Center Slide Library

Dates of Photographs: 1960s–1980s

Collection Origins

National Museum of American Art (NMAA) staff created the collection to document American and, to a lesser degree, European art works and international architecture, for use by educators, researchers, staff, and students. Every object in each changing NMAA exhibit from the 1970s and 1980s was photographed for the collection. Photographers and studios represented include the Bostonian Society, McKim, Mead & White, and NMAA and OPPS staff.

Physical Description

There are 85,000 photographs including color dye coupler slides and silver gelatin slides.

Subjects

The photographs document graphic prints, paintings, and sculpture by American and European artists, primarily in NMAA permanent holdings, and architecture throughout the world, including NMAA buildings. American structures shown include the Boston Public Library and Trinity Church in Boston; the Chrysler Building, Ellis Island buildings, the Seagram Building, and Statue of Liberty in New York; and the Alice Pike Barney Studio House, Jefferson Memorial, Old Patent Office Building, Renwick Gallery, and U.S. Treasury Building in Washington, D.C. European structures include the Roman Theater in Arles, France, and St. Peter's Square in Rome.

Artists whose work is reproduced include Anni Albers, Stephen Antonakos, Diane Arbus, Will Barnet, Cecilia Beaux, Frank W. Benson, Solon H. Borglum, Romaine Brooks, Jacques Callot, George Catlin, Howard N. Cook, Arthur B. Davies, T.W. Dewing, Werner Drewes, George Fuller, Adolph Gottlieb, Charles Grafly, Marsden Hartley, William H. Holmes, Peter Hurd, John F. Kensett, John LaFarge, Jacob Lawrence, Morris Louis, Man Ray, Paul H. Manship, John Marin, Tina Modotti, Robert Motherwell, Rembrandt Peale, Philip Pearlstein, Hiram Powers, Theodore Roszak, Albert Pinkham Ryder, Horatio Shaw, Raphael Soyer, Walter Stuempfig, Jr., Abbott H. Thayer, Elihu Vedder, Samuel Lovett Waldo, and Julian A. Weir.

Arranged: In two series. 1) Public lending slides. 2) Non-circulating slides. Then alphabetically by artist or location, then by subject or title of the art work.

Captioned: Art works with artist, date, dimensions, medium, owner, NMAA accession number, and title.

Finding Aid: Four computer-generated indexes for art works. 1) Artist index, arranged alphabetically by the artist's last name, lists life dates, medium, and title. 2) Location index, arranged alphabetically by the repository or owner location, lists artist, artist's life dates, date, medium, and title. 3) Subject index, arranged alphabetically by the art work's subject, lists artist, date, medium, and title. 4) Number index, arranged by NMAA accession number, lists artist, date, medium, and title.

Restrictions: Open to the public; researchers are encouraged to write or call in advance. Up to 50 public lending slides may be borrowed at one time for two weeks, for non-commercial use only. Non-circulating slides are open to the public for viewing, but are loaned only to Smithsonian Institution staff. Contact Joan Stahl, Coordinator of Image Collections, Slide and Photograph Archives, National Museum of American Art, Room 331, Washington, D.C., 20560, (202) 357-1348.

AM·15

Walter Rosenblum Photonegative Collection

Dates of Photographs: Circa 1945–1962

Collection Origins

Walter Rosenblum (1919–) created the collection while working as a free-lance photographer documenting the work of New York City artists, collectors, and galleries. Rosenblum studied at the College of the City of New York and under Sid Grossman, Lewis W. Hine, and Paul Strand. He joined New York City's Photo League in 1937 and eventually became president (1941–1948), editor of *Photo Notes,* and chair of the exhibit committee. Rosenblum also worked as a photographer for *PM* newspaper and *Life* magazine, where he was an assistant to Eliot Elisofon. After serving as a staff photographer with the Agricultural Adjustment Administration in 1942, Rosenblum became a professor at Brooklyn College, where he taught photography from 1947 until 1986. Between 1952 and 1978 he was a professor at the Yale Summer School of Music and Art in New Haven, Connecticut, and an adjunct instructor at the Cooper Union school in New York City.

Rosenblum was also a member of the board of directors of the Photographers' Forum and a founding member of the Society for Photographic Education. Known primarily for his black-and-white documentary images of urban life, he remains active as a freelance photographer, specializing in photographs for artists and galleries in New York. The National Museum of American Art acquired the collection in 1976.

Physical Description

There are 7,500 silver gelatin photonegatives.

Subjects

The photographs document American and European art works, primarily from the late 19th and 20th centuries. Artists whose works are reproduced include Samuel M. Adler, Calvin Alberts, Milton Avery, Ernst Barlach, Leonard Baskin, Rosa Boris, Georges Braque, Nancy Brown, Norman Carton, Robert Cenedella, Nicolai Cikovsky, Robert M. Cronbach, Willem de Kooning, Beauford Delaney, José de Rivera, Burgoyne A. Diller, Camilo Egas, Philip Evergood, Alberto Giacometti, Maxwell Gordon, Adolph Gottlieb, Lorrie Goulet, Chaim Gross, Joseph Hirsch, Wassily Kandinsky, Frederic C. Knight, René Magritte, Edouard Manet, Ad Reinhardt, Mark Rothko, Aaron Shikler, David Slivka, Raphael Soyer, Clyfford Still, Charles White, and Robert Jay Wolff. There are also some photographic portraits of artists.

Arranged: Alphabetically by artist or gallery, then by negative number.

Captioned: With negative number.

Finding Aid: Preliminary checklist, alphabetical by artist or gallery.

Restrictions: Available by appointment only. Contact Joan Stahl, Coordinator of Image Collections, Slide and Photograph Archives, Research and Scholars Center, National Museum of American Art, Room 331, Washington, D.C., 20560, (202) 357-1348. Researchers must describe their research topic, the type of material that interests them, and their research aim.

Renwick Gallery

Renwick Gallery of the National Museum of American Art
Smithsonian Institution
Washington, D.C. 20560
Ellen Myette, Exhibitions Coordinator
(202) 357-2531
Hours: By appointment.

Scope of the Collection
There is one photographic collection with approximately 200 photographs.

Focus of the Collection
The photographs document the restoration and use of the Renwick building, designed by James Renwick for the original Corcoran Gallery of Art and renovated and reopened in 1972 as the Renwick Gallery. The building houses 20th century art, craft, and design objects in many media including clay, fiber, glass, metal, and wood. There also are images of other buildings in Washington, D.C.

Photographic Processes and Formats Represented
The collection contains color dye coupler photonegatives and photoprints and silver gelatin photonegatives and photoprints.

Other Materials Represented
The collection also contains magazine clippings, newspaper clippings, photomechanicals (photogravures), and xerographic copies.

Access and Usage Policies
Available for scholarly research only. No photographic copies may be made. Researchers should call or write for an appointment, describing their research topic, the type of material that interests them, and their research aim.

Publication Policies
No photographic or xerographic copies may be made.

AM·16

Renwick Gallery Historical Photography Collection

Dates of Photographs: 1968–Present

Collection Origins

National Museum of American Art (NMAA) Renwick Gallery staff created the collection to document the history of the Renwick Gallery building. James Renwick designed the building, which was constructed between 1859 and 1891, to house the art collection of Washington, D.C., businessman and art collector William Wilson Corcoran. Shortly before its completion, the U.S. Army appropriated the building for use by the Quartermaster General's Corps during the Civil War. Restored between 1869 and 1873, the building served as the Corcoran Art Gallery until 1897, then housed the Court of Claims from 1899 to 1964. In 1965 President Lyndon B. Johnson approved the Smithsonian's request to renovate the building and use it as a gallery of arts, crafts, and design. It was renamed the Renwick Gallery in honor of its architect and opened to the public in 1972.

Photographers and studios represented include William Edmund Barrett, Mathew Brady, Columbia Historical Society, Charles S. Cudlip, Library of Congress, National Archives and Records Administration, OPPS, Photogravure & Colors Co., and the *Washington Star.*

Physical Description

There are 200 photographs including color dye coupler photonegatives and photoprints and silver gelatin photonegatives and photoprints (most are copy prints). Other materials include magazine clippings, newspaper clippings, photomechanicals (photogravures), and xerographic copies.

Subjects

The photographs document the exterior and interior of the Renwick Gallery building from 1861 to the present, with emphasis on the restoration of the building in the late 1960s and early 1970s. Many images document architectural details or repair work, and a few show objects in the Renwick Gallery's permanent American crafts collection. There are also images of other buildings in Washington, D.C., and photographic reproductions of architectural drawings of the Renwick building, as well as early maps of Washington, D.C.

Arranged: No.

Captioned: Some with date, photographer, and subject.

Finding Aid: No.

Restrictions: Available for scholarly research only. No photographic copies may be made. Contact Ellen Myette, Exhibitions Coordinator, Renwick Gallery, Room B9, Smithsonian Institution, Washington, D.C., 20560, (202) 357-2531.

CH

THE COOPER-HEWITT MUSEUM

Dianne Pilgrim, Director

The Cooper Union Museum for the Arts of Decoration was founded in 1897 as part of philanthropist Peter Cooper's tuition-free public institution, the Cooper Union for the Advancement of Science and Art in New York City. Cooper's granddaughters Amelia (Amy), Eleanor (Nelly), and Sarah (Sally) Hewitt created the Cooper Union Museum in emulation of Paris's Musée des Arts Décoratif. Used as a teaching museum by Cooper Union instructors, the museum's holdings included examples of international decorative arts and design.

In 1963 the Cooper Union trustees resolved to close the museum due to financial difficulties. The museum's holdings were donated to the Smithsonian Institution on July 1, 1968, and the Cooper Union's name was changed to the Cooper-Hewitt Museum of Decorative Arts and Design. The historic Andrew Carnegie Mansion and nearby Miller House, donated to the Smithsonian in 1969 by the Carnegie Corporation, have housed the museum collections since 1970. In October 1976, following restoration of the facilities, the Cooper-Hewitt Museum opened its exhibits to the public in the Carnegie Mansion on New York City's historic Museum Row. In 1978 the museum was renamed the Cooper-Hewitt National Museum of Design; 11 years later, the museum's name officially became the Cooper-Hewitt Museum, the Smithsonian Institution's National Museum of Design.

Assembled over nearly a century of collecting, the Cooper-Hewitt's holdings include more than 170,000 contemporary and historical objects including architectural ornaments, ceramics, drawings, furniture, glassware, graphic prints, metalwork, photographs, textiles, wallpaper, and woodwork. The museum's holdings serve as a resource to scholars and design professionals by representing most major movements, periods, and styles of decorative arts.

The Cooper-Hewitt Museum promotes the study of design through exhibits, publications, and educational programs including classes, colloquia, conferences, lectures, seminars, tours, and workshops. The museum offers a two-year Master of Arts program in the history of European decorative arts in conjunction with the Parsons School of Design. The 40,000-volume fine and applied arts reference library contains over 3,000 rare books, as well as a classified picture file of 1.5 million illustrations and photographs.

Although the Cooper-Hewitt does not have a separate department of fine art photography, the museum contains both artifactual and documentary images. The Cooper-Hewitt's 365,630 photographs are contained in 36 photographic collections that document decorative art objects and the history of design worldwide, as well as Cooper-Hewitt activities, educational programs, exhibits, staff, and visitors.

CH

Department of Decorative Arts

Department of Decorative Arts
Cooper-Hewitt Museum, the Smithsonian Institution's National
Museum of Design
2 East 91st Street
New York, New York 10128-9990
Curator of Decorative Arts
(212) 860-6960
Hours: By appointment.

Scope of the Collections

There are three photographic collections with approximately 16,500 photographs.

Focus of the Collections

The photographs document the department's 14,000 objects including architectural elements, ceramics, costumes, enamelware, furniture and wood-carvings, glassware, jewelry, lacquerware, lighting devices, metalwork, miniatures, timepieces and measuring devices, toys and games, and other decorative objects, dating from 1500 B.C. to the present.

Photographic Processes and Formats Represented

There are color dye coupler slides and silver gelatin photoprints.

Other Materials Represented

The department holdings also include original decorative arts objects.

Access and Usage Policies

Most of the photograph collections are open to researchers by appointment. Researchers should write to the curator in advance and describe their research topic, the type of material that interests them, and their research aim. All inquiries concerning photographic rights in connection with scholarly or trade use should be addressed to the Department of Photographic Services, Cooper-Hewitt Museum, 2 East 91st Street, New York, New York, 10128-9990.

Publication Policies

Researchers must obtain permission from the Cooper-Hewitt Museum to reproduce a photograph and may also have to obtain permission from the copyright holder, which is not necessarily the Smithsonian Institution. The preferred credit line is "Courtesy of the Department of Decorative Arts, Cooper-Hewitt Museum, the Smithsonian Institution's National Museum of Design." The photographer's name, when known, also should appear.

CH·1

CH Decorative Arts Accessioned Object Catalog Card Collection

Dates of Photographs: Late 1930s–Present

Collection Origins

The Cooper-Hewitt (CH) Decorative Arts Department curator created the collection as an administrative record of the accessioned objects in departmental holdings.

Images from the collection appear in the following books, all published by the Cooper-Hewitt Museum in New York except where noted: 1) Nancy Aakre, ed. *The Smithsonian Illustrated Library of Antiques: Miniatures.* 1983. 2) Susan Benjamin. *The Smithsonian Illustrated Library of Antiques: Enamels.* 1983. 3) Robert C. Bishop and Patricia Coblentz. *The Smithsonian Illustrated Library of Antiques: Furniture: Prehistoric through Rococo.* 1979. 4) Cooper-Hewitt Museum. *American Art Pottery.* 1987. 5) Cooper-Hewitt Museum. *Buttons in the Collection of the Cooper-Hewitt Museum.* 1982. 6) Cooper-Hewitt Museum. *Furniture in the Collection of the Cooper-Hewitt Museum.* 1979. 7) Cooper-Hewitt Museum. *Glass in the Collection of the Cooper-Hewitt Museum.* 1979. 8) Cooper-Hewitt Museum. *Matchsafes in the Collection of the Cooper-Hewitt Museum.* 1981. 9) Cooper-Hewitt Museum. *Porcelain in the Collection of the Cooper-Hewitt Museum.* 1979. 10) Cooper-Hewitt Museum. *Pottery in the Collection of the Cooper-Hewitt Museum.* 1981. 11) Cooper-Hewitt Museum. *Silver in the Collection of the Cooper-Hewitt Museum.* 1980. 12) Cooper-Hewitt Museum. *Tiles in the Collection of the Cooper-Hewitt Museum.* 1980. 13) Cooper-Hewitt Museum. *Tsuba and Japanese Sword Fittings in the Collection of the Cooper-Hewitt Museum.* 1980. 14) Paul Vickers Gardner. *The Smithsonian Illustrated Library of Antiques: Glass.* 1979. 15) Carlotta Kerwin, ed. *The Smithsonian Illustrated Library of Antiques: Pottery.* 1981. 16) William C. Ketchum. *The Smithsonian Illustrated Library of Antiques: Boxes.* 1982. 17) William C. Ketchum. *The Smithsonian Illustrated Library of Antiques: Furniture #2: Neoclassic to the Present.* 1981. 18) William C. Ketchum. *The Smithsonian Illustrated Library of Antiques: Toys and Games.* 1981. 19) Russell Lynes. *More Than Meets the Eye: The History and Collections of Cooper-Hewitt Museum.* 1981. 20) Marie-Louise d'Otrange Mastai. *The Smithsonian Illustrated Library of Antiques: Jewelry.* 1981. 21) Jessie McNab. *The Smithsonian Illustrated Library of Antiques: Silver.* 1981. 22) Christine Minter-Dowd. *Finders' Guide to Decorative Arts in the Smithsonian Institution.* Washington, D.C.: Smithsonian Institution Press, 1984. 23) Jerry E. Patterson. *The Smithsonian Illustrated Library of Antiques: Porcelain.* 1979. 24) Douglas H. Shaffer. *The Smithsonian Illustrated Library of Antiques: Clocks.* 1980.

Physical Description

There are 9,000 silver gelatin photoprints mounted on index cards, of which 7,000 are duplicates.

Subjects

The photographs document CH accessioned decorative art objects, which include international handcrafted and mass-produced items dating from 1500 B.C. to the 20th century, with an emphasis on European objects from the 17th through 20th centuries. Objects documented include ceramics, enameled objects, furniture, glassware, glyptics (engraved precious stones), hardware, Japanese costume and sword fittings, jewelry, lighting devices, metalwork, papier-mâché objects, seals, timepieces, and toys.

Ceramics documented include earthenware, porcelain, and stoneware such as figures, tableware, and vessels. Enameled objects illustrated include boxes, plaques, tableware, and teaware. Furniture and woodcarvings shown include boxes, chairs, desk items, ornaments, and woodenware. Glass items shown include clocks, decorative pieces, jewelry, snuff boxes, tableware, and vessels. Hardware depicted includes furniture mounts and pulls, keys, knockers, and locks. Japanese artifacts include *inrō* (box-like seal holders attached to a cloth sash); *netsukes* (clothing toggles); and sword fittings such as *fuchi, kashira, kozuka, menuki,* and *tsuba.* Lacquer items shown include boxes, screens, teaware, and writing implements. Lighting devices shown include betty lamps, candlesticks, candelabra, chandeliers, grease lamps, lanterns, rush holders, and sconces. Metalwork illustrated includes birdcages, boxes, desk accessories, figures, food molds, frames, furniture, hardware, matchsafes, medals, plaques, swords, and tableware in a variety of media including brass, bronze, copper, gold, iron, pewter, silver, steel, and tin. Toys shown include marionettes, puppets, toy theaters, and Venetian *commedia dell'arte* figures. Timepieces depicted include clocks and watches.

Furniture depicted includes lacquer, marquetry, papier-mâché, and wooden pieces by designers such as Jules Dessoir, Jean Dunand, Charles Eames, Jean Michel Frank, Hector Guimard, Josef Hoffmann, Louis Majorelle, Eugenio Quarti, Terrence Robsjohn-Gibbings, David Roentgen, and Frank Lloyd Wright. Glassware illustrated was created by artists such as René Lalique and Louis C. Tiffany. Metalwork depicted includes examples by Edgar Brandt, William Fawdery, and Thomas Heming.

Arranged: By object's medium, then country, century, and accession number.

Captioned: With object's accession number, artist, date, description, dimensions, material, origin, and source.

Finding Aid: The collection is a card catalog, listing accession number, artist, date, description, dimensions, material, origin, remarks, source, and type of object.

Restrictions: Available only to Smithsonian Institution staff and, by appointment, to outside specialized researchers. Other researchers are referred to similar files in the Registrar's Office.

CH·2

CH Decorative Arts Master Slide Collection

Dates of Photographs: 1976–Present

Collection Origins

The Cooper-Hewitt (CH) Department of Decorative Arts assembled the collection to document accessioned objects in the department's holdings for accessions management, lectures, publications, and student research. See the *Collection Origins* section of *CH·1* for a bibliography of publications in which the photographs are reproduced. Photographers represented include CH staff and contract photographers.

Physical Description

There are 3,000 color dye coupler slides (about two-thirds are duplicates).

Subjects

The photographs document CH accessioned decorative arts objects, dating from 1500 B.C. to the present, including architectural elements; birdcages; boxes; buttons; ceramics; clocks and watches; enameled items; furniture and woodwork; glassware; glyptics (engraved precious stones); hardware including furniture mounts and pulls, keys, knockers, and locks; Japanese sword fittings; jewelry; lacquerware; lighting devices; metalwork; and toys and games. See the *Subjects* section of *CH·1* for further information.

Arranged: By object's material or medium, then accession number.

Captioned: With object's accession number; artist; date; filing code indicating century, medium, and place of origin; name or title; and size.

Finding Aid: Card catalog arranged by object's accession number listing artist, date, description, dimensions, material, origin, and remarks.

Restrictions: Available to Cooper-Hewitt staff only.

CH·3

CH Decorative Arts Photoprint Notebook Collection

Dates of Photographs: 1930s–Present

Collection Origins

In 1978, the Cooper-Hewitt (CH) Department of Decorative Arts curator assembled the collection to provide images of accessioned objects in the department's holdings for publication and study. For a listing of publications in which the photographs are reproduced, see the *Collection Origins* section of *CH·1*.

Physical Description

There are 4,500 silver gelatin photoprints.

Subjects

The photographs document CH accessioned decorative art objects, dating from 1500 B.C. to the 20th century, including architectural elements; birdcages; boxes; buttons; ceramics; clocks and watches; enameled items; furniture and woodwork; glassware; glyptics (engraved precious stones); hardware including furniture mounts and pulls, keys, knockers, and locks; Japanese sword fittings; jewelry; lacquerware; lighting devices; metalwork; and toys and games. See the *Subjects* section under *CH·1* for further information.

Arranged: By material or type of object and then by country of origin and date.

Captioned: With object's accession number; most also with artist, date, description, dimensions, medium, origin, remarks, and source.

Finding Aid: Card catalog listing artist, date, description, dimensions, medium, origin, remarks, and source.

Restrictions: Available by appointment only.

CH

Department of Drawings and Prints

Department of Drawings and Prints
Cooper-Hewitt Museum, the Smithsonian Institution's National
  Museum of Design
2 East 91st Street
New York, New York 10128-9990
Curator of Drawings and Prints
(212) 860-6893
Hours: Tuesday–Friday, 10 a.m.–5 p.m.

Scope of the Collections

There are ten photographic collections with approximately 33,900 images.

Focus of the Collections

The images include fine art photographs; historical landscape photographs of Yosemite, California; photographic genre scenes; portraits; scenes from Cooper-Hewitt Museum history; and travel photographs showing international architecture and culture from the 1870s to the 1930s. The collections also contain photographs of departmental holdings of drawings and prints from Asia, Europe, and the United States, dating from 1400 to the 20th century. Some of these images are housed at and managed by the Photographic Services Division.

Photographic Processes and Formats Represented

There are albumen photoprints (some cartes-de-visite, postcards, and stereographs); collodion wet plate lantern slides (some tinted) and stereographs; collodion gelatin photoprints (POP, some stereographs); color dye coupler slides; color screen plate phototransparencies (Autochrome); platinum photoprints; silver gelatin dry plate lantern slides (some tinted); silver gelatin photoprints (some cartes-de-visite and stereographs); and tintypes.

Other Materials Represented

The department also collects drawings including architectural plans and textile designs; graphic prints including decorated book papers, engravings, etchings, fashion plates, greeting cards, peep-show prints, and woodblock prints; and photomechanicals; as well as calligraphy, oil sketches, silhouettes, and watercolors.

Access and Usage Policies

The photograph collections are open to researchers by appointment. Researchers should write or telephone the department in advance and describe their research topic, the type of material that interests them, and their research aim. All inquiries concerning photographic rights in connection with scholarly or trade use should be addressed to the Department of Photographic Services, Cooper-Hewitt Museum, 2 East 91st Street, New York, New York, 10128-9990.

Publication Policies

Researchers must obtain permission from the Cooper-Hewitt Museum to reproduce a photograph and may also have to obtain permission from the copyright holder, which is not necessarily the Smithsonian Institution. The preferred credit line is "Courtesy of the Department of Drawings and Prints, Cooper-Hewitt Museum, the Smithsonian Institution's National Museum of Design." The photographer's name, when known, also should appear.

CH·4

CH Drawings and Prints Cooper-Hewitt Historical Photograph Collection

Dates of Photographs: 1890s–Present

Collection Origins

Cooper-Hewitt (CH) Drawings and Prints Department staff assembled the collection for exhibition, publication, and research purposes from donations by the Hewitt family and others. Photographers and studios represented include L.A. Dubernet for Holmes & Mrf. and Thompson Photographers.

Physical Description

There are 250 photographs including albumen photoprints, collodion wet plate lantern slides (tinted), color screen plate phototransparencies (Autochrome), and silver gelatin photoprints. One lantern slide is a diascope.

Subjects

The photographs document the history of the CH Museum—previously known as the Cooper Union Museum—and the lives and homes of its founding members from the 1890s to the present. Houses shown include the Old Ship House in New York City and Ringwood Manor (the New Jersey estate owned by the Cooper and Hewitt families) and its gardens. There are images of Cooper Union Museum and Cooper Union women's art school interiors including art galleries, classrooms and lecture halls, engine rooms, and laboratories for chemistry, electricity, and physics. The museum's art holdings also are documented. People portrayed include members of both the Cooper and Hewitt families such as Peter Cooper and Sarah (Sally) Hewitt.

Arranged: No.

Captioned: Some with subject.

Finding Aid: Box list.

Restrictions: Available by appointment only.

CH·5

CH Drawings and Prints Fine Arts Photograph Collection

Dates of Photographs: 1870–1960

Collection Origins

Cooper-Hewitt Department of Drawings and Prints staff assembled the collection from donations, exchanges, and purchases for exhibition, publication, and research. Photographers and studios represented include Mathew Brady, Joseph Byron, Alfred Cook, David Davidson, Davis and Sanford, Aimé Dupont, Lafayette, Burr McIntosh, Baron Adolf De Meyer, Emily W. Miles, Wallace Nutting, Evelyn A. Pitschke, Marc Riboud, Ernst Schneider, and George Yates.

Physical Description

There are 95 photographs including albumen photoprints (cartes-de-visite), silver gelatin photoprints (some tinted), and a tintype.

Subjects

The photographs include photographic genre scenes (often posed pictorialist photographs); portraits; still lifes; and travel photographs of architecture, landscapes, and sculptures in Europe and New York dating from 1870 to 1960.

Genre scenes represented include the following titles: *At the Fender, Bewhiskered Man, Camel Caravan at Rest, Country Road, Dainty China, A Grandmother, Hands Lacing a Shoe, Head of Negro Woman, Portrait of a Czech, A Sunset, A Tap at the Squire's Door, Three Women, Two Pigs,* and *The Village Prattlers.* People portrayed include Ethel Barrymore as Mme. Trenton in *Captain Jinks of the Horse Marines,* Sara Bernhardt as L'Aiglon, Andrew Carnegie, Chauncey Depew, Elsie DeWolfe, Eleanora Duse as Cleopatra, Ferdinand Foch, Clara Hatzfeldt as Queen Esther, Prince Henry of Prussia, James Hazen Hyde, Isabel Irving, Prince de Joinville, Duc de Montpensier, Duc de Nemours, Comte and Comtesse de Paris, Mme. Rejane, Gladys L. (Mrs. Edward G.) Robinson, Lillian Russell (signed), Baroness Schwachheim (of Russia), General James Watson Webb (with his family), and J. Louis Webb as Robin Hood.

There are still lifes of flowers including cacti in bloom, flowering fruit trees, Christmas roses, jonquils, and snowbells; insects including praying mantisses; and seashells including conch and crab shells. Travel photographs show the Arno River, a cathedral, and the Leaning Tower in Pisa, Italy; the Austrian Alps; bridges in Bern, Switzerland; the Church of Santa Clara in Assisi, Italy; the Frick Garden on Long Island, New York; a street scene in Pressburg (now Bratislava), Czechoslovakia; and the terminal pavilion at the Cooper-Hewitt Museum in New York City. Some photographs reproduce art works by León Bakst, Stuart Benson, and Carolus Duran. Several images from the collection are reproduced in the illustration section of this volume.

Arranged: By photographer.

Captioned: Some with photographer, subject, or title.

Finding Aid: Inventory sheet listing accession number, date, photographer, and title.

Restrictions: Available by appointment only.

CH·6

CH Drawings and Prints Ely Jacques Kahn Collection

Dates of Photographs: 1930–1940, Most 1934

Collection Origins

Architect Ely Jacques Kahn (1884–1972) created the collection to document his 1934 trip to the Far East. Kahn received a degree in architecture from Columbia University in 1907, and in 1911 he received a diploma and the LaBarre prize for design from the École des Beaux Arts in Paris. Kahn became a professor of design at Cornell University in 1915. In 1929 he designed the Metropolitan Museum of Art's contemporary arts show, and in 1934 and 1940 he designed the museum's industrial arts exhibition. Kahn served as a consultant to the United States Housing Authority and the New York City Sanitation Department, a fellow of the American Institute of Architects, and president of the New York Municipal Art Society. In 1970 Kahn donated the collection to the Cooper-Hewitt Museum, where it received accession numbers 1970-35-1 and 1977-122-1.

Physical Description

There are 55 photographs including silver gelatin dry plate lantern slides and silver gelatin photoprints. Other materials include drawings, etchings, graphic prints, and watercolor paintings mounted in an album.

Subjects

The photographs document Ely Jacques Kahn's 1934 trip to the Far East with stops in Agra, Bali, Benares (now Varanasi), the Ganges (Ganga) River in India, and Lahore in Pakistan. Activities shown include folk dancing in Bali and buying and selling at a market in Lahore. There also are images of village life in Bali and Lahore. People portrayed include Kahn with family and friends, a Balinese princess in a pool, and a snake charmer. Balinese architecture shown includes architectural details, ornamentation, and shrines.

Arranged: In two parts. 1) An album, unarranged. 2) Lantern slides, arranged chronologically according to Kahn's itinerary.

Captioned: With slide number; some also with subject.

Finding Aid: Caption list including location, slide number, and subject.

Restrictions: Available by appointment only.

CH·7

CH Drawings and Prints Lantern Slide Collection

Dates of Photographs: 1905–1930

Collection Origins

Cooper-Hewitt (CH) staff assembled the collection from several anonymous donations. Photographers represented include T.H. McAllister. The collection has not yet been accessioned.

Physical Description

There are 440 collodion wet plate lantern slides (some tinted).

Subjects

These travel photographs document cityscapes, monuments, people, and scenic locales in Asia, Europe, the Middle East, and the United States between 1905 and 1930. Asian nations shown are Burma (now Myanmar) including Mandalay; Cambodia including Angkor; Hong Kong; India including Agra, Bali, Benares (now Varanasi), Calcutta, and Delhi; Indonesia including Celebes (now Sulawesi); Pakistan including Lahore; Siam (now Thailand) including Bangkok; and Singapore. European locales such as England including London; France including Paris; Germany; Norway; Scotland; and Switzerland including Geneva, Interlaken, and Montreux also are shown.

There are architectural studies and details of French cathedrals (such as Châtres) and chateaux, as well as Indian monuments, temples, and tombs (such as the Taj Mahal). There are cityscapes including informal portraits of people in markets, parks, and streets. The photographs also reproduce art objects including 19th century academic sculpture by A.J. Aller, Girolamo Fontana, and J.L. Villa, as well as decorative art objects such as porcelains. In addition, there are theatrical and vaudeville announcement slides that list theater rules and "header" and "trailer" slides that indicate the beginning or end of magic lantern, motion-picture, theatrical, or vaudeville programs. Many of these slides contain stereotypical images of children, minorities, and women.

Arranged: By locale such as cities, states, and countries.

Captioned: A few with location or name of the building or site.

Finding Aid: Box lists.

Restrictions: Available by appointment only.

CH·8

CH Drawings and Prints Palladian Architecture Photograph Collection

Dates of Photographs: 1976–1977

Collection Origins

Photographers Joseph M. Farber and Phyllis Massar created the collection to document American architecture in the Palladian style for a Cooper-Hewitt exhibit, "Andrea Palladio in America," held between June 7 and October 5, 1977. Italian Renaissance architect Andrea Palladio (1508–1580) designed and built Roman-influenced villas in Vicenza, Italy. In 1570 he published *The Four Books of Architecture,* which was reprinted in London in 1715 as *The Architecture of A. Palladio in Four Books.* Following the re-publication, Palladio's designs were copied widely and reproduced in Europe and the United States, serving as sources for such structures as Thomas Jefferson's Monticello.

The photographs were published in the following book: James Ackerman. *Palladio Revisited.* New Orleans: School of Architecture, Tulane University, 1978. The collection also contains images of historic American homes, taken by other photographers. These photographs were purchased for and used in a small CH exhibit held in conjunction with the 1977 Palladio show.

Physical Description

There are 100 silver gelatin photoprints.

Subjects

The photographs document European buildings designed by Italian Renaissance architect Andrea Palladio and American structures, built centuries later, that were based on or inspired by Palladio's ideas.

Arranged: No.

Captioned: With architect, date, location, and name of the building; some also with photographer. Phyllis Massar's photographs also list their corresponding page number in James Ackerman's book, *Palladio Revisited.*

Finding Aid: Box lists.

Restrictions: Available by appointment only. Some images are under copyright protection and may not be reproduced.

CH·9

CH Drawings and Prints Photograph Albums

Dates of Photographs: 1874–Early 1930s

Collection Origins

Cooper-Hewitt (CH) Drawings and Prints staff assembled the collection from photograph albums given by several donors. James Hazen Hyde (1876–1959), son of Equitable Life Assurance Society founder Henry B. Hyde, donated at least five of the photograph albums. Hyde lived in France for 34 years after selling his controlling interest in Equitable. He also donated a collection of 7,500 photoprints and photonegatives illustrating the iconography of the "Four Continents" to the Library of Congress on September 26, 1960, which are now on loan to the Cooper-Hewitt. Photographs from the collection appear in the following publication: Cooper Union for the Advancement of Science and Art. *The Four Continents: From the Collection of James Hazen Hyde.* New York: Cooper Union Museum, 1961. Another album was donated by genealogist Winchester Fitch, and others are anonymous gifts. Photographers represented include Cagliari, Mr. and Mrs. Max Farrand, and Winchester Fitch. The collection has been assigned CH accession numbers 1948-30-1 through 1948-30-50, 1948-125-1, 1955-72-1, 1956-38-10, and 1961-105-76.

Physical Description

There are 1,000 photographs including albumen photoprints, platinum photoprints, and silver gelatin photoprints (some cartes-de-visite and stereographs), mounted in 11 photograph albums. Some images are tinted. Other materials include photomechanicals.

Subjects

The photographs are formal and informal portraits and travel images dating from the 1870s to the 1930s. The travel photographs show architecture, cityscapes, landscapes, market scenes, ruins, and street scenes in Asia and Europe including Abydos and Karnak, Egypt; Constantinople (now Istanbul), Turkey; Crete, Greece; Elbe, Germany; Paris, France; Rhodes, South Africa; and Sardinia and Sicily, Italy; as well as in Asia Minor and Japan. Architecture, cityscapes, and landscapes illustrated include chateaux, churches, and the Loire Valley and Touraine in France; excavations at Karnak, Egypt; ruins in Delos, Greece; the temple of Set I in Egypt; and American tourists eating a formal luncheon outdoors in Abydos, Egypt.

There are portraits of American and European actors, artists, political figures, and writers; Asian and European royalty; Egyptian villagers; French farmers and fox and stag hunters at Chantilly Chateau; Japanese fieldworkers; Swiss villagers; and Turkish attendants and soldiers of the sultan. Artists shown include Rosa Bonheur, Gustave Courbet at his easel, Gustav Doré, Jean Léon Gérôme, and Edwin Landseer. Writers portrayed include William Cullen Bryant, Thomas Carlyle, Wilkie Collins, Charles Dickens, Alexandre Dumas, Ralph Waldo Emerson, Victor Hugo, Henry Wadsworth Longfellow, John Ruskin, George Sand, and Anthony Trollope. Royalty depicted includes the Duc de Châtres, the Empress of China, Empress Joséphine de Beauharnais of France, the Empress of Russia, Napoleon I, the Prince of Wales, and Queen Victoria. Actors portrayed include Sarah Bernhardt, Nelly Bromley, Molly Clary, Henry Irving, Amy Sheridan, and Ellen Wallis (as Cleopatra). Other portrait subjects include English prime ministers Benjamin Disraeli and Henry John T. (Lord) Palmerston and English nursing pioneer Florence Nightingale. There are also photographs of automobiles, steam engines, and yachts including the *Emerald*. Several images from this collection are reproduced in the illustrations section of this volume.

Arranged: No.

Captioned: Some with date, location, and subject.

Finding Aid: 1) Box lists. 2) Card catalog. 3) Database inventory.

Restrictions: Available by appointment only.

CH·10

CH Drawings and Prints Slide Reference File

Dates of Photographs: 1974–Present

Collection Origins

Cooper-Hewitt (CH) Drawings and Prints Department staff created the collection to document the department's holdings, with funds provided by two grants from the New York State Council for the Arts. Photographers represented include Scott Hyde and Carmel Wilson.

Photographs from this collection are included in the following publications: 1) Gerhard Bott. *Idee und Anspruch der Architektur Zeichnungen des 16. bis 20. Jahrhunderts aus dem Cooper-Hewitt Museum, New York.* Köln: Museen der Stadt Köln, 1979. 2) Lynda Corey Claassen. *Finders' Guide to Prints and Drawings in the Smithsonian Institution.* Washington, D.C.: Smithsonian Institution Press, 1981. 3) Cooper-Hewitt Museum. *Crosscurrents: Neoclassical Drawings and Prints from the Cooper-Hewitt Museum.* Washington, D.C.: Smithsonian Institution Press, 1978. 4) Cooper-Hewitt Museum. *Kata-gami: Japanese Stencils in the Collection of the Cooper-Hewitt Museum.* New York: Cooper-Hewitt Museum, 1979. 5) Elaine Evans Dee and Thomas S. Michie. *Japanese Woodblock Prints in the Collection of the Cooper-Hewitt Museum.* New York: Cooper-Hewitt Museum, 1979. 6) Elaine Evans Dee. *Master Printmakers from Cooper-Hewitt Museum of Decorative Arts and Design.* New York: American Federation of Arts, 1970. 7) Elaine Evans Dee. *The Two Sicilies: Drawings from the Cooper-Hewitt Museum.* New York: Finch College, 1970. 8) Donald H. Karshan. *The Smithsonian Illustrated Library of Antiques: Prints.* New York: Cooper-Hewitt Museum, 1980. 9) Russell Lynes. *More Than Meets the Eye: The History and Collections of Cooper-Hewitt Museum.* New York: Cooper-Hewitt Museum, 1981. 10) Richard P. Wunder. *Five Centuries of Drawing: The Cooper Union Centennial Exhibition.* New York: Cooper Union Museum, 1961.

Physical Description

There are 30,000 color dye coupler slides, about 40 percent of which are originals.

Subjects

The photographs document the department's holdings of drawings and graphic prints from Europe, Japan, and the United States, dating from the 1400s to the present. Types of work reproduced include architectural drawings; book illustrations; engravings; etchings; *katagami* (Japanese stencils); lithographs; paper toys such as dolls and games; posters; silhouettes; sketches for murals, paintings, and stage designs; *ukiyo-e* (Japanese woodblock) prints; and watercolors. The drawings and graphic prints reproduced include abstract designs; anatomical studies; botanical studies; fashion illustrations; landscapes; portraits and studies of craftsmen, mythological figures, and saints; and theatrical designs. The photographs also reproduce designs for objects such as altars, fans, funerary monuments, furniture, lighting devices, ornaments, and textiles.

Artists whose works are represented include Robert Adam, Albrecht Altdorfer, Giuseppe Barberi, Stefano della Bella, the Bibiena family, François Boucher, Edward Burne-Jones, G.B. Castiglione, Thomas Chippendale, Frederic Edwin Church, Charles-Louis Clerisseau, Kenyon and Allyn Cox, Frederick Crace, Lucas Cranach the Elder, Jean François Cuvilliés, Jean Delafosse, Isaac de Moucheron, Donald Deskey, Henry Dreyfuss, Louis-Albert Du Bois, Albrecht Dürer, Hugh Ferriss, Girolamo Fontana, Felice Giani, Francisco José de Goya, Francesco Guardi, Hector Guimard, William Stanley Haseltine, Childe Hassam, Ando Hiroshige, William Hogarth, Katsushika Hokusai, Winslow Homer, Daniel Huntington, Filippo Juvarra, E. McKnight Kauffer, Käthe Kollwitz, Utagawa Kunisada, Charles Le Corbusier, Jean Le Pautre, Romolo Liverani, Andrea Mantegna, Carlo and Filippo Marchionni, Flaminio Innocenzio Minozzi, Thomas Moran, John Nash, Gilles-Marie Oppenort, Jean Baptiste Pillement, Giovanni Battista Piranesi, Matthäus Daniel Poppelman, Andrea Pozzo, Augustus Charles Pugin, Marcantonio Raimondi, Rembrandt van Rijn, Hubert Robert, Martin Schongauer, J.A. Seethaler, Isadore Solda, Giovanni Battista Tiepolo, Lucas van Leyden, Israhel van Meckenem, Elihu Vedder, Whitney Warren, James Abbott McNeill Whistler, and Frank Lloyd Wright.

Arranged: In two series. 1) Browsing slides, by object's medium, subject matter, or artist. 2) Master slides, by object's accession number.

Captioned: Browsing slides with accession number and artist of the object shown, slot number of the slide tray, and subject heading or title.

Finding Aid: 1) Card catalog to accessioned objects, arranged by accession number and cross-referenced by artist, listing the object's accession number, artist, bibliography, country of origin, dimensions, inscription, material, source, and watermark. 2) Shelf list (titled "Box Listings") to accessioned objects, arranged by country, then period, then subject.

Restrictions: Available by appointment only.

CH·11

CH Drawings and Prints Stereograph Collection

Dates of Photographs: 1860–1910

Collection Origins

Cooper-Hewitt Department of Drawings and Prints staff assembled the collection from many donations including images from Eleanor and Sarah Hewitt. Photographers and studios represented include Mathew Brady, James Cramer, De Young Palace Dollar Store in Philadelphia, E. & H.T. Anthony Company, and Underwood and Underwood.

Physical Description

There are 1,555 photographs including albumen photoprints (some postcards and stereographs), collodion gelatin photoprints (POP, some stereographs), collodion wet plate lantern slides and stereographs, and silver gelatin stereographs and postcards. Other materials include graphic prints such as engravings and etchings.

Subjects

The photographs document cityscapes, landscapes, objects, and people worldwide. Places documented include Austria, Belgium, China, Egypt (100 views), England, France, Germany, Italy, Japan, Mexico, Palestine (now Israel), Peru, the Philippines, Russia, Sweden, Switzerland (Lake Lucerne), and California, Massachusetts, Montana, New York, North Carolina, Pennsylvania, Rhode Island, Tennessee, Virginia, and Wyoming in the United States. Architecture shown includes Egyptian monuments, pyramids, temples (such as the temple of Abu Simbel), and tombs; English abbeys, cathedrals, churches, country houses, and exhibition buildings (such as the Crystal Palace), as well as the London Zoo; French chateaux; Italian architecture (including the Vatican) and monuments; and U.S. Civil War fortifications in Virginia. Events documented include the Centennial Exposition, Philadelphia, 1876 (15 views); the U.S. Civil War (50 views); and the International Exhibition of 1862, London (80 views); as well as ship sinkings. The collection also includes theatrical stills depicting scenes from plays. Stereographs of the U.S. Civil War by Mathew Brady include scenes of Petersburg, Richmond, and Yorktown, Virginia. Landscapes pictured include French gardens and American natural wonders such as Niagara Falls in New York and Yellowstone National Park in Montana and Wyoming. Objects depicted include Egyptian antiquities, graves, and sculptures. People portrayed include General Rufus King, other Civil War officers, and Emperor Napoleon III and Empress Eugénie of France. The collection also contains genre scenes, many of which are sentimental portraits of French and German women and children. A Civil War image from this collection is reproduced in the illustrations section of this volume.

Arranged: By location and subject. Major headings are American Civil War, Animals of the London Zoo, Cathedrals, Egyptian Antiquities (Pyramids), English Abbeys, the Holy Land, Underwood & Underwood slides of Lake Lucerne, and Yellowstone National Park.

Captioned: Some with creator and subject.

Finding Aid: 1) Inventory notebooks. 2) Card catalog file. 3) Database inventory.

Restrictions: Available by appointment only.

CH·12

CH Drawings and Prints Karl Vogel Lantern Slide Collection

Dates of Photographs: 1909–1922

Collection Origins

Physician Karl Vogel (1877–1968) created the collection to document his service in World War I and his travels between 1909 and 1922. Vogel received an M.D. in 1900 from Columbia University, where he later served as an associate clinical professor of medicine. He was a fellow of the New York Academy of Medicine and the American College of Physicians. A frequent traveler, Vogel visited the American Southwest on horseback in 1909, when he took 55 of these slides. In 1910 he visited the Mediterranean, particularly Morocco and Spain, where he took another 51 of the slides. During World War I he served in the American Ambulance Service at the Ancien College de Juilly at Dammartin-en-Goële, France, in 1914 and 1915, when another 48 of these slides were made. In 1921 and 1922 Vogel traveled around the world on Arthur Curtiss James's square-rigged sailing yacht *Aloha*, visiting Hawaii, India, Japan, and Southeast Asia, where he took the last 145 slides and purchased another 71 from Japanese vendors. Photographers represented include Karl Vogel and F. Saito of Japan. Many of the slides were published in the Karl Vogel's book *Aloha Around the World*. New York: G.P. Putnam's Sons, 1922. The collection's CH accession numbers are 1968-77-1 through 1968-77-372.

Physical Description

There are 370 silver gelatin dry plate lantern slides (tinted).

Subjects

The photographs document three trips taken by Vogel between 1909 and 1922 and his World War I medical service at Dammartin-en-Goële, France, during 1914 and 1915. Photographs from Vogel's 1909 trip to the American Southwest show men on horseback in landscapes such as the Grand Canyon, Arizona, and Kayenta and Mesa Verde, Colorado; Anasazi Indian (pre-Columbian Pueblo Indians) cliff dwellings in Arizona, New Mexico, and Utah; and portraits of William Mac-Callum and Clayton Wetherill, an early guide to the cliff dwellings.

The photographs of Vogel's 1910 trip to the Mediterranean illustrate markets and streets in Algiers, Algeria; Tangiers, Morocco; and Palermo, Sicily. The photographs of Spain show bullfights, markets, and streets in Mallorca and Seville, as well as images of the Alhambra (museum) in Granada.

World War I images show the American Ambulance Corps in the Dammartin-en-Goële area of France, as well as bombed buildings; hospital exteriors (particularly that of the Ancien College de Juilly), grounds, and interiors; and trenches. There are also informal portraits of doctors and nurses in French hospitals around 1914 and on the ship *Lusitania*, as well as patients, including wounded *poilus* (French foot soldiers), both in hospital wards and recovering on the hospital grounds.

Photographs from Vogel's 1921 to 1922 around-the-world trip show street scenes in Rangoon, Burma (now Myanmar); Ceylon (now Sri Lanka); Peking (Beijing), China; Hong Kong; Agra, Bombay, and Darjeeling (Dārjiling), India; Nikkō, Japan; Java (Jawa); Seoul, Korea; Baalbek, Lebanon; and the Philippines. Other landscapes shown include Hawaiian volcanoes, such as Hilo, and the Panama Canal. Japanese scenes show the river Tachiani and various temples in cities such as Ieyasu and Nikkō and the Shokonsha Temple in Tokyo. Occupations portrayed include Indian snake charmers and Japanese workers such as agricultural workers hulling rice in a mill, a blind masseuse, and sumo wrestlers.

Arranged: Chronologically by trip in four series. 1) American Southwest in 1909. 2) Mediterranean in 1910. 3) World War I service in France. 4) Worldwide yacht trip in 1921–1922, in three subseries: a) slides made by Vogel; b) a slide set purchased in Japan; and c) a second slide set purchased in Japan.

Captioned: With location and subject.

Finding Aid: Summary sheet listing dates and itineraries of each trip and the number of slides taken.

Restrictions: Available by appointment only.

CH·13

CH Drawings and Prints Carlton Eugene Watkins Yosemite Photograph Collection

Dates of Photographs: Circa 1860s

Collection Origins

Cooper-Hewitt (CH) Drawings and Prints Department staff assembled the collection from donations by California photographer Carleton E. Watkins (1829–1916). In 1851 during California's gold rush, Watkins left Oneonta, New York, for San Francisco. During his apprenticeship under photographer Robert Vance around 1854, Watkins learned the daguerreotype process. After mastering the collodion wet plate process in 1858, Watkins set up his own gallery, the Watkins Yosemite Art Gallery, which he owned and operated until the 1906 San Francisco earthquake.

Beginning in 1861, Watkins made many trips to Yosemite to make mammoth-plate size collodion wet plate photonegative views of the landscapes, which he published in an 1863 portfolio titled *Yo-Semite Valley: Photographic Views of the Falls and Valley*. For the next several years, Watkins served as a member of several geographical and geological surveys including the 1866 Geological Survey of California. By 1867 Watkins was widely recognized as one of the foremost landscape photographers in California, winning the 1868 International Exposition medal in Paris. Besides documenting the natural landscape of California, Watkins photographed the state's cities, mining camps, missions, ranches, and towns. Most of Watkins's prints and plates, along with his studio, were destroyed in the great San Francisco earthquake and fire of 1906; few large prints survive. The CH assigned this collection accession numbers 1976-23-1 through 1976-23-30.

Physical Description

There are 30 albumen photoprints (17″ × 22 1/2″). Most of the photoprints are signed "C.E. Watkins."

Subjects

The photographs document the rugged landscape of Yosemite (now Yosemite National Park) in east central California in the 1860s. The landscapes illustrated include cliffs, forests, mountains such as Mount Star King, rivers, valleys, and waterfalls. A photograph from the collection is reproduced in the illustration section of this volume.

Arranged: By object's accession number.

Captioned: With Watkins' signature; one also with the name of the mountain.

Finding Aid: 1) Box lists. 2) Card catalog file. 3) Database inventory.

Restrictions: Available by appointment only.

CH

Department of Textiles

Department of Textiles
Cooper-Hewitt Museum, the Smithsonian Institution's National
  Museum of Design
2 East 91st Street
New York, New York 10128-9990
Textile Curator
Hours: By appointment.

Scope of the Collections

There are two photographic collections with approximately 61,200 images.

Focus of the Collections

The photographs document the department's holdings of over 20,000 textile-related objects, including embroidered, printed, woven, and non-woven fabric, dating from the third century B.C. to the present. The departmental artifacts document the history of textile dyeing, needlework, printing, and weaving processes, structures, and techniques worldwide.

Photographic Processes and Formats Represented

There are color dye coupler slides and silver gelatin photoprints.

Other Materials Represented

No other materials are accessible to the public.

Access and Usage Policies

The photograph collections are open to researchers by appointment. Researchers should call or write to the department in advance and describe their research topic, the type of material that interests them, and their research aim. All inquiries concerning photographic rights in connection with scholarly or trade use should be addressed to the Department of Photographic Services, Cooper-Hewitt Museum, 2 East 91st Street, New York, New York, 10128-9990.

Publication Policies

Researchers must obtain permission from the Cooper-Hewitt Museum to reproduce a photograph and may also have to obtain permission from the copyright holder, which is not necessarily the Smithsonian Institution. The preferred credit line is "Courtesy of the Department of Textiles, Cooper-Hewitt Museum, the Smithsonian Institution's National Museum of Design." The photographer's name, if known, also should appear.

CH·14

CH Textiles Research File

Dates of Photographs: 1970s–Present

Collection Origins

Cooper-Hewitt (CH) Textiles Department staff assembled the collection to document activities such as conservation, exhibits, loans, and research involving the department's textile holdings.

The photographs appear in the following publications: 1) Alice Baldwin Beer. *Trade Goods: A Study of Indian Chintz in the Collection of the Cooper-Hewitt Museum.* Washington, D.C.: Smithsonian Institution Press, 1970. 2) Adolph Cavallo. *The Smithsonian Illustrated Library of Antiques: Needlework.* New York: Cooper-Hewitt Museum, 1979. 3) Walter B. Denny. *The Smithsonian Illustrated Library of Antiques: Oriental Rugs.* New York: Cooper-Hewitt Museum, 1979. 4) Russell Lynes. *More Than Meets the Eye: The History and Collections of Cooper-Hewitt Museum.* New York: Cooper-Hewitt Museum, 1981. 5) Christine Minter-Dowd. *Finders' Guide to Decorative Arts in the Smithsonian Institution.* Washington, D.C.: Smithsonian Institution Press, 1984. 6) Milton Sonday. *Lace in the Collection of the Cooper-Hewitt Museum.* New York: Cooper-Hewitt Museum, 1982. 7) Milton Sonday and Gillian Moss. *Western European Embroidery in the Collection of the Cooper-Hewitt Museum.* New York: Cooper-Hewitt Museum, 1978.

Physical Description

There are 1,200 silver gelatin photoprints.

Subjects

The photographs document the department's textile holdings, dating from the third century B.C. to the present, such as dyed and printed fabrics including intaglio, relief, resists (for example batik, ikat, and tie-dye), and roller-printed fabrics; embroidery including book covers, pictures, and samplers; non-woven fabrics including appliqué, beading, knitting, knotting, lace (for example, needle and bobbin lace), looping, punched fabric, and tatting; dyers' record books; and woven fabrics including cotton, linen, silk, and wool. These textiles are primarily from Europe, although there are also pieces from China, Egypt, India, Indonesia, Japan, Persia (now Iran), and Peru.

Arranged: By the object's accession number.

Captioned: Some with subject.

Finding Aid: No.

Restrictions: Available by appointment only.

CH·15

CH Textiles Slide Collection

Dates of Photographs: 1976–Present

Collection Origins

Cooper-Hewitt Textiles Department staff assembled the collection as a research file to provide an alternative to viewing the department's original textile holdings. For a list of publications in which the photographs appear, see the *Collection Origins* section in *CH·14.* Photographers represented include Smithsonian Institution Conservation Analytical Laboratory staff.

Physical Description

There are 60,000 color dye coupler slides (Kodachrome).

Subjects

The photographs document the department's more than 20,000 accessioned textiles including international dyed and printed fabrics, embroidery, and both woven and non-woven fabrics, dating from roughly the third century B.C. to the present. Objects documented include carpetbags; carpet fragments; costumes and accessories such as printed handkerchiefs and scarves; ecclesiastical panels and vestments; and embroidered pictures. Fabrics illustrated are block printed; copper-plate printed; pigment printed; resist dyed including batik, ikat, and tie-dye; roller printed; and screen printed items. Printed materials shown include leathers, silks, and wools. Printing accessories illustrated include 19th century dyers' record books and printing blocks.

Embroidered textiles documented date from the 19th and 20th centuries and include costumes such as embroidered caps, coifs, hats, dresses, shawls, and waistcoats; embroidery on leather; pictures such as mourning pictures; religious embroidery; samplers; silk-on-silk embroidery; trapunto quilting; and whitework embroidery. There are images of embroidery from Africa, Central America, and Scandinavia, as well as nations such as Austria, Belgium, China, Crete, Czechoslovakia, Egypt, Formosa (now Taiwan), France, Germany, Greece, India, Indonesia, Italy, Japan, Mexico, Morocco, the Philippines, Portugal, Spain, Sri Lanka, Tibet (now Xizang), Turkey, and the United States.

Non-woven fabrics illustrated include appliqué on gauze, on knotted net, and on net; basketware; beadwork; bebilla netting; braiding; card weaving; cutwork fabric with needlework fillings and embroidery; crocheting; deflected element work; drawnwork; knitting by hand, by machine, and with beads; knotting; lace including Brussels-style lace, machine-made lace, needle lace, pre-made tape lace, and Valenciennes lace; looping and beaded looping; macramé; needlework on gauze, on knotted net, and on net; openwork including machine-made openwork; perforated and punched fabric; and tatting.

Woven objects documented include church vestments and weavings, handkerchiefs, towels, and woven trimmings. Woven fabrics documented include examples from China, Egypt, England, India, Italy, Persia (now Iran), Peru (including pre-Columbian textiles), Russia, Scandinavia, Spain, Turkey, and the United States.

Arranged: In four series containing identical slides used for different purposes. 1) Slide carousels, by object's medium or process. 2) Master file, by object's accession number. 3) Duplicator file, by object's accession number. 4) Spare set, by object's accession number.

Captioned: Some with object's accession number.

Finding Aid: No.

Restrictions: Available by appointment only.

CH

Department of Wallcoverings

Department of Wallcoverings
Cooper-Hewitt Museum, the Smithsonian Institution's National
*   Museum of Design*
2 East 91st Street
New York, New York 10128-9990
Keeper, Department of Wallcoverings
(212) 860-6896
Hours: By appointment.

Scope of the Collections

There are three photographic collections with approximately 50,780 images.

Focus of the Collections

The photographs document the department's holdings of international wallcoverings and wallpaper production tools dating from the 17th to the 20th centuries.

Photographic Processes and Formats Represented

There are color dye coupler slides and phototransparencies and silver gelatin photoprints.

Other Materials Represented

The department also contains accessioned bandboxes, wallcoverings, and wallpaper production tools.

Access and Usage Policies

The photograph collections are open to researchers by appointment. Researchers should call or write to the department in advance and describe their research topic, the type of material that interests them, and their research aim. All inquiries concerning photographic services, materials, and rights in connection with scholarly or trade use should be addressed to the Department of Photographic Services, Cooper-Hewitt Museum, 2 East 91st Street, New York, New York, 10128-9990.

Publication Policies

Researchers must obtain permission from the Cooper-Hewitt Museum to reproduce a photograph and may also have to obtain permission from the copyright holder, which is not necessarily the Smithsonian Institution. The preferred credit line is "Courtesy of the Department of Wallcoverings, Cooper-Hewitt Museum, the Smithsonian Institution's National Museum of Design." The photographer's name, if known, also should appear.

CH·16

CH Wallcoverings Color Phototransparency File

Dates of Photographs: 1976–Present

Collection Origins

Former Cooper-Hewitt (CH) Department of Wallcoverings keeper Ann H. Dorfsman assembled the collection from photographs produced by the CH Department of Photographic Services. Photographers represented include Scott Hyde and Kenneth Pelka. The photographs have appeared in the following publications: 1) Cooper-Hewitt Museum. *Wallpaper in the Collection of the Cooper-Hewitt Museum*. New York: Cooper-Hewitt Museum, 1981. 2) Russell Lynes. *More Than Meets the Eye: The History and Collections of Cooper-Hewitt Museum*. New York: Smithsonian Institution Press, 1981. 3) Catherine Lynn. *Wallpaper in America: From the Seventeenth Century to World War I*. New York: W.W. Norton, 1980. 4) Christine Minter-Dowd. *Finders' Guide to Decorative Arts in the Smithsonian Institution*. Washington, D.C.: Smithsonian Institution Press, 1984.

Physical Description

There are 280 color dye coupler phototransparencies.

Subjects

The photographs document international wallcoverings, dating from the 17th through the 20th centuries, in the Department of Wallpaper's holdings. Most pieces illustrated are from Asia, Europe, and the United States.

The cloth, leather, and paper wallcoverings illustrated are hand-drawn and painted; painted including Swedish *bonaders* (folk scenes); flocked; printed including mechanically printed items and woodblock prints; printed and stenciled; stenciled; or waxed including *wachstuch* (wax cloth). There are illustrations of objects covered with wallpaper such as bandboxes, fireboards, folding screens, and window shades.

Arranged: By object's accession number.

Captioned: With object's accession number.

Finding Aid: No.

Restrictions: No access. Restricted private research collection.

CH·17

CH Wallcoverings Reference Notebook File

Dates of Photographs: 1930s–Present

Collection Origins

Former Cooper-Hewitt (CH) Department of Wallcoverings keeper Ann H. Dorfsman assembled the collection from photographs created by the CH Department of Photographic Services to document departmental holdings for publication and research. The photographs have appeared in numerous publications, some of which are listed under the *Collection Origins* section in *CH·16*.

Physical Description

There are 2,500 silver gelatin photoprints.

Subjects

The photographs document international wallcoverings, dating from the 17th through the 20th centuries, in the Department of Wallcoverings' holdings. Most pieces illustrated are from Asia, Europe, and the United States.

The cloth, leather, and paper wallcoverings illustrated are hand-drawn and painted; painted including Swedish *bonaders* (folk scenes); flocked; printed including mechanically printed items and woodblock prints; printed and stenciled; stenciled; or waxed including *wachstuch* (wax cloth). There are illustrations of objects covered with wallpaper such as bandboxes, fireboards, folding screens, and window shades. Wallcoverings represented include architectural motifs such as dadoes and friezes; chinoiseries; exotic, fantastic, historical, or mythological landscapes; geometric designs; medallions; motifs derived from nature; and *ombré* (design showing a single color's range of tints) papers. Design movements represented in the wallcoverings reproduced include art deco, art nouveau, arts and crafts, baroque, Bauhaus, empire or neoclassical, gothic revival, Greek revival, and rococo including chinoiserie.

Arranged: By object's accession number.

Captioned: With object's accession number, country of origin, date, description, and medium.

Finding Aid: No.

Restrictions: Available by appointment only.

CH·18

CH Wallcoverings Slide Library

Dates of Photographs: 1976–Present

Collection Origins

Former Cooper-Hewitt (CH) Department of Wall-coverings keeper Ann H. Dorfsman assembled the collection to document the history of wallpaper and the department's accessioned objects. Part of the collection was created for the Department of Wallcoverings by the CH Photographic Services Division.

Physical Description

There are 48,000 color dye coupler slides (Kodachrome), 35,000 of which are duplicates.

Subjects

The photographs document international wallcoverings, dating from the 17th through the 20th centuries, in the Department of Wallcoverings' holdings. Most pieces illustrated are from Asia, Europe, and the United States. Wallcovering designers and manufacturers represented include Frederick Crace; Walter Crane; Jean Zuber et Cie; J.H. Dearle; Jules Defossé; Joseph Dufour; Zecheriah Mills; William Morris; Charles L.L. Muller; Jean Baptiste Réveillon; S.A. Maxwell and Co.; Louis C. Tiffany; Charles F.A. Voysey; and the Wiener Werkstätte.

The cloth, leather, and paper wallcoverings illustrated are hand-drawn and painted; painted including Swedish *bonaders* (folk scenes); flocked; printed including mechanically printed items and woodblock prints; printed and stenciled; stenciled; or waxed including *wachstuch* (wax cloth). There are illustrations of objects covered with wallpaper such as bandboxes and window shades.

Wallcoverings represented include architectural motifs such as dadoes and friezes; chinoiseries; exotic, fantastic, historical, or mythological landscapes; geometrical designs; medallions; motifs derived from nature; and *ombré* (design showing a single color's range of tints) papers. Design movements represented in the photographs include art deco, art nouveau, arts and crafts, baroque, Bauhaus, empire or neoclassical, gothic revival, Greek revival, and rococo including chinoiserie.

Arranged: By function in four series. 1) Inventory slides, by object's accession number. 2) Duplicate slides, by object's accession number. 3) Master slides, by object's accession number. 4) Reference slides, by subject heading, then by medium, then by country of origin, then by date.

Captioned: With object's accession number, country of origin, date, and type of object and function of slide.

Finding Aid: No.

Restrictions: Available by appointment only.

CH

Education Department

Education Department
Cooper-Hewitt Museum, the Smithsonian Institution's National
*   Museum of Design*
2 East 91st Street
New York, New York 10128-9990
Senior Program Coordinator
(212) 860-6899
Hours: By appointment.

Scope of the Collection

There is one photographic collection with approximately 700 images.

Focus of the Collection

The photographs document activities and events at the Cooper-Hewitt Museum between 1976 and the present including arts and crafts demonstrations; classes, lectures, and seminars on topics related to the decorative arts; concerts; and exhibit openings.

Photographic Processes and Formats Represented

There are color dye coupler slides and silver gelatin photonegatives and photoprints.

Other Materials Represented

None.

Access and Usage Policies

The photograph collection is open to researchers by appointment. Smithsonian Institution employees should call or write the division in advance. Other researchers should call or write the Public Information Office and describe their research topic, the type of material that interests them, and their research aim. All inquiries concerning photographic rights in connection with scholarly or trade use should be addressed to the Department of Photographic Services, Cooper-Hewitt Museum, 2 East 91st Street, New York, New York, 10128-9990.

Publication Policies

Researchers must obtain permission from the Cooper-Hewitt Museum to reproduce a photograph and may also have to obtain permission from the copyright holder, which is not necessarily the Smithsonian Institution. The preferred credit line is "Courtesy of the Education Department, Cooper-Hewitt Museum, the Smithsonian Institution's National Museum of Design." The photographer's name, if known, also should appear.

CH·19

CH Education Department Newsletter and Departmental Photograph Collection

Dates of Photographs: 1976–Present

Collection Origins

Cooper-Hewitt (CH) Education Department program coordinator Susan Yelavich created the collection to document CH activities and for occasional use in the following publication: *Cooper-Hewitt Newsletter.* New York: Cooper-Hewitt Museum, 1977– . Photographs also appeared in the museum's previous newsletter: *The Cooper Union Museum Chronicles.* New York: Cooper Union Museum, 1935–1963. Photographers represented include Pat Tine and Susan Yelavich.

Physical Description

There are 700 photographs including color dye coupler slides (Ektachrome) and silver gelatin photonegatives and photoprints (some contact sheets).

Subjects

The photographs document activities and events at the CH Museum between 1976 and the present including classes, concerts, demonstrations, lectures, openings, seminars, and staff parties. There are also images of CH buildings.

Arranged: By format, then in four series by subject. 1) Personalities and staff. 2) Parties for exhibit openings, programs, and miscellaneous events. 3) Physical plant. 4) Programs and Miscellaneous.

Captioned: No.

Finding Aid: No.

Restrictions: Available by appointment only.

CH

Department of Exhibitions

Department of Exhibitions
Cooper-Hewitt Museum, the Smithsonian Institution's National
  Museum of Design
2 East 91st Street
New York, New York 10128-9990
Lucy Fellowes, Exhibitions Research
(212) 860-6115
Hours: By appointment.

Scope of the Collection	There is one photographic collection with approximately 25,000 photographs.
Focus of the Collection	The photographs document all exhibits presented at or by the Cooper-Hewitt Museum since 1975, including shows organized by the museum and traveling exhibits.
Photographic Processes and Formats Represented	There are color dye coupler slides and silver gelatin photonegatives and photoprints.
Other Materials Represented	None.
Access and Usage Policies	The photograph collection is open only to Smithsonian staff, who should write or call in advance for an appointment. All inquiries concerning photographic rights should be addressed to the Department of Photographic Services, Cooper-Hewitt Museum, 2 East 91st Street, New York, New York, 10128-9990.
Publication Policies	Potential publishers must obtain permission from the Cooper-Hewitt Museum to reproduce a photograph and may also have to obtain permission from the copyright holder, which is not necessarily the Smithsonian Institution. The preferred credit line is "Courtesy of the Exhibitions Office, Cooper-Hewitt Museum, the Smithsonian Institution's National Museum of Design." The photographer's name, if known, also should appear.

CH·20

CH Department of Exhibitions Installation Photograph Collection

Dates of Photographs: 20th Century, most 1975–Present

Collection Origins

The Cooper-Hewitt (CH) Department of Exhibitions created the collection to document exhibits presented at or by the museum since 1975. Photographers represented include Bill Jacobson, Jennifer Kotter, Norman McGrath, Tom Rose, and Graydon Wood.

Physical Description

There are 25,000 photographs including color dye coupler slides and silver gelatin photonegatives and photoprints.

Subjects

The photographs document CH exhibits installed at the museum since 1975. Exhibits documented focus on the history of architecture, design, drawings, graphic prints, textiles, wall coverings, and the decorative arts including boxes, buttons, ceramics, enamel, furniture, glassware, jewelry, lacquerware, lighting devices, metalwork, timepieces, and toys and games.

Exhibits documented include "Advertising America"; "Alvar Aalto"; "American Drawings from the Cooper-Hewitt Collection: Training the Hand Eye"; "American Enterprise: Nineteenth Century Patent Models"; "The American Landscape"; "American Picture Palaces"; "Americans in Glass"; "The Amsterdam School: Dutch Expressionists Architecture, 1915–1930"; "Andrea Palladio in America"; "Annual Reports"; "Arches for Galveston"; "Architectural Drawings from the 19th Century"; "Architectural Fantasy and Reality"; "Art Nouveau Bing: The Paris Style 1900"; "The Art of the European Goldsmith: From the Schroder Collection"; "Art That Is Life: The Arts and Crafts Movement in America"; "Artist's Postcards Series II"; "Basketry: Tradition in New Form"; "Beach, Boardwalk, Boulevard"; "Berlin 1900–1933: Architecture and Design"; "Bon Voyage! Designs for Travel"; and "Button, Button."

Other exhibits depicted are "Canes and Walking Sticks"; "The Carnegie Mansion"; "The Carnegie Mansion Embellished"; "Carnegie's Libraries: A Sesquicentennial Celebration"; "Catalan Spirit: Gaudí and His Contemporaries"; "Central Park"; "A Century of Ceramics in the United States: 1878–1978"; "Ceramics of the Weimar Republic, 1919–1933"; "Chicago Furniture: Art, Craft and Industry, 1833–1983"; "Chinese Gold and Silver from the Tang Dynasty (A.D. 618–907) in the American Collections"; "Circles of the World: Traditional Art of the Plains Indians"; "City Dwellings and Country Houses: Robert Adam and His Style"; "Close Observations: The Oil Sketches of Frederic E. Church"; "Color by the Yard: Printed Fabrics, 1760–1860"; "Color Light Surface: Recent Textiles"; "The Column: Structure and Ornament"; "Contemporary Continuous Pattern"; "The Cooper-Hewitt Collection: Furniture"; "The Copper-Hewitt Collection: Glass"; "The Copper-Hewitt Collection: Porcelain"; "The Cooper-Hewitt Collection: Silver"; "The Countess's Treasury: Gems & Curiosities from Burghley House"; "Courts and Colonies: The William and Mary Style in Holland, England, and America"; "Crosscurrents: Neoclassical Drawings and Prints"; "Crystal Palaces"; and "Cut Paper."

Other exhibits shown are "Damask"; "Designed for Theater"; "Design in the Service of Tea"; "Design Sales Gallery"; "The Doghouse"; "Drawing Toward a More Modern Architecture"; "Drawings by Francesco & Giovanni Carlo Bibiena"; "Dream King: Ludwig II of Bavaria"; "E. McKnight Kauffer: Graphic Art and Theater Design"; "Electroworks"; "Embellished Calendars: An Illustrated History"; "Embroidered Samplers"; "Embroidered Ship Portraits"; "Embroidery through the Ages"; "English Majolica"; "Ephemeral Images: Recent American Posters"; "Erich Mendelsohn: 1887–1953"; "Etchings by the Tiepolos: From the Cooper-Hewitt Collection"; "European Illustration: 1974–1984"; "Fabergé: Jeweller to Royalty"; "Fabled Cloth: Batik from Java's North Coast"; "Fantastic Illustration and Design in Britain"; "Fashion Prints: 125 Years of Style"; "Finished in Beauty: Southwest Indian Silver"; "Flora Danica and the Heritage of Danish Porcelain"; "Folding Fans from the Cooper-Hewitt Collection"; "Form Follows Film"; "The Four Continents"; "Frank Lloyd Wright and the Johnson Wax Buildings: Creating a Corporate Cathedral"; "Frank Lloyd Wright and the Prairie School"; "Gardens of Delight"; "The Golden Eye"; and "Gold of Greece: Jewelry and Ornaments from the Benaki Museum."

The collection also features images from exhibits such as "Hair"; "Hawai'i: The Royal Isles"; "Henry C. Mercer Tiles"; "Hollywood: Legend and Reality"; "Honor & Glory: Triumphal Arches"; "Immovable Objects: Lower Manhattan from Battery Park to the Brooklyn Bridge"; "Immovable Objects: Subways"; "Immovable Objects: Urban Open Spaces"; "In Celebration of Water"; "Indelible Images: Contemporary Advertising Design"; "Innovative Furniture in America"; "Interior Design: The New Freedom"; "In Small

Stages: Puppets from the Cooper-Hewitt Collection"; "The Intimate World of Alexander Calder"; "The Jacquard Loom: Recent Experiments"; "Jewelry: A Selection from the Cooper-Hewitt Collection"; "John Henry Belter and the Rococo Revival"; "Kata-Gami"; "Lace"; "La Nijinska: A Dancer's Legacy"; "L'Art de Vivre: Decorative Arts and Design in France 1789–1989"; "Look Again"; "Looking at Los Angeles"; "Louis Sullivan: The Function of Ornament"; "Magazine Covers"; "Manhattan Skyline: New York Skyscrapers Between the Wars"; "ManTRANSforms"; "MA, Space/Time in Japan"; "Matchsafes"; "Memphis/Milano"; "Milestones: 50 Years of Goods and Services"; "The Modern Dutch Poster: The First 50 Years, 1890–1940"; "The Modern Spirit: Glass from Finland"; "Mondo Materials"; "More Than Meets the Eye"; "The Moving Image"; "Museum of Drawers"; "Mustard Pots from the Colman Collection"; "Netsuke: Japanese Design in Miniature"; "Newcomb Pottery: An Enterprise for Southern Women"; "New Vistas: American Art Pottery, 1880–1920"; "Nineteenth Century German Stage Design"; and "Now I Lay Me Down to Eat."

Other exhibits shown include "Objects of Adornment: 500 Years of Jewelry from Walters Art Gallery, Baltimore"; "The Oceanliner: Speed, Style, Symbol"; "Old Master Prints from the Wallerstein Collection"; "Ornament in the 20th Century"; "The Outdoor Chair"; "Palaces for the People"; "Paris Opera on Stage: Designs, Costumes, Jewels"; "Paris Recorded: The Thérèse Bonney Collection"; "A Penny Saved: Architecture in Cast-Iron Toy Banks"; "Perspective: The Illusion of Space"; "Photography and Architecture: 1839–1939"; "Place, Product, Packaging"; "Playing Cards"; "Pottery"; "Puppets: Art and Entertainment"; "Purses, Pockets, Pouches"; "Recollections: A Decade of Collecting"; "Resorts of the Catskills"; "Robert Adam and Kedleston Hall"; "Roma Intereotta"; and "The Royal Pavilion at Brighton."

Other shows documented are "Safe and Secure: A World of Design in Locks and Keys"; "Scandinavian Modern 1880–1980"; "The Shopping Bag: Portable Graphic Art"; "Smithsonian"; "Spectacular Spaces: Drawings from the Cooper-Hewitt Collection"; "Suburbs"; "Surprise! Surprise! Pop-up and Moveable Books"; "Take Your Choice: Contemporary Product Design"; "Tiffany Studios: Metalwork and Other Decorative Arts"; "Tiles"; "Timeless Sources: Rare Books from the Cooper-Hewitt Museum"; "To Celebrate the Moment"; "Toys from the Nuremburg Spielzug Museum"; "Treasures from Hungary: Gold and Silver from the 9th–19th Centuries"; "The Triumph of Simplicity: 350 Years of Swedish Silver"; "Tsuba"; "Turned Wood Bowls"; "Two Hundred Years of American Architectural Drawing"; "Underground Images: Subway Posters from the School of Visual Arts"; "Urban Documents: Twentieth Century American Prints"; "Versailles: The View from Sweden, Drawings from the National Museum and Royal Palace, Stockholm"; "Vienna Moderne 1898–1918"; "Vienna/New York: The Work of Joseph Urban, 1872–1933"; "Views of Rome: Drawings and Watercolors from the Collection of the Biblioteca Apostolica Vaticana"; "Visual Spaces in Music: Drawings by John Decesare"; "Wallpaper from the Cooper-Hewitt Collection"; "Western European Embroidery"; "What Could Have Been: Unbuilt Architecture of the '80s"; "Wine: Celebration and Ceremony"; "Winslow Homer"; and "Writing and Reading."

Arranged: In four series. 1) Master slides and photoprints, chronologically by exhibit. 2) Spare slides, chronologically by exhibit. 3) Contact prints and photonegatives, alphabetically by exhibit. 4) Slides of pre-1975 exhibits, uncataloged.

Captioned: No.

Finding Aid: List of CH exhibits since October 1975 arranged by date.

Restrictions: Available by appointment only.

CH

Cooper-Hewitt Library

Cooper-Hewitt Library
Cooper-Hewitt Museum, the Smithsonian Institution's National
* Museum of Design*
2 East 91st Street
New York, New York 10128-9990
Stephen Van Dyk, Librarian
(212) 860-6887
Hours: By appointment.

Scope of the Collections

There are eight photographic collections with approximately 130,300 images.

Focus of the Collections

The photographs document Cooper-Hewitt Museum holdings and the history of the decorative arts worldwide, from prehistory to the present. There are images of architecture, ceramics, color usage, furniture, industrial design, metalwork, product design, textiles, and wallcoverings.

Photographic Processes and Formats Represented

There are albumen photoprints, collodion gelatin photoprints (POP), color dye coupler photoprints and slides, dye diffusion transfer photoprints, and silver gelatin photonegatives and photoprints.

Other Materials Represented

The library also contains advertisements; awards; blueprints; books; color cards; color charts; color keys; correspondence; drawings; dye samples; exhibit catalogs; exhibit labels; exhibit panels; fabric samples; graphic prints such as engravings, etchings, illustrations, and lithographs; lectures; magazine clippings; manuscripts; newspaper clippings; notebooks; notes; object samples; pamphlets; photomechanicals such as duotones and halftones; portfolios; press kits; publications; questionnaires; rare books; reprints; sample books; scrapbooks; sketches; speeches; and xerographic copies.

Access and Usage Policies

Most photograph collections are open to researchers by appointment. Researchers should call or write to the library in advance and describe their research topic, the type of material that interests them, and their research aim. All inquiries concerning photographic rights in connection with scholarly or trade use should be addressed to the Department of Photographic Services, Cooper-Hewitt Museum, 2 East 91st Street, New York, New York, 10128-9990.

Publication Policies

Researchers must obtain permission from the Cooper-Hewitt Museum to reproduce a photograph and may also have to obtain permission from the copyright holder, which is not necessarily the Smithsonian Institution. The preferred credit line is "Courtesy of the Library, Cooper-Hewitt Museum, the Smithsonian Institution's National Museum of Design." The photographer's name, if known, also should appear.

CH·21

CH Library Art History Slide Collection

Dates of Photographs: 1980s

Collection Origins

Cooper-Hewitt (CH) Museum staff assembled the collection in 1986 for use by faculty and students of the Master of Arts program at the Parsons School of Design. The images are used in presentations, slide shows, and seminars. Photographers represented include Ken Peters.

Physical Description

There are 9,000 color dye coupler slides.

Subjects

The photographs document the history of decorative arts and design, particularly those of 17th through 19th century Europe and 19th century United States. Some accessioned objects from the museum's collection also are shown. Objects documented date from the 6th to the 20th centuries and include architectural drawings, architectural interiors, birdcages, boxes, buttons, ceramics, drawings, enamelwork, furniture, glassware, graphic prints, industrial designs, interior designs, jewelry, lacquerware, lighting devices, metalwork, mosaics, musical instruments, paintings, pottery, silver pieces, tiles, timepieces, toys, wallcoverings, and woodwork.

Arranged: By medium of the illustrated object, then by country of origin, century, and artist.

Captioned: With artist, date, dimensions, location, and name of object or building.

Finding Aid: No, although there is an authority file which lists the sources of the images.

Restrictions: Available to Cooper-Hewitt staff and Parsons School of Design faculty only.

CH·22

CH Library Picture Collection

Dates of Photographs: 1890s–Present

Collection Origins

Eleanor (Nelly) and Sarah (Sally) Hewitt, who with their sister Amelia founded the Cooper Union Museum, began assembling this collection in 1896 as a series of graphic illustration albums modeled on the browsing albums of the Musée des Arts Décoratifs in Paris. The Hewitts wanted the albums to serve as a source of inspiration for practicing architects, artists, and designers. The images were primarily drawings; graphic prints such as engravings, etchings, and lithographs; photomechanicals; and photographs, many taken from books and magazines. The albums were later taken apart and the illustrations were filed individually in the collection. Cooper Union and later Cooper-Hewitt Library staff continued to add to the collection.

Physical Description

There are 100,000 photographs including albumen photoprints, collodion gelatin photoprints (POP), color dye coupler photoprints, dye diffusion transfer photoprints, and silver gelatin photoprints. Other materials (approximately 200,000 items) include drawings; graphic prints, such as engravings, etchings, and lithographs; magazine clippings; newspaper clippings; and photomechanicals.

Subjects

The photographs reproduce international architecture, design, and objects from the decorative and fine arts, dating from the Middle Ages to the present, with an emphasis on 17th to 20th century Europe and 19th century United States.

Objects shown include aqueducts and dams, arms and armor, baskets, Bibles, birdcages, bookbindings, boxes, bridges, buttons, calvaries and shrines, camera equipment, costumes, desk accessories, dolls, embroideries, enameled items, Fabergé objects, flooring, folding fans, folk art, games, glassware, globes, glyptics (engraved precious stones), goldwork, graphic prints (such as advertisements), handcrafts, hardware, heating appliances, heraldic emblems, icons, inlaid woodwork, jewelry, kites, lace, lacquer work, leatherwork, lighting devices, machinery, maps, marble items, masks, masonry, medallions and plaques, metalwork, miniatures, mosaics, musical instruments, needlework, numismatics, office equipment, paper handcrafts, paperweights, plastic items, portraits, puppets, religious furnishings, reliquaries, ribbons and bows, robots, rugs, scientific instruments, ships and boats, signs and signboards, silhouettes, silverwork, smoking accessories, snuff boxes and scrapers, spinning wheels, stencil work, street furniture, subways, tapestries, tents, textiles, toilet accessories, tools, totem poles, toys, travel accessories, trophies, urns, vases, wall hangings, wallpapers, wax objects, weathervanes, and window displays.

Motifs documented include angels, animals, birds, cigar store figures, circuses, cupids and cherubs, fish, flowers, food, fruit, gardens, gods and goddesses, insects, Madonnas, mummies, parades, patterns, plants, pyrotechnics, reptiles, saints, sea life, shells, symbols, tattoos, trees, vegetables, and wine.

Thematic topics illustrated include allegorical works, amusements, astrology, astronomy, celebrations, ceremonies, *commedia dell'arte,* communications, countries, dance, decoration and ornament, design, display, Easter, fantastic art, farming, history, house and home, movement and locomotion, mythology, occupations, religion, restoration, space, street scenes, time, transportation, and zoos.

There are portraits of artists and artisans, barbers, blacksmiths, civil servants, cowboys, peddlers, printers and newsboys, and shepherds. There are also images showing workers involved in the clothing industry, the construction industry, deep-sea diving, farming, fishing, the food industry, glassmaking, handcrafts, medicine, and mining, including women laborers. Images of architecture include aerial views of buildings, exterior decoration and details, interior decoration, and landscaping for commercial, domestic, educational, factory, government, military, recreational, and religious structures worldwide.

Arranged: In two series by size. 1) Images measuring 8″ × 10″ or smaller. 2) Oversize images. Then alphabetically by the categories listed in the *Subjects* section, then by numerous sub-categories.

Captioned: With subject heading.

Finding Aid: A "Picture Library Index," which is a classified and partially cross-referenced list of approximately 170 subject headings and numerous sub-categories used in filing the images, adapted from the picture collection authority file at the Musée des Arts Décoratifs in Paris.

Restrictions: Available by appointment only. Photographic reproduction of some items is permitted.

CH·23

CH Library Vertical File Collection

Dates of Photographs: 1890s–Present

Collection Origins

Cooper Union Museum and Cooper-Hewitt Museum library staff assembled the collection with clippings from publications such as magazines and newspapers and photographs received from various donors.

Physical Description

There are 500 silver gelatin photoprints. Other materials include exhibit catalogs, magazine clippings, newspaper clippings, and pamphlets.

Subjects

The photographs document architecture and commercial, decorative, and fine arts from prehistory to the present.

Arranged: In two series by size, then alphabetically by subject headings.

Captioned: With subject heading; some also with their source including author of article, date, journal, page numbers, title, and volume and number.

Finding Aid: No.

Restrictions: Available by appointment only.

CH·24

CH Dreyfuss Study Center Mabel Thérèse Bonney Collection

Dates of Photographs: 1925–1940

Collection Origins

Photojournalist Mabel Thérèse Bonney (1897–1978) assembled the collection from photographs provided by news agencies, photographers, and stock photographic vendors, as well as images she took herself, to document design in Paris between 1925 and 1940. Born in California, Bonney went to France in 1919 as head of the first international student exchange program. There she became active in the international expatriate community. After receiving a doctorate from the Sorbonne, Bonney founded the first American illustrated press service in Europe. Most of the photographs in this collection were taken during this early period of Bonney's journalistic career.

As a columnist and correspondent for the French daily newspaper *Le Figaro* during the second World War, Bonney covered the Soviet invasion of Finland and the Nazi invasion of France. She also undertook missions for the United States during the war. Later in her career, she helped found the "Meals on Wheels" program and the UNESCO organization while also remaining active in Paris's art and literary communities. Bonney wrote many books including the following: 1) *Buying Antique and Modern Furniture in Paris.* New York: R.M. McBride, 1929. 2) *Europe's Children, 1939 to 1943.* New York: Plantin Press, 1943. 3) *War Comes to the People.* London: Pendock Press, 1944. Bonney also worked on an exhibition titled "To Whom the Wars Are Done."

Photographers and studios represented include Bernès, Marouteau & Cie Photographes; Mabel Thérèse Bonney; Georges Buffotot; Photo Industrielle; and Photo Rep.

Physical Description

There are 4,000 silver gelatin photoprints.

Subjects

The photographs document predominantly Parisian commercial displays, decorative arts, fine arts, landscaping, and interiors created by artists, designers, and design firms working in Paris between 1925 and 1940. Objects documented include ceramics, costume, display mannequins, furniture, gardens and terraces, glassware, graphic arts, jewelry, lighting devices, paintings, sculpture, silverwork, textiles, and window displays, many in the art deco or art moderne style. Artists and companies whose works are documented include J.J. Adnet, Bally, Pierre Barbe, Robert Bonfils, Leon Bouchet, Da Silva Bruhns, Chim, Jacques and Francis Challou, Pierre Chareau, Pierre Dumont, Jean Dunand, Michel Duran, Albert Fau, Raymond Fischer, Fjerdingstad, Georges Fouquet, Jean Fouquet, Alexis Jean Fournier, Paul Francis, Jean Michel Frank, Paul T. Frankl, Martita Garcia, Ghislain-Ringuet, Marcel Gimond, Maurice Glaize, Gouffe, Marcel Goupy, Madeleine Gras, Gaspard Grigori, Guerin Frères, Marcel Guillemard, Francis Guiraud, Hermés, Lucie Holt-Le-Son, Ile de France, Jacquemin Frères, Joubert & Petit, Francis Jourdain, Robert Lalemant, René Lalique, Jeanne Langrand, Henri Laurens, Charles Le Corbusier, Paul Le Masson, Rob Mallet-Stevens, Mercier Frères, Madame Myrbor, Navarre, Pierre Petit, Paul Poiret, Maurice Pré, Primavera, Edmond Regy, Lucie Renaudot, François Roques, Gustav Sandoz, Guy Schwob, Sèvres, Stele Evolution, Studium-Louvre, Sue et Mare, Tassinari and Chatel, Vuitton, and Wiener Werkstätte.

Arranged: Alphabetically by subject heading such as architecture, ceramics, or interior design; then by subheading such as commercial, domestic, educational, or fine arts; then by type of structure or object, for example, aquarium, factory, shop, or school.

Captioned: With assigned number; some also with narrative subject including information such as artist, artist's influences or intent, design information, location, medium, and patron.

Finding Aid: Three indexes containing caption information in notebooks. Two arranged by designer and then by assigned number; one arranged by assigned number.

Restrictions: Available for reference use by appointment only. No reproductions may be made.

CH·25

CH Dreyfuss Study Center Color in Design Collection

Dates of Photographs: 1915–1978

Collection Origins

Cooper-Hewitt museum staff assembled the collection—which documents the use of color in design, domestic, and industrial applications—from materials received from four sources: 1) Raymond K. Briden, 2) the Color Association of the United States, Inc., 3) *House and Garden* magazine, and 4) the Inter-Society Color Council.

Textile designer Raymond K. Briden assembled a portion of this collection while teaching at the Rhode Island School of Design and working in various New

England cotton mills from 1925 to 1960. Briden researched the history of the jacquard loom and other cotton-weaving equipment and techniques, as reflected in the correspondence, patterns, swatches, record books, textbooks, and workbooks he assembled.

The Color Association of the United States, Inc. (CAUS), formerly the Textile Color Card Association of the United States, was a nonprofit organization active from 1915 to 1975. Supported by a membership of dye houses and fashion manufacturers, CAUS was dedicated to keeping color identification constant by assigning numerical codes to colors, regardless of fashion industry names. CAUS's donation consists mainly of color cards for fashion and furnishings issued by the Association and other domestic and foreign companies. Note: The Briden material was integrated into the CAUS donation.

The non-profit Inter-Society Color Council (ISCC) was formed in 1932 to standardize and describe colors for its membership, which included architects, associations such as the American Philatelic Society, ceramic companies, food companies, interior designers, and paint and chemical companies. The ISCC portion of the collection deals with the National Bureau of Standards' Guest Worker Project, which identified the differences between the Swedish Natural Color System and the Munsell Color System created by the Munsell Color Company of Baltimore. ISCC Secretary Dorothy Nickerson donated the ISCC records to the Cooper-Hewitt.

The final component of the collection, donated by *House and Garden,* consists of records of home furnishing colors promoted on a special or yearly basis by the publication.

Photographers represented include A. Clavel, F. Lindenmeyer, and Georges Meyer. Studios represented include the following organizations: the American Society for Testing Materials, American Standard Association, British Colour Council, Commission Internationale d'Éclairage, Illuminating Engineering Society, National Bureau of Standards, Natural Color System, Nuances Classiques Syndicales, Optical Society of America, Societé des Nouveautes Textiles, Technical Association of the Pulp and Paper Industry, Textile Argus, Textiles Paris Echos, and Union des Syndicats. Other studios include A. Leimgruber and Company; Bale; Bartels, Dierichs and Company; Bilbille and Company; California Port of Call; Centurieres de St. Étienne; Ciba; Ente Moda Cartieda Colori; Fischer Frères; Florida Port of Call; *House and Garden* magazine; Jacques Isler and Company; J. Claude Frères et Cie; *Journal of the Optical Society;* Judkins and McCormick; Munsell Color Company of Baltimore; the National Silk Dyeing Company; U.S. Army; and the United Nations.

Physical Description

There are 2,500 photographs including color dye coupler slides and silver gelatin photoprints. The bulk of the collection consists of almost 1,700 color cards. Other materials include book manuscripts, color charts, color chips, color keys, correspondence, crayons, data sheets, drawings, dye samples, fabric swatches, illustrations from books, magazine clippings, newspaper clippings, notes on color promotions, publications, questionnaires, reports, sample books, scrapbooks, textile swatches, watercolor sketches, weaving patterns, and weavers' record books and workbooks. The Cooper-Hewitt Library contains a small reference library of books and reprints on color, which the museum received with the CAUS component of the collection.

Subjects

The photographs document color use in the fashion industry, primarily for women's clothing but also for accessories, carpets, children's clothing, dyes, gloves, handbags, house paint, interior decorating schemes, men's clothing, millinery, plastic floor coverings, ribbons, rugs, shoe leather, straw-hat braids, textiles, and thread. There are also illustrations of color use by colleges and universities for pennants and by the governments of United Nations member countries, such as Canada, Great Britain, Japan, and the United States, for flags and uniforms.

Arranged: In three series by creator. 1) Color Association of the United States (includes Raymond K. Briden materials). 2) Inter-Society Color Council. 3) *House and Garden* magazine.

Captioned: No.

Finding Aid: 1) Card index with two sections: a) cards filed by date of the color chart; b) cards filed by drawer number, listing contents of the file, date, and file drawer number of the item. 2) Shipping list of CAUS materials.

Restrictions: No access due to remote storage, lack of complete access guide, and physical condition.

CH·26

CH Dreyfuss Study Center Donald Deskey Collection

Dates of Photographs: 1920s–1930s

Collection Origins

American industrial and interior designer Donald Deskey (1894–1989) created these papers to document his life and work. An early practitioner of streamlined industrial design, Deskey studied at the Art Institute of Chicago, the Art Students League of New York City, L'École de la Grandechamière in Paris, the Mark Hopkins Art School in San Francisco, and the University of California at Berkeley. Known for his work on club, factory, home, hotel, office, and restaurant interiors, Deskey also designed machines such as printing presses, space heaters, and vending machines. In addition, Deskey pioneered modern furniture designs using aluminum, bakelite, chrome, glass, lacquer, plastic laminates, and tubular steel, as well as a high-pressure laminate called Weldtex, which he invented.

Deskey designed the interior of Radio City Music Hall in New York City in 1932 and the interior and furnishings of the R.H. Mandell House in Mount Kisco, New York, in collaboration with architect Edward Durrell Stone from 1933 to 1935. Director of both Donald Deskey Associates, founded in 1928, and Sculley, Deskey & Scott, Inc., Deskey also designed exhibitions for trade fairs and world's fairs including the New York World's Fair (1939–1940) and the Seattle World's Fair (1962). Deskey taught at Juniata College in Huntington, Pennsylvania, and at New York University, where he became the director of the industrial design department. He also wrote articles for the journal *London Studio*.

Physical Description

There are 3,000 silver gelatin photoprints. Other materials include blueprints, correspondence, lectures, newspaper clippings, notebooks, publications, reprints, speeches, and xerographic copies.

Subjects

The photographs document the design projects Donald Deskey completed during the 1920s and 1930s. Objects illustrated include bowling ball racks; boxes; furniture such as chairs, lamps, and tables; and machinery such as printing presses, space heaters, and vending machines. There are also images of apartments, clubs, factories, hotels, offices, restaurants, showrooms, trade shows, and world's fairs including the New York World's Fair (1939–1940) and the Seattle World's Fair (1962). Packaging and product designs illustrated include Aqua Velva after-shave, Bounty paper towels, Cheer laundry detergent, Crisco shortening, Gleem toothpaste, Jif peanut butter, Pampers disposable diapers, Prell shampoo, and Sanka coffee. Corporate clients whose products are illustrated include Beechnut Baby Foods, DuPont, Fuller Brush, Johnson & Johnson, Maidenform, Nestle's, Proctor and Gamble, Radio City Music Hall, and Union Carbide. Private clients whose apartments are illustrated include Mr. and Mrs. Adam Gimbel, Mrs. John D. Rockefeller, and William Rosenfeld Roxy.

Arranged: Alphabetically by client, then by type of project and type of interior, packaging, or product.

Captioned: No, although the folders are labeled.

Finding Aid: No.

Restrictions: Available for reference use only. No reproductions may be made without the written permission of the donor's heirs.

CH·27

CH Dreyfuss Study Center Henry Dreyfuss Collection

Dates of Photographs: 1926–1972

Collection Origins

Industrial designer Henry Dreyfuss (1904–1972) created the collection to document his career. After graduating from the Ethical Culture School in New York City in 1922, Dreyfuss apprenticed with theatrical designer Norman Bel Geddes, for whom he designed costumes, scenery, and stage sets. From 1923 until December 1927, Dreyfuss designed costumes, lighting, and scenery for the Strand Theatre. He then worked briefly for the William Fox Theatres, before leaving for a lengthy visit to Europe.

While in Europe, Dreyfuss received a job offer from R.H. Macy's department store in New York to improve the appearance of its products. Returning to America in 1928, Dreyfuss instead decided to start his own business. He opened a small New York industrial design office and began convincing American manufacturers of the need for inexpensive, low-maintenance, and safe products whose simplified appearance emphasized their function. Dreyfuss designed building interiors, consumer and household products, farm and industrial products, public transportation vehicles, and theatrical costumes and sets. In the 1940s, he opened a second office in Pasadena, California, and in 1952 he formed Henry Dreyfuss & Associates with partners Julian Everett, Robert Hose, and William Purcell.

The photographs appear in the following publications, all written by Dreyfuss: 1) *Designing for People.* New York: Simon and Schuster, 1955. 2) *Measure of Man: Human Factors in Design.* New York: Whitney Library of Design, 1959. 3) *Symbol Sourcebook: An Authoritative Guide to International Graphic Symbols.* New York: McGraw-Hill, 1972. Photographs also appear in a number of small presentation books published by Henry Dreyfuss and Associates for corporate clients, including "Coast to Coast Train," "New York World's Fair, 1939," and "United States Peace Corps." The collection was given to the Cooper-Hewitt Museum in 1972 by Henry Dreyfuss. Additional materials, part of a small accession deeded by Dreyfuss in 1962, were given to the museum by the University of California at Los Angeles in 1973.

Physical Description

There are 6,300 photographs including color dye coupler slides and silver gelatin photonegatives and photoprints. Other materials include advertisements, awards, blueprints, books, correspondence, drawings, exhibit captions, exhibit panels, fabric samples, manuscripts, microfilm, newspaper clippings, notes, object samples, publications, press kits, reprints, and sketches.

Subjects

The photographs document Henry Dreyfuss's industrial- and interior-design work between 1926 and 1972. Products and product models shown, occasionally in before-and-after shots, include Bell Laboratories telephones; Capstan glass storage containers; Chrysler automobiles; Cities Service Petroleum gas stations; Crane bathroom fixtures; General Electric refrigerators; Hoover irons, toasters, and vacuum cleaners; Mosler safes; Radio Corporation of America (RCA) air conditioners, phonographs, radios, stoves, and television sets; Seth Thomas clocks and watches; and Singer sewing machines. Farm and industrial machinery illustrated includes American Machine & Foundry Company (AMF) bread-making, button-stitching, and cigarette-manufacturing machines, bowling lane equipment, and fast-food restaurant fixtures; Byron Jackson oil-well tools; John Deere tractors; Mergenthaler linotype machines; National Supply oil-well equipment; and Warner and Swasey turret lathes.

Interior-design work documented includes commercial buildings and models of commercial buildings such as cafes, hotels, offices, and restaurants; private dwellings such as apartments and houses; and transportation vehicles such as airplanes, oceanliners, and trains. Building interiors illustrated include rooms Dreyfuss designed for the Bankers Trust Company, the Hotels Statler Company, and the Park Lane and Plaza Hotels of New York City. There are photographic reproductions of Dreyfuss's theatrical designs including the sets for such stage productions as *An Affair of State* (1930), *The Gang's All Here* (1931), *A Midsummer Night's Dream* (1925), *Pagan Lady* (1930), and *Strike Me Pink* (1933); photographs of the RKO Denver Theater made in 1931; and images of costume and lighting designs. There are photographic reproductions of graphic symbols published in Dreyfuss's *Symbol Sourcebook*; photographic portraits of Henry Dreyfuss; and photographs of Dreyfuss's first industrial design office; as well as some installation photographs of a Dreyfuss retrospective exhibit held in 1971 at Hall's Exhibition Gallery, Kansas City, Missouri.

Arranged: In 20 series by subject, format, or medium, for example theater designs or oversized symbols.

Captioned: No.

Finding Aid: A 71-page guide titled "Industrial Design Archive: Henry Dreyfuss (1904–1972)," which also contains a bibliography, historical notes, a folder list, and an appendix listing Dreyfuss's clients.

Restrictions: Available by appointment only.

CH·28

CH Dreyfuss Study Center Ladislav Sutnar Collection

Dates of Photographs: 1920s–1976

Collection Origins

Czechoslovakian designer Ladislav Sutnar (1897–1976) created the collection. Sutnar, who studied at the Technical University and Academy of Applied Arts in Prague, served as a professor (1923–1932) and trustee (1932–1939) at the State School of Graphic Arts. In

1939, while working as head designer for the Czech Pavilion at the New York World's Fair, Sutnar decided to remain in the United States. Working as director of Sweet's Catalogue Services, Sutnar soon became designer of corporate image projects for McGraw-Hill and Printex. He also served as a consultant for many other firms and wrote several books on design, including the following: 1) *Design for Point of Sale*. New York: Pellegrini & Cudahy, 1952. 2) *Package Design: The Force of Visual Selling*. New York: Arts, Inc., 1953. 3) *Visual Design in Action: Principles, Purposes*. New York: Hastings House, 1961.

Physical Description

There are 5,000 photographs including silver gelatin photonegatives and photoprints. Other materials include albums, books, correspondence, drawings, exhibit panels, newspaper clippings, reprints, and scrapbooks.

Subjects

The photographs document 20th century industrial design in Czechoslovakia, Europe, and the United States, with an emphasis on the work of Ladislav Sutnar. Industrial design work documented includes exhibit, graphic, package, and product design, produced for corporations such as McGraw-Hill and Sweet's Catalogue Services. There is also an image of an International Book Design exhibit.

Arranged: By format, then by project.

Captioned: No.

Finding Aid: A guide.

Restrictions: Available by appointment only.

CH

Department of Photographic Services

Department of Photographic Services
Cooper-Hewitt Museum, the Smithsonian Institution's National
  Museum of Design
2 East 91st Street
New York, New York 10128-9990
(212) 860-6868
Hours: Not open to the public.

Scope of the Collections

There are three photographic collections with approximately 32,050 images.

Focus of the Collections

The photographs document the museum's holdings of international decorative arts objects, which date from prehistory to the present and include ceramics, decorative objects, drawings, furniture, glassware, graphic prints, metalwork, textiles, wallcoverings, and woodwork. The photographs also document the history of the Cooper Union Museum, the predecessor of the Cooper-Hewitt, including images of early buildings, major donors, and the founders.

Photographic Processes and Formats Represented

There are silver gelatin photonegatives and photoprints.

Other Materials Represented

None.

Access and Usage Policies

The photograph collections are not accessible to the public. However, the Department handles all requests for photographic services, materials and rights of Cooper-Hewitt-owned objects in connection with scholarly and trade publication use.

Publication Policies

Researchers must obtain permission from the Cooper-Hewitt Museum to reproduce a photograph and may also have to obtain permission from the copyright holder, which is not necessarily the Smithsonian Institution. Requests for information on publication policies, credits and captions, permissions, fees, and other matters associated with trade or scholarly publication of Cooper-Hewitt material should be addressed to this department.

CH·29

CH Photographic Services Historical Photograph Collection

Dates of Photographs: 1895–1970s

Collection Origins

Cooper Union and Cooper-Hewitt staff assembled this collection from a variety of sources to document the museum's holdings for collections management, publication, and research purposes. Relatives of Peter Cooper and the Hewitt family and early employees of the Cooper Union Museum took many of the photographs. The photographs have appeared in Russell Lynes's catalog of the collections of the Cooper-Hewitt Museum: *More Than Meets the Eye: The History and Collections of the Cooper-Hewitt Museum*. New York: Cooper-Hewitt Museum, 1981.

Physical Description

There are 1,050 photographs including silver gelatin photonegatives and photoprints.

Subjects

The photographs document the founders, major donors, operations, and origins of the Cooper Union Museum, the predecessor to the Cooper-Hewitt Museum. People portrayed include Andrew Carnegie and his family, Peter Cooper and his family, and Amelia (Amy), Eleanor (Nelly), and Sarah (Sally) Hewitt. Buildings documented include the Carnegie Mansion and the Cooper Union's library, museum (including early exhibits), and school.

Arranged: By object's accession number, photograph's negative number, or the name and page of the publication in which the image appears.

Captioned: With object's accession number, photograph's negative number, or the full citation of the publication for which the image was created.

Finding Aid: No.

Restrictions: Available by appointment only.

CH·30

CH Photographic Services Museum Record Photonegative Collection

Dates of Photographs: 1930s–Present

Collection Origins

Cooper Union and Cooper-Hewitt (CH) staff created the collection to provide an ongoing record of the museum's holdings for staff use. Photographers represented include Almonte, Bernhardt, George D. Cowdery, Scott Hyde, John Parnell, Kenneth Pelka, Thomas Rose, and Carmel Wilson.

Physical Description

There are 22,000 silver gelatin photonegatives.

Subjects

The photographs document the artifactual holdings of the Cooper-Hewitt Museum. The objects, which date from prehistory to the 20th century, are mainly from 15th through 20th century Asia, Europe, and the United States. Objects shown include decorative objects, drawings, furniture, glassware, graphic prints, jewelry, metalwork, textiles, wallcoverings, and woodwork.

Arranged: By object's accession number.

Captioned: With object's accession number.

Finding Aid: A card index to part of the collection in three parts. 1) By type of object. 2) By object's accession number. 3) By photographer.

Restrictions: Available to Smithsonian Institution staff only. Reproductions may be purchased for study or publication (subject to restrictions) from the CH Department of Photographic Services.

CH·31

CH Photographic Services Museum Record Photoprint Collection

Dates of Photographs: 1930s–Present

Collection Origins

The staff of the Cooper-Hewitt (CH) Museum Department of Photographic Services created the collection to provide an ongoing photographic record of most of the museum's holdings.

Physical Description

There are 9,000 silver gelatin photoprints.

Subjects

The photographs document the accessioned objects of the CH Departments of Decorative Arts, Drawings and Prints, Textiles, and Wallcoverings, and the holdings of the CH Library. The objects illustrated date from prehistory to the present and are international in scope, with a special emphasis on work from Asia, Europe, and the United States. Objects shown include decorative items, drawings, furniture, glassware, graphic prints, jewelry, metalwork, textiles, wallcoverings, and woodwork.

Arranged: By object's accession number.

Captioned: No.

Finding Aid: No.

Restrictions: Not available to the public. Copies of prints can be purchased for study or publication (subject to restrictions).

CH

Public Information Office

Public Information Office
Cooper-Hewitt Museum, the Smithsonian Institution's National
*   Museum of Design*
2 East 91st Street
New York, New York 10128-9990
Public Information Officer
(212) 860-6894
Hours: Monday–Friday, 9:00 a.m.–5:00 p.m.

Scope of the Collection

There are three photographic collections with approximately 8,300 images.

Focus of the Collections

The photographs document exhibits and other events, such as classes, demonstrations, lectures, performances, and programs, held at the Cooper-Hewitt Museum and its predecessor, the Cooper Union, from the 1950s to the present. Exhibit photographs include images of individual objects such as ceramics, drawings, glassware, graphic prints, metalwork, and textiles. There are also images of buildings and people related to the museum.

Photographic Processes and Formats Represented

There are color dye coupler slides and silver gelatin photonegatives and photoprints.

Other Materials Represented

The office also contains brochures, correspondence, exhibit catalogs, labels, notes, press releases, and programs.

Access and Usage Policies

The photograph collections are open by appointment to Smithsonian Institution employees, who should call or write to the office in advance and describe their research topic, the type of material that interests them, and their research aim. All inquiries concerning photographic rights in connection with scholarly or trade use should be addressed to the Department of Photographic Services, Cooper-Hewitt Museum, 2 East 91st Street, New York, New York, 10128-9990.

Publication Policies

Researchers must obtain permission from the Cooper-Hewitt Museum to reproduce a photograph and may also have to obtain permission from the copyright holder, which is not necessarily the Smithsonian Institution. The preferred credit line is "Courtesy of the Public Information Office, Cooper-Hewitt Museum, the Smithsonian Institution's National Museum of Design."

CH·32

CH Public Information Office Exhibits Collection

Dates of Photographs: 1940s–Present

Collection Origins

Cooper-Hewitt Museum staff members, including Public Information officers, created the collection to document the exhibits and public events of the Cooper-Hewitt Museum. Photographers represented include Scott Hyde and Carmel Wilson. Photographs have appeared in the following books: 1) Russell Lynes. *More Than Meets the Eye: The History and Collections of the Cooper-Hewitt Museum.* New York: Cooper-Hewitt Museum, 1981. 2) Wim de Wit, ed. *The Amsterdam School: Dutch Expressionist Architecture, 1915–1930.* New York and Cambridge, Massachusetts: Cooper-Hewitt Museum and Massachusetts Institute of Technology Press, 1983.

Physical Description

There are 4,000 photographs including color dye coupler slides and silver gelatin photonegatives and photoprints (some contact prints). Other materials include correspondence, exhibit catalogs, labels, notes, and programs.

Subjects

The photographs document the exhibit installations and other events held at the Cooper Union Museum from the 1950s to 1976 and at the Cooper-Hewitt Museum from 1976 to the present. Events documented include classes, performances, and programs. Exhibit images show entire installations, individual objects, labels, and museum shop displays. Artifacts shown, dating from prehistory to the present and originating in Asia, Europe, and the United States, include architecture, drawings, embroidery, glassware, graphic prints, jewelry, metalwork, ornaments, patent models, postcards, pottery, and textiles.

Arranged: In two series. 1) Materials prior to 1976, unarranged. 2) Materials from 1976 to the present, chronologically by exhibit or program.

Captioned: With credit line; date and name of the event or exhibit; and object's accession number, creator, date, description, donor, and place of origin.

Finding Aid: No, although there is a master list of CH exhibits held since 1976.

Restrictions: Available by appointment to Smithsonian Institution employees only.

CH·33

CH Public Information Office Photograph Collection

Dates of Photographs: 1895–Present

Collection Origins

Cooper-Hewitt (CH) Public Information Office staff assembled the collection to document activities and projects of the museum.

Physical Description

There are 4,000 photographs including color dye coupler slides and silver gelatin photonegatives and photoprints.

Subjects

The photographs document the Carnegie Mansion from 1895 to the present, the CH Museum from 1976 to the present, and the Cooper Union Museum, the CH's predecessor, from 1895 to 1976. The photographs show CH and Cooper Union buildings, exhibits, founders, staff (such as former CH director Lisa Taylor), and visitors. Among the people portrayed are the the Peter Cooper family and the Hewitt family including Eleanor (Nelly) and Sarah (Sally) Hewitt.

Arranged: In three series. 1) Press photographs of former CH director Lisa Taylor. 2) Publication photographs. 3) Historical photographs.

Captioned: No.

Finding Aid: No.

Restrictions: Available by appointment to Smithsonian Institution employees only.

CH·34

CH Public Information Office Press Kit Collection

Dates of Photographs: 1976–Present

Collection Origins

Cooper-Hewitt (CH) Public Information staff created the collection to publicize exhibits, events, and programs at the CH Museum. The Public Information Office keeps copies of each press kit, complete with photographs and cut-lines, as a permanent record of the museum's activities.

Physical Description

There are 300 silver gelatin copy photoprints. Other materials include brochures and press releases.

Subjects

The photographs document the events and exhibits at the CH Museum from 1976 to the present. Events documented include classes, demonstrations, lectures, openings of exhibits, and seminars. Topics of events shown include architecture, decorative arts, design, and the fine arts. Exhibits documented feature drawings, embroidery, glassware, graphic prints, lighting devices including Tiffany lamps, magazine covers, metalwork, ornaments, packages, patterns in contemporary art, Plains Indian art, postcards, pottery, prints, products, puppets, and weaving. There are also images of buildings, landscaping, and subways.

Arranged: Chronologically by exhibit or event.

Captioned: With subject.

Finding Aid: No, although there is a master list of CH exhibits held since 1976.

Restrictions: Available by appointment to scholarly researchers only.

CH

Publications Office

Publications Office
Cooper-Hewitt Museum, the Smithsonian Institution's National
  Museum of Design
2 East 91st Street
New York, New York 10128-9990
(212) 860-6908
Hours: No access.

Scope of the Collection	There is one photographic collection with 3,000 photographs.
Focus of the Collection	The photographs are used to illustrate Cooper-Hewitt (CH) publications that document the history of the decorative and fine arts. The collection includes images of architecture, ceramics, gardens, glassware, jewelry, textiles, and theatrical designs, in CH collections and other museums and private collections around the world.
Photographic Processes and Formats Represented	There are color dye coupler photoprints and silver gelatin photoprints, which are found with pre-publication versions of books, called designer's production mechanicals.
Other Materials Represented	The office mechanicals also contain graphics and photomechanical prints.
Access and Usage Policies	No access. All inquiries concerning photographic rights in connection with scholarly or trade use should be addressed to the Department of Photographic Services, Cooper-Hewitt Museum, 2 East 91st Street, New York, New York, 10128-9990.
Publication Policies	Researchers must obtain permission from the Cooper-Hewitt Museum to reproduce a photograph and may also have to obtain permission from the copyright holder, which is not necessarily the Smithsonian Institution.

CH·35

CH Editor's Office Publication Mechanicals Collection

Dates of Photographs: 1976–Present

Collection Origins

The Cooper-Hewitt (CH) Editor's Office staff created the collection during the production of Cooper-Hewitt Museum publications. The photographs came from Cooper-Hewitt Museum collections, other Smithsonian Institution collections, and outside repositories.

Physical Description

There are 3,000 photographs including color dye coupler photoprints and silver gelatin photoprints. The photographs are part of designer's production mechanicals, which are pre-publication versions of books. Other materials, also with the mechanicals, include graphic and photomechanical prints.

Subjects

The photographs were used as illustrations in CH publications and document decorative arts from prehistory to the present. Objects depicted include ceramics, jewelry, pottery, shopping bags, textiles, tiles, and written documents. There are also images of architecture, gardens, and theatrical designs. Some of the photographs illustrate topics such as the history of reading and writing and the impact of human creativity on the environment.

Arranged: By book series, then by publication title.

Captioned: No.

Finding Aid: No.

Restrictions: No access.

CH

Registrar's Office

Registrar's Office
Cooper-Hewitt Museum, the Smithsonian Institution's National
  Museum of Design
2 East 91st Street
New York, New York 10128-9990
(212) 860-6910
Hours: By appointment

Scope of the Collection

There is one photographic collection with approximately 4,200 photographs.

Focus of the Collection

The photographs document decorative art objects that are loans made from or to the Cooper-Hewitt (CH) Museum, new accessions, and potential gifts to the Museum.

Photographic Processes and Formats Represented

There are dye diffusion transfer photoprints and silver gelatin photoprints.

Other Materials Represented

The collection also contains accession records, correspondence, loan records, newspaper clippings, and xerographic copies.

Access and Usage Policies

The photograph collection is open by appointment only. Researchers should call or write the office in advance and describe their research topic, the type of material that interests them, and their research aim. Some materials on accessions and incoming loans are restricted due to their confidential nature.

Publication Policies

No photographic or xerographic copies may be made. However, images of CH objects can be obtained from the CH Department of Photographic Services, Cooper-Hewitt Museum, 2 East 91st Street, New York, New York, 10128-9990, (212) 860-6868.

CH·36

CH Registrar's Files

Dates of Photographs: 1930s–Present

Collection Origins

The Cooper-Hewitt (CH) Registrar's Office staff and its predecessor office at the Cooper Union Museum (1897–1965) assembled the collection to document the museum's object holdings and loans for administrative purposes. Photographers represented include donors, potential donors, and gallery owners.

Physical Description

There are 4,200 photographs including dye diffusion transfer photoprints and silver gelatin photoprints. Other materials include accession records, correspondence, loan records, newspaper clippings, and xerographic copies. Note: According to the registrar, these are not publication-quality photographs.

Subjects

The photographs record loans to and from the CH, newly accessioned objects in CH holdings (approximately 600 per year), and potential gifts to CH departments. Objects depicted include birdcages, boxes, ceramics, clocks, decorative objects, drawings, furniture, glassware, graphic prints, jewelry, metalwork, textiles, toys such as puppets, wallpaper, and woodwork.

Arranged: In two series. 1) Loans (3,500 images), in two subseries: a) photographs attached to condition reports that document incoming loans (confidential records) and b) photographs that document outgoing loans. 2) Accessions records (700 images), in two subseries: a) correspondence with donors (confidential) and b) catalog cards.

Captioned: No.

Finding Aid: No.

Restrictions: Available by appointment only. No reproductions may be made.

FG

FREER GALLERY OF ART

Milo C. Beach, Director

The legacy of Detroit businessman and art collector Charles Lang Freer (1856–1919), the Smithsonian Institution's Freer Gallery of Art (FGA) contains more than 26,000 Asian and late-19th century American art works. The museum's holdings include Chinese bronzes, calligraphy, ceramics, jades, lacquer, paintings, and stone sculptures; Indian miniature paintings and sculptures; Japanese ceramics, graphic prints, lacquerware, paintings, and sculptures; Korean ceramics; Persian glass, metalwork, and miniatures; and American drawings, graphic prints, and paintings.

In 1906 Freer donated the core of the Gallery's holdings, as well as funds for the construction of the museum (designed by Charles Adams Platt) and an endowment for research and future purchases. A founder of the American Car & Foundry Company, Freer began purchasing Japanese objects in 1887 and first visited Asia in 1895. After the turn of the century he increasingly turned his attention to acquiring east Asian objects.

Influenced by his associations with such scholars and aesthetes as Ernest Fenollosa, Tomitarō Hara, Baron Takashi Masuda, and James Abbott McNeill Whistler, Freer acquired over 9,000 art objects during his lifetime. Freer began collecting art works by Whistler in the 1880s, and the two met and became friends in 1890. Freer came to own nearly 1,300 works by Whistler, including drawings, graphic prints, paintings, and the Peacock Room, originally a dining room in the London mansion of Frederick R. Leyland, decorated by Whistler. After Freer's retirement at age 44, he devoted his life to his art collections and travel.

Since Freer's death in 1919, when the bulk of his art works was moved to Washington, D.C., the museum's holdings have nearly tripled through gifts and purchases. Freer's will prohibits the FGA from lending objects in its permanent collection or borrowing art works for exhibits; however, the museum maintains a growing study collection of related materials, which is used for educational purposes and laboratory analysis.

Opened to the public in 1923, the FGA also maintains a library containing 55,000 volumes of monographs and serials, 800 rare books, a 53,000-image slide collection, and an archives containing manuscript collections, personal papers, and expeditionary records of several archaeologists, art historians, and scholars of Asia and the Near East. The FGA conducts an annual series of slide lectures on Asian art, co-sponsors the scholarly journal *Ars Orientalis*, and publishes *Occasional Papers, Oriental Studies*, and exhibit and research catalogs.

The FGA shares its administration, staff, and research facilities with the Arthur M. Sackler Gallery (ASG), another Smithsonian museum specializing in Asian art. (ASG collections are described elsewhere in this volume.) The FGA contains 69 photographic collections with nearly 384,100 images documenting art objects, museum activities, and the Asian world. Many of the collections were created jointly by Freer and Sackler staff.

FG

Freer Gallery of Art and Arthur M. Sackler Gallery Archives

Freer Gallery of Art and Arthur M. Sackler Gallery Archives
Freer Gallery of Art and Arthur M. Sackler Gallery
Smithsonian Institution
Washington, D.C. 20560
Lily Kecskes, Head Librarian
Colleen Hennessey, Archivist
(202) 357-2091
Hours: Monday–Friday, 10 a.m.–5 p.m.

Scope of the Collections

There are 57 photographic collections with approximately 210,900 images in the Archives.

Focus of the Collections

The photographs document Asian architecture, art, and artifacts, including pieces from the holdings of the Freer Gallery of Art and the Arthur M. Sackler Gallery, as well as other museums and private collectors. There are also images of architecture and objects shown in their original locations throughout Asia. Most of the images depict architecture, calligraphy, ceramics, graphic prints, paintings, and sculptures.

Subjects extensively documented include Chinese archaeology, ceramics, and paintings; Indian folk art; and religious architecture including Buddhist temples and Islamic mosques. There are many images of daily life in 20th century Asia, especially in China, India, Japan, and Persia (now Iran), taken by travelers and participants in expeditions. The collections also contain photographs of the Freer and Sackler buildings, events, staff, and visitors, as well as photographic portraits of Charles Lang Freer and James Abbott McNeill Whistler. There are also photographs of paintings by Whistler and other Western artists.

Photographic Processes and Formats Represented

There are albumen photoprints (some cabinet cards, cartes-de-visite, and stereographs); collodion gelatin cartes-de-visite and photoprints (POP); collodion wet plate lantern slides and photonegatives; color dye coupler photonegatives, photoprints, phototransparencies, and slides; color screen plate lantern slides and phototransparencies (Autochromes); cyanotypes; dye transfer photonegatives and photoprints; platinum photoprints; silver gelatin dry plate lantern slides and photonegatives; and silver gelatin photonegatives (some on nitrate), photoprints (some cartes-de-visite and stereographs), phototransparencies, and slides.

Other Materials Represented

The Archives also contains announcements, architectural drawings and plans, articles, awards, bibliographies, book reviews, books, cards, ceramics, charts, correspondence, diagrams, diaries, drawings, genealogies, ink rubbings, inventories, journals, lectures, ledger books, manuscripts, maps, newspaper clippings, notebooks, notes, pamphlets, papier-mâché copies of architectural details (squeezes), photograph albums, photomechanicals, postcards, registers, reports, research files, scrapbooks, subject files, tracings, typescripts, and xerographic copies.

Access and Usage Policies

Most collections are open to the public by appointment. Researchers should call or write in advance and describe their research topic, the type of material that interests them, and their research aim. Some collections are accompanied by finding aids. Certain materials may be restricted due to copyright status or preservation conditions. There is a charge for photographic and xerographic copies of unrestricted photographs, based on rates set by the Freer Gallery of Art and Arthur M. Sackler Gallery.

Publication Policies

Requests to reproduce items from the collections must be made in writing, indicating how the reproduction will be used. Researchers must also obtain permission from the holder of the original copyright, which is not necessarily the Smithsonian Institution. The credit line should list the collection name, photographer, negative number, and "Courtesy of the Freer Gallery of Art and Arthur M. Sackler Gallery Archives, Smithsonian Institution."

Copies of photographs may be ordered by contacting Laveta Emory, Supervisor, Mail Order Department, Gallery Shop, FGA, Smithsonian Institution, Washington, D.C., 20560. Those wishing to publish an image must complete a Permission Request Form, obtained from the Rights and Reproductions Office, FGA, Smithsonian Institution, Washington, D.C., 20560, (202) 786-2088. All permissions to publish are for one-time use, only for the publication specified, and may not be sold or transferred. A copy of the publication must be sent gratis to the FGA library. No FGA images may be cropped, overprinted with type, or altered in any way without prior written approval from the Gallery.

FG·1

"Art Treasures from Japan" Photograph Album

Dates of Photographs: Circa 1963–1965

Collection Origins

Freer Gallery of Art (FGA) staff created the collection to document an exhibit titled "Art Treasures from Japan," which traveled in the United States in 1965 and 1966. The exhibit was sponsored by the Detroit Institute of Arts, the Japanese National Commission for the Protection of Cultural Properties, the Los Angeles County Museum of Art, the Philadelphia Museum of Art, and the Royal Ontario Museum.

Writer and FGA director Harold P. Stern (1922–1977) served as a member of the Canadian-U.S. committee of specialists that worked on the exhibit. Stern, who received a Ph.D. in Japanese Studies from the University of Michigan, began working at the FGA in 1949, while still a graduate student. In 1950 he joined the museum's curatorial staff. He also served as an advisor on a 1953 Japanese government loan exhibit and a 1957–1958 Korean government loan exhibit. Stern wrote and lectured on Korean imperial treasures, Tokugawa painting, and *ukiyo-e* paintings and woodblock prints. Stern became director of the FGA in 1971 and served until his death in 1977.

Photographs from this collection were used in the exhibit catalog: *Art Treasures from Japan.* Tokyo: Kodansha International, 1965.

Physical Description

There are 165 silver gelatin photoprints.

Subjects

The photographs document Japanese artifacts, dating from prehistory to the 20th century, included in the exhibit "Art Treasures from Japan." Japanese artists whose work is reproduced include Ogata Kōrin, Momoda Ryūei, Sesshū, and Hasegawa Tōhaku. Objects documented include albums, armor, bronze mirrors and vases, calligraphy, fan holders, folding fans, graphic prints, lacquerware, lanterns, metalwork, narrative paintings, screens (such as Momoyama-period golden screens), scrolls, swords, textiles, and *tsubas* (sword guards).

Art objects reproduced include parodies of contemporary society such as animal cartoons; scenes of court life; *ukiyo-e* prints of courtesans; and views of the natural world such as bamboo, landscapes, and monkeys.

Buddhist religious figures, objects, and scenes reproduced include *bosatsu* (Buddhist saints), the *Butsu Nehan* (death of Buddha), the *Jigoku Zōshi* (Hell Scrolls), and Zen priests, as well as *sutra* illustrations. There are also reproductions of Japanese narrative picture scrolls such as the *Eshi no Shoshi* (the story of a painter), the *Heiji Monogatari Emaki* (the story of the Heiji clan), and the *Ippen Shōnin Eden* (the story of the Buddhist preacher Ippen).

Arranged: By assigned number, in the order objects appear in the exhibit catalog.

Captioned: No.

Finding Aid: No.

Restrictions: Available by appointment only.

FG·2

"Art Treasures of Turkey" Photographs

Dates of Photographs: 1966

Collection Origins

Freer Gallery of Art (FGA) staff created the collection to document an exhibit of art from Turkey held at the National Gallery of Art in 1966 and circulated by the Smithsonian through 1968. Richard Ettinghausen (1906–1979), then head curator of Near Eastern art at the Freer, served on the exhibit's executive committee, selected the Islamic art objects, and wrote part of the exhibit catalog. Ettinghausen, who received a doctorate in Islamic history and art history from the University of Frankfurt, was a research associate at the American Institute of Persian Art and Archaeology from 1934 to 1937. He taught at New York University (1937–1938) and the University of Michigan (1938–1944) before joining the FGA in 1944, where he later served as head curator of Near Eastern art (1961–1967).

The photographs appeared in the following exhibit catalog: *Art Treasures of Turkey.* Washington, D.C.: Smithsonian Institution Press, 1966.

Physical Description

There are 425 photographs including silver gelatin photonegatives and photoprints.

Subjects

The photographs document artifacts from Turkey, dating from 6000 B.C. through the 18th century, that appeared in the exhibit "Art Treasures of Turkey." Objects shown include armor, ceramics, clothing, decorative items, Korans, manuscripts (in Arabic and Persian), a map, ornaments, paintings (such as royal portraits), porcelain objects (primarily from China), rugs, sculptures, and weapons.

Arranged: By catalog number.

Captioned: Photonegatives with catalog number; photoprints with catalog number and description.

Finding Aid: No.

Restrictions: Available by appointment only.

FG·3

Esin Atil Photographs

Dates of Photographs: 1979–1981

Collection Origins

Freer Gallery of Art (FGA) curator and writer Esin Atil (1938–) created the collection in preparation for a 1981 exhibit titled "Renaissance of Islam: Art of the Mamluks." Circulated by the Smithsonian Institution Traveling Exhibition Service (SITES), the exhibit was shown at the Smithsonian's National Museum of Natural History before traveling to six other U.S. museums. The exhibit included objects from institutional and private collections in Canada, Egypt, England, France, Ireland, Syria, and the United States. Photographic murals depicting objects from FGA holdings also were displayed.

Atil, who received a Ph.D. from the University of Michigan in 1969, worked as a research librarian in New York City (1961–1966) and as a curator at Queens College of the City University of New York (1963–1966). She joined the FGA in 1970 as curator of Near Eastern Art and later became head of special programs at the Arthur M. Sackler Gallery (ASG). She is now the historian of the FGA/ASG. Author and translator of many works on Islam and the Arab world, Atil is on the boards of directors or advisory councils of several organizations, including the Asia Society, the Middle East Studies Association, the Society for the Preservation of Architectural Resources in Egypt, and the American Turkish Association of Washington, D.C.

Photographers and studios represented include the Chester Beatty Library; FGA Photography Laboratory staff members James T. Hayden and Stanley E. Turek; Pieterse Davison International, Ltd.; Justin Andrews Schaffer; and the Walters Art Gallery (Baltimore). Some of the photographs in this collection appeared in the following catalog: Esin Atil. *Renaissance of Islam: Art of the Mamluks.* Washington, D.C.: Smithsonian Institution Press, 1981.

Physical Description

There are 1,250 photographs including color dye coupler phototransparencies and silver gelatin photonegatives, photoprints, and phototransparencies.

Subjects

The photographs document the exhibit "Renaissance of Islam: Art of the Mamluks." The objects in the exhibit originated in the Mamluk Empire, which existed from 1250 to 1500 A.D. and included areas that are now Egypt, Israel, Saudi Arabia, Syria, and parts of Libya and Sudan.

Objects documented include basins, bowls, boxes, candlesticks, ceramics, decorative arts objects, glassware, incense burners, inlaid metalwork, a Koran box, lamps, manuscript illustrations, miniature paintings, perfume atomizers, rugs, swords, textiles, tiles, and weapons. Also included are views of Mamluk architecture in Cairo.

Arranged: Exhibit objects by exhibit catalog number; architectural images by building name and location.

Captioned: Some with photographer or subject.

Finding Aid: No.

Restrictions: Available by appointment only.

FG·4

Carl Whiting Bishop Papers

Dates of Photographs: 1923–1934

Collection Origins

Carl Whiting Bishop (1881–1942), an archaeologist and associate curator at the Freer Gallery of Art (FGA), created the collection to document his research activities. Born in Tokyo to missionary parents, Bishop received an M.A. in anthropology at Columbia University in 1913. He began his career in archaeology as a member of the Peabody Museum Expedition to Central America, then served as assistant curator of Oriental art at the University of Pennsylvania Museum from 1914 to 1918. Bishop went on an archaeological excavation in China from 1915 to 1917 and remained in the country two more years as an assistant naval attaché. From 1921 to 1922, he was a professor of archaeology at Columbia University.

In 1922 Bishop became an associate curator at the FGA, a position he held until his death. Bishop set up an agreement with the Historical Museum in Peking (Beijing) to encourage cultural exchanges between China and the United States. In addition to purchasing items for the museum's collections, Bishop conducted archaeological field research in China, working closely with Chinese scientists. He conducted two major archaeological expeditions in northern and central China (1923–1927 and 1929–1934) to uncover the large neolithic site at Wan-ch'üan Hsien, Shansi, and to complete a reconnaissance of the entire area. Bishop's other excavations in China included the altar of Hou t'u, sixth century tombs in Shansi, and the Shang dynasty site at Anyang. Photographers represented include Carl Whiting Bishop and his assistant, K.Z. Tung.

Physical Description

There are 10,000 photographs including silver gelatin dry plate photonegatives (2,000), silver gelatin photonegatives on nitrate (2,000), silver gelatin photonegatives on safety film (2,000 on S0015 film), and silver gelatin photoprints (4,000, some tinted). Other materials include drawings, journals, a manuscript, maps, notecards, and postcards from China and Korea.

Subjects

The photographs document Bishop's two major archaeological expeditions to China. Most of the photographs illustrate archaeological sites in the Honan (Henan) and Shansi (Shanxi) provinces. Other sites documented are located in Hebei province, Manchuria; the city of Nanking (Nanjing); and Mongolia. The photographs also document the cultures and environments of surrounding areas.

Specific digs shown include a neolithic site; the Shang site at Anyang; the altar for the official worship of the goddess of earth, Hou t'u; and sixth century A.D. tombs near Fen-yin. The photographs show artifacts such as bronze vessels and weapons (including details of animal mask decorations on the bronzes), ceramic sculptures and vessels, jade ritual implements (such as blades), sculptures of animals, and shell oracle bones, both on-site and in a conservation laboratory. There are also photographs of the Anyang and Nanking tombs, as well as the American and Chinese archaeologists and laborers who worked on the excavation.

The photographs include Chinese cityscapes, landscapes, and waterscapes of Peking (Beijing), Shanghai, and Szechwan (Sichuan), depicting boats, bridges, city walls, courtyards, gates, pagodas, palaces, rice fields, rickshaws, rubbings, statues of Buddha, temples, the T'ien-lung Shan Buddhist caves, villages, and wall paintings. There are also portraits of a calligrapher and Mongol peoples in Korea.

Arranged: In two series. 1) Photographs of field work in China from 1923 to 1927, arranged by subject headings using Bishop's decimal system. 2) Four notebooks on field work in China from 1930 to 1933, arranged by negative numbers. The photographs are keyed to charts documenting types of ceramics found and containing classification and number, color, date, impressed pattern, plate number, section and dwelling pit, and shape.

Captioned: With date, description, location, and negative number.

Finding Aid: 1) Unpublished index: Sarah L. Newmeyer. "The Bishop Collection." Freer Gallery of Art, 1976. 2) Box/container index listing negative number and subject.

Restrictions: Available by appointment only.

FG·5

Burke Collection: Tosa Mitsunori *Genji Monogatari* Album

Dates of Photographs: Circa 1970s–1980s

Collection Origins

Freer Gallery of Art assembled the collection from photographs created by New York-based photographer O.E. Nelson. The images reproduce a group of ink drawings by Tosa Mitsunori (1583–1638), used to illustrate the Fujiwara-era Japanese romance novel *Genji*

Monogatari (The Tale of Genji) written by Lady Murasaki Shikibu (978–1031). The ca. 1620 drawings are in the *hakubyo* (white drawing) style. The original drawings, part of the Mary and Jackson Burke Collection, were exhibited at the Metropolitan Museum of Art in 1975.

Printer and book designer Jackson Burke (1908–1975) attended the University of California at Berkeley and worked for Stanford University Press after World War II. From 1948 to 1963 he served as director of typographic development at the Mergenthaler Linotype Company, where he designed newspaper texts and book faces. He and Mary Burke, his wife, collected Japanese art and supported the acquisition and study of Japanese art at the Metropolitan Museum of Art.

Japanese artist Tosa Mitsunori (1583–1638) studied painting techniques under Mitsuyoshi (1539–1613) in Sakai, Izumi province, Japan. After moving to Kyoto, Mitsunori supplied ceremonial fans to the court and painted miniatures and genre scenes, often in album format. Known for his delicate ink lines, Mitsunori painted in an archaic style then popular with the aristocracy, which came to be known as the Tosa school.

Some of these images have been published in the following catalog: Miyeko Murase. *Japanese Art: Selections from the Mary and Jackson Burke Collection.* New York: Metropolitan Museum of Art, 1975.

Physical Description

There are 60 silver gelatin photoprints.

Subjects

The photographs are reproductions of two albums of ink drawings by Tosa Mitsunori, illustrating the Japanese romance novel *Genji Monogatari (The Tale of Genji)*. The novel is about the life and adventures of Prince Genji ("the Shining One") in Fujiwara-era Japan (897–1185 A.D.).

The photographs illustrate vignettes, such as the departure of Nyosan (Genji's wife) to a Buddhist nunnery and Genji's courtship of Princess Asagao. Other images include informal scenes of court life, such as nobles warming themselves at braziers; attending concerts; courting; making ceremonial visits; playing with children and animals; producing calligraphy; and viewing flowers, scrolls, and the moon.

Arranged: In the order of the original albums, which roughly follow the book's chapter sequence.

Captioned: A few with subject.

Finding Aid: No.

Restrictions: Available by appointment only.

FG·6

James F. Cahill Photographs

Dates of Photographs: 20th Century

Collection Origins

Freer Gallery of Art (FGA) staff created the collection for research purposes by making copy photographs of images assembled by art historian, educator, and writer James F. Cahill (1926–). Cahill, who received a Ph.D. from the University of Michigan in 1958, served as curator of Chinese art at the FGA from 1958 to 1965. He has been a professor of art history and a curator of Oriental art at the University of California at Berkeley since 1965. He also was the Charles Eliot Norton Professor of poetry at Harvard University from 1978 to 1979. He has written numerous works on Chinese and Japanese painting and Chinese bronzes including the following: 1) *Chinese Painting.* New York: Rizzoli, 1977. 2) *Scholar Painters of Japan: The Nanga School.* New York: Asia Society, 1972. Photographs from this collection appear in the former publication.

The FGA Photography Laboratory copied Cahill's slides of China and Chinese paintings to create the collection. Photographers and studios represented include Henry Beville, James F. Cahill, and the Freer Gallery of Art Photography Laboratory.

Physical Description

There are 595 copy silver gelatin copy photoprints.

Subjects

The photographs document Chinese painting dating from prehistory to the twentieth century, including art works from the Soochow (or Su-chou or Suzhou) and *che* (or *jer*) schools of painting and from the Ch'ing (or Qing), early Ming, and Yüan dynasties. The paintings reproduced show horses, human figures, and landscapes.

Titles of paintings include *Bamboo by Stream, Early Spring,* and *Fisherman Scroll.* Artists whose work is represented include Chao Meng-fu, Ch'iu Ying, Chu Ta (*A.K.A.* Pa-ta-shan-jen), Kuo Hsi, Ma Lin, Ni Tsan, Ts'ui Po, Wang Meng, Wên Cheng-ming, and Wu Chen.

Arranged: In four series. 1) China Series I. 2) China Series II. 3) China Series III. 4) Study collection. Photographs in these series then are arranged by assigned letter, then assigned number.

Captioned: No.

Finding Aid: Indexes to each series. Each China series index lists description, editorial comments, and negative numbers. The study collection index lists paintings photographed by Henry Beville.

Restrictions: Available by appointment only. Photographs in the study collection available for reference only. To reproduce images from the China series, permission from the owners of the painting is required.

FG·7

Chinese Painting of the Song, Yüan, Ming, and Qing Periods Picture Set

Dates of Photographs: Circa 1960

Collection Origins

The Freer Gallery of Art staff assembled the collection from selected copy photoprints purchased from the Asian Art Photographic Distribution Service (AAPDS), Department of the History of Art, University of Michigan. Established in the 1970s, AAPDS is a non-profit enterprise that distributes photoprints and slides of Asian art from private collections and exhibits to educational institutions for use in research.

AAPDS created the photographs for the following catalogs, which document masterpieces of Chinese painting lent by Japanese collections for two exhibits held at the Tokyo National Museum: 1) *Chūgoku Minshin Bijutsuten Mokuroku (Chinese Arts of the Ming and Ch'ing Periods)*. Tokyo: Kokuritsu Hakubutsukan, 1963. 2) *Chūgoku Sōgen Bijutsuten Mokuroku (Chinese Arts of the Sung and Yüan Periods)*. Tokyo: Kokuritsu Hakubutsukan, 1961. The photographs also have appeared in two monographs: 1) Tokyo National Museum, ed. *Min shin no Kaiga*. Tokyo: Benrido, 1964. 2) Tokyo National Museum, ed. *Sō-gen no Kaiga*. Tokyo: Benrido, 1962.

Physical Description

There are 500 silver gelatin copy photoprints.

Subjects

The photographs document Chinese landscape painting, dating from the ninth century A.D. to the 1800s,

mainly by artists of the Ch'ing (or Qing), Ming, Sung (or Song), and Yüan dynasties. There are images of paintings in albums and on fans and scrolls, with some shown in detail. Painters whose works are reproduced include Ch'ai Tzu-ang, Chang Ssu-kung, Chang Yü, Chao Ch'ang, Chao Tso, Cheng So-nan, Ch'ien Hsuan, Ching-ch'u, Fang Ts'ung-i, Hsüeh-ch'uang, Liang K'ai, Li Ch'üeh, Li Ti, Lo-ch'uang, Sheng Mao-yeh, Sh'êng Tzu-chao, Sun Chün-tse, Sung Ju-chih, Wang Hui, Wen Cheng-ming, Wu T'ai-su, Yen Hui, and Yü Chien. Paintings reproduced include *Autumn Landscape, Bamboo by the Rock, Plum Blossoms, Poets Making Tea,* and *Scroll of Flowers.*

Arranged: By AAPDS archive number.

Captioned: No.

Finding Aid: AAPDS finding aid listing archive number, artist, catalog number, date, dimensions, format, material, owner, and title.

Restrictions: Available by appointment only. Photonegatives are stored in Japan and are copyrighted by the Tokyo National Museum. Researchers interested in purchasing copies should contact the Asian Art Photographic Distribution Service, Department of the History of Art, University of Michigan, Tappan Hall, Room 50, 519 South State Street, Ann Arbor, Michigan, 48109-1357, (313) 764-1817. For permission to publish, write the Tokyo National Museum (Tokyo Kokuritsu Habubutsukan), 13-9, Ueno-koen, Taito-ku, Tokyo, Japan, or telephone 011-03-822-1111.

FG·8

John M. Crawford, Jr., Picture Set

Dates of Photographs: Early 1960s

Collection Origins

Freer Gallery of Art (FGA) staff assembled the collection from photographs created for research purposes by Asian Art Photographic Distribution Service (AAPDS), Department of the History of Art, University of Michigan. For information on AAPDS, see the *Collection Origins* field of *FG·7*. These photographs document Chinese calligraphy and paintings from the collection of John McAllister Crawford, Jr., and were taken by New York-based photographer O.E. Nelson.

Crawford (1913–) graduated from Brown University in 1937. He first visited Asia while on a world tour during 1937 and 1938. Crawford's interest in Chinese art grew after he attended a Wildenstein and Company exhibit of Ming and Ch'ing (or Qing) paintings in March 1949. He became a student of Chinese art and began collecting Chinese bronzes (gilt sculptures and ritual vessels), calligraphy, ceramics, jades, paintings in albums and on scrolls, porcelains, and sculptures (gilt bronze and wood). Crawford was on the Visiting Committee of the Fogg Art Museum at Harvard University from 1961 to 1966. He also has been a member of the Art Advisory Committee of Brown University since 1974 and a trustee and member of the Acquisitions Committee of the Metropolitan Museum of Art in New York since 1982.

A collector of bibliographic materials, Crawford acquired extensive holdings of medieval manuscripts, early printed books, proofs, and rare books (including arts and crafts movement works such as Kelmscott Press books), which he gave to the Pierpont Morgan Library, New York, in 1975.

Calligraphy and paintings from Crawford's collection appeared in a 1962 traveling exhibit held at the the Fogg Art Museum, Harvard University; the Musée Cernuschi, Paris; the National Museum of Stockholm; the Nelson-Atkins Gallery of Art, Kansas City; Pierpont Morgan Library, New York; and the Victoria and Albert Museum, London. Many of these images appear in the following catalogs: 1) John M. Crawford, Jr. *Chinese Calligraphy and Painting in the Collection of John M. Crawford, Jr.* New York: Pierpont Morgan Library, 1962. 2) Vito Giacalone. "The John M. Crawford, Jr., Collection of Calligraphy and Painting in the Metropolitan Museum of Art." *Oriental Art.* 31(4) (1985): 433–439. 3) *The Individualists: Chinese Painting and Calligraphy of the 17th Century from the Collection of John M. Crawford, Jr.* Providence, Rhode Island: Brown University, 1980. 4) Wan-go Weng. *Chinese Painting and Calligraphy: A Pictorial Survey; 69 Fine Examples from the John M. Crawford, Jr., Collection.* New York: Dover, 1978. 4) Marc F. Wilson and Kwan S. Wong. *Friends of Wen Cheng-ming: A View from the Crawford Collection.* Kansas City, Missouri: Nelson-Atkins Art Gallery, 1975.

Physical Description

There are 375 silver gelatin copy photoprints.

Subjects

The photographs document Chinese calligraphy and paintings dating from the eighth century A.D. through the 1700s, from the T'ang through the Ch'ing (or Qing) dynasties. The paintings include agricultural scenes, floral sketches, seasonal landscapes, and water-scapes. There are also reproductions of colophons, which are inscriptions or emblems often placed at the beginning of a work. Artists whose work is represented include Ch'iao Chung-ch'ang, Huang T'ing-chien, Ku Hung-chung, Ma Yüan, Mi Fu, and Tung Yüan.

Arranged: By AAPDS archive number.

Captioned: No.

Finding Aid: AAPDS finding aid listing archive number, artist, dimensions, painting format, and title.

Restrictions: Available by appointment only. The photographs are copyrighted by the Asian Art Photographic Distribution Service. For information on how to order copies, see the *Restrictions* field of *FG·7*.

FG·9

Peter F. Drucker Photographs *A.K.A.* The *Sansō* Collection

Dates of Photographs: 1970s–1990s

Collection Origins

Author and educator Peter F. Drucker (1909–) created the photographs and donated them to the Freer Gallery of Art (FGA). The photographs show Drucker's *Sansō* Collection of Japanese paintings. Drucker, who received an LL.D. from the University of Frankfurt in 1931, was an economist at the London Banking House (1933–1937); an American adviser to British banks (1937–1942); and an American correspondent for British newspapers (1937–1942). He also served as a consultant to major American businesses (1940–); a professor of philosophy and politics at Bennington College (1942–1949); a professor of management at New York University (1950–1972); chairman of the Management Department at New York University (1957–1962); and a lecturer at the Department of Art at Pomona College in California (1979–1985). Author of many management textbooks, Drucker also has produced audiotape casette and motion-picture film series and received numerous awards and honorary doctorates.

In 1959 Peter and Doris Drucker, his wife, began to collect Japanese Kamakura, Muromachi, Momoyama, and Edo period masterworks, particularly monochrome ink paintings such as *suiboku-ga* landscape paintings, *zenga* paintings, and *sumi-e* landscape and still life ink paintings of *nanga* painters. The Druckers named this group of paintings "*Sansō*," meaning mountain cottage. The Druckers continue to notify the Freer of additions to or sales of their *Sansō* paintings.

The paintings were described and reproduced in the following exhibit catalogs: 1) *Sansō Collection: Japanese Paintings Collected by Professor and Mrs. P. F. Drucker.* Osaka: Osaka Municipal Museum of Art and Nihon Keizai Shinbun, 1986. 2) *Song of the Brush: Japanese Paintings from the Sansō Collection.* Seattle, Washington: Seattle Art Museum, 1979. In 1979 and 1980, the latter exhibit traveled to the Asian Art Museum of San Francisco; Denver Art Museum; Fogg Art Museum, Harvard University; Japan House Gallery, New York; and the Seattle Art Museum.

Physical Description

There are 200 silver gelatin photoprints.

Subjects

The photographs document Peter and Doris Drucker's *Sansō* Collection of Japanese paintings including hanging scrolls and diptychs from three schools of Japanese art: 1) *suiboku-ga* (ink painting) of the Muromachi (1336–1573) and Momoyama (1573–1615) periods; 2) *zenga* (Zen paintings) by painters of the Edo period (1615–1868); and 3) *nanga* ink paintings by Japanese masters of the 18th and 19th centuries (based on the works of the *nan tsung hua,* or literati school, of the Ming dynasty).

Painters whose work is reproduced include Tani Bunchō, Tanomura Chikuden, Nakabayashi Chikutō, Kuwayama Gyokushū, Ekaku Hakuin, Gyokuran Ikeno, Taiga Ikeno, Nukina Kaioku, Noro Kaiseki, Kantei, Watanabe Kazan, Gibon Sengai, Soga Shōhaku, Uragami Shunkin, Toki Tōbun, Eii Unkei, and Yukinobu.

Arranged: By negative number.

Captioned: With artist, date, description, medium, mount format, origin, and size of the painting, as well as assigned number.

Finding Aid: No.

Restrictions: Available for reference use by appointment only. No reproductions may be made.

FG·10

Egyptian Architecture Photograph Album

Dates of Photographs: Early 20th Century

Collection Origins

Unknown.

Physical Description

There are 50 collodion gelatin photoprints (POP), mounted in an album.

Subjects

The photographs document 20th century Egypt, with an emphasis on architecture. Besides aerial views of towns, there are photographs of architectural details, cityscapes, razed buildings, street scenes, and temples. There are also images of children playing.

Arranged: No.

Captioned: No.

Finding Aid: No.

Restrictions: Available for reference use by appointment only. No reproductions may be made.

FG·11

Milton S. Eisenhower Library South Asian Architecture Photograph Collection

Dates of Photographs: Early 20th Century–Circa 1920s

Collection Origins

The Milton S. Eisenhower Library of Johns Hopkins University assembled the collection from photographs created by Lala Dean Dayal & Sons, Johnston &

Hoffmann, and others. Dayal (1844–1910) was an Indian engineer who graduated from the University of Roorkee in 1862. In the 1860s, Dayal founded the photographic firm of Lala Deen Dayal & Sons, based in Hyderabad, India. Through the 1880s, the studio produced images of Indian architecture, landscapes, and peoples. The firm's photographs have been reproduced in the following books: 1) J.H. Furneaux, ed. *Glimpses of India; A Grand Photographic History of the Land of Antiquity, the Vast Empire of the East.* London: International Art Co., 1896. 2) Sir Lepel Henry Griffin. *Famous Monuments of Central India.* London: Southeran, Autotype Co., 1886.

British photographers Johnston & Hoffmann worked in Calcutta, Darjeeling, and Simla in India, as well as Dacca, Bangladesh, and Burma (now Myanmar), from 1865 until the 1890s. They were known for their cartes-de-visite and other photoprints of Eastern peoples and landscapes.

Physical Description

There are 255 photographs including albumen photoprints, collodion gelatin photoprints (POP), platinum photoprints, and silver gelatin photoprints. Other materials include photomechanical prints.

Subjects

The photographs document prehistoric through fifth century A.D. architecture in India, Java (Jawa), and Burma (now Myanmar), including religious and secular structures and engineered works. There are also landscapes showing the sites of early structures in Kashmir, India (now a region of India and Pakistan). Structures shown include bridges, Buddhist temples (with sculptures), dwellings (such as caves and huts), pagodas, ruins, and walls (with sculpture). The photographs also include informal portraits of a young girl and group portraits of men and women washing in the Ganges (Ganga) River in India.

Arranged: No.

Captioned: Some with description, location, and name of building or site.

Finding Aid: No.

Restrictions: Available by appointment only.

FG·12

Facsimile Photonegatives of the Washington Manuscript of Deuteronomy and Joshua in the Freer Collection

Dates of Photographs: 1908

Collection Origins

Charles Lang Freer, founder of the Freer Gallery of Art (FGA), assembled the collection from photographs made by George R. Swain to function as a facsimile of an original fifth century parchment manuscript of two books of the Bible, Deuteronomy and Joshua. For a biography of Freer, see the FGA introduction. Freer purchased the original manuscript from Ali al-Arabi in Egypt in 1906 and later gave the manuscript to the FGA. The original probably was copied from a single parent manuscript by a fifth century Egyptian scribe.

This facsimile photographic version of the manuscript was published in an edition of 265 copies with the following title: *Facsimile of the Washington Manuscript of Deuteronomy and Joshua in the Freer Collection.* Ann Arbor: University of Michigan, 1910. The first facsimile copy was presented to Freer and is now in the museum's library. The negatives are stored in the museum's archives.

Physical Description

There are 200 silver gelatin photonegatives. Note: A facsimile of the Deuteronomy and Joshua manuscript, created from these negatives, is contained in the museum's library.

Subjects

The photographs reproduce a fifth century parchment manuscript, written in Greek, of the Old Testament books Deuteronomy and Joshua.

Arranged: In the order of the original manuscript.

Captioned: No.

Finding Aid: No.

Restrictions: Available by appointment only. Researchers are encouraged to use the facsimile copy of the manuscript in the Freer Gallery of Art and Arthur M. Sackler library.

FG·13

Facsimile Photoprints of the Washington Manuscript of the Four Gospels in the Freer Collection

Dates of Photographs: 1908

Collection Origins

Charles Lang Freer assembled the collection from photographs created by George R. Swain as a facsimile of an original fourth century parchment manuscript of the four Gospels of the New Testament. The main body of the original of this manuscript was written in fourth century Egypt by a single scribe. However, the first 16 pages of the book of John appear to date from an earlier time and to be written by a different hand. Freer purchased the original manuscript from Ali al-Arabi in Egypt in 1906 and later donated it to the Freer Gallery of Art (FGA). For a biography of Freer, see the FGA introduction.

The facsimile was published in an edition of 435 copies with the following title: *Facsimile of the Washington Manuscript of the Four Gospels in the Freer Collection*. Ann Arbor: University of Michigan, 1912. The first copy was presented to Freer and now is housed in the Freer Gallery of Art and Arthur M. Sackler library along with the photographs.

Physical Description

There are 370 silver gelatin photoprints. Other materials include a printed facsimile edition of the four Gospels.

Subjects

The photographs duplicate a fourth century A.D. parchment manuscript, written in Greek, of the four Gospels (Matthew, Mark, Luke, and John) of the New Testament.

Arranged: In the order of the original manuscript.

Captioned: No.

Finding Aid: No.

Restrictions: Available by appointment only. Researchers are encouraged to use the facsimile copy of the manuscript in the museum's library.

FG·14

FGA and ASG Slide Library

Dates of Photographs: 20th Century

Collection Origins

Staff of the Freer Gallery of Art (FGA) and Arthur M. Sackler Gallery (ASG) created the collection for use as a resource for research on Asian art.

Physical Description

There are 53,000 photographs including color dye coupler slides (Kodachrome) and silver gelatin slides.

Subjects

The photographs document art objects owned by the FGA and the ASG since the 1920s. There are also photographs of other art objects and architecture, dating from the Neolithic period through the early 20th century, from Asia Minor, Byzantium (now Istanbul, Turkey), Egypt, India, Indo-China, Persia (now Iran), Iraq, Japan, North Korea, South Korea, Syria, Tibet (now Xizang), and the United States.

Artifacts depicted include bronzes, calligraphy, ceramics, glassware, ivory carvings, jade items, lacquerware, manuscripts, metalwork, paintings, screens, scrolls, and sculpture. Genres of images reproduced include landscapes, narrative paintings, portraits, religious scenes, still lifes, and waterscapes.

Arranged: In two series. 1) Slides of Asian and Islamic art and architecture, by medium and then by country and period. 2) Slides of American art related to the FGA collection, alphabetically by artist and then by medium and location.

Captioned: With description; some also with date.

Finding Aid: 1) Card index for slides of FGA and ASG holdings. 2) Computer database.

Restrictions: Available by appointment only.

FG·15

FGA Building Records

Dates of Photographs: 1916–Present

Collection Origins

Freer Gallery of Art (FGA) staff assembled the collection to document the history of the FGA museum building, designed by American architect and painter Charles Adams Platt (1861–1933) in the style of a Florentine Renaissance palace as specified by FGA founder Charles Lang Freer. For a biography of Freer, see the introduction to the FGA. Freer presented his collections and related funds to the Smithsonian in 1906, and the gallery's construction began in 1916. The George A. Fuller Company was responsible for the actual construction work. In November 1920, a year after Freer's death, his art holdings arrived at the new gallery. The museum building was accepted by the Smithsonian Institution in 1921 and opened to the public in 1923. Photographers and studios represented include FGA staff, the George A. Fuller Company, and Charles Adams Platt.

Physical Description

There are 350 photographs including color dye coupler slides, silver gelatin dry plate photonegatives, and silver gelatin photonegatives and photoprints (some copy). Other materials include architectural records and blueprints.

Subjects

The photographs document the construction and development of the physical plant (exteriors and interiors) of the FGA from 1916 to the present. Images trace the construction of the building, from the groundbreaking in 1916 to its completion in 1921, including shots taken from the tower of the Smithsonian Institution Building (the Castle).

Later FGA images, from the 1920s to the 1990s, include both exteriors (such as the facade) and interiors (such as the interior courtyard with peacocks and James Abbott McNeill Whistler's Peacock Room). There are also photographs of nearby buildings, including the Arts & Industries Building of the Smithsonian Institution, the Central Market, the Post Office Building, the Smithsonian Institution Building (the Castle), the U.S. Capitol, and the Washington Monument.

Arranged: Construction photographs in chronological order; the rest loosely arranged.

Captioned: With architect, assigned number, builder, building, city, and date.

Finding Aid: No.

Restrictions: Available by appointment only.

FG·16

FGA Lantern Slide Collection

Dates of Photographs: Early 20th Century

Collection Origins:

Freer Gallery of Art (FGA) staff assembled the collection from materials owned by FGA founder Charles Lang Freer and from items donated by other institutions. Freer originally owned many of the lantern slides, which were donated when the FGA opened. For a biography of Freer, see the introduction to the FGA. The collection also includes many images created or owned by orientalist and educator Ernest F. Fenollosa (1853–1908), which were later purchased by Freer.

Fenollosa, who graduated from Harvard University in 1874, was a professor of political economy and philosophy at the University of Tokyo from 1878 to 1880 and served as the imperial fine arts commissioner of Japan in 1886 and 1887. He later became professor of aesthetics and manager of the Tokyo Fine Arts Academy and the Art Department of the Imperial Museum in Tokyo. After returning to the United States in 1890, Fenollosa served as curator at the Department of Oriental Art at the Boston Museum of Fine Arts until 1896. He then returned to Japan and taught English literature for a year at the Imperial Normal School, Tokyo. Decorated by the emperor of Japan with the Sacred Mirror and the Order of the Rising Sun, Fenollosa is the author of two volumes of poems and numerous works on Japanese and Chinese art. Note: Photographs of Fenollosa's Japanese funeral service appear in the illustrations. Photographers represented include Louis C. Bennett, Ernest F. Fenollosa, and T.H. McAllister.

Physical Description

There are 2,730 photographs including color screen plate lantern slides and silver gelatin dry plate lantern slides (some tinted).

Subjects

The photographs document Far-, Middle-, and Near-Eastern architecture, artifacts, and art works (some in FGA collections) dating from prehistory to the early 20th century, as well as 19th century American paintings. Freer's travel photographs include cityscapes of China, Hong Kong, India, and Japan, as well as informal portraits of their peoples, including Buddhist monks, Chinese mendicants, and Japanese geishas.

Architecture and art objects shown include American paintings (by artists such as Thomas W. Dewing, Willard L. Metcalf, Albert Pinkham Ryder, Abbott H. Thayer, and Dwight William Tryon); Byzantine art; Cambodian bronze sculptures; Chinese architecture (such as buildings in the Forbidden City of Peking [Beijing]), bronzes, and fountains (such as Peking's Grotto Fountain); Indian architecture and sculpture; Iraqi painting; Japanese architecture and paintings; Middle Eastern mosaics; Persian ceramics, metalwork, and paintings from the 14th, 15th, and 16th centuries; and Syrian metalwork.

Arranged: By art movement, country, or school.

Captioned: With country, date, notations, origin, period, school, style, and subject.

Finding Aid: No.

Restrictions: Available by appointment only.

FG·17

FGA Personnel and Special Events Photographs

Dates of Photographs: 1920s–1980s

Collection Origins

Freer Gallery of Art (FGA) staff assembled the collection to document special events at the museum and to serve as a portrait file of FGA personnel. Photographers and studios represented include FGA staff pho-

tographers, Arnold Genthe, Harris & Ewing, Richard Hofmeister, Yousuf Karsh, OPPS, Ed Roseberry, and the Woodward and Lothrop Studio.

Physical Description

There are 400 photographs including color dye coupler photoprints and slides, platinum photoprints, and silver gelatin photonegatives and photoprints.

Subjects

The photographs document FGA award presentations, exhibit openings, parties, receptions, staff members, and visitors. Special events documented include visits by royalty and political figures, such as the king of Nepal in 1960, the prince of Japan in 1965, the empress of Iran in 1973, and the crown prince of Jordan in 1975. Other events documented include the 50th anniversary of the FGA in 1973, the opening of the "Art of the Arab World" exhibit in 1975, a reception for Agnes E. Meyer, and retirement parties for John A. Pope (FGA director), Helen Quail, and Burns A. Stubbs.

FGA staff portrayed include curators Carl W. Bishop, James F. Cahill, and Richard Ettinghausen and museum directors Thomas Lawton, John Ellerton Lodge, Harold P. Stern, and Archibald G. Wenley. Informal portraits show Esin Atil (former FGA curator, now FGA/ASG historian), Sarah Newmeyer (FGA/ASG assistant director, administration), S. Dillon Ripley (former Smithsonian secretary), Mary Ripley (his wife), and Technical Laboratory personnel.

Arranged: No.

Captioned: About half with negative number, subject, or both.

Finding Aid: No.

Restrictions: Available by appointment only.

FG·18

FGA Reference Photograph Collection

Dates of Photographs: 20th Century

Collection Origins

Freer Gallery of Art (FGA) staff assembled the collection for study purposes. Charles Lang Freer originally owned many of the images, which were received from his estate when the FGA opened. For a biography of Freer, see the introduction to the FGA. Other images were received through exchange agreements with other institutions.

Photographers represented include M. Arpad, Félix Bonfils, Samuel Bourne, Avery Brundage, Mrs. Lin Ho, E.C. Jacobs, John Pope, Tai, and Scotty Tsuchiya. Studios represented include the Boston Museum of Fine Arts, British Museum, Cambridge University Library, C.C. Wang Collection, City Art Museum of St. Louis, Cleveland Museum of Art, Field Museum of Natural History, Fogg Art Museum, Gellatly Collection, Indian Museum in Calcutta, Kevorkian Collection, King of Sweden Collection, Medelhavsmuseef, Metropolitan Museum of Art, Musée Guimet, National Museum of India, Nelson-Atkins Gallery, Pierpont Morgan Library, Royal Ontario Museum, Tehrān Architecture Museum, Toledo Museum of Art, and Virginia Museum of Fine Arts.

Physical Description

There are 8,000 photographs including albumen photoprints and silver gelatin photoprints.

Subjects

The photographs document architecture, artifacts, and art objects dating from prehistory to the present, from Afghanistan, Cambodia, China, Egypt, India, Iraq, Japan, Java (Jawa), Persia (now Iran), Syria, Turkey, and Yemen.

Chinese art and artifacts shown include bronzes; Buddhist sculptures; ceramics (blue-and-white vases and other Ming-era vessels); enamelware; lacquerware; metalwork; monuments; mortuary urns; paintings (such as *Itinerant Folks and Street Performers* by Chou Ch'en, landscapes by Tung Ch'i-Ch'ang, *Nymph of the Lo River* attributed to Ku K'ai-chih, and *Portrait of An-Ch'i* by Wang Hui); sculpture; and textiles from the Chou through the Ch'ing dynasties. Views of the Chinese natural and built environments include bridges, cities, and mountains. There are images of the Great Wall; Honan (Henan) province; the Lung-men Caves; Peking (Beijing); and the Yangtze River (or Yangzi Jiang or Chang Jiang) gorges.

Photographs of India reproduce architecture, carvings, lacquerware, metalwork, paintings, and sculpture. Images of Japan show architecture (such as Himeji Castle, Kinkakuji Pavilion in Kyoto, and a Buddhist temple); ceramics; graphic prints; lacquerware; metalwork; paintings (such as *Death of Buddha* from the Kamakura period); and sculpture. There are also photographs of Egyptian sculpture and temples; Javanese architecture; Persian manuscripts; and Islamic art from Iraq, Syria, Turkey, and Yemen; as well as a relief sculpture from Persepolis (now Istakhr), Persia (now Iran).

Arranged: By country and then by dynasty, period or medium.

Captioned: With accession number, country of origin, date, dynasty, medium, and title.

Finding Aid: No.

Restrictions: Available by appointment only.

FG·19

Charles Lang Freer Papers

Dates of Photographs: 1870s–1930s

Collection Origins

The collection was created by Charles Lang Freer (1856–1919), founder of the Freer Gallery of Art (FGA). In 1906 Freer donated over 8,000 art works, as well as these papers, to the FGA. For a biography of Freer, see the FGA introduction.

The collection contains three distinct photograph series. The first documents Freer's life, including his art holdings, colleagues, and travels. The second set of photographs was taken by Utai, a photographer who traveled with Freer to the Lung-men Caves in China. These images appear in the following magazine article: Frederick McCormick. "China's Treasures." *National Geographic.* 23(10) (1912): 996–1040. The final series depicts 150 Chinese art objects sent on approval to Freer from a Shanghai art collector in 1919. The photographs were mounted in an album with caption descriptions in English. Freer purchased the majority of the works depicted, and most are now part of the FGA holdings. A few remaining paintings were purchased by friends of Freer.

Photographers represented in the collection include Alvin Langdon Coburn; George C. Cox; P. Dittrich; M. Dornac; Arnold Genthe; K. Maekawa; Marceau; S. Matsubara; T. Morita; Napolean Sarony; Edward Steichen; Alfred Stieglitz; Tingley; Utai; and D.W.C. Ward. Studios represented include Bacard Fils; Bracy, Diehl & Company; Ferd Stark Company; C.M. Hayes & Company; R. Kohno Photo Studio; London Stereoscopic Company; the University of Michigan; and W. & D. Downey.

Physical Description

There are 820 photographs including albumen photoprints, color screen plate phototransparencies (Autochrome), platinum photoprints, silver gelatin dry plate photonegatives, and silver gelatin photonegatives and photoprints. Other materials include correspondence, diaries, financial records, genealogies, inventories, letterpress copybooks, newspaper clippings, notes, and scrapbooks.

Subjects

Most of the photographs document Charles Lang Freer's life, his art holdings, his friends and associates, and his travels between 1895 and 1911, primarily to China, Egypt, Italy, and Japan. Structures depicted include the Charles Lang Freer memorial in Kyoto, Japan; Chinese temples (including the Lung-men Caves); Freer's Detroit home; Japanese temples (such as Hōmyōin Temple); James Abbott McNeill Whistler's Peacock Room; Whistler's studio in Paris (ca. 1892–1894); and Whistler's tomb in London.

Artifacts shown include Freer's death mask and author Lafcadio Hearn's desk. There are images of silk paintings including landscapes (such as mountain scenes), a portrait, studies of animals (particularly birds), and waterscapes (such as views of waterfalls). The collection also contains photographs of art works by Abbott H. Thayer and Whistler, as well as portraits of Thayer and Dwight William Tryon.

Individuals portrayed include U.S. Ambassador to Japan William C. Castle, American painter Thomas W. Dewing; American author and curator Ernest F. Fenollosa; American businessman Frank J. Hecker; the king of Sweden; American artist Katherine Nash Rhoades (by Alfred Stieglitz); American sculptor Augustus Saint-Gaudens; Louisine Waldron (the wife of American sugar refiner Henry O. Havemeyer); and American artist James Abbott McNeill Whistler and his family, specifically Anna Mathilda Whistler (his mother), George Washington Whistler (his father), and Rosaline Birnie Philip (his sister-in-law). Other photographs show Freer drinking from a stream and in the tea room of a Japanese temple. Workers portrayed include a Chinese rickshaw driver and Chinese servants. There are also views of Ernest F. Fenollosa's funeral at Hōmyōin Temple and a memorial to Fenollosa.

There are photographs that document the seventh century cave temples at Lung-men, Honan (Henan), China. Lung-men cave temples shown include Feng-hsien ssu, Ku-Yang, Lien-hua, and Ping-yang. Sculpture and stone figures from the caves shown include Buddha, Buddha's disciple Ananda, and other divinities such as cave guardians.

Other Chinese art works documented in the collection date from the 12th century B.C. to the 1800s and include ceramics such as porcelain bowls, cups, and vases (from the Sung Dynasty); jades; metalwork including brass and bronze objects; paintings including scrolls; and sculptures including ceramic human figures from the Han dynasty and jade and brass inlaid cowrie shell animals. Photographs from this collection are reproduced in the illustrations section of this volume.

A group of photographs recently has been removed from this collection including images of the FGA (both exterior and interior views, with peacocks in the interior courtyard); photographs of art works by Korean and Tibetan artists, Korean ceramics, Nepalese brass sculpture, a sketch of Freer by Katherine Nash Rhoades, and Syrian architecture; and portraits of a Japanese calligrapher and Japanese musicians. Contact the archivist for further information.

Arranged: In three series. 1) Photographs of Charles Lang Freer's life. 2) Lung-men cave photographs, organized by assigned number and location of sculpture in caves, then in three sub-series: a) original photoprints; b) copy photoprints; c) original photonegatives. 3) Chinese art photographs, organized by format of art work shown.

Captioned: 1) Photographs of Freer's life with subjects; some also with date and photographer. 2) Most Lung-men photographs with information on subject, location, or title. 3) Chinese art photographs with album number, artist, dynasty, and title; images of objects now in the FGA also have accession numbers.

Finding Aid: List of some of the Lung-men photographs, titled "Photographs of the Buddhist Caves at Lung-men, Honan, Freer Gallery of Art," which provides the photographs' assigned numbers and descriptions, as well as some citations for books on the subject.

Restrictions: Available by appointment only.

FG·20

Henry Clay Frick Photograph Collection

Dates of Photographs: 1970s

Collection Origins

The collection was created as a visual inventory of the Chinese porcelains purchased by industrialist and art patron Henry Clay Frick (1849–1919) from the estate of financier J. Pierpont Morgan (1837–1913).

Frick was president and chairman of the board of the H.C. Frick Coke Company. An associate of Andrew Carnegie, Frick also served on the board of directors of Carnegie Brothers & Company and the United States Steel Corporation. Frick's extensive art holdings later formed the nucleus of the Frick Collection, a New York City art gallery, which opened to the public in 1935. Frick purchased the Chinese porcelains depicted in this collection from the estate of J. Pierpont Morgan in 1915. During the late 19th and early 20th centuries Morgan controlled several banking partnerships including Dabney, Morgan & Company; J.S. Morgan and Company; Drexel, Morgan & Company; and the J.P. Morgan Company. One of the most well known art collectors of his day, Morgan served as president of the Metropolitan Museum of Art in New York. His holdings were shown in galleries around the United States. The Chinese porcelains depicted in this photograph collection were exhibited at the Metropolitan Museum of Art.

Photographs from this collection also appeared in the following publication: The Frick Collection. *The Frick Collection, an Illustrated Catalogue.* Vol. 7, *Porcelains.* New York: The Frick Collection, 1974. John A. Pope, former FGA director, prepared the text concerning the Asian pieces.

Physical Description

There are 90 silver gelatin photoprints.

Subjects

The photographs document late 16th century Chinese porcelains, purchased by Henry Clay Frick from the estate of J. Pierpont Morgan. Types of porcelain depicted include enameled figurines, stem cups, and vases in the *famille noire, famille rose,* and *famille verte* styles.

Arranged: No.

Captioned: No.

Finding Aid: No.

Restrictions: Available by appointment only.

FG·21

Elizabeth Gordon Papers *A.K.A. Shibui* Archives

Dates of Photographs: 1947–1964

Collection Origins

Elizabeth Gordon (1907-   ) created the collection to document her research on *shibui*, a Japanese aesthetic concept denoting naturalness and simplicity. Gordon served as editor of *House Beautiful* magazine from 1941 to 1964. In 1959 and 1960 she traveled to Japan to investigate Japanese home design. *House Beautiful* subsequently devoted two 1960 issues to the concept of *shibui* and its application in American design and architecture. After enthusiastic public response, Gordon arranged *shibui* exhibits throughout the United States.

Photographers represented include Akio Kawasumi, Maynard L. Parker, and Ezra Stoller. Many of the photographs in the collection were published in the August and September 1960 issues of *House Beautiful*.

Physical Description

There are 405 photographs including color dye coupler phototransparencies and slides, silver gelatin dry plate lantern slides, and silver gelatin photoprints and phototransparencies. Some of the photographs are in an album. Other materials include announcements, an award, books, correspondence, drafts of articles, drawings, newspaper clippings, notes, periodicals, a photograph album, reprints, and speeches.

Subjects

The photographs document Japanese interior design and landscape architecture, as well as Western adaptations of this design in the United States. The photographs show architecture such as home exteriors and interiors; artifacts such as handcrafts and fine arts objects; and landscaping such as gardens in Japan and the United States.

Artifacts shown include a birdbath, bowls, costumes, foil decorations, lacquerware, paintings (such as screens and scrolls), sculptures, textiles, trays, and vases. Some objects are shown in installations for the U.S. *shibui* exhibits. There are also informal portraits of Japanese children, men, and women posed in gardens and rooms.

Arranged: By topic.

Captioned: Some with date, photographer, and subject.

Finding Aid: Box list, identifying each item.

Restrictions: Available by appointment only.

FG·22

Raymond A. Hare Photographs

Dates of Photographs: 1930s–1960s

Collection Origins

Diplomat Raymond A. Hare (1901–   ) created the collection and donated it to the Freer Gallery of Art (FGA). Hare received a B.A. from Grinnell College in 1924. Often called the country's first career diplomat, he joined the Foreign Service in 1927. By the time he retired in 1966, Hare had served as U.S. ambassador to Egypt, Lebanon, Saudi Arabia, Turkey, and the United Arab Republic. He also served as the director general of the U.S. Foreign Service (1956–1958) and has been affiliated with the Middle East Institute in Washington, D.C., as its president (1966–1969), national chairman (1969–1976) and chairman emeritus (1976–   ). An amateur photographer, Hare documented Islamic architecture during his extensive travels in the Middle East, especially in Egypt, Syria, and Turkey. Photographers represented include Ara Guler and Raymond A. Hare.

Physical Description

There are 2,300 photographs including color dye coupler slides (Kodachrome and Ektachrome) and silver gelatin photoprints, mounted in albums.

Subjects

The photographs document the architecture, cities, and landscapes of the Middle East, including Afghanistan, Egypt, Greece, Iraq, Jordan, Palestine (now Israel), Persia (now Iran), Syria, Turkey, and Yemen. Images of Egypt and Turkey include aerial views.

There are architectural studies, cityscapes, and street scenes of many Middle Eastern cities including Aleppo (Halab), Syria; Ani, Turkey; Ankara, Turkey; Beirut, Lebanon; Bethlehem, Jordan (West Bank); Cairo, Egypt; Constantinople (now Istanbul), Turkey; Damascus, Syria; Esfahān (Isfahan), Iran; Palmyra (now Tadmur),

Syria; Samarkand, U.S.S.R. (Uzbekistan); and Tehrān, Iran.

Architectural details documented include arches, courtyards, facades, minarets, mosaics, and portals. Buildings and other structures shown include bridges, citadels, hospitals, inns, mausoleums, and mosques. Religious sites and structures in Jerusalem documented include the Church of St. Anne, the Dome of the Rock, the Holy Seph, the Mount of Olives, and the Wailing Wall. Photographs of Yemen document agriculture, architecture, landscapes, and royalty.

Arranged: Slides by country and city or country and subject; then by Hare's use of the material. The photoprints are mounted in albums in original collation order.

Captioned: Slides with description including city, country, and subject; some prints with date, name, and subject.

Finding Aid: 1) Box container list. 2) Index to the slides, consisting of 12 notebooks arranged partly by country and city and partly by topic.

Restrictions: Available by appointment only.

FG·23

Ernst Herzfeld Papers

Dates of Photographs: 1903–1980s

Collection Origins

Architect, archaeologist, and historian Ernst Herzfeld (1879–1948) created the collection to document his research on the history of the Near East. After training as an architect and studying archaeology under Friedrich Delitzsch in the excavations at Assur in Mesopotamia, Herzfeld received a doctorate in humanistic studies at the universities of Munich and Berlin in 1907. Working with Friedrich P.T. Sarre, Herzfeld surveyed the monuments of the Tigris and Euphrates valleys, which resulted in his landmark studies in architectural history published in 1911 and 1920.

In 1920 Herzfeld began his excavation at Sāmarrā, Iraq, often called the "Islamic Pompeii." Other projects completed and published by Herzfeld include a study of the Dome of the Rock (1911); writings on the Syrian cities of Aleppo (Halab), Damascus, and Homs; the authoritative dating of the facade of the Mschatta palace; drawings of the ruins of Pāikūlī, Persia (now

Iran); and reports on excavations in Persia at Pasargadae, *A.K.A.* Tall-i Nokhodi (1929), and of the Royal Palace at Persepolis, now Istakhr (1930–1934). From 1936 to 1945 Herzfeld was a research fellow at the Institute for Advanced Study at Princeton.

Herzfeld wrote extensively on the sources of Islamic and pre-Islamic architecture and ornament. A bibliography of 203 articles and books by Herzfeld was compiled by George C. Miles in *Ars Islamica*, 7 (1940): 82–92. A supplement appeared in the following publication: George Carpenter Miles. *Archaeologia Orientalia in Memoriam Ernst Herzfeld*. Locust Valley, New York: J.J. Augustin, 1952.

Photographers and studios represented include H.F.R. Bassewitz, Gertrude L. Bell, Félix Bonfils, Otto Burchard, Ernst Herzfeld, Friedrich Krefter, Joseph Lackner, Ladislas Lorent, Percy Lorraine, the Oriental Institute of the University of Chicago, Arthur U. Pope, Profeldt, Friedrich P.T. Sarre, Antoin Sevruguin, Cl. Thevenet, Max van Berchem, and Max A.S. von Oppenheim.

Physical Description

There are 20,000 photographs including albumen photoprints, collodion wet plate lantern slides (many tinted) and photonegatives, cyanotypes, dye transfer photonegatives, silver gelatin dry plate photonegatives, and silver gelatin photonegatives (some on nitrate film) and photoprints. There are copy photoprints of the original cyanotypes and some duplicate photoprints. Formats represented include panoramas. Other materials include artifacts, correspondence, drawings, field notes, inventories, journals, maps, papier-mâché "squeeze" copies of architectural details and inscriptions, plans, and sketchbooks.

Subjects

The photographs document Islamic and pre-Islamic archaeology, architecture, and artifacts in Mesopotamia (an ancient civilization located between the Tigris and Euphrates Rivers, encompassing parts of modern Iran, Iraq, Syria, and Turkey), Persia (now Iran), and Syria dating from prehistory through 1945, as well as 20th century life in those regions including cityscapes, landscapes, peoples, and street scenes.

Photographs show cities and regions in Persia including Esfahān (Isfahan), Firūzābād (now Rask), Hamadān, Harsin, Khārg (Khark) Island, Muhammadabad (now Darreh Gaz), Pasargadae (now Tall-i Nokhodi), Persepolis (Istakhr), Shīrāz, Sistan, Tehrān, and Tepe Giyan. Other areas documented include Afghanistan; Alamut (a city of 12th century southeast Asia); Cairo, Egypt; Delhi, India; Baghdād and Sāmarrā, Iraq; Baalbek, Lebanon; Jaffa (now Tel Aviv-Yafo), Palestine (now Israel); Aleppo (Halab) and Damascus, Syria; the Tigris River, Iraq; and Samarkand, U.S.S.R. (Uzbekistan).

Architectural images include burial structures such as mausoleums and tombs including the Tomb of Darius, the Tomb of Omar Khayyám, and the Varāmīn Tomb Tower; religious structures such as al-Aqsa Mosque (in Jerusalem), the Dāmghān citadel (in Iran), and the Great Mosque and a synagogue (in Aleppo); and royal dwellings such as the Palace of Darius at Persepolis (bas-reliefs), the castle in Alamut, and Gulistan Palace (in Tehrān).

Other Persian structures shown include Chehel Sutun (Dome Fountain, now in Esfahān); Herzfeld's living room (in Tehrān, 1929); Herzfeld Library (in Tehrān); a hospital; Masjid-i-'Ali (in Esfahān); the Shah's Museum; and the Taq-e Bostan (grottoes in Kirmanshah). There are also photographic reproductions of papier-mâché "squeezes" made from bas reliefs, friezes, and inscriptions on the walls of mausoleums, mosques, and palaces.

Artifacts illustrated include bronzeware; ceramics (such as bowls, jars, pitchers, pot-shards, stoneware, and urns); coins; foundation tablets (some made of gold and silver); ironwork; jewelry (such as bracelets, pins, and rings made of engraved copper and inlaid bronze); religious or ritual objects (such as fertility symbols, fetishes, idols, and scarabs); sculptures (such as busts, relief sculpture, sculpture-in-the-round, steles, and other statues in bronze, copper, iron, and stone); signature seals; textiles (such as embroidered saddle covers); tools; and weapons (such as arrows, quivers, and spears). Persian monarchs depicted in sculpture include Artaxerxes I, Darius, Mithradates I, Mithradates II, and Xerxes. Xerxes' tomb also is shown.

Photographs of daily life show Arab workers at Sāmarrā (in Iraq), brick kilns and brickmaking in Kurdish villages, a lumberyard in Tehrān, musicians with drums and fifes in Kurdish villages, prayers at the Great Mosque of Aleppo, street scenes in Aleppo, and a tent city in the desert.

Individuals and groups portrayed include the German Legation, 1930; Charlotte Herzfeld (Ernst Herzfeld's sister); Ernst Herzfeld at his post in Kurdistan during World War I; the Persian Minister in the Gulistan Palace Museum; German Minister Friedrich von der Schulenberg on a horse in 1930; and Moritz Sobernheim and his family.

Arranged: In four series by type of material. 1) Photonegatives on glass, arranged by Herzfeld's assigned number. 2) Photonegatives on cut film, arranged by topical category. 3) Original cyanotypes, arranged by Herzfeld's assigned topic. 4) Photo File (consisting primarily of modern copy photoprints and a few original albumen photoprints, cyanotypes, and silver gelatin photoprints), arranged by topic. Photographs are then arranged according to archaeological site, location, source of the image, or type of artifact.

Captioned: Most photographs with image sequence number, location, Herzfeld's negative number, and occasionally with photographer. Cyanotypes with location, Herzfeld's negative number, and a citation for any publication in which the image appeared. Lantern slides with location, description, and negative number. Photonegatives with Herzfeld's negative number.

Finding Aid: 1) A nine-volume index to the collection, titled "Catalogue to Herzfeld Archives," which lists any published use of the image, description and geographic location of the subject, image sequence number, and negative number. 2) A card catalog to the drawings, photonegatives, and papier-mâché "squeezes," which lists the date, description, and negative number. 3) Topical files in the Photo File (series 4) serve as a rough subject index.

Restrictions: Available by appointment only. Persepolis photographs from the Oriental Institute are restricted due to their copyright status. For reproductions and permission to publish the Persepolis images, write the Oriental Institute Museum of the University of Chicago, 1155 East 58th Street, Chicago, Illinois, 60637, or call (312) 962-9520.

FG·24

Hobart Collection of Chinese Paintings Picture Set

Dates of Photographs: 1969

Collection Origins

Freer Gallery of Art staff assembled this collection from images created by Asian Art Photographic Distribution Service (AAPDS), Department of the History of Art, University of Michigan. For information on AAPDS see the Collection Origins field of FG·7. Photographers represented include Raymond Schwartz.

The photographs are of Chinese paintings and porcelains owned by Richard Bryant Hobart. Hobart first became acquainted with the arts of Asia while on a trip to China and Korea in 1909 and 1910, and he went on to acquire a large collection of Oriental art. These paintings were photographed in 1969 before the public auction of Hobart's ceramics and paintings held by Parke-Bernet Galleries, Inc. The Parke-Bernet Galleries auction catalogs were titled as follows: 1) *Richard Bryant Hobart Collection of Oriental Ceramics, May*

23, 1969. Sale No. 2869. 2) *Richard Bryant Hobart Estate: Chinese Porcelains and Paintings, December 12, 1969*. Sale No. 2958.

Physical Description

There are 175 silver gelatin photoprints.

Subjects

The photographs document Chinese landscape paintings dating from the Ch'ing (or Qing, 1644–1912) and Ming (1368–1644) dynasties. Most of the paintings shown are in albums or on hanging scrolls. Artists whose work is represented include Shêng Mao-hua and Wang Hui.

Arranged: By AAPDS archive number.

Captioned: No.

Finding Aid: AAPDS finding aid listing archive number, artist's name, and painting description and format.

Restrictions: Available by appointment only. The photographs are copyrighted by the AAPDS. Researchers interested in purchasing or publishing copies should contact AAPDS (see the Restrictions field of FG·7).

FG·25

In Pursuit of Antiquity: Chinese Paintings of the Ming and Ch'ing Dynasties from the Collection of Mr. and Mrs. Earl Morse: Photographs, 1969

Dates of Photographs: 1969

Collection Origins

Staff of the Far Eastern Art Research Photographic Archive of the Department of Art and Archaeology at Princeton University created the collection to document an exhibit of Chinese paintings owned by Mr.

and Mrs. Earl Morse, held at Princeton's Art Museum from May 17 to July 27, 1969.

Earl Morse (1907–1988), who earned a law degree from Harvard in 1930, was vice president of the Doughnut Corporation of America and chairman of the Union of American Hebrew Colleges. He and Irene Levitt Morse, his wife, collected historic Chinese paintings, with special emphasis on the work of Wang Hui (1632–1717), an eclectic master painter of the Ch'ing (or Qing) dynasty. The Morse collection puts Wang Hui's work in a historical context by including paintings by his Ming predecessors, his teachers, his contemporaries, and his orthodox school successors.

The photographs appeared in the following catalog: Roderick Whitfield. *In Pursuit of Antiquity: Chinese Paintings of the Ming and Ch'ing Dynasties from the Collection of Mr. and Mrs. Earl Morse.* Princeton, New Jersey: Princeton University, 1969. The Far Eastern Art Research Photographic Archive gave the collection to the Freer Gallery of Art.

Physical Description

There are 240 silver gelatin photoprints.

Subjects

The photographs document Chinese paintings by Wang Hui and other related masters of the Ming and Ch'ing (or Qing) dynasties, dating from the 15th to 18th centuries. Artists whose work is represented include Ch'en Hung-shou, Fang Shih-shu, Lan Ying, Shen Chou, T'ang Yin, Tung Ch'i-ch'ang, Wang Chien, Wang Hui, Wang Shih-min, Wen Cheng-ming, Yang Chin, and Yün Shou-p'ing.

Paintings reproduced are in screen and scroll format and include images of architecture (such as a scholar's hut and a tea house), landscapes (such as mountains), and waterscapes (such as waterfalls). There are also photographic reproductions of calligraphy and colophons (emblems and inscriptions found at the beginning of a book or manuscript).

Arranged: By catalog number.

Captioned: With artist, catalog number, dimensions, format, medium, and title.

Finding Aid: No.

Restrictions: Available by appointment only.

FG·26

Konishi Family Collection of Kōrin Sketches and Calligraphy

Dates of Photographs: 1970s–1980s

Collection Origins

The collection was created by an unknown photographer to document a collection of calligraphy and sketches by Ogata Kōrin (1658–1716), preserved by the Konishi family of Japan, who are descendents of Kōrin.

A Japanese calligrapher, lacquerer, painter, potter, and textile designer of the *rimpa* school, Kōrin lived in Edo (now Tokyo), where he was considered the foremost decorative painter of his time. From 1699 to 1712 Kōrin worked in ceramics at the Narutaki kiln. Some of the photographs appeared in the following book: Yamane Yūzō. *The Life and Work of Kōrin.* Vol. 1, *The Konishi Collection.* Tokyo: Chuo-Koron Bijutsu Shuppan, 1962.

Physical Description

There are 60 silver gelatin photoprints.

Subjects

The photographs document sketches and calligraphy produced by the Japanese artist Kōrin from 1670 through 1716. The work shown was done primarily on *washi* (Japanese handmade papers). The photographs reproduce calligraphy in running grass script and sketches of abstract patterns, banners, fans, and motifs from nature, such as flowers, leaves, and ocean waves.

Arranged: No.

Captioned: No.

Finding Aid: No.

Restrictions: Available by appointment only.

FG·27

Leventritt Chinese Porcelain Photograph Collection

Dates of Photographs: 1965

Collection Origins

Roy C. Leventritt created the collection to document his Chinese porcelain collection, exhibited at the De-Young Memorial Museum in San Francisco in 1965. Photographs in the collection were reproduced in the following article: John C. Pope. "The Roy Leventritt Collection." *Art Quarterly* 28(1, 2) (1965): 69–80.

Physical Description

There are 90 silver gelatin photoprints, mounted in albums.

Subjects

The photographs document the blue-and-white Chinese porcelain objects owned by Roy C. Leventritt, which date from the 14th through 19th centuries. The collection also documents the installation and exhibition of these porcelains at the DeYoung Memorial Museum in San Francisco in 1965.

Porcelain objects depicted include basins, beakers, bowls, brush holders, brush pens with caps, brush washers, candlesticks, cup stands, cups, dishes, covered ewers, flower pots, fly whisks, fountain fixtures, hot water bowls, incense burners, inkstands, jars, *kendi* (drinking vessels or ewers), *kogo* (round ceramic boxes), oil lamps, paperweights, pitchers, plates, scholar's inkscreens, seed cups, spoons, tankards, teapots, temple seals, tripod incense vases, utensils, vases (including small-mouthed vases in *mei-p'ing* and bottle vases in *yü-hu-ch'un p'ing* form), wall vases, water containers, water droppers, and wine pots with cosies.

Arranged: In order of the exhibit arrangement.

Captioned: With catalog number.

Finding Aid: Unpublished catalog titled "The Roy Leventritt Collection of Blue-and-White Porcelain," by William D.Y. Wu, listing date, description, dimensions, and image number.

Restrictions: Available by appointment only.

FG·28

Li Chi Reports

Dates of Photographs: 1926–1929

Collection Origins

Archaeologist Li Chi (1896–1979) created the collection to document his excavations in the Shansi (Shanxi) and Honan (Henan) provinces of northern China, where he worked in association with the Freer Gallery of Art (FGA). Li came to the United States in 1918 and received a Ph.D. in anthropology from Harvard University in 1923. In 1925 he became a professor at Tsing Hua Research Institute in Peking. In 1926, working in association with the FGA, Li and a colleague discovered and excavated the prehistoric site of Hsi-yin Ts'un, Hsia-hsien. He conducted another FGA-sponsored excavation at Anyang, Honan province, in 1929.

Li was the first to study ancient Chinese civilization through the combined use of archaeological excavation, epigraphic scholarship, and a humanistic/anthropological outlook. His career included positions at Academia Sinica, Peking (Beijing), China; the National Research Institute of History and Philology, Taipei, Taiwan; and the National Taiwan Normal University in Taipei.

In addition to publishing some 150 titles, Li edited three periodicals, *Archaeologia Sinica*, the *Bulletin of the Department of Archaeology and Anthropology* (of National Taiwan Normal University), and the Chinese *Journal of Archaeology*. Photographers include T'ang Hsui-ping and P.L. Yuan of the Geological Survey of China.

Physical Description

There are 280 silver gelatin photoprints. Other materials include correspondence, drawings, field reports, ink rubbings, and reproductions.

Subjects

The photographs document Li Chi's archaeological excavations and surveys in the Shansi (Shanxi) and Honan (Henan) provinces of northern China. The photographs illustrate an archaeological surveying trip along the lower part of the Feng River Valley and excavations at the sites of Hsi-yin Ts'un in the Shansi province and Yin-hsü in the village of Hsiao-t'un at Anyang in the Honan province.

People portrayed include Li Chi, P.L. Yuan, and Chinese soldiers and villagers. Structures illustrated include a bell tower, a stone pillar, temples, and un-identified Chinese villages. There are also images of "fairy caves" and a mule cart. Prehistoric items depicted include bones, ceramics, inscribed plastrons, ornaments, pot-shards, and tools.

Arranged: Chronologically.

Captioned: With description, location, number, and subject's name.

Finding Aid: No.

Restrictions: Available by appointment only.

FG·29

Maharaja Sawai Man Singh II Museum Photographs

Dates of Photographs: 1970s

Collection Origins

Staff of the Maharaja Sawai Man Singh II Museum of the City Palace of Jaipur, India, created the collection to document two of its illustrated manuscripts, the *Rāmāyana* and *Razam-Nameh.* Prepared for Emperor Akbar (1542–1605) during the 16th century, the manuscripts are related to *Mahābhārata,* a Hindu epic poem describing an ancient war between two families that occurred near Delhi, India. The *Rāmāyana* is a religious folk legend, purported to be at least 5,000 years old, that appears in outline form in the third book of the *Mahābhārata.* The *Razam-Nameh* is a Persian translation of sections of the *Mahābhārata.*

This *Rāmāyana* manuscript arrived in Jaipur in the 1740s. This *Razam-Nameh* manuscript was part of the Imperial Library at Delhi until the Emperor of Delhi, Muhammad Shah, gave it to the Maharaja of Jaipur in the mid-18th century. The Maharaja Sawai Man Singh II Museum sent the photographs on exchange to the Freer Gallery of Art (FGA) in the early 1970s. FGA staff later supplemented the *Razam-Nameh* photographs with copy photoprints from a rare book in the Freer library: Alban G. Widgery. *Mahābhārata: Book of Photographs of the Paintings in the Razam-Nameh at the Palace, Jaipur, India.* n.p., n.d. Alban G. Widgery acquired the original photoprints in the book from the City Palace at Jaipur sometime before 1924.

Physical Description

There are 300 silver gelatin photoprints.

Subjects

The photographs reproduce two illustrated manuscripts, the *Rāmāyana* and *Razam-Nameh,* housed in the Maharaja Sawai Man Singh II Museum of the City Palace, Jaipur, India.

The *Rāmāyana* manuscript, with 176 full-page miniature paintings, recounts a religious folk legend that traces the life and adventures of the human god Rāma Dasarathi and his wife Sītā. The *Razam-Nameh* manuscript, containing 169 full-page miniature paintings, is a Persian translation of a section of the Hindu epic *Mahābhārata,* a religious poem that recounts a war between two families that took place near Delhi, India.

Arranged: Generally in the same order as they appear in the manuscripts.

Captioned: With catalog or negative number.

Finding Aid: Caption list to the *Razam-Nameh* manuscript.

Restrictions: Available by appointment only.

FG·30

Curt Maury Papers

Dates of Photographs: Late 1950s–1977

Collection Origins

Social services administrator, writer, and Indian art scholar Curt Maury (1909–1989) created the collection during the preparation of an unpublished manuscript titled "India's Folk Tradition as the Mirror of Mankind's Religious History." Born in Germany, Maury received a Ph.D. in German literature from the University of Vienna in 1935 and emigrated to the United States in 1939. He developed an interest in India, which he visited several times in the 1950s, 1960s, and 1970s. Maury produced extensive photographic records while conducting research on Indian folk art.

Some of the photographs in the collection were published in an earlier work: Curt Maury. *Folk Origins of Indian Art.* New York: Columbia University Press, 1969. After Maury's death, his brother, Hans Tischler, donated the collection to the Freer Gallery of Art.

Physical Description

There are 13,440 photographs including color dye coupler slides and silver gelatin photoprints. Other materials include books, ledgers, maps, notecards, a sketchbook, travel notebooks, and a typescript of the book.

Subjects

The photographs document Indian folk art, primarily religious artifacts and structures with applied decorative detailing, as well as Indian cultural activities and natural surroundings. Areas of India documented include the states of Andhra Pradesh, Gujarat, Karnataka, Kerala, Madhya Pradesh, Maharashtra, Rajasthan, and Tamil Nadu.

Religious buildings and architectural elements shown include the altar of Mahaprabhu (a Hindu yogi), cave temples, a shrine to the Hindu god Ganesh, the Taj Mahal, and temples to the Hindu gods Mahalakshmi, Shiva, and Vishnu-Rama. Other images of the built environment include bridges, cemeteries, city gates, city streets, a country market, forts, a high school, a laundry, a peacock courtyard in a palace, a private house, villages, and a zoo.

Natural surroundings illustrated include landscapes (showing caves, chalk rocks, cliffs, coffee trees, and mountains) and waterscapes (such as beaches, oceans, and ponds). There are images of modes of transportation (such as animals, bicycles, and chariots); religious objects (such as paintings and statues of gods and symbolic wooden clubs); sculptures (such as animal sculptures, figurative sculptures, and portrait sculptures, in both relief and free-standing form); and textiles (such as wall hangings). Some of the paintings and sculptures shown are of the Hindu gods Vishnu and Yellamma.

Activities and events illustrated include a bicycle race, a parade, a pilgrimage to a temple, a soccer game, and a wedding. Occupations illustrated include basket weavers, coconut vendors, merchants (selling holy images at a bazaar), and pastry chefs.

Arranged: By region, then by city or village.

Captioned: With codes keyed to index.

Finding Aid: Index titled "Appendix III," arranged geographically with a code for each location.

Restrictions: Available by appointment only.

FG·31

Miao Manuscript Photographs

Dates of Photographs: Circa 1960s

Collection Origins

Scholar Li Lin-ts'an created the collection during his research on a Chinese manuscript documenting the Miao people of China. The title and location of the manuscript are unknown. Li, who worked at the National Palace Museum in Peking (Beijing) from the 1940s through the 1970s, studied Chinese calligraphy and painting. A regular contributor to the *National Palace Museum Bulletin* in the 1960s and 1970s, Li was a visiting scholar at the Freer Gallery of Art (FGA) in the 1960s.

Originally inhabitants of central China's river valleys, the Miao were forced into south China by the Han Chinese around 300 B.C. During the 18th and 19th centuries, numerous battles against Han Chinese authorities and regular skirmishes with local bandits led the Miao to emigrate into Laos, Thailand, and Vietnam, where they were referred to as the Hmong or Meo.

Physical Description

There are 200 silver gelatin photoprints.

Subjects

The photographs reproduce drawings and text from an unidentified Chinese manuscript or picture book that provides an ethnographic study of the Miao (*A.K.A.* Hmong or Meo) people. The illustrations show Miao culture and environments, probably in southern China.

Photographs show drawings of Miao people bending crossbows, butchering animals, carrying water, courting, driving oxen, eating, emptying fish traps, fishing, forging metal, hunting, performing acupuncture, making baskets, playing games and sports, planting rice, plowing rice paddies, praying, relaxing by a fire, shearing sheep, spinning wool, sweeping courtyards, traveling, and walking in procession.

Drawings of structures reproduced include aqueducts, buildings such as shrines, and gates. There are drawings of art objects, farms and other landscapes, and occupations such as craftsmen, farmers, fishermen, metalsmiths, musicians, and soldiers. There are also images of calligraphy.

Arranged: By assigned number according to the order of the manuscript collection.

Captioned: With assigned number; accompanied by a page of text.

Finding Aid: No.

Restrictions: Available by appointment only.

FG·32

Philip Miles Photographs

Dates of Photographs: Circa 1920s

Collection Origins

Freer Gallery of Art (FGA) staff found the photonegatives within the *Carl Whiting Bishop Papers* and made copy photoprints. The photographs are attributed to Philip Miles. See the *Collection Origins* field of *FG·4* for further information on the Bishop Papers.

Physical Description

There are 35 photographs including silver gelatin dry plate photonegatives and silver gelatin photoprints (recent prints made from the vintage negatives).

Subjects

The photographs document Chinese architecture at the imperial Summer Palace in Peking (Beijing) near a hill known as Wan Shou Shan (meaning 10,000-year mountain). Architecture shown includes a building on a shore, a royal ceremonial hall, pagodas, and a pavilion. Other Peking structures illustrated include the Altar of Heaven, the Temple of Heaven, and the Yellow Temple with its Indian pagoda. There are also photographs of roads leading to the Ming tombs northwest of Peking, lined with monumental sculptures of camels, elephants, lions, and people.

Arranged: No.

Captioned: With subject.

Finding Aid: Caption list.

Restrictions: Available by appointment only.

FG·33

Ming and Qing Exhibit Picture Set

Dates of Photographs: 1970

Collection Origins

Freer Gallery of Art (FGA) staff assembled the collection with photographs purchased from the Asian Art Photographic Distribution Service (AAPDS), Department of the History of Art, University of Michigan. For information on AAPDS see the *Collection Origins* field of *FG·7*. AAPDS created the photographs for a catalog documenting an exhibit of calligraphy and paintings of the Ming and Ch'ing (or Qing) dynasties, sponsored by the Urban Council and the Min Ch'iu Society. The exhibit was curated by John Warner and shown at the City Museum and Art Gallery, Hong Kong, in 1970. Eddie Chan photographed the art work, which was lent by a private collector in Hong Kong. The photographs appear in the catalog: *Ming Ch'ing Hui Hua Chan Lan (Exhibition of Paintings of the Ming and Ch'ing Periods)*. Hong Kong: City Museum and Art Gallery, Urban Council, 1970.

Physical Description

There are 250 silver gelatin photoprints.

Subjects

The photographs document Chinese calligraphy and paintings created in the 1400s through the 1700s by major artists of the Ming and Ch'ing (Qing) dynasties. There are details and full views of the art works. The majority of the paintings are landscapes (such as mountain scenes and village views) and waterscapes (such as boats on a river). There are also images of animals (such as birds on branches) and Chinese families. Artists whose work is represented include Hsieh Shih-ch'en, Wang Chien, and Wang Hui.

Arranged: By AAPDS archive number.

Captioned: No.

Finding Aid: The AAPDS finding aid lists archive number, artist, and exhibit catalog number for each item.

Restrictions: Available by appointment only. The photographs are copyrighted by the Asian Art Photographic Distribution Service. Researchers interested in purchasing or publishing copies should contact AAPDS. See the *Restrictions* field of *FG·7* for the address.

FG·34

Monuments Modernes de la Perse Photographs

Dates of Photographs: 20th Century

Collection Origins

The collection was created to reproduce original graphic illustrations from a French book on Persian architecture, titled *Monuments Modernes de la Perse*. The book was purchased around 1950 by Islamic scholar Myron Bement Smith for his personal library. Smith (1897–1970) studied architecture in Persia from 1933 to 1937 and received a Ph.D. in Islamic archaeology from Johns Hopkins University in 1947. He was associated with the Library of Congress for 32 years (1938–1970), as well as Columbia University (1955), the Department of State Bureau of Educational and Cultural Exchange (1957–1960), the Pratt Institute (1962–1965), Pennsylvania State University (1967–1968), and UNESCO (1969).

Smith purchased the volume from *Bernard Quaritch's Catalogue No. 685*, which described the book as "very scarce. One of the few authentic works on Persian architecture with accurate measurements, elevations, sections, details, and ornaments." In 1972 the Smith Collection (see *FG·45*) was transferred to the Smithsonian Institution and officially donated the following year by Smith's wife, Katharine Dennis Smith. The original illustrations that these photographs reproduce appear in the following folio: Pascal Coste. *Monuments Modernes de la Perse; Mesures, Dessines et Decrits par Pascal Coste.* Paris: A. Morel, 1867. Copies of this book are housed in the Smithsonian's National Museum of Natural History anthropology library and Cooper-Hewitt Museum library.

Physical Description

There are 30 silver gelatin photoprints.

Subjects

The photographs reproduce graphic illustrations from the book *Monuments Modernes de la Perse*. The illustrations show the architecture of Persia (now Iran), particularly in Esfahān (Isfahan) and Tehrān, including private spaces (such as garden follies, gardens, and houses); public spaces (such as baths, bazaars, bridges, caravansaries, cemeteries, palaces, pavilions, and universities); religious structures (such as minarets, mosques, and tombs); and ruins (such as fortified towers and ruin reconstructions).

The architectural book plates reproduced include architectural elevations (both exterior and interior); detail drawings (such as cupolas and ornamentation); perspective drawings (such as exterior perspectives, interior perspectives, and partial perspectives); plans (such as city plans and floor plans); and sections (such as cross sections, longitudinal sections, and partial sections).

Bazaars illustrated include the Adji-Seid-Hussen in Kachan and the Bazar des Tailleurs in Esfahān. Illustrations depicting caravansaries (inns built to accommodate caravans) are captioned "Caravanserail Amin-Abad sur la Route d'Isphahan a Schiraz," "Caravanserail Chah Sultan-Hussein" (in Esfahān), and "Caravanserail Passengan su la Route de Teheran a Ispahan."

Illustrations of mosques illustrated are captioned "Mosque Djum'ah" (in Esfahān), "Mosquee du Medreceh Maderi-Chah Sultan-Hussein," "Mosquee Mesdjïd-I-Chah," "Mosquee de Sunni" (in Tabrīz), and "Mosquee et Tombeau d'Ismael Khoda-Bendeh." Pavilions illustrated include the "Pavilion des Huit Paradis" and "Pavilion des Miroirs" in Esfahān; "Pavilion Tchehel Souton, Dit des 40 Colonnes;" and the Pavilion of the Throne in Tehrān.

Private houses illustrated include the "Chateau de Kasr-i-Kadjar" in Tehrān, "Grande Maison a Ebher," "Maison a Tauris," and "Maison au Village d'Alvar." Other buildings illustrated include the "College Medresseh Maderi-chah-Sultan-Hussein," the "Palais Tchar-Bach," and the "Parallele des Voussures."

Other illustrations of the built environment are captioned "d'un Colombier in Isfahan," "Jmam et Cimetiere a Farseidjeh," "Minaret de Chah-Roustan," "Pont Allah Verdy-Khan" in Isfahan, the "Pont Hassan-Beg sur le Zeinderoud" in Esfahān, the Public Bath in Kachan, and the "Ruines de Rei." Also reproduced are drawings of the "Jardin Tchehel Souton, Dit des 40 Colonnes" and the "Palace Royale Mesdjïd-I-Chah."

Arranged: No.

Captioned: No.

Finding Aid: Index in French.

Restrictions: Available by appointment only.

FG·35

Nihon Ukiyo-e Kyōkai (Japan Ukiyo-e Society) Photographs

Dates of Photographs: 1972

Collection Origins

Members of the Nihon Ukiyo-e Kyōkai (Japan Ukiyo-e Society) created the collection to document the opening of an *ukiyo-e* (Japanese woodblock print) exhibit in Tokyo in 1972. The exhibit honored six prominent *ukiyo-e* artists, whose works date primarily from 1765 to 1868 and illustrate daily life in Edo-period Japan (1615–1868). The exhibit was one of several sponsored by the Society to commemorate its 10th anniversary.

Physical Description

There are 60 photographs including color dye coupler photoprints and silver gelatin photoprints.

Subjects

The photographs document an opening of an *ukiyo-e* (Japanese woodblock print) exhibit, part of the 10th anniversary celebration of Nihon Ukiyo-e Kyōkai (Japan Ukiyo-e Society). The photographs show visitors and dignitaries attending the opening, including Prince and Princess Takamatsu of Japan, as well as views of the exhibit installation. *Ukiyo-e* prints reproduced were designed by Suzuki Harunobu, Andō Hiroshige, Katsushika Hokusai, Torii Kiyonaga, Saitō Sharaku, and Kitagawa Utamaro. These prints depict Edo-era Japan including portraits of actors, courtesans, and geishas; cityscapes such as street scenes; landscapes, often with people; and scenes of human activity including theatrical productions.

Arranged: In original exhibit order.

Captioned: No.

Finding Aid: No.

Restrictions: Available by appointment only.

FG·36

Yoichi Okamoto Photographs

Dates of Photographs: 1979

Collection Origins

Yoichi Okamoto (1915–1985) created the collection to document a visit made in 1979 by Zhuo Lin, wife of Vice Premier Deng Xiaoping of China, to the Freer Gallery of Art (FGA). Okamoto was Lyndon Johnson's personal photographer during his presidency and later worked as a free-lance photographer for such publications as *Smithsonian* magazine. Okamoto's wife, Paula Okamoto, donated these negatives to the FGA in 1989. FGA staff created contact prints from the negatives.

Physical Description

There are 140 photographs including silver gelatin photonegatives and photoprints (contact prints).

Subjects

The photographs document a 1979 reception at the FGA for Zhuo Lin, wife of Chinese Vice Premier Deng Xiaoping. The photographs portray Zhuo Lin, former FGA director Thomas Lawton, other FGA staff members, and guests. There are also images of FGA exhibit galleries, including an exhibit of ceramics, graphic prints, and sculptures.

Arranged: No.

Captioned: No.

Finding Aid: No.

Restrictions: Available by appointment only.

FG·37

The People of India Collection

Dates of Photographs: 1850s–1860s

Collection Origins

John Forbes Watson and John William Kaye assembled this ethnological study collection from photographs made by British photographers in India. The collection documents the caste and culture groups of India for a British India Office multi-volume publication.

A graduate of Aberdeen University in England, John Forbes Watson (1827–1892) served as an assistant surgeon in the Bombay Medical Service from 1850 to 1853. While in India, Watson began to research Indian agricultural resources. In 1858 he became reporter on the products of India for the India Office in England. A year later, he began directing the India Office's India Museum, devoted to promoting trade in the British Empire. While there, he published several monographs on Indian plants and textiles. In 1867 he was appointed keeper of the museum and served in that capacity until he retired in 1879. John William Kaye was secretary of the India Office's Political and Secret Department.

The photographs appeared in the following publication: John William Kaye and John Forbes Watson, eds. *The People of India: A Series of Photographic Illustrations, with Descriptive Letterpress, of the Races and Tribes of Hindustan.* 8 vols. London: India Museum, 1868–1875. The India Office published 200 sets of the volumes, half for official use.

Photographers represented include J.C.A. Dannenberg, R.H. De Montmorency, E. Godfrey, Willoughby W. Hooper, H.C. McDonald, J. Mulheran, G. Richter, Shepherd & Robertson, B. Simpson, B.W. Switzer, H.C.B. Tanner, C.C. Taylor, and James Waterhouse. The Freer Gallery of Art and Arthur M. Sackler Gallery Archives obtained the volumes at an auction in London in May 1990.

Physical Description

There are 470 albumen photoprints, mounted in published volumes alongside text.

Subjects

Taken in the 1850s and 1860s, the photographs portray people of many castes, culture groups, and occupations in India, posed individually and in groups. Indian peoples portrayed include Bhogta, Bhoti, Chero, Dombo, Gond, Gujarati, Ho, Kachari, Kishangarh, Kotah, Lepcha, Mishmi, Munda, Naga, Pahari, Paithan, Rajput, Saora, Singpho, Thakur, Tharu, and Toda. Peoples portrayed are from India and surrounding areas, some of which are now in Bangladesh, Iran, and Pakistan, including Assam, Bareli, Behat, Cachar, Chittagong, Delhi, Hazara, Hisar, Kohat, Lahore, Madras, Munjpur, Mysore, Palamau, Shahabad, Shahjahanpur, Sikkim, and Sind.

Occupations illustrated include barbers, blacksmiths, carpenters, charcoal carriers, farmers, fish vendors, horse dealers, interpreters, landlords, mendicants, merchants, officials, priests, warriors, and water carriers. Activities shown include dancing and knitting. Artifacts documented include books, buildings, devotional objects, a *hookah* (smoking pipe), tools, and weapons such as bows, clubs, guns, and spears.

Arranged: By region.

Captioned: With culture group and region, some also with name and occupation of subject.

Finding Aid: Table of contents listing culture group and region for each image.

Restrictions: No.

FG·38

Photographic Archive from the Chinese National Palace and Central Museums

Dates of Photographs: Early 1960s

Collection Origins

The Department of the History of Art of the University of Michigan created this collection in the early 1960s to document the holdings of the Kuo Li Ku Kung Po Wu Yüan (National Palace Museum) in Taipei, Taiwan. The Department of the History of Art distributes copy photographs identical to this collection to educational institutions for use in research. Photographers represented include James R. Dunlop and Raymond Schwartz.

Physical Description

There are 4,250 silver gelatin photoprints.

Subjects

The photographs document selected Chinese artifacts, dating from prehistory to the 20th century, in the National Palace Museum, Taipei, Taiwan. There are photographs of bronze vessels, calligraphy, ceramic vessels, cloisonné, ink sticks, inkstones, lacquerware, paintings, silver objects, tapestries, and wood objects.

Many photographs reproduce landscape scrolls that incorporate scenes of agriculture, birds, family gatherings, flowers, and mountain pavilions and temples. Artists whose work is reproduced include Chao Meng-fu, Chü-jan, Fan K'uan, Kuo Hsi, Li Ti, Ma Yüan, Ni Tsan, Su Han-Ch'ên, Wang Hui, Wang Meng, and Wang Yüan-ch'i.

Arranged: Most numerically by University of Michigan archive number; some images of paintings arranged chronologically by dynasty and then by scroll format.

Captioned: With artist, date, format, inscription, medium, period, seal, subject, and title.

Finding Aid: 1) Card index arranged by archive number. 2) James F. Cahill's "Concordance to the Palace Museum Paintings." 3) "Taiwan Archives—Master List," divided into three parts arranged by archive number: a) lists of hanging scrolls including artist, concordance number, dynasty, format, and title; b) list of bronzes and ceramics including provenance, dynasty, form of vessel, and glaze or kiln site; and c) calligraphy lists, including artist, concordance number, dynasty, format, and title. 4) Inventory of photoprints listed in the *Chien Mu,* a National Palace Museum catalog, arranged by dynasty and scroll format according to Cahill's concordance.

Restrictions: Available by appointment only.

FG·39

James Marshall Plumer Papers

Dates of Photographs: 1930s

Collection Origins

James Marshall Plumer (1899–1960), a scholar of Asian art, created the collection for personal research and publication purposes. After receiving a B.A. from Harvard University, Plumer served as an administrative officer with the Chinese Government Service in Maritime Customs. From 1935 until his death, he taught art history at the University of Michigan and and continued to visit and work in China and Japan. In 1935 and 1937, Plumer discovered ancient kiln sites in the Chinese provinces of Fukien (Fujian) and Chekiang (Zhej-

iang). He wrote extensively on Chinese ceramics and edited the *Far Eastern Ceramic Bulletin* from 1950 to 1958.

Photographers and studios represented include the Fogg Art Museum of Harvard University, Charles B. Hoyt, Herbert Ingram, C.T. Loo, the Museum of Fine Arts (Boston), and James Marshall Plumer. Photographs from this collection were used in a 1938 exhibit, "Early Chinese Pottery: An Exhibition at Ann Arbor," held at the Institute of Fine Arts, University of Michigan. Some of the photographs also appeared in the following: 1) James Marshall Plumer. "Certain Celadon Potsherds from Samarra Traced to Their Source." *Ars Islamica.* 4 (1937): 195–200. 2) James Marshall Plumer. *Temmoku: A Study of the Ware of Chien.* Tokyo: Idemitsu Art Gallery, 1972. Caroline I. Plumer (Plumer's wife) donated the collection to the Freer Gallery of Art in 1961.

Physical Description

There are 250 photographs including silver gelatin photonegatives and photoprints. Other materials include correspondence, drawings, manuscripts, maps, notes, and printed material.

Subjects

The photographs document Chinese ceramics and kilns that were discovered by James Marshall Plumer in Fukien (Fujian) and Chekiang (Zhejiang) provinces, dating from the ninth and tenth centuries. Many of the images depict ceramics both at their original archaeological sites and in the laboratory. Most of the items are "wasters," imperfect ceramic objects that were broken at the kiln site at the time of manufacture. They include bowls, candlesticks, jars, tea cups, and vases. Other photographs show archaeological field workers including Plumer and local staff, field work activities, kilns, and the landscape surrounding the kilns.

Arranged: No.

Captioned: Some with descriptions including date, location, site, or other information.

Finding Aid: No.

Restrictions: Available by appointment only.

FG·40

John A. Pope Papers

Dates of Photographs: Early 20th Century–1978

Collection Origins

John A. Pope (1906–1982), former director of the Freer Gallery of Art (FGA), created the collection. Pope, who received a Ph.D. from Harvard University in 1955, first went to China in 1929 as a volunteer ambulance driver for the Red Cross. After returning to the United States, Pope studied Chinese art and subsequently lectured on the subject at Columbia University. During World War II he served in the Far East as an interpreter.

Pope joined the FGA staff in 1943 as a research associate. He then served as the museum's first curator of Chinese ceramics and became assistant director in 1946. Pope served as the FGA's director from 1962 until his retirement in 1972, after which he continued to serve as research curator of Chinese ceramics and director emeritus at the FGA until his death in 1982.

Pictures from this collection appear in two books by Pope: 1) *Chinese Porcelains from the Ardebil Shrine.* Washington, D.C.: Smithsonian Institution, Freer Gallery of Art, 1956. 2) *Fourteenth-Century Blue-and-White, a Group of Chinese Porcelains in the Topkapu Sarayi Müzesi, Istanbul.* Washington, D.C.: Smithsonian Institution, Freer Gallery of Art, 1952.

Photographers and studios represented include FGA staff, Lund University (Sweden), the Oriental Institute of the University of Chicago, John A. Pope, Robert Skelton, and the University of Wisconsin. The photographs were donated by Annamarie H. Pope (Pope's wife) in 1988, 1989, and 1990.

Physical Description

There are 10,020 photographs including color dye coupler photonegatives, photoprints, phototransparencies, and slides; dye transfer photoprints; silver gelatin dry plate lantern slides and photonegatives; and silver gelatin photonegatives and photoprints (including an infrared photoprint). Other materials include articles, bibliographies, biographical information, book reviews, ceramics, correspondence, drawings, lectures, manuscripts, maps, newspaper clippings, notebooks, notes, pamphlets, photostatic copies, research files, and subject files.

Subjects

Most of the photographs show Chinese Ming dynasty blue-and-white ceramic vessels, as well as pot-shards from such vessels. There are also photographs of other art objects from China, Japan, and Thailand; informal portraits of Pope's acquaintances and colleagues; and travel photographs of Asia, such as architectural studies, cityscapes, and landscapes of China, Egypt, Iran, Japan, and Thailand.

Other objects depicted include bamboo items, ceramics (from Japan and Thailand), costumes, funerary figures (from China), glassware, graphic prints, ivory work (from China), jade items, lacquerware (from China and Japan), paintings, pillar tombs, and sculptures.

Travel photographs show irrigated fields and villages in China; ruins in Egypt; the Ardebil (or Ardabil) Shrine in Persia (now Iran); and buildings, gardens, and pottery kilns in Japan. There are also photographic reproductions of maps of China. People portrayed include Chinese (such as children and workers); Egyptians; and Japanese.

Arranged: No.

Captioned: Some with date, owner, title, or type of ceramics.

Finding Aid: No.

Restrictions: Available by appointment only.

FG·41

Restless Landscape: Chinese Painting of the Late Ming Period Picture Set

Dates of Photographs: Circa 1970

Collection Origins

Freer Gallery of Art (FGA) staff assembled the collection from photographs created by the Asian Art Photographic Distribution Service (AAPDS) of the Department of the History of Art at the University of Michigan. For a history of AAPDS, see the *Collection Origins* field of *FG·7*. The FGA purchased the photographs from AAPDS used in the following exhibit catalog: James F. Cahill, ed. *Restless Landscape: Chinese Painting of the*

Late Ming Period. Berkeley, California: University Art Museum, 1971. The catalog documents an exhibit curated by James F. Cahill, held in 1971 and 1972 at the University Art Museum (University of California at Berkeley) and the Fogg Art Museum (Harvard University). The photographs were taken by Colin McRae.

Physical Description

There are 295 silver gelatin photoprints.

Subjects

The photographs reproduce Chinese landscape paintings and calligraphy from the late 16th and 17th centuries. Paintings reproduced include *The Chih Garden, Men Seated in a Bamboo Grove, View of Mount Sung,* and *Waterfall on Mount Lu.* Some paintings are shown in detail.

Arranged: By AAPDS archive number.

Finding Aid: AAPDS finding aid listing archive number, catalog number, artist, painting format, and title.

Restrictions: Available by appointment only. The photographs are copyrighted by the Asian Art Photographic Distribution Service. Researchers interested in purchasing or publishing copies should contact AAPDS. See the *Restrictions* field of *FG·7* for the address.

FG·42

Kenneth X. Robbins Photograph Collection

Dates of Photographs: 1927–1947

Collection Origins

Psychiatrist, collector of south Asian art, and writer Kenneth X. Robbins assembled the collection to document Indian society, particularly court nobles. The limited edition souvenir photograph album included was created to commemorate the 1945 Silver Jubilee of the last Nawab of Junagadh (now Gujarat, India), whose full name was Mahabat Khanji Rasukhanji Babi Bahadur. The Nawab, notorious for the money he spent on his dogs, was ousted in 1947 after repeatedly attempting to unite his country with Pakistan.

Photographers represented include the Photo Color Company (Ajmer) and K.L. Syed & Company (State Photographers, Palanpur). Kenneth X. Robbins donated the collection to the Freer Gallery of Art and Arthur M. Sackler Gallery Archives in 1990.

Physical Description

There are 45 photographs including collodion gelatin photoprints (POP) and silver gelatin photoprints, most (42) mounted in an album.

Subjects

The photographs document the Silver Jubilee celebration of Mahabat Khanji Rasukhanji Babi Bahadur, the last Nawab of Junagadh (now Gujarat, India), in 1945, including entertainment, events, and formal and informal portraits of participants.

The Nawab is shown being saluted by government officials, being weighed in silver, and receiving a gift. Performances by dancing women and marching bands are documented, as are sports such as horseback riding, rock lifting, and running. People portrayed include government officials, prisoners (in chains), the Nawab, the Nawab's son, nobles such as Kau Mull Ladha with his daughter in a limousine, prominent citizens of Junagadh, and uniformed men marching.

Arranged: Loosely grouped by subject in the album.

Captioned: With subject.

Finding Aid: A caption list.

Restrictions: No.

FG·43

Seal Photonegative Collection

Dates of Photographs: 1930s

Collection Origins

The collection is believed to have been assembled by former Freer Gallery of Art (FGA) director Archibald G. Wenley as part of a project to document seal impressions found on Asian paintings. Wenley (1898–1962) graduated from the University of Michigan and later studied at the Library School of the New York Public Library, L'École des Langues Orientales Vivantes, Institut de Hautes Études Chinoises, and the College of France. After working as an archaeological field assistant on an FGA-sponsored expedition in China (1923–1926), Wenley went on to serve as a research associate (1930–1942) and director (1943–1962) of the FGA.

Photographers and studios represented include H.F. Meyer, Nan T'ang Chao, Kan Chiu, Kan T'u, Tong Ying and Company, and Yananaka and Company. Some of the photographs appear in the following publication: Victoria Contag and Wang Chi Ch'ien. *Seals of Chinese Painters and Collectors of the Ming and Ch'ing Period.* Hong Kong: Hong Kong University Press, 1966.

Physical Description

There are 1,160 silver gelatin dry plate photonegatives.

Subjects

The collection reproduces Chinese and Japanese censor and signature seal impressions and inscriptions found on drawings, graphic prints, and paintings at the FGA. In Asian art, a seal imprint (made by a small die or disk) routinely served as a mark of approval, a signature, or a sign of ownership. The collection includes photographs of impressions made by censor's seals and signature seals. One image shows a seal impression on a Japanese graphic print or a theater announcement for the play *Mongaku.*

Arranged: By volume and FGA negative number.

Captioned: With date, donor, and an unidentified number.

Finding Aid: No.

Restrictions: Available by appointment only.

FG·44

Antoin Sevruguin Photographs

Dates of Photographs: Circa 1875–Circa 1920s

Collection Origins

Photographer Antoin Sevruguin (*A.K.A.* Antoin Khan, Antoine Sevruguine Dvarjanin, and Antoin Sevruguin Parvarde-ye-Iran) created the collection as part of his day-to-day operation of a commercial photographic studio in Tehrān, Persia (now Iran), from the 1870s until 1933. According to Sevruguin family correspon-

dence, Antoin Sevruguin (ca. 1830s–1933) initially trained as a painter before studying photography under the Russian photographer Ermakov. In the 1870s Sevruguin and his brothers Kolia and Emanuel conducted a photographic survey of several regions in northern Persia, photographing archaeological sites, landscapes, and tribal customs. Later, Sevruguin conducted a documentary trip in southern Iran for the German archaeologist Friedrich P.T. Sarre.

The Sevruguins settled in Tehrān and established a photographic studio. A well-known figure in Persia during the late 19th and early 20th centuries, Antoin Sevruguin photographed the Persian architecture, landscapes, peoples, and private and public events. His clients included two shahs (Nasir Al-Din Shah and Reza Shah), as well as members of Persia's political and social elite and middle class, including doctors, lawyers, and well-to-do merchants. In addition to his studio, Sevruguin operated a photographic sales shop where he sold his more sensational images of life in Tehrān, including photographs of criminal punishments, culture groups, religious figures, and women.

Family members credit Sevruguin with producing over 7,000 glass plate negatives during his lifetime. During a period of political turmoil in Persia, looters destroyed all but 2,000 of Sevruguin's original photonegatives. The surviving images were confiscated and ordered destroyed by the government of Reza Shah. Some photographs were spared destruction and were bought in Jerusalem by Jay Bisno, who donated them to the Freer Gallery of Art and Arthur M. Sackler Archives in 1985. Note: *FG·45* contains duplicates of some of these images.

Physical Description

There are 18 albumen photoprints.

Subjects

The photographs show scenes in Tehrān including cityscapes; portraits; and studies of criminal punishment. Cityscapes include images of the Jewish quarter and a temple in Tehrān. Portraits include a man with a falcon, members of a religious fraternity, and royalty such as Muzaffar Al-Din Shah and Nasir Al-Din Shah in front of the Peacock Throne. Nasir Al-Din Shah's funeral also is shown.

Images of criminal punishment include a bastinado (a whipping on the soles of the feet); the display (in chains) and hanging of the Shah's assassin; an execution in a public square; a live burial of a man (up to his neck); and prisoners with guards.

Arranged: No.

Captioned: With subject.

Finding Aid: List of subjects.

Restrictions: Available by appointment only.

FG·45

Myron Bement Smith Collection *A.K.A.* Islamic Archives

Dates of Photographs: 1870s–1966

Collection Origins

Myron Bement Smith, a scholar of Islamic and Iranian architecture and history, created the collection for research and publication purposes. For a biography of Smith, see the *Collection Origins* field of *FG·34*. In 1948, with the assistance of John Albert Wilson and T. Cuyler Young, Smith established the Islamic Archives, consisting of photographs and other archival material, to be administered jointly by the Committee for Islamic Culture and the American Council of Learned Societies. Seventy-five percent of the collection consists of Smith's work; the remainder was obtained from other sources by donation, loan, or purchase.

Smith used materials from the Islamic Archives to write over 50 publications and papers, including the following articles: 1) "Masjid-i Juma, Demawend." *Ars Islamica.* 2(2) (1935): 153–173. 2) "Manar and Masjid, Barsian (Isfahan)." *Ars Islamica.* 4 (1937): 7–41.

Material from other sources in this collection includes photographs taken by Antoin Sevruguin *(A.K.A. Antoin Khan, Antoine Sevruguine Dvarjanin, and Antoin Sevruguin Parvarde-ye-Iran)*, a photographer in Tehrān (active 1870s–1920s) and the court photographer for two shahs of Iran. For more details on Sevruguin, see the *Collection Origins* field of *FG·44*. Additional sources include the Pennsylvania Museum of Fine Arts, the Museo Nacionale d'Art Orientale, and the Wisconsin Historical Society.

In 1972 the Smith Collection was transferred to the Smithsonian Institution. It officially was donated to the Institution in 1973 by Smith's wife, Katharine Dennis Smith. The study collection of architectural objects and pot-shards went to the Freer Gallery of Art; the rest of the collection was housed in the National Anthropological Archives of the National Museum of Natural History's Department of Anthropology. In 1977 the photographic portion of the collection was transferred to the Freer Archives.

Several exhibits have used materials from this collection including a 1940 exhibit of Persian art in New York City; a photographic exhibit of Islamic architecture from Persia at the Library of Congress (1953); and "Antoin Sevruguin: Photographs of Iran" at the Arthur M. Sackler Gallery (1990–1991).

Photographers and studios represented include Basin-Yanin, V. Derounian Beyrouth, Bierstadt, Paul Neil Bombardier, Louise Dahl-Wolfe, William O. Douglas, Werner Ellinger, Henry Field, Henri Goblot, Harold D. Gresham, Elgin Groseclose, Guiragossian, Raymond A. Hare, Mohibul Hasan Khan, Y. Dugan Kuban, Aptallah Kuran, Fred P. Latimer, Richard Marshall, Charles W. Moore, Harold K. Parsons, Louise Pfeiffer, John A. Pope, Josephine Powell, Hossein Ravanabod, Hushang Sanai, Paul Schumacher, Henri Sevrig, Antoin Sevruguin (*A.K.A.* Anton Kahn), Abdul Grafu Sheikh, Cyril Stanley Smith, Myron Bement Smith, Reverend Thompson, Paul Vanderbilt, Lee Wallace, Bettina Warburg, Francis D. Weeks, Owen Maynard Williams, Ernest E. Wolfe, and T. Cuyler Young. Note: *FG·44* contains duplicates of some of these images.

Physical Description

There are 74,880 photographs including albumen photoprints; collodion wet plate lantern slides; color dye coupler photoprints, phototransparencies, and slides; silver gelatin dry plate lantern slides and photonegatives; and silver gelatin photonegatives (some nitrate) and photoprints (some copies, duplicates, and stereographs). Photographic formats represented include panoramas and stereographs. Other materials include architectural plans, correspondence, drawings, field notes, maps, minutes, photomechanicals (Woodburytypes), registers, reprints, sketches, and tracings.

Subjects

The photographs primarily document Islamic architecture in the Middle and Near East, dating from prehistory through 1966, as well as the daily life of the people in these areas. Regions documented include Central Asia, Europe, the Far East, the Middle East, the Near East, Southeast Asia, and the U.S.S.R. Cities shown include Agra, India; Jerusalem and Nazareth in Israel; and Esfahān (or Isfahan), Hamadān, Persepolis, Qom, Tabrīz, and Tehrān in Iran; and Rabat in Morocco.

Buildings and structures shown include the Damascus Gate in Jerusalem, Gulistan Palace in Tehrān (including the Peacock Throne), Mary's Well in Nazareth, mosques in Esfahān, and the Taj Mahal, as well as numerous bridges (such as Baghi Shah Bridge and the Rasht Road Bridge) and villages. Architectural details illustrated include ornamental patterns in mosaics and wall frescoes. Some photographs document the gothic influence in Islamic architecture. There are also city-scapes including bazaars, gardens, palaces, street scenes, and tent camps outside a palace.

Culture groups documented include Armenians; Bohemians (Bedouins); Persians; and Turks including children and women. Religious groups portrayed include Christian, Jewish, and Islamic peoples (including dervishes).

Other people and activities portrayed include criminals being executed (such as a man buried up to his neck), families posed outside their homes, laundresses, men praying, merchants (such as ice vendors), missionaries, musicians, roadside mendicants, rug weavers, shoppers in a bazaar, snake charmers, soldiers (some on military maneuvers), and wrestlers. There are also portraits of military figures such as Thomas E. Lawrence (Lawrence of Arabia), shahs such as Reza Shah and Nasir Al-Din Shah, and scholars such as Myron Bement Smith. Photographs from this collection are reproduced in the illustrations section of this volume.

Arranged: In two series. 1) Materials created by Smith, organized by negative number, then by geographic area. 2) Materials that were donated, lent, or sold to Smith, divided into two sections: a) photoprints and photonegatives produced by Sevruguin and b) photoprints, photonegatives, and slides produced by others. Sevruguin's photographs are arranged as follows: i) royal and military portraits; ii) village views and bridges; iii) bazaar and genre scenes; iv) architecture; v) arts; and vi) original photographs.

Captioned: Smith's silver gelatin photoprints and lantern slides with country, date, detail, district, monument, negative number, photographer, and town. Stereographs with date and subject or location and period. Sleeves containing photonegatives on nitrate with date, exposure information, light conditions, and time. Some of Sevruguin's photoprints with location including country, district, and town and subject.

Finding Aid: 1) Six-volume photographer's negative log book titled "M.B. Smith Leica Negative Register and Print Record," which incorporates 35mm contact photoprints, arranged by negative number and listing country, district, monument, and town; date; description; and photographer. 2) Self-indexing file of duplicate silver gelatin photoprints and index cards, containing date, dimensions, geographical area, site, specific architectural features, and style of architecture, as well as negative, print, or slide number. The file is divided into three sub-series: a) monument file, consisting of index cards arranged by geographical area, then by architectural type; b) architectural file, consisting of index cards and photoprints arranged by architectural features; and c) geographical file, consisting of photoprints arranged by location. 3) Index arranged

by city or site, monument, province, and type of image. 4) Smith's list of field photographs, listing date, f-stop setting, shutter speed, and subject. 5) Two-volume index to the Sevruguin sub-series arranged by negative number, incorporating xerographic prints, and listing image titles, negative numbers, parallel titles, photographer, process, and publication histories.

Restrictions: Available by appointment only. Many materials are restricted due to copyright status or preservation conditions. In particular, some of Smith's images and photographs from the Museo Nazionale D'Art Orientale/Roma, the Pennsylvania Museum of Art in Philadelphia, and the Wisconsin Historical Society may not be reproduced without written permission from the copyright holder, which is not necessarily the Smithsonian.

FG·46

Tessai Exhibition Photograph Collection

Dates of Photographs: 1958

Collection Origins

The collection was created by an unknown donor to document an exhibit of the work of Tomioka Tessai (1836–1924), a Japanese Buddhist bishop and artist. The exhibit, consisting of Tessai paintings and *kanji* (calligraphy) housed in the Kiyoshikojin Temple in Japan, toured the United States in 1958. The photographs appeared in a catalog: *Tomioka Tessai—The Commemorative Picture Album of Tessai's Circulating Exhibition in the U.S.A.* Takarazuka, Japan: Kiyoshi-Kojin, 1960. According to Freer Gallery of Art staff, the donor may be Kojo Sakamoto, Bishop of Kiyoshikojin Seichoji Temple, from which the paintings came.

Physical Description

There are 65 silver gelatin photoprints.

Subjects

The photographs document a 1958 traveling exhibit of paintings and *kanji* (calligraphy) by Buddhist Bishop Tomioka Tessai. Titles of the paintings reproduced include *Children Piling Stones to Make a Stupa; Flowers and Birds; A Haven for Immortals in the Eastern*

Sea; A Pleasant Life in a Gourd; and *The Zen Master Feng Kan.*

Arranged: In the same order as the exhibit catalog.

Captioned: No.

Finding Aid: 1) The catalog *Tomioka Tessai—The Commemorative Picture Album of Tessai's Circulating Exhibition in the U.S.A.* 2) Index in Japanese.

Restrictions: Available by appointment only.

FG·47

Topkapi Photograph Collection

Dates of Photographs: 1960s

Collection Origins

The collection was created for research purposes by an unidentified donor to document the artifacts and art objects in the Topkapi Saray Museum in Istanbul, Turkey.

Physical Description

There are 570 silver gelatin photoprints.

Subjects

The photographs document art work, dating from prehistory to the 17th century, in the Topkapi Saray Museum in Istanbul, Turkey. There are photographic reproductions of Chinese paintings, Islamic and Persian miniature paintings, decorative ornaments, and details from larger paintings. Painting details reproduced show animals, autumn scenes, battle scenes, beggars, birds on flowering branches, demons, landscapes, men on horseback, musicians, royal ceremonies, and women.

Arranged: No.

Captioned: No.

Finding Aid: No, although there is an illustrated guide to the objects in the Topkapi Saray Museum.

Restrictions: Available by appointment only.

FG·48

Dwight William Tryon Papers

Dates of Photographs: Late 19th Century–1920s

Collection Origins

Freer Gallery of Art (FGA) staff assembled the collection to document the life and work of American landscape painter Dwight William Tryon (1849–1925). The collection was begun in 1989 with an anonymous donation to the Freer Gallery of Art and Arthur M. Sackler Gallery Archives and supplemented later that year by a donation from FGA curator Linda Merrill.

Tryon studied art in Paris under Charles F. Daubigny and Henri-Josef Harpignies before returning to the United States in 1881. He taught art at Smith College from 1886 until his retirement in 1923, when he endowed the Smith College art museum. Photographers represented include Daniel S. Camp, R.S. De Lamater, Garber, and Lovell.

Physical Description

There are 30 photographs including albumen photoprints (some cabinet cards and cartes-de-visite) and silver gelatin photonegatives and photoprints. Other materials include correspondence, newspaper clippings, and a sketchbook.

Subjects

The photographs primarily document Dwight William Tryon's personal life. Portraits of Tryon show him in his youth and middle age, as well as fishing in a boat. Tryon family members portrayed include Alice Belden (his wife) and Delia R. Tryon (his mother). There are photographs of Tryon's summer house in South Dartmouth, Massachusetts, and the interior of his New York City apartment. There is also a photographic reproduction of one of his paintings.

Arranged: No.

Captioned: Some with date and name.

Finding Aid: No.

Restrictions: Available by appointment only.

FG·49

Tun-huang Photograph Collection

Dates of Photographs: 20th Century

Collection Origins

Freer Gallery of Art (FGA) staff assembled the collection from diverse sources to document the Tun-huang Buddhist cave temple in China. Tun-huang is one of a series of excavated caves dating from ca. 480 A.D. that contain paintings and statues of Buddha. Photographers and studios represented include the Art History Archives in Paris, the Louvre, the Musée Guimet, and John A. Pope.

Physical Description

The collection contains 125 silver gelatin copy photoprints.

Subjects

The photographs document Buddhist paintings and sculptures dating from 206 B.C. to 1100 A.D. in the Tun-huang cave temple in western Kansu, China. The art work depicts the life of Buddha, his incarnations, and his disciples. The photographs reproduce details and entire works of Buddhist figurative paintings and painted ceramic and wooden figurative sculptures.

Arranged: No.

Captioned: With description in French, museum stamp, and negative number.

Finding Aid: No.

Restrictions: Available by appointment only.

FG·50

Tz'u-hsi, Empress Dowager of China, 1835–1908, Photographs

Dates of Photographs: Circa 1903–1905, Late 1920s

Collection Origins

According to Freer Gallery of Art (FGA) staff, these photographs may have been taken by Hsün-ling *(A.K.A. Shun Ling)* (1874–1943), the son of Lady Yü-keng, senior lady-in-waiting to the last empress dowager of China, Tz'u-hsi (1835–1908).

Hsün-ling studied photography as a hobby while living in Tokyo and Paris. At the time the photographs were taken, he was an official of the Electricity Division of the Imperial Household. The photographs were acquired by Hsün-ling's brother-in-law, Thadeus C. White, and later by Mrs. Ernst von Harringa, who sold them to the FGA in 1963 and 1964. The photographs have appeared in the following publication: Katharine A. Carl. *With the Empress Dowager of China.* New York: The Century Company, 1907. Note: A possibly related collection is listed in a May 5, 1979, sales catalog for Philips, a New York-based auction house. On page 183, the catalog describes a group of "silver prints" of Chinese portraits by Shun Ling of China.

Physical Description

There are 110 photographs including silver gelatin dry plate photonegatives (some copy) and silver gelatin photonegatives (copy) and photoprints (some copy).

Subjects

The photographs document the last empress dowager of China, Tz'u-hsi, and her court in both the Forbidden City and the Summer Palace, probably between 1903 and 1905. The empress dowager is shown alone and with ladies and eunuchs of the court.

There are portraits of Tz'u-hsi in formal attire, in a garden, on the imperial barge on K'un-ming Lake, with the imperial throne, in a sedan chair, and in a snow-covered courtyard. Members of the royal court portrayed include Princess Der Ling and Lady Roongling, Hsün-ling's sisters; Li Lien-ying, the chief eunuch; Lily, Hsün-ling's daughter; and Lady Yü-keng. Other portraits include 18 young Chinese ladies-in-waiting; Kuang-hsü, Emperor of China (1871–1908), and his wife Empress Hsiao-ting (1868–1913); and P'u-i

(1906–1967) and his wife Wan-jung. There are photographic reproductions of a jade Buddha and two paintings of the empress dowager.

Arranged: No.

Captioned: Some with negative number or subject.

Finding Aid: Index listing negative number and subject.

Restrictions: Available by appointment only.

FG·51

University of Glasgow Photographs

Dates of Photographs: 1980s

Collection Origins

The University of Glasgow in Scotland created the collection as part of the on-going exchange of information about American painter James Abbott McNeill Whistler between the University's library and the Freer Gallery of Art (FGA). The FGA and the University of Glasgow own the world's two largest collections of Whistler's paintings and drawings.

American-born James Abbott McNeill Whistler (1834–1903) first studied art at the Russian Imperial Academy when his father, military engineer George Washington Whistler, was hired to build a railroad from St. Petersburg to Moscow. Whistler returned to the United States in 1849 and studied at West Point from 1851 to 1854.

After moving to Paris in 1855, Whistler studied painting under Charles Gleyre and published his first set of etchings. In 1859 Whistler went to London, where he became celebrated for his elegant figure and acerbic wit, as well as for his etchings, lithographs, and portrait paintings. Rejected by the Paris Salon, Whistler's *Symphony in White* appeared in the Salon des Refusés in 1863. A successful libel lawsuit in 1878 against art critic John Ruskin led to Whistler's bankruptcy. While living in Venice in 1879 and 1880, Whistler produced two groups of etchings that salvaged his career and brought him international acclaim.

Whistler returned to England in 1881 and became a leading proponent of the "art for art's sake" doctrine. He wrote books such as *The Gentle Art of Making Enemies* (1890) and served as president of the Royal Society of British Artists (1886–1888). After marrying artist and model Beatrix Godwin in 1888, Whistler opened the Academy Carmen in Paris, where he was active as an etcher, lithographer, and teacher until 1901.

The University of Glasgow received its Whistler materials from Rosalind Birnie Philip, Whistler's sister-in-law and executor of his will. The FGA's Whistlers were donated by museum founder Charles Lang Freer, a prominent patron of Whistler. For a biography of Freer, see the introduction to the FGA. These photographs were donated to the FGA in 1984 by the University of Glasgow.

Physical Description

There are 405 silver gelatin duplicate photoprints.

Subjects

The photographs document Whistler's drawings, etchings, lithographs, and paintings, dating from 1890 to 1900, housed at the University of Glasgow's Hunterian Art Gallery in Scotland. There are also photographs of objects owned by Whistler and a painting by Alfred Stevens (1857).

Works by Whistler reproduced include *Florence Leyland Standing; Girl in a Long Dress Seated in Profile to the Left; A Grey Note: Village Street; Nude Girl Standing with Both Elbows Resting on a Rail; Off the Dutch Coast; Red and Gold: Salute Sunset; Resting; Rose Drapery; Rose et Vert—Une Étude; A Shop with a Balcony; Study of Four Hands; Two Caricatures of Oscar Wilde as a Pig and a Jockey;* and *Venus: A Nude on the Shore.*

Arranged: No.

Captioned: With an assigned number; most also with date, dimensions, donor, medium, and name of person or subject depicted.

Finding Aid: No.

Restrictions: Available by appointment only. No reproductions may be made.

FG·52

University of Michigan Museum of Art Shāhnāma Manuscript Photoprints

Dates of Photographs: 1960s–1980s

Collection Origins

Freer Gallery of Art (FGA) staff assembled the collection from copy photoprints of a 15th century Persian manuscript at the University of Michigan Museum of Art in Ann Arbor.

Physical Description

There are 35 silver gelatin photoprints.

Subjects

The photographs document a *Shāhnāma,* an illuminated King's Book of Kings, containing illustrated stories of the lineage of Persian rulers from mid-15th century Persia (now Iran). The photographs reproduce calligraphy and miniature paintings from the manuscript. Painting details show beheadings, combat, courtship, demons, devils, dragons, prisoners, and members of the royal court.

Arranged: By location of the image in the original manuscript.

Captioned: With location headings.

Finding Aid: No.

Restrictions: Available by appointment only.

FG·53

Vever Family Photograph Album

Dates of Photographs: 1881–1930

Collection Origins

The collection was created by Vever family members, including Henri Vever (1854–1942), an owner of and designer for Maison Vever, a Paris jewelry firm. Member of an elite circle of art collectors in Paris at the turn of the century, Vever purchased French impressionist paintings, Japanese *ukiyo-e* woodblock prints, and Persian manuscripts containing miniature paintings. Jacqueline Mautin, Vever's granddaughter, donated the collection to the Freer Gallery of Art and Arthur M. Sackler Gallery Archives in 1988.

Physical Description

There are 100 photographs including albumen cartes-de-visite, collodion gelatin cartes-de-visite (POP), and silver gelatin photoprints (some cartes-de-visite). Other materials include a communion card.

Subjects

The photographs document jeweler Henri Vever, his family, and their estate in France. Vever family members are shown attending family weddings, dining, hunting, playing (as children) with toys, sewing, and traveling. Modes of transportation illustrated include animals (such as camels, donkeys, and a horse with buggy), automobiles, and bicycles. There are also landscapes of the Vever estate in France showing several views of the house and gardens, with plants and ponds.

Vever family members portrayed include Henri Vever, Jean-Jacques Ernest Vever (his father), Paul Vever (his brother), and his mother. There are portraits of Jeanne Vever (Henri's wife) and Mr. and Mrs. Jean Hilaire Monthiers (his wife's parents). Marguerite Vever Mautin (Henri Vever's daughter), Andre Mautin (her husband), and François and Jacqueline Mautin (their children) also are portrayed.

Arranged: Chronologically.

Captioned: Most with date and name.

Finding Aid: No.

Restrictions: Available by appointment only.

FG·54

Henri Vever Papers

Dates of Photographs: Circa 1864–1930

Collection Origins

The collection was created by art collector and jeweler Henri Vever (1854–1942), who owned Maison Vever, a jewelry company in Paris. For a biography of Vever, see the *Collection Origins* field in *FG.53*. Photographers represented include Chiltin Berger, J. Caron, A. Dietsch, and Abel Paris. Vever's grandson, François Mautin, donated the papers in 1988 to the Freer Gallery of Art.

Physical Description

There are 24 photographs including albumen photoprints (some cartes-de-visite), collodion gelatin photoprints (POP), platinum photoprints, and silver gelatin photoprints. Other materials include diaries, ledgers, a list of dinner guests, postcards, and a reproduction of a sword pommel. The diaries have been reproduced on microfilm.

Subjects

The photographs document jewelry designer and art collector Henri Vever, his family, and his home. People portrayed include Henri Vever, Jeanne Vever (his wife), and Marguerite Vever Mautin (his daughter). There is a photographic reproduction of a drawing of Jean Hilaire Monthiers (Vever's father-in-law). There are also landscapes of Vever's estate in France and scenes of family members with bicycles.

Arranged: No.

Captioned: Some with date and name.

Finding Aid: No.

Restrictions: Available by appointment only.

FG.55

Wan-go Weng Collection: Tung Ch'i Ch'ang Paintings, 1555–1636

Dates of Photographs: 20th Century

Collection Origins

An unknown photographer created the collection to document Wan-go Weng's holdings of paintings by Chinese artist Tung Ch'i Ch'iang. Weng, an American filmmaker and historian of Chinese art, produced a 13-part film documentary called *China: The Enduring Heritage.* He also served as the president of the China Institute in New York (1982–1986). He has written several publications, including the following: 1) *China: A History of Art.* New York: Harper & Row, 1973. 2) *Chinese Painting and Calligraphy: A Pictorial Survey; 69 Fine Examples from the John M. Crawford, Jr., Collection.* New York: Dover, 1978. 3) *The Palace Museum: Treasures of the Forbidden City.* New York: Harry N. Abrams, Inc., 1982.

Tung Ch'i Ch'iang (1555–1636) was a widely traveled member of the class of scholar/officials who governed Ming-era China. Eventually ascending to the presidency of the Board of Rites, Tung was known both as a calligrapher and a painter. Working with Ch'ên Chi-ju and Mo Shih-lung, Tung studied the historical techniques of Chinese brush and ink painting. He developed a classification system that grouped Chinese paintings into two schools—southern (spiritual or philosophical) and northern (courtly and decorative). This distinction greatly influenced later writings on Chinese art.

Physical Description

There are 75 silver gelatin photoprints.

Subjects

The photographs document Chinese landscape paintings by Tung Ch'i-Ch'ang, dating from 1555 to 1636 (the late Ming dynasty), owned by filmmaker and art historian Wan-go Weng. Images include full views and details of the paintings.

Arranged: No.

Captioned: With artist, collection, date, format, and title in Chinese and English.

Finding Aid: No.

Restrictions: Available by appointment only.

FG.56

Gus L. Wolf Photograph Collection

Dates of Photographs: Circa Early 1940s

Collection Origins

Gus L. Wolf discovered the collection abandoned behind an antique store in New Jersey. He donated the photographs to the Freer Gallery of Art and Arthur M. Sackler Gallery Archives in 1989. Copy photoprints were made by OPPS.

Physical Description

There are 50 photographs including silver gelatin photonegatives and photoprints.

Subjects

The photographs document art and architecture of southeast Asia. Structures shown include buildings, gates, monuments, ruins, sculptures (some of Buddha), and tombs. There are also portraits of an Asian woman and child and a Western man.

Arranged: No.

Captioned: No.

Finding Aid: No.

Restrictions: Available by appointment only.

FG·57

Kaihō Yūshō Photograph Collection

Dates of Photographs: 1970s

Collection Origins

Bettina Geyger-Klein of the University of Heidelberg assembled this collection to document the panel and screen paintings of Kaihō Yūshō, a painter from 16th and 17th century Japan. As the younger son of a military family, Kaihō Yūshō (1533–1615) became a Buddhist monk at Tōfukuji Temple. A student of Kanō Motonobu, Yūshō's patrons included Hideyoshi and Emperor Goyōzei, whom Yūshō had tutored in art while the emperor was the imperial prince. A popular Momoyama screen and wall painter, Yūshō is credited with assisting Eitoku in painting Hideyoshi's palace at Jurakudai and for creating panels and screen paintings for Kennin-ji Temple in Kyoto. Yūshō's Zen-inspired brush line and use of color influenced the work of decorative school painters such as Kōetsu and Sōtatsu.

Photographs in the collection have appeared in the following publication: Takeda Tsuneo. *Kennin-ji*. Vol. 7, *Shōhekiga Zenshū*. Tokyo: Bijutsu Shuppan-sha, 1968. Geyger-Klein donated the collection to the Freer Gallery of Art in the 1970s.

Physical Description

There are 90 silver gelatin photoprints.

Subjects

The photographs reproduce 16th and early-17th century panel and screen paintings by Kaihō Yūshō for the sliding doors and walls of the Kennin-ji Temple in Kyoto, Japan. Images include details of such paintings as *Birds and Flowers*, *Clouds and Dragons*, *Four Pleasures*, *Landscape*, and *Seven Sages in Bamboo Grove*.

Arranged: No.

Captioned: No.

Finding Aid: No.

Restrictions: Available by appointment only.

FG

Photography Laboratory

Photography Laboratory
Freer Gallery of Art and Arthur M. Sackler Gallery
Smithsonian Institution
Washington, D.C. 20560
John G. Tsantes, Photography Department
(202) 357-2029
Hours: Monday–Friday, 10 a.m.–5 p.m.

Scope of the Collections	There are six collections with 77,400 images. Note: The Photography Laboratory also houses two related Arthur M. Sackler Gallery collections containing 22,550 images. For descriptions of these collections, see *SG·1* and *SG·2*.
Focus of the Collections	The photographs document the Freer Gallery of Art (FGA) buildings, events, holdings, and staff members. Artifacts illustrated date from prehistory to the present and include calligraphy, ceramics, graphic prints, manuscripts, metalwork, paintings, and sculptures. The works are from the Far East including China, Japan, Korea, and Tibet (now Xizang); India and Indo-China; and the Near East including Asia Minor, Byzantium (now Istanbul, Turkey), Egypt, Iraq, and Syria; as well as from Europe and the United States.
Photographic Processes and Formats Represented	There are color dye coupler photonegatives, photoprints, phototransparencies, and slides; silver gelatin dry plate photonegatives; and silver gelatin photonegatives and photoprints.
Other Materials Represented	The Photography Laboratory also contains videotapes.
Access and Usage Policies	The collections are open to the public for research by appointment only. The registrar's database serves as a finding aid to the accessioned objects collections. Photographic copies of unrestricted images are ordered through the Museum Shop, which determines the charge.
Publication Policies	Researchers must obtain permission from the appropriate Freer Gallery of Art staff of the Smithsonian Institution to reproduce a photograph and may also have to obtain permission from the copyright holder, which is not necessarily the Smithsonian Institution. Each reproduction must bear the credit line "Courtesy of the Freer Gallery of Art, Smithsonian Institution, Washington, D.C.," together with the accession number and any additional information required by the Gallery.
	Copies of photographs may be ordered by contacting Laveta Emory, Supervisor, Mail Order Department, Gallery Shop, FGA, Smithsonian Institution, Washington, D.C., 20560. Those wishing to publish an image must complete a Permission Request Form, obtained from the Rights and Reproductions Office, FGA, Smithsonian Institution, Washington, D.C.,

20560, (202) 786-2088. All permissions to publish are for one-time use, only for the publication specified, and may not be sold or transferred. A copy of the publication must be sent gratis to the FGA library. No FGA images may be cropped, overprinted with type, or altered in any way without prior written approval from the Gallery.

FG·58

FGA Accessioned Objects Photograph Collection

Dates of Photographs: 1940s–Present

Collection Origins

Freer Gallery of Art (FGA) and Arthur M. Sackler Gallery (ASG) Photography Laboratory staff created the collection to document FGA accessioned objects for use by FGA and ASG staff. Staff photographers represented include Jeffrey Crespi, James T. Hayden, Kim Nielsen, Ray Schwartz, Bernard Shoper, and John G. Tsantes.

Some of the photographs have been published in the following books: 1) Esin Atil. *Art of the Arab World.* Washington, D.C.: Smithsonian Institution, Freer Gallery of Art, 1975. 2) Esin Atil, W.T. Chase, and Paul Jett. *Islamic Metalwork in the Freer Gallery of Art.* Washington, D.C.: Smithsonian Institution, Freer Gallery of Art, 1985. 3) Freer Gallery of Art. *Masterpieces of Chinese and Japanese Art: Freer Gallery of Art Handbook.* Washington, D.C.: Smithsonian Institution Press, 1976. 4) Susan Hobbs. *The Whistler Peacock Room.* 4th ed. Washington, D.C.: Freer Gallery of Art, Smithsonian Institution, 1980. 5) John A. Pope. *The Freer Gallery of Art.* Washington, D.C.: Columbia Historical Society, 1971. 6) John A. Pope, Josephine H. Knapp, and Esin Atil. *Oriental Ceramics: The World's Great Collections.* Tokyo: Kodansha, 1975, 1981.

Physical Description

There are 65,340 photographs including color dye coupler photonegatives, photoprints, phototransparencies, and slides; silver gelatin dry plate photonegatives; and silver gelatin photonegatives and photoprints.

Subjects

The photographs document most of the 27,000 art works in the FGA's holdings, dating from prehistory to the 20th century. Art works shown originate from the Far East including China, Japan, Korea, and Tibet (now Xizang); India and Indo-China; and the Near East including Asia Minor, Byzantium (now Istanbul, Turkey), Egypt, Iraq, Turkey, Persia (now Iran), and Syria; as well as from Europe and the United States.

Asian art works reproduced are in many formats, processes, and techniques including bronzeware; calligraphy; ceramic objects; glassware; ivory carvings; jade objects; lacquerware; manuscripts; metalwork; paintings including albums, screens, and scrolls; porcelains; and sculptures. Art genres represented include landscapes, narrative paintings, portraits, religious scenes, still lifes, and waterscapes.

Artists whose work is reproduced include Chinese calligraphers such as Wang Hsi-chih; Chinese painters such as Chao Meng-fu, Ch'ien Hsuan, and Kung K'ai; Japanese ceramic artists such as Ogata Kenzan; Japanese painters such as Kawanabe Gyōsai, Ogata Kōrin, Minagawa Kien, Sesson, and Nonomura Sōtatsu; and Japanese *ukiyo-e* (woodblock print) artists such as Andō Hiroshige and Katsushika Hokusai.

Western art works illustrated include 19th century American and European graphic work such as drawings, engravings, etchings, lithographs, and pastels, as well as paintings such as oils and watercolors. Visual genres depicted in the Western works include landscapes, portraits, religious scenes, still lifes, and waterscapes.

American and European artists represented include American architects such as Charles Adams Platt; American painters such as George Butler, Thomas W. Dewing, Childe Hassam, Winslow Homer, Gari Melchers, Willard L. Metcalf, John F. Murphy, Albert Pinkham Ryder, John Singer Sargent, Abbott H. Thayer, Dwight William Tryon, John Henry Twachtman, and James Abbott McNeill Whistler; British painters such as Joseph Lindon Smith; and French painters such as Charles Gillot.

Arranged: By object's accession number.

Captioned: With object's accession number; some also with date and description.

Finding Aid: Registrar's database, listing object's accession number, country of origin, date, and medium.

Restrictions: No.

FG·59

FGA and ASG Historical Photograph File

Dates of Photographs: 1940s–Present

Collection Origins

Freer Gallery of Art (FGA) and Arthur M. Sackler Gallery (ASG) Photography Laboratory staff assembled the collection to document the history of the two museums. Photographers and studios represented include Alvin Langdon Coburn, Jeffrey Crespi, James T.

Hayden, Yousuf Karsh, Kim Nielsen, Edward Steichen, and John G. Tsantes.

Physical Description

There are 3,300 photographs including color dye coupler photonegatives, photoprints, and slides and silver gelatin photonegatives and photoprints (some copies).

Subjects

The photographs document the history of the FGA and the ASG from their beginnings to the present. Images of the museum buildings include construction, exteriors and interiors, the garden, and renovations. Events documented include artists demonstrating their work, the ASG's opening, and exhibits such as "The Noble Path." There are also images of museum advertisements and publicity.

Individuals portrayed include artists such as James Abbott McNeill Whistler and Yani, FGA and ASG director Milo Beach, founders Charles Lang Freer and Arthur M. Sackler, staff, and visitors such as the empress of Japan and the queen of Jordan.

Arranged: By negative number, roughly chronologically.

Captioned: Some with event or subject.

Finding Aid: No.

Restrictions: No.

FG·60

FGA and ASG Personnel Photograph File

Dates of Photographs: 1982–Present

Collection Origins

Freer Gallery of Art (FGA) and Arthur M. Sackler Gallery (ASG) Photography Laboratory staff created the collection to document museum staff. Pictures originally were used for passports and for public relations. Photographers represented include Kim Nielsen and John G. Tsantes.

Physical Description

There are 1,550 photographs including color dye coupler photonegatives and photoprints and silver gelatin photonegatives and photoprints.

Subjects

The photographs portray FGA and ASG staff since 1982. Many images are studio portraits; others show staff members at work and posing with museum objects.

Arranged: Chronologically.

Captioned: With date and name.

Finding Aid: No.

Restrictions: No.

FG·61

FGA and ASG Public Relations File

Dates of Photographs: 1971–Present

Collection Origins

Freer Gallery of Art (FGA) and Arthur M. Sackler Gallery (ASG) Photography Laboratory staff created the collection to document museum events for publications and public relations purposes.

Physical Description

There are 4,500 photographs including color dye coupler photonegatives and photoprints and silver gelatin photonegatives and photoprints.

Subjects

The photographs document museum events from 1971 to the present at the FGA and ASG. Exhibit openings documented include "Decade of Discovery," "The Imperial Image," "Timur and the Princely Vision: Persian Art and Culture in the Fifteenth Century," and "Warring States." Other events documented include a calligraphy workshop, restoration of James Abbott McNeill Whistler's Peacock Room, tours, and visits from Asian and Near Eastern leaders and officials.

Arranged: Chronologically.

Captioned: With date and event.

Finding Aid: No.

Restrictions: No.

FG·62

FGA and ASG Staff Photograph File

Dates of Photographs: 1940s–Present

Collection Origins

Freer Gallery of Art (FGA) and Arthur M. Sackler Gallery (ASG) Photography Laboratory staff assembled the collection for FGA and ASG staff research and publications. Many of the images were taken by Photography Laboratory photographers at staff request; others were received from outside sources.

Physical Description

There are 900 photographs including color dye coupler phototransparencies and slides and silver gelatin photonegatives and photoprints. Some of the photographs are copies.

Subjects

The photographs document FGA and ASG staff research projects. Images include Asian art objects, book illustrations, building plans, field photos, and FGA and ASG staff portraits.

Arranged: Alphabetically by staff member.

Captioned: Some with subject.

Finding Aid: No.

Restrictions: Available by appointment only. Some materials are under copyright protection and may not be reproduced.

FG·63

FGA and ASG Study and Vault Photograph Collection

Dates of Photographs: 1940s–Present

Collection Origins

Freer Gallery of Art (FGA) and Arthur M. Sackler Gallery (ASG) Photography Laboratory staff created the collection to document unaccessioned objects for research purposes. Staff photographers represented include James T. Hayden, Kim Nielsen, and John G. Tsantes.

Physical Description

There are 1,800 photographs including color dye coupler photonegatives, photoprints, and phototransparencies and silver gelatin photonegatives and photoprints.

Subjects

The photographs document unaccessioned Asian art objects in the FGA. Artifacts shown include bronzeware, ceramics, porcelain objects, pot-shards, rubbings, and sculptures.

Arranged: In two series. 1) Study objects. 2) Vault objects. Then arranged by medium.

Captioned: No.

Finding Aid: No.

Restrictions: Available for research only. No reproductions may be made.

FG

Technical Laboratory

Technical Laboratory
Freer Gallery of Art and Arthur M. Sackler Gallery
Smithsonian Institution
Washington, D.C. 20560
W. Thomas Chase, Head Conservator
(202) 357-2014
Hours: Monday–Friday, 10 a.m.–5 p.m.

Scope of the Collections

There are five photographic collections with approximately 31,830 images.

Focus of the Collections

The Technical Laboratory was created by R.J. Gettens in 1951 to restore and stabilize the Freer Gallery of Art (FGA) fine art holdings. Most objects examined by the Laboratory are FGA accessions or items being considered for acquisition. The Technical Laboratory also has served the Arthur M. Sackler Gallery (ASG) since it opened in 1987. The photographs are before-and-after shots showing the deterioration and restoration of fine art objects at the FGA and ASG, as well as in other museums and private holdings. Some of the images are photomicrographs, radiographs, and scanning electron microscope (SEM) photomicrographs created in the process of studying an object. Objects documented include Chinese, Japanese, Korean, Near Eastern, and Western art work, such as ceramics, glassware, metalwork, paintings, and sculptures, dating from prehistory to the present. Note: Since this volume was completed the Technical Laboratory has changed its name to the Department of Conservation and Scientific Research.

Photographic Processes and Formats Represented

There are color dye coupler photomicrographs, photonegatives, photoprints, phototransparencies, and slides (Kodachrome and Ektachrome); dye diffusion transfer photomicrographs and photoprints (Polaroid); silver gelatin dry plate photonegatives; and silver gelatin photonegatives and photoprints (some photomicrographs, radiographs, and SEMs).

Other Materials Represented

The technical laboratory also contains audiotape cassettes, correspondence, examination reports, memos, microprobe printouts, notes, xerographic copies, and x-ray specifications.

Access and Usage Policies

Open to scholarly researchers, who should call or write in advance for an appointment, describing their research topic, the type of material that interests them, and their research aim.

Publication Policies

Researchers must obtain permission from the Smithsonian Institution's Freer Gallery of Art Technical Laboratory to reproduce a photograph and may also have to obtain permission from the copyright holder, which is not necessarily the Smithsonian Institution. The preferred credit line is "Courtesy of the Department of Conservation and Scientific Research, Freer Gallery of Art and Arthur M. Sackler Gallery, Smithsonian Institution."

Copies of photographs may be ordered by contacting Laveta Emory, Supervisor, Mail Order Department, Gallery Shop, FGA, Smithsonian Institution, Washington, D.C., 20560. Those wishing to publish an image must complete a Permission Request Form, obtained from the Rights and Reproductions Office, FGA, Smithsonian Institution, Washington, D.C., 20560, (202) 786-2088. All permissions to publish are for one-time use, only for the publication specified, and may not be sold or transferred. A copy of the publication must be sent gratis to the FGA library. No FGA images may be cropped, overprinted with type, or altered in any way without prior written approval from the Gallery.

FG·64

FGA and ASG Technical Laboratory Negative Collection

Dates of Photographs: Circa 1900–Present

Collection Origins

Freer Gallery of Art (FGA) Technical Laboratory and other staff created the collection, beginning in the early 1900s, to document the physical condition and restoration of the museum's artifactual holdings. For a history of the laboratory, see the department introduction. Note: Since this volume was completed the Technical Laboratory merged with the East Asian Paintings Conservation Studio and changed its name to the Department of Conservation and Scientific Research.

Physical Description

There are 4,950 photographs including color dye coupler photonegatives, photoprints, and phototransparencies; dye diffusion transfer photomicrographs (some SEMs) and photoprints (Polaroid); silver gelatin dry plate photonegatives; and silver gelatin photonegatives and photoprints.

Subjects

The photographs document deterioration and restoration of objects in the Freer Gallery of Art collections. Objects shown include American paintings such as a James Abbott McNeill Whistler oil painting; Chinese bronzes such as caldrons, mirrors, and ceremonial vessels; Chinese, Japanese, Korean, and Mamluk metalware such as bowls, chaplets, knife money, and mirrors; and Japanese *ukiyo-e* paintings.

Arranged: In four series. 1) FGA objects, by accession number. 2) Study and vault collections, by vault or registration number. 3) Photomicrographs, by subject. 4) 8″ × 10″ negatives and transparencies.

Captioned: With object's accession, registration, or vault number; date of photograph; description of object; exposure information including the length of exposure, magnification, and type of film, lens, and light; and the nature of damage suffered by the object.

Finding Aid: No.

Restrictions: Available by appointment only.

FG·65

FGA and ASG Technical Laboratory Notebook Collection

Dates of Photographs: 1965–Present

Collection Origins

The Freer Gallery of Art (FGA) and Arthur M. Sackler (ASG) Technical Laboratory staff assembled the collection to serve as evidence for technical studies, to document object deterioration and restoration, and to function as a master control file for the study of collection objects. For a history of the laboratory, see the introduction to the department. Photographers represented include staff of the Photography Laboratory and Technical Laboratory. Note: Since this volume was completed the Technical Laboratory merged with the East Asian Paintings Conservation Studio and changed its name to the Department of Conservation and Scientific Research.

Physical Description

There are 11,180 photographs including color dye coupler photomicrographs and photonegatives and silver gelatin photoprints. Other materials include correspondence, examination reports, memos, microprobe printouts, notebooks, xerographic copies, and x-ray specifications.

Subjects

The photographs document artifacts held by the FGA and ASG since 1923. Most of the photographs illustrate object deterioration and subsequent restoration work and technical studies undertaken by FGA/ASG Technical Laboratory staff. Objects shown include art works from the Far East including China, Japan, North and South Korea, and Tibet (now Xizang); India and Indo-China; and the Near East including Asia Minor, Byzantium (now Istanbul, Turkey), Egypt, Iraq, Persia (now Iran), and Syria; as well as from Europe and the United States.

Asian art shown includes bronzeware; calligraphy; ceramics; glassware; ivory carvings; jade objects; lacquerware; manuscripts; metalwork; paintings including albums, screens, and scrolls; and sculptures. Genres represented include landscapes, narrative paintings, portraits, religious scenes, still lifes, and waterscapes. Artists whose work is shown include Chinese calligraphers such as Wang Hsi-chih; Chinese painters such as Chao Meng-fu, Ch'ien Hsuan, and Kung K'ai; Japanese ceramic artists such as Ogata Kenzan; Japanese painters such as Kawanabe Gyōsai, Ogata Kōrin, Minagawa Kien, Sesson, and Nonomura Sotatsu; and Japanese *ukiyo-e* (woodblock print) artists such as Andō Hiroshige and Katsushika Hokusai.

Western art works reproduced include 19th century American drawings, engravings, etchings, lithographs, oils, pastels, and watercolors. Genres represented include landscapes, narrative paintings, portraits, religious scenes, seascapes, and still lifes. American artists represented include George de Forest Brush, George Butler, Thomas W. Dewing, Childe Hassam, Winslow Homer, Gari Melchers, Willard L. Metcalf, John F. Murphy, Charles Adams Platt, Albert Pinkham Ryder, John Singer Sargent, Joseph L. Smith, Abbott H. Thayer, Dwight William Tryon, John Henry Twatchman, and James Abbott McNeill Whistler. European artists whose work is represented include Charles Gillot, Mortimer Menpes, Thomas Robert Way, and Beatrix Godwin Whistler (Whistler's wife). Most of the European art works are portraits of or by James Abbott McNeill Whistler.

Arranged: In four series. 1) Vault objects, by vault number. 2) Study collection objects, by registration number. 3) Freer Gallery of Art accessioned objects, by accession number. 4) Laboratory general records. Within these series, photographs are in chronological order, by date of examination report.

Captioned: Some with date, number, and scale. Most images are attached to notes with description and repair history.

Finding Aid: Card index listing accession or registration number, owner, and type of object.

Restrictions: Available by appointment only.

FG·66

FGA and ASG Technical Laboratory Scanning Electron Microscope (SEM) Photomicrograph Collection

Dates of Photographs: 1972–Present

Collection Origins

The Freer Gallery of Art (FGA) and Arthur M. Sackler Gallery (ASG) Technical Laboratory staff created the collection to document deterioration, preservation, and restoration of the FGA's accessioned objects and for use in technical studies. Most of the photographs were taken by John Winter. For a history of this laboratory, see the department introduction. Note: Since this volume was completed the Technical Laboratory merged with the East Asian Paintings Conservation Studio and changed its name to the Department of Conservation and Scientific Research.

Some of the photographs from this collection have been published in the following: 1) R.J. Gettens and E.W. FitzHugh. "Malachite and Green Verditer." *Studies in Conservation.* 19 (1974): 2–23. 2) R.J. Gettens, E.W. FitzHugh, and R.L. Feller. "Calcium Carbonate Whites." *Studies in Conservation.* 19 (1974): 157–184. 3) John Winter. "The Characterization of Pigments Based on Carbon." *Studies in Conservation.* 28 (1983): 49–66. 4) John Winter. "Preliminary Investigations on Chinese Ink in Far Eastern Paintings." *Archaeological Chemistry.* 138 (1975): 207–225.

Physical Description

There are 1,270 photographs including silver gelatin photonegatives and photoprints. All are scanning electron microscope (SEM) photomicrographs.

Subjects

These SEM photomicrographs are microscopic images of FGA objects used for technical studies and conservation purposes. Most of the images are details of Chinese, Japanese, and Korean paintings including samples of carbon, fiber, gold leaf, and inks and other pigments. Some images show conservation treatment materials prepared under controlled conditions.

Arranged: In two series. 1) Photoprints, arranged chronologically. 2) Photonegatives, by negative number.

Captioned: With alphanumeric notations.

Finding Aid: Photographer's log listing date of sample, date of SEM, description of object, location of sample, magnification, and type of photonegative.

Restrictions: Available by appointment only.

FG·67

FGA and ASG Technical Laboratory Slide Collection

Dates of Photographs: 1965–Present

Collection Origins

Freer Gallery of Art (FGA) and Arthur M. Sackler Gallery (ASG) Technical Laboratory staff assembled the collection from materials produced by R.J. Gettens and FGA and ASG Photography Laboratory staff. For a description of this laboratory, see the the department introduction. Other studios represented include the Metropolitan Museum of Art. Note: Since this volume was completed the Technical Laboratory merged with the East Asian Paintings Conservation Studio and changed its name to the Department of Conservation and Scientific Research.

Physical Description

There are 12,930 color dye coupler slides (Kodachrome and Ektachrome). Other materials include audiotape cassettes.

Subjects

The photographs document art objects, dating from prehistory to the present, in the ASG and FGA, as well as other art galleries, museums, and private collections. Some images document deterioration, examination, and restoration of artifacts.

Art objects documented are from the Far East (including China and Japan) and the Middle East (including Egypt and the Dead Sea area), as well as Europe and the United States. FGA and ASG objects reproduced include artifacts made out of bamboo, bone, bronze, ceramics, copper, crystal, glass, gold, ivory, jade, lacquer, metal, shells, textiles, and wood. Media and techniques illustrated include calligraphy, cloisonné, drawings, graphic prints, paintings, rubbings, and sculptures. Other objects illustrated include furniture, manuscripts, and Whistleriana.

Artifacts from outside collections illustrated include the Dead Sea Scrolls and objects made of bone, bronze, ceramics, copper, diopside, Egyptian blue, fluorite, gold, iron, ivory, jade, jadeite, lacquer, lead, plastic, precious and semiprecious stones, silver, and wood.

There are photographs of objects from other museums, including the Carnegie Institute (Pittsburgh, Penn-

sylvania), the Fogg Museum (Harvard University), the Isabella Stewart Gardner Museum (Boston), the Metropolitan Museum of Art (New York City), the National Collection of Fine Arts (now the National Museum of American Art, Washington, D.C.), the National Gallery (London), the National Gallery of Art (Washington D.C.), the University Museum (Philadelphia), and the Walters Art Gallery (Baltimore).

Arranged: Most by accession number; some unarranged.

Captioned: With description; some also with date of photograph, lighting conditions, location, origin, time of day, and type of film.

Finding Aid: Index titled "Slide File Guide—Third Revised List, September 29, 1982," in two parts, arranged by slide number and subject: 1) FGA and ASG items and 2) outside items. Entries also list object's location.

Restrictions: Available by appointment only.

FG·68

FGA and ASG Technical Laboratory X-Radiography Collection

Dates of Photographs: 1976–Present

Collection Origins

Freer Gallery of Art (FGA) and Arthur M. Sackler Gallery (ASG) Technical Laboratory staff created this collection of x-ray images of objects for examination, restoration, publication, and research purposes. For a brief history of the laboratory, see the introduction to the department. Most objects shown are FGA accessions or items being considered for acquisition. Photographers represented include W. Thomas Chase, Paul R. Jett, Janet S. Douglas, John Winter, and Lynda Aussenberg Zycherman. Note: Since this volume was completed the Technical Laboratory merged with the East Asian Paintings Conservation Studio and changed its name to the Department of Conservation and Scientific Research.

Physical Description

There are 1,500 silver gelatin radiographs.

Subjects

The radiographs document objects from FGA and ASG holdings including the study and temporary vault storage collections. Art works depicted, dating from prehistory to the 20th century, are from the Far East including China, Japan, North and South Korea, and Tibet (now Xizang); India and Indo-China; and the Near East including Asia Minor, Byzantium (now Istanbul, Turkey), Egypt, Iraq, Persia (now Iran), and Syria; as well as Europe and the United States.

Asian artifacts shown include bronzes; calligraphy; ceramics; glassware; ivory carvings; jade objects; lacquerware; manuscripts; metalwork; paintings (including albums, screens, and scrolls); and sculptures. Western art reproduced includes 19th century American drawings, engravings, etchings, lithographs, oil paintings, pastels, and watercolors, along with European etchings and paintings (primarily portraits).

Arranged: By medium or subject, then location of origin, then laboratory record number.

Captioned: With accession number and description of the object; date of photograph; equipment, film, and filters used; position of object; radiograph number; remarks; and special conditions.

Finding Aid: Two photographer's log books called "X-Ray Notes" and "X-Radiography Log," which list date of the radiograph; object's accession, registration, or vault number, description, dimensions, medium, and position; development information, focal shot, screen filters, time, and type of film; notes; and x-ray number.

Restrictions: Available by appointment only.

FG

Registrar's Office

Registrar's Office
Freer Gallery of Art and Arthur M. Sackler Gallery
Smithsonian Institution
Washington, D.C. 20560
Eleanor Radcliffe, Registrar, Freer Gallery of Art
Bruce Young, Registrar, Arthur M. Sackler Gallery
(202) 357-4960
Hours: Monday–Friday, 10 a.m.–5 p.m.

Scope of the Collection

There is one photographic collection with approximately 64,000 images.

Focus of the Collection

The photographs document accessioned objects at the Freer Gallery of Art and Arthur M. Sackler Gallery. These include artifacts from the Far East, India and Indo-China, and the Near East, as well as Europe and the United States. Objects shown include ceramics, drawings, graphic prints, manuscripts, metalwork, paintings, and sculptures.

Photographic Processes and Formats Represented

The collection contains silver gelatin photoprints.

Other Materials Represented

The Registrar's Office also has catalog cards (on which the photoprints are mounted) for the Freer collection.

Access and Usage Policies

The collection is open to the public by appointment with the director's permission.

Publication Policies

Researchers must obtain permission from the Freer Gallery of Art or Arthur M. Sackler Gallery to reproduce a photograph and may also have to obtain permission from the copyright holder, which is not necessarily the museum. The preferred credit line is "Courtesy of the [Freer Gallery of Art or Arthur M. Sackler Gallery], [specific donor, if any], Smithsonian Institution."

Copies of photographs may be ordered by contacting Laveta Emory, Supervisor, Mail Order Department, Gallery Shop, FGA, Smithsonian Institution, Washington, DC, 20560. Those wishing to publish an image must complete a Permission Request Form, obtained from the Rights and Reproductions Office, FGA, Smithsonian Institution, Washington, D.C., 20560, (202) 786-2088. All permissions to publish are for one-time use, only for the publication specified, and may not be sold or transferred. A copy of the publication must be sent gratis to the FGA library. No FGA images may be cropped, overprinted with type, or altered in any way without prior written approval from the Gallery.

FG·69

FGA and ASG Registrar's Card Catalog

Dates of Photographs: 1923–Present

Collection Origins

The Freer Gallery of Art (FGA) and Arthur M. Sackler Gallery (ASG) Registrar's Office staff created the collection to document the two museums' accessioned objects. See the introductions to both museums for histories of their collections. Photographers represented include Jeff Crespi, James T. Hayden, Kim Nielsen, and John G. Tsantes of the Freer Photography Laboratory.

Physical Description

There are 64,000 silver gelatin photoprints.

Subjects

The photographs document the accessioned objects, dating from prehistory to the present, in the holdings of the FGA and ASG. Objects shown include works of art from the Far East, including China, Japan, North and South Korea, and Tibet (now Xizang); India and Indo-China; and the Near East, including Asia Minor, Byzantium (now Istanbul, Turkey), Egypt, Iraq, Persia (now Iran), and Syria.

Asian art objects shown include carvings, manuscripts, paintings, and sculptures made from materials such as bronze and other metals, ceramics, glass, ivory, jade, and lacquer. Visual genres illustrated include floral designs, landscapes, narrative paintings, portraits, religious paintings, still lifes, and waterscapes.

Western art shown includes 19th century drawings, engravings, etchings, lithographs, oil paintings, pastels, and watercolors by American and European artists including Childe Hassam, Winslow Homer, Gari Melchers, Albert Pinkham Ryder, John Singer Sargent, and James Abbott McNeill Whistler.

Arranged: In four series, three by the accession number and one by medium, country, era, and school or artist.

Captioned: With accession number; artist; country of origin; description including format, genre, medium, size, and special marks or notations; dynasty or period; and negative number.

Finding Aid: No. The collection itself is a finding aid to the accessioned objects at the FGA and ASG.

Restrictions: Available by appointment only, with the director's permission.

HM

HIRSHHORN MUSEUM AND SCULPTURE GARDEN

James T. Demetrion, Director

Created by an act of Congress on November 7, 1966, the Hirshhorn Museum and Sculpture Garden (HMSG) is the Smithsonian Institution's museum of modern and contemporary art. The museum contains over 12,500 drawings, graphic prints, paintings, and sculptures created by 19th and 20th century artists, primarily from Europe and North and South America.

The nucleus of the HMSG holdings was given by Latvian-born philanthropist and financier Joseph H. Hirshhorn (1899–1981), who donated the founding gift of 5,685 art works in 1966. Construction of the building began in March 1970, and the museum opened to the public in October 1974. Since then, donations from private collectors, a major bequest of the remainder of Hirshhorn's private collection in 1981, and a purchase program have enlarged the depth and scope of the HMSG holdings.

Offering an ongoing exhibit program and frequent concerts, films, symposia, tours, and other educational programs, the Hirshhorn also contains an archives of curatorial records, a unique painting study and storage area, and a 36,000-volume reference library. The archives maintains the primary documentation on HMSG holdings, contains some personal papers of American artists, and houses documentation on curatorial interpretive research.

Ongoing research programs at the HMSG include studies of HMSG art objects, an international biographical survey of living artists represented in the HMSG permanent holdings, investigations into the history of casting modern sculpture, and in-depth research in support of the HMSG exhibit program. Although the HMSG does not maintain a separate department of photography, photographs are included in archival holdings, collection documentation files, departmental research files, and exhibits. In addition, nearly 300 photographs are accessioned into the museum's permanent holdings. The HMSG's 19 photographic collections contain 178,000 photographs that document fine-art objects; HMSG activities, exhibits, staff, and visitors; and 19th and 20th century American and European artists and their work.

HM

Department of Administration and Museum Support Services

Department of Administration and Museum Support Services
Hirshhorn Museum and Sculpture Garden
Smithsonian Institution
Washington, D.C. 20560
Anna Brooke, Librarian, (202) 357-3222
Sidney S. Lawrence III, Public Affairs Officer, (202) 357-1618
M. Lee Stalsworth, Chief Photographer, (202) 357-3098
Hours: Monday–Friday, 10 a.m.–5 p.m.

Scope of the Collections

There are ten photographic collections with approximately 147,700 images within three administrative offices: the Hirshhorn Museum and Sculpture Garden (HMSG) Library (four collections with 13,500 images), the HMSG Photographic Services Office (four collections with 127,100 images), and the HMSG Public Information Office (two collections with 7,100 images).

Focus of the Collections

The photographs document HMSG activities such as ceremonies, events, and openings; the HMSG building and facilities; HMSG exhibits; and HMSG object holdings including 19th and 20th century American and European drawings, graphic prints, paintings, and sculptures. There also are formal and informal portraits of artists, HMSG staff, and visitors to the museum.

Photographic Processes and Formats Represented

There are color dye coupler photonegatives, photoprints, phototransparencies, and slides and silver gelatin photonegatives and photoprints.

Other Materials Represented

The department holdings also include calendars, correspondence, exhibit label copy, invitations, lecture schedules, magazine clippings, magazine reprints, manuscripts, newsletters, newspaper clippings, pamphlets, press releases, radio scripts, and television scripts.

Access and Usage Policies

The unrestricted collections are open to scholarly researchers by appointment. Researchers should call or write two weeks in advance describing their research topic, the type of material that interests them, and their research aim. The Public Information Office materials are open primarily to professional art critics and journalists, although other requests will be considered.

Publication Policies

Researchers must obtain permission from the Smithsonian Institution, particularly the HMSG Photographic Services Office, to reproduce a photograph and may also have to obtain permission from the copyright holder, which is not necessarily the Smithsonian Institution. The preferred credit line is "Courtesy of the (Library, Photographic Services Office, or Public

Information Office), Hirshhorn Museum and Sculpture Garden, Smithsonian Institution." The photographer's name, if known, also should appear. Researchers are asked to provide the HMSG Library with copies of any publications created using HMSG research materials or that include a reproduction of an object in the HMSG collection.

HM·1

HMSG Library Accessioned Objects Photograph Collection

Dates of Photographs: 1966–Present

Collection Origins

Hirshhorn Museum and Sculpture Garden (HMSG) Library staff assembled the collection for reference purposes to document objects accessioned into HMSG holdings. This collection duplicates images held in the HMSG Photographic Services Office and in the HMSG Collection Archives.

Photographers represented include Jon Abbot, Cradoc Bagshaw, Helen Bate, Anthony Bergman, Diane Church, Geoffrey Clements, Bevan Davis, J. Ferrari, James W. Flannery, Lothar Frank, Marianne B. Gurley, Bruce C. Jones, Julius Kozlowski, Paulus Lesser, Kim Lim, O.E. Nelson, Eric Pollitzer, John D. Schiff, M. Lee Stalsworth, John R. Tennant, and George Yates. Studios represented include the American Federation of Arts; Brenwasser; Brigadier Studios; Freer Gallery of Art; Galerie Claude Bernard; Graham Gallery; Greenberg, Wrotzen, and May; Herbert Johnson Museum; HMSG Photographic Services Office; Lefebre Gallery; Molton Gallery; and the Whitney Museum of American Art.

Physical Description

There are 7,400 silver gelatin photoprints (many are duplicate or copy images).

Subjects

The photographs document HMSG accessioned objects—primarily 19th and 20th century American and European drawings, graphic prints, paintings, and sculptures—as well as HMSG exhibits. Artists whose work is represented include Pat Adams, Robert D. Adams, Samuel M. Adler, Yaacov Agam, Josef Albers, Richard J. Anusziewicz, Alexander Archipenko, Kenneth Armitage, Robert Arneson, Jean Arp, Milton Avery, Francis Bacon, Saul Baizerman, Ernst Barlach, Leonard Baskin, William A. Baziotes, Romare H. Bearden, Robert P. Beauchamp, Max Beckmann, Leland Bell, Harry Bertoia, Albert Bierstadt, Ralph A. Blakelock, Oscar F. Bluemner, Louise Bourgeois, Constantin Brancusi, Georges Braque, Alexander Calder, Sandro Chia, Bruce Conner, Joseph Cornell, Honoré Daumier, Arthur B. Davies, José de Creeft, Edgar Degas, Willem de Kooning, Mark di Suvero, and Jean Dubuffet.

Other artists whose work is represented include Thomas Eakins, Louis M. Eilshemius, Max Ernst, Philip Evergood, Eric Fischl, Lucian Freud, Alberto Giacometti, Gregory Gillespie, Arshile Gorky, Philip Guston, Robert Henri, Barbara Hepworth, Jess (Collins), Jasper Johns, Anselm Kiefer, Edward Kienholz, Nancy Reddin Kienholz, Fernand Léger, David P. Levine, Jacques Lipchitz, George B. Luks, Man Ray, Giacomo Manzù, Henri Matisse, Mario Merz, Henry Moore, Robert Moskowitz, and Elizabeth Murray.

The collection also features photographs of works by Elie Nadelman, Louise Nevelson, Kenneth Noland, Pablo Picasso, Sigmar Polke, Martin Puryear, Gerhard Richter, Larry Rivers, Auguste Rodin, James A. Rosenquist, Mark Rothko, Ed Ruscha, Morgan Russell, Anne Ryan, Lucas Samaras, John Singer Sargent, Sean Scully, George Segal, Richard Serra, Ben Shahn, David Smith, Moses Soyer, Raphael Soyer, Joseph Stella, Harold Tovish, Anne Truitt, Nahum Tschacbasov, William Wiley, Jack Zajac, Carl Zerbe, R.F. Zogbaum, and William Zorach.

Arranged: In three series, then alphabetically by artist. 1) Accessioned objects. 2) Thomas Eakins materials. 3) Unidentified photoprints.

Captioned: With negative number and the object's accession number, artist, dimensions, and medium.

Finding Aid: No.

Restrictions: Available by appointment only. Contact Anna Brooke, Librarian, HMSG Library, Room 427, Smithsonian Institution, Washington, D.C., 20560, (202) 357-3222.

HM·2

HMSG Library Hirshhorn Publicity Notebooks

Dates of Photographs: 1950s–Present

Collection Origins

Hirshhorn Museum and Sculpture Garden (HMSG) Library and Public Affairs staff assembled this collection from materials received from the Hirshhorn family and other sources to document the HMSG and its founder, Joseph H. Hirshhorn. Hirshhorn (1899–1981) was born in Latvia and emigrated to the United States in 1905. He began his career as a stock broker in 1916 and became a successful financier. He purchased his first art work when he was 18 and eventually amassed a collection of over 11,000 pieces. Hirshhorn donated 5,685 art works to the HMSG during his lifetime and left another 5,888 items to the museum after his death. Photographers and studios represented include the Boston Museum of Fine Arts; Arthur Ellis, *Washington Post;* Los Angeles County Museum of Art; M.H. De Young Memorial Museum, San Francisco; Museum of Fine Arts, Houston; and the Walker Art Center, Minneapolis.

Physical Description

There are 120 photographs including a color dye coupler photoprint and silver gelatin photoprints, mounted in notebooks. Other materials, also in notebooks, include invitations, lecture schedules, magazine articles, and newspaper clippings.

Subjects

The photographs document activities and events involving Joseph H. Hirshhorn, his art holdings, and the HMSG. Events documented include an award presentation to Hirshhorn at the White House by President and Mrs. Lyndon B. Johnson; Hirshhorn collection exhibits during the 1950s including "Sculpture in Our Time," "A View of the Protean Century," and a show at the Toronto Art Gallery; HMSG ground-breaking ceremonies on January 8, 1969, including images of Smithsonian Secretary S. Dillon Ripley with President Lyndon B. Johnson; and the museum's opening on October 4, 1974. There is also an image of Hirshhorn's New York office interior in 1958.

Arranged: By date.

Captioned: With the exhibit dates, location, and name.

Finding Aid: No.

Restrictions: Available to scholars by appointment only. Contact Anna Brooke, Librarian, HMSG Library, Room 427, Smithsonian Institution, Washington, D.C., 20560, (202) 357-3222.

HM·3

HMSG Library Museum Reference Slide File

Dates of Photographs: 20th Century

Collection Origins

Hirshhorn Museum and Sculpture Garden (HMSG) Librarian Anna Brooke assembled the collection from slides created by HMSG curators, Education Department staff, and Photographic Services Office staff, as well as from donations by artists. The collection serves as a reference file for research purposes, although some slides may be borrowed. Photographers and studios represented include Marianne B. Gurley, OPPS, Rosenthal Art Slide Company, Scala, M. Lee Stalsworth, and John R. Tennant.

Physical Description

There are 750 color dye coupler slides (85 percent are duplicates).

Subjects

The slides document HMSG art objects, sometimes shown in HMSG exhibit installations, as well as art objects and buildings (both interiors and exteriors) of other museums such as the J. Paul Getty Museum and the Norton Simon Museum. HMSG accessioned objects shown include American and European drawings, graphic prints, paintings, and sculptures, dating primarily from the 19th and 20th centuries. Artists whose work is reproduced include Jean Arp, Milton Avery, Francis Bacon, Leonard Baskin, Pierre Bonnard, Honoré Daumier, Willem de Kooning, Jim Dine, Max Ernst, Richard Lindner, André Masson, László Moholy-Nagy, Henry Moore, Barnett Newman, Larry Rivers, Auguste Rodin, Mark Rothko, John Singer Sargent, John Sloan, Paolo Soleri, Saul Steinberg, and Andy Warhol.

Painting genres illustrated include abstract art, architectural studies, cityscapes, landscapes, portraits, and still lifes. Art movements represented include abstract expressionism, the ash can school, concrete art, constructivism, cubism, dadaism, de stijl, expressionism, fauvism, futurism, minimalism, neo-impressionism (pointillism), pop art, post-impressionism, realism, suprematism, and surrealism.

Arranged: In four series. 1) Duplicate slides from the HMSG Photographic Services Office, arranged alphabetically by artist and then by accession number. 2) Non-collection slides donated by artists, galleries, and HMSG staff, arranged alphabetically by artist. 3) Views of other museums. 4) Miscellaneous and unlabeled slides.

Captioned: Some with artist, date, medium, size, and title of work or name of museum.

Finding Aid: No.

Restrictions: Available by appointment only. Non-collection slides may be borrowed. Contact Anna Brooke, Librarian, HMSG Library, Room 427, Smithsonian Institution, Washington, D.C., 20560, (202) 357-3222.

HM·4

HMSG Library Non-Hirshhorn Object Photographs *A.K.A.* Modern Art Photographic File

Dates of Photographs: 1950s–Present

Collection Origins

Hirshhorn Museum and Sculpture Garden (HMSG) staff created the collection to document four types of art objects: 1) art works offered to the HMSG as donations, but not accepted; 2) art works offered as potential purchases, but not purchased; 3) art works once in HMSG's holdings, but since deaccessioned; and 4) art works received as loans for HMSG exhibits.

Photographers represented include Pat Cope, Marianne B. Gurley, Bill Lundberg, Eric Pollitzer, John D. Schiff, Harry Seager, M. Lee Stalsworth, John R. Tennant, and Rodney Todd-White. Studios represented include the Adam L. Gimpel Gallery, New York; Betty Parsons Gallery, New York; Detroit Institute of Arts; Gilman Galleries, Chicago; Gimpel Fils Gallery, London; Guggenheim Museum, New York; Hanson Fuller Goldeen Gallery, San Francisco; Knoedler and Company, New York; Midtown Galleries, New York; Museum of Contemporary Art, Chicago; and the National Museum of American Art, Smithsonian Institution.

Physical Description

There are 5,230 photographs including color dye coupler phototransparencies and slides (Ektachrome) and silver gelatin photonegatives and photoprints (some copy images).

Subjects

The photographs document art objects offered to the HMSG as potential donations or purchases, HMSG art works that have since been deaccessioned, and art works on loan for HMSG exhibits. Art objects shown include 19th and 20th century American and European drawings, graphic prints, paintings, and sculptures.

Arranged: Alphabetically by artist.

Captioned: With artist, date, exhibit history, medium, and title of the work.

Finding Aid: No.

Restrictions: Available by appointment only. Contact Anna Brooke, Librarian, HMSG Library, Room 427, Smithsonian Institution, Washington, D.C., 20560, (202) 357-3222.

HM·5

HMSG Photographic Services Bequest Objects Photograph File

Dates of Photographs: 1985

Collection Origins

Hirshhorn Museum and Sculpture Garden (HMSG) staff created the collection preparatory to accessioning items bequeathed by financier Joseph H. Hirshhorn (1899–1981). For Hirshhorn's biography, see the *Collection Origins* field of *HM·2*. Photographers represented include Marianne B. Gurley and M. Lee Stalsworth of the HMSG Photographic Services Office.

Physical Description

There are 575 photographs including color dye coupler phototransparencies and slides and silver gelatin photonegatives and photoprints.

Subjects

The photographs document a portion of Joseph H. Hirshhorn's posthumous bequest of 5,888 art objects including American and European drawings, graphic prints, paintings, and sculptures, predominately from the 19th and 20th centuries. Approximately 100 artists are represented in this collection, including Joseph Albers, Milton Avery, Francis Bacon, Georges Braque, Alexander Calder, Mary Cassatt, Stuart Davis, Willem de Kooning, Max Ernst, Alberto Giacometti, Arshile Gorky, Red Grooms, Barbara Hepworth, Edward Hopper, Paul Klee, Jack Levine, Aristide Maillol, Henri Matisse, Joan Miró, Piet Mondrian, Henry Moore, Pablo Picasso, Larry Rivers, Auguste Rodin, David Smith, Raphael Soyer, and Abraham Walkowitz.

Arranged: Alphabetically by artist.

Captioned: Photoprints (on folders) with artist and bequest number. Photonegatives and phototransparencies with artist, bequest number, and date.

Finding Aid: No.

Restrictions: Available by appointment only. Contact M. Lee Stalsworth, Chief Photographer, Photographic Services Office, HMSG, Room G24, Smithsonian Institution, Washington, D.C., 20560, (202) 357-3098.

HM·6

HMSG Photographic Services Exhibit Documentation File

Dates of Photographs: 1973–Present

Collection Origins

Hirshhorn Museum and Sculpture Garden (HMSG) staff created the collection to document HMSG exhibits for administrative and curatorial reference purposes. Photographers represented include Marianne B. Gurley, M. Lee Stalsworth, and John R. Tennant of the HMSG Photographic Services Office.

Physical Description

There are 8,050 photographs including silver gelatin photonegatives and photoprints (some contact sheets).

Subjects

The photographs document exhibits held at HMSG from 1974 to the present, as well as HMSG events, facilities, staff, and visitors. Exhibits documented— primarily of 19th and 20th century American and European drawings, graphic prints, paintings, and sculptures—include "Alberto Giacometti 1901–1966"; "Artistic Collaborations in the Twentieth Century"; "Artists, Authors, and Others: Drawings by David Levine"; "The Avant-Garde in Russia, 1910–1930: New Perspectives"; "Bay Area Figurative Art, 1950–1965"; "Cornell Boxes"; "David Smith: Painter, Sculptor, Draftsman"; "Dennis Adams"; "Different Drummers"; "Directions" (series); "Drawings: 1974–1984"; "Dreams and Nightmares: Utopian Visions in Modern Art"; "The Eight and the Independent Tradition in American Art"; "Friedel Dzubas"; "The Golden Door: Artist-Immigrants of America, 1876–1976"; "Gregory Gillespie"; "Hans Hofmann"; "Jim Dine: Five Themes"; "Kenneth Snelson"; "Lucian Freud Paintings"; "Miró: Selected Paintings"; "Morris Louis"; "Nancy Graves: A Sculpture Retrospective"; "A New Romanticism: Sixteen Artists from Italy"; "The Noble Buyer: John Quinn, Patron of the Avant-Garde"; "Numbers/Letters/Images"; "The Photographs of Leland Rice"; "Probing the Earth: Contemporary Land Projects"; "Purchases by the Hirshhorn Museum and Sculpture Garden: 1974–1983"; "Red Grooms: The Hirshhorn Museum and Sculpture Garden Collection"; "Representation Abroad"; "Robert Arneson: A Retrospective"; "The Sculpture and Drawings of Elie Nadelman"; "Soto: A Retrospective Exhibition"; "Summer Sculpture '77: Jules Olitski"; "The Thomas Eakins Collection of the Hirshhorn Museum and Sculpture Garden"; and "Works on Paper: Genre Scenes."

HMSG events documented include the ground-breaking ceremonies; presentation of a Smithsonian Institution medal to Joseph H. Hirshhorn in April 1973; installation of the HMSG sculpture garden in August 1974; opening the museum to the public on October 4, 1974; and the unveiling of Alexander Calder's *Flamingo*, a sculpture for the blind, in October 1975. HMSG facilities shown include the library, lobby, lower level, museum shop, general museum views, Joseph H. Hirshhorn's office, painting study-storage screens, registrar's office, sculpture storage, styrofoam mock-ups of the plaza garden, and storage warehouses used by Joseph H. Hirshhorn in New York City, as well as Hirshhorn's house in Greenwich, Connecticut. Staff and other HMSG-related people portrayed include docents, employees-of-the-month, Joseph H. Hirshhorn, Abram Lerner (the first HMSG director), and trustees. Visitors portrayed include the empress of Iran, Richard Estes, First Lady Betty Ford, Henry Moore, Georgia O'Keeffe, and Mrs. Kurt Waldheim.

Arranged: Alphabetically by name or subject.

Captioned: No.

Finding Aid: No.

Restrictions: Available to HMSG staff only on a "need-to-know" basis.

HM·7

HMSG Photographic Services Master Slide File

Dates of Photographs: 1966–Present

Collection Origins

Hirshhorn Museum and Sculpture Garden (HMSG) Photographic Services staff created the collection to document art works in HMSG holdings, as well as museum-related artists, events, and staff. New acquisitions are photographed as they arrive at the museum. The resulting images are used for publications such as books, calendars, exhibit catalogs, magazines, and posters; for publicity; and for reference and research by HMSG staff and outside researchers. HMSG photographers represented include Marianne B. Gurley, M. Lee Stalsworth, and John R. Tennant.

Physical Description

There are 48,000 color dye coupler slides (Kodachrome). The collection contains both original and duplicate images.

Subjects

The photographs portray artists whose work is represented in HMSG collections, as well as documenting HMSG art objects, exhibits, museum events, and staff members. Art objects reproduced include drawings, graphic prints, paintings, and sculptures by the following artists: Yaacov Agam, Josef Albers, Alexander Archipenko, Robert Arneson, Francis Bacon, Saul Baizerman, Aaron Bohrod, Pierre Bonnard, Samuel P. Bookatz, Roger Brown, Alexander Calder, Carroll Cloar, Bruce Conner, Ralston Crawford, Robert Cumming, Edwin Dickinson, Burgoyne A. Diller, Jim Dine, William Dole, Enrico L. Donati, Arthur G. Dove, Jean Dubuffet, Friedel Dzubas, Thomas Eakins, Louis M. Eilshemius, Richard Estes, Vernon Fisher, Lucian Freud, Franz Gertsch, Alberto Giacometti, Gregory Gillespie, Arshile Gorky,

Nancy Graves, Red Grooms, Philip Guston, Barbara Hepworth, David Hockney, Walt Kuhn, David P. Levine, Jacques Lipchitz, Seymour Lipton, Morris Louis, Louis Lozowick, George B. Luks, Henri Matisse, Joan Miró, Henry Moore, Robert Moskowitz, Elizabeth Murray, Samuel A. Murray, Elie Nadelman, Reuben Nakian, Louise Nevelson, Arnold Newman, Kenneth Noland, Jules Olitski, Pablo Picasso, Jackson Pollock, Gerhard Richter, Ed Ruscha, Kenneth Smelson, Saul Steinberg, Joseph Stella, Max Weber, William Wiley, and William Zorach.

Events documented include the construction of the HMSG from 1969 to 1974; HMSG exhibit openings; the move of the Joseph H. Hirshhorn art donations from New York and Hirshhorn's home in Greenwich, Connecticut, to Washington, D.C., including views of Hirshhorn's home in Greenwich; and the museum opening ceremonies in October 1974 including views of the museum building, plaza, and sculpture garden. People portrayed include artists whose work is represented in the collection, Joseph H. Hirshhorn, Abram Lerner (the first HMSG director), and HMSG staff.

Exhibit installations documented include "Alberto Giacometti 1901–1966"; "Alexander Calder"; "American Collages: Selections from the Museum's Collection"; "Arnold Newman Photographs Artists"; "Art Deco Posters from the Library of Congress"; "Artistic Collaborations in the Twentieth Century"; "Artists, Authors, and Others: Drawings by David Levine"; "The Avant-Garde in Russia, 1910–1930: New Perspectives"; "Bay Area Figurative Art, 1950–1965"; "Brancusi as Photographer"; "Bridging the Century: Images of Bridges from the Hirshhorn Museum and Sculpture Garden"; "British Sculpture since 1965: Cragg, Deacon, Flanagan, Long, Nash, Woodrow"; "Central European Art"; "Contemporary Paintings from Pakistan"; "Content: A Contemporary Focus, 1974–1984"; "Culture and Commentary: An Eighties Perspective"; "David Hockney: Travels with Pen, Pencil, and Ink"; "Different Drummers"; "Direct Carving in Modern Sculpture"; "Dreams and Nightmares: Utopian Visions in Modern Art"; "Edwin Dickinson: Selected Landscapes"; "The Eight and the Independent Tradition in American Art"; and "European Modernism: Selections from the Museum's Collection."

Other exhibits shown include "The Fifties: Aspects of Painting in New York"; "Francis Bacon"; "Franz Gertsch: Large Scale Woodcuts"; "Gerhard Richter"; "German Expressionist Sculpture"; "The Golden Door: Artist-Immigrants of America, 1876–1976"; "Gregory Gillespie"; "Heirs of de Stijl"; "Images of American Industry from the Museum's Collection"; "Jim Dine: Five Themes"; "Joseph Stella: The Hirshhorn Museum and Sculpture Garden Collection"; "Kenneth Snelson"; "Kin and Communities"; "Louis M. Eilshemius"; "Lucian Freud Paintings"; "Metaphor: New Projects by Contemporary Sculptors"; "Modern Indian Paintings from the Collection of the National Gallery of Modern Art, New Delhi"; "Morris Louis"; "Murals Without Walls: Arshile Gorky's Aviation Murals Rediscovered"; "Nakian"; "Nancy Graves: A Sculpture Retrospective"; "A New Romanticism: Sixteen Artists from Italy"; "New York: The Artist's View"; and "Numbers/Letters/Images."

The collection also includes photographs of "Paintings from Pakistan"; "Patterned Images: Works on Paper from the Museum's Collection"; "Prints and Collages;" "Prints and Drawings of the Sixties from the Museum's Collection"; "Probing the Earth: Contemporary Land Projects"; "Purchases by the Hirshhorn Museum and Sculpture Garden, 1974–1983"; "Ralston Crawford Photographs"; "Red Grooms: The Hirshhorn Museum and Sculpture Garden Collection"; "Representation Abroad"; "Richard Estes: The Urban Landscape"; "Robert Arneson: A Retrospective"; "Robert Moskowitz"; "Roger Brown"; "Samuel Murray: The Hirshhorn Museum and Sculpture Garden Collection"; "Saul Steinberg"; "The Sculpture and Drawings of Elie Nadelman"; "Selections from the Collection of Marion and Gustave Ring"; "Soto: A Retrospective Exhibition"; "Summer Sculpture '77: Jules Olitski"; "The Thomas Eakins Collection of the Hirshhorn Museum and Sculpture Garden"; "Thomas Eakins Photographs: A Selection from the Permanent Collection"; and "Works on Paper: Genre Scenes."

Two special post-1987 HMSG exhibit series also are featured—"Directions" with exhibits by Erika Beckman, Mel Chin, Ilya Kabakov, Sherrie Levine, Christian Marclay, Walter Pichler, Joel Shapiro, Susana Solano, and Keith Sonnier; and "Works" with exhibits by Dennis Adams, Daniel Buren, Kathryn Clark, Houston Conwill, Ann Hamilton, David Ireland, Sol Lewitt, Matt Mullican, Buster Simpson, and Krzysztof Wodiczko.

Arranged: In two series. 1) Art objects, alphabetically by artist and then by accession number. 2) Events, exhibits, and staff, grouped by subject.

Captioned: Most with artist, slide number, and title.

Finding Aid: No.

Restrictions: No. Contact M. Lee Stalsworth, Chief Photographer, Photographic Services Office, HMSG, Room G24, Smithsonian Institution, Washington, D.C., 20560, (202) 357-3098.

HM·8

HMSG Photographic Services Permanent Holdings Photograph File

Dates of Photographs: 20th Century

Collection Origins

Hirshhorn Museum and Sculpture Garden (HMSG) Photographic Services Office staff created the collection to document the accessioned objects in the HMSG's permanent holdings. HMSG photographers represented include Marianne B. Gurley, M. Lee Stalsworth, and John R. Tennant.

Physical Description

There are 70,500 photographs including color dye coupler photonegatives and phototransparencies and silver gelatin photonegatives and photoprints.

Subjects

The photographs document HMSG accessioned art objects—19th and 20th century American and European drawings, graphic prints, paintings, and sculptures—by artists such as Alexander Archipenko, Milton Avery, Saul Baizerman, Charles E. Burchfield, Bruce Conner, Joseph Cornell, E.E. Cummings, Louis M. Eilshemius, Max Ernst, Sam Francis, Paul Gauguin, Alberto Giacometti, Arshile Gorky, Chaim Gross, David Hockney, Edward Hopper, Wassily Kandinsky, Alexander R. Katz, Anselm Kiefer, Nancy Reddin Kienholz, Man Ray, Henri Matisse, Robert Moskowitz, Robert Motherwell, Gerhard Richter, Larry Rivers, Auguste Rodin, Mark Rothko, Lucas Samaras, John Singer Sargent, W. Lee Savage, George Segal, Moses Soyer, and Frank Stella.

Arranged: Alphabetically by artist.

Captioned: Most photographs with object's accession number, artist, and title. Folders with format of the photograph and object's accession number, artist, date, medium, size, and title.

Finding Aid: No.

Restrictions: No. Contact M. Lee Stalsworth, Chief Photographer, Photographic Services Office, HMSG,

Room G24, Smithsonian Institution, Washington, D.C., 20560, (202) 357-3098.

HM·9

HMSG Public Affairs Files

Dates of Photographs: 1970–1986

Collection Origins

Hirshhorn Museum and Sculpture Garden (HMSG) Public Affairs Office staff created the collection as part of their working files to supply journalists and art critics with information about HMSG activities, such as acquisitions, exhibit openings, and staff changes.

Photographers represented include Marianne B. Gurley, M. Lee Stalsworth, and John R. Tennant of the HMSG Photographic Services Office; and Kim Nielsen and Steven Sloman. These photographs have appeared in magazines and newspapers such as *ARTnews, Art in America,* the *Baltimore Sun, Newsweek,* the *New York Times,* the *Philadelphia Inquirer, Smithsonian, Time, Vanity Fair, Vogue,* and the *Washington Post.*

Physical Description

There are 1,500 photographs including color dye coupler photoprints, phototransparencies, and slides and silver gelatin photonegatives and photoprints. Other materials include calendars, correspondence, exhibit scripts, magazine clippings, newsletters, newspaper clippings, press releases, radio scripts, and television scripts.

Subjects

The photographs document art objects owned by or lent to the HMSG; HMSG events, exhibits, and facilities; and HMSG staff and visitors from 1974 to 1986.

Artists whose exhibits are illustrated include Josef Albers, Francis Bacon, Thomas Hart Benton, Oscar F. Bleumner, Fernando Botero, Constantin Brancusi, Daniel Buren, Alexander Calder, Arthur B. Carles, E.E. Cummings, Edwin Dickinson, Jim Dine, Friedel Dzubas, Thomas Eakins, Louis M. Eilshemius, Richard Estes, Philip Evergood, Gregory Gillespie, George Grosz, David Hockney, Hans Hofmann, Winslow Homer, R.B. Kitaj, Alfred Leslie, David P. Levine, Jacques Lipchitz, Alfred Maurer, Joan Miró, Henry Moore, Samuel A. Murray, Elie Nadelman, Reuben Nakian, Robert Natkin, Ben Nicholson, Kenneth Noland, Jules Olitski, Robert Rauschenberg, Leland Rice, Larry Rivers, David Smith, Kenneth Snelson, and Saul Steinberg.

Exhibits documented include "Arshile Gorky: The Hirshhorn Museum and Sculpture Garden Collection"; "Art Deco Posters from the Library of Congress"; "Art from Italy: Selections from the Museum's Collection"; "Artistic Collaborations in the Twentieth Century"; "The Avant-Garde in Russia, 1910–1930: New Perspectives"; "Conservation of Modern Art"; "Contemporary Paintings from Pakistan"; "Content: A Contemporary Focus, 1974–1984"; "De Stijl: 1917–1931, Visions of Utopia"; "Direct Carving in Modern Sculpture"; "Directions" (series); "Drawings: 1974–1984"; "Dreams and Nightmares: Utopian Visions in Modern Art"; "The Eight and the Independent Tradition in American Art"; "European Modernism: Selections from the Museum's Collection"; "The Fifties: Aspects of Painting in New York"; "Five Distinguished Alumni: The WPA Federal Art Project"; "Fourteen Canadians: A Critic's Choice"; "German Expressionist Sculpture"; "The Golden Door: Artist-Immigrants of America, 1876–1976"; "Modern Indian Paintings from the Collection of the National Gallery of Modern Art, New Delhi"; "Murals Without Walls: Arshile Gorky's Aviation Murals Rediscovered"; "A New Romanticism: Sixteen Artists from Italy"; "New York: The Artist's View"; "The Noble Buyer: John Quinn, Patron of the Avant-Garde"; "Orozco, Rivera, Siqueiros"; "Probing the Earth: Contemporary Land Projects"; "Els Quatre Gats: Art in Barcelona around 1900"; "Red Grooms: The Hirshhorn Museum and Sculpture Garden Collection"; "Representation Abroad"; "Selections from the Collection of Marion and Gustave Ring"; "Seven Belgian Artists: Selections from the Hirshhorn Museum Collection"; and "Variations on a Musical Theme: Selections from the Museum's Collection."

People portrayed include artists such as Jim Dine; donors such as Joseph H. Hirshhorn; HMSG staff such as James T. Demetrion (the present HMSG director) and Abram Lerner (the first HMSG director); Smithsonian administrative staff such as S. Dillon Ripley (former SI secretary); and visitors such as President and Mrs. Lyndon B. Johnson. There are also images of HMSG art objects, including graphic prints, paintings, photography, and sculpture, and exterior and interior views of the museum.

Arranged: In six series. 1) Working files, including accession information, exhibit catalogs, film/lecture series, ideas for future exhibits, in-house calendars, publication schedules, and visitor statistics. 2) Current and future exhibit files. 3) Portrait files of key staff members. 4) Old exhibit files. 5) Chronological correspondence files. 6) Duplicate photographs of current exhibits. Note: Photographs of art objects appear in all of these series.

Captioned: Approximately half of the photoprints with date, names, and subject. Most phototransparencies with artist, catalog number, date, medium, size, and title of the work; date and title of exhibit; and name of lender.

Finding Aid: No.

Restrictions: Available to art critics, journalists, and researchers by appointment. Contact Sidney S. Lawrence III, Public Affairs Officer, HMSG, Room 406, Smithsonian Institution, Washington, D.C., 20560, (202) 357-1618.

HM·10

HMSG Public Affairs Press Archives

Dates of Photographs: 1974–Present

Collection Origins

Hirshhorn Museum and Sculpture Garden (HMSG) Public Affairs Office staff created the collection to document HMSG exhibit openings. Photographers represented include Freer Gallery of Art and Arthur M. Sackler Gallery photographer Kim Nielson and HMSG Photographic Services Office staff Marianne B. Gurley, M. Lee Stalsworth, and John R. Tennant. Photographs have been published in magazines and newspapers such as *Art in America, ARTnews,* the *Baltimore Sun,* the *Los Angeles Times, Newsweek,* the *New York Times,* the *Philadelphia Inquirer, Portfolio, Smithsonian, Time, Vanity Fair, Village Voice, Vogue, Wall Street Journal,* and the *Washington Post.* These slides also have been used for promotional television spots.

Physical Description

There are 5,600 photographs including color dye coupler slides and phototransparencies and silver gelatin photonegatives and photoprints (some contact prints). Other materials include calendars, correspondence, magazine articles, manuscripts, newspaper clippings, pamphlets, and press releases.

Subjects

The photographs primarily document HMSG exhibits, as well as the HMSG building, events, staff, and visitors from 1974 to the present. Artists whose exhibits are illustrated include Josef Albers, Thomas Hart Benton, Oscar F. Bluemner, Fernando Botero, Constantin Brancusi, Alexander Calder, Arthur B. Carles, Ralston Crawford, E.E. Cummings, Edwin Dickinson, Jim Dine, Friedel Dzubas, Thomas Eakins, Louis M. Eilshemius, Richard Estes, Philip Evergood, Franz Gertsch, Gregory Gillespie, George Grosz, David Hockney, Hans Hofmann, Winslow Homer, R.B. Kitaj, Alfred Leslie, David P. Levine, Jacques Lipchitz, Alfred Maurer, Joan Miró, Henry Moore, Samuel A. Murray, Elie Nadelman, Reuben Nakian, Robert Natkin, Ben Nicholson, Kenneth Noland, Jules Olitski, Walter Pichler, Robert Rauschenberg, Leland Rice, Larry Rivers, David Smith, Kenneth Snelson, and Saul Steinberg.

Exhibits documented include "Alberto Giacometti 1901–1966"; "Arnold Newman Photographs Artists"; "Art Deco Posters from the Library of Congress"; "Art from Italy: Selections from the Museum's Collection"; "Artistic Collaborations in the Twentieth Century"; "The Avant-Garde in Russia, 1910–1930: New Perspectives"; "Bridging the Century: Images of Bridges from the Hirshhorn Museum and Sculpture Garden"; "British Sculpture since 1965: Cragg, Deacon, Flanagan, Long, Nash, Woodrow"; "Central European Art"; "Conservation of Modern Art"; "Contemporary Paintings from Pakistan"; "Content: A Contemporary Focus, 1974–1984"; "De Stijl: 1917–1931, Visions of Utopia"; "Different Drummers"; "Direct Carving in Modern Sculpture"; "Directions—Erika Beckman"; "Directions—Joel Shapiro: Painted Wood"; "Directions—Keith Sonnier: Neon"; "Directions 1979"; "Directions 1981"; "Directions 1983"; "Drawings: 1974–1984"; "Dreams and Nightmares: Utopian Visions in Modern Art"; "The Eight and the Independent Tradition in American Art"; "European Modernism: Selections from the Museum's Collection"; "The Fifties: Aspects of Painting in New York"; "Five Distinguished Alumni: The WPA Federal Art Project"; "Fourteen Canadians: A Critic's Choice"; "Francis Bacon"; "Gerhard Richter"; "German Expressionist Sculpture"; "The Golden Door: Artist-Immigrants of America, 1876–1976"; "Lucian Freud Paintings"; "Modern Indian Paintings from the Collection of the National Gallery of Modern Art, New Delhi"; "Morris Louis"; "Murals Without Walls: Arshile Gorky's Aviation Murals Rediscovered"; "Nancy Graves: A Sculpture Retrospective"; "A New Romanticism: Sixteen Artists from Italy"; "New York: The Artist's View"; "The Noble Buyer: John Quinn, Patron of the Avant-Garde"; "Numbers/Letters/Images"; "Orozco, Rivera, Siqueiros"; "Patterned Images: Works on Paper from the Museum's Collection"; "Probing the Earth: Contemporary Land Projects"; "Els Quatre Gats: Art in Barcelona around 1900"; "Ralston Crawford Photographs"; "Red Grooms: The Hirshhorn Museum and Sculpture Garden Collection"; "Relief Sculpture"; "Representation Abroad"; "Robert Arneson: A Retrospective"; "Robert Moskowitz"; "Roger Brown"; "Selections from the Collection of Marion and Gustave Ring"; "Seven Belgian Artists: Selections from the Hirshhorn Museum Collection"; "Thomas Eakins Photographs: A Selection from the Permanent Collection"; "Variations on a Musical Theme: Selections from the Museum's Collection"; and "Works: Buster Simpson."

Arranged: In four series. 1) Exhibits (90 percent of the collection). 2) Building materials. 3) Film releases and other public relations materials. 4) Portraits of HMSG staff members.

Captioned: Some with the object's artist and title and the exhibit title and date.

Finding Aid: No.

Restrictions: Available to professional art critics, journalists, and researchers by appointment. Contact Sidney S. Lawrence III, Public Affairs Officer, HMSG, Room 406, Smithsonian Institution, Washington, D.C., 20560, (202) 357-1618.

HM

Department of Painting and Sculpture

Department of Painting and Sculpture
Hirshhorn Museum and Sculpture Garden
Smithsonian Institution
Washington, D.C. 20560
Valerie J. Fletcher, Curator of Sculpture, (202) 357-3230
Frank Gettings, Curator of Prints and Drawings, (202) 357-3286
Judith K. Zilczer, Curator of Paintings, (202) 357-3230
Hours: By appointment.

Scope of the Collections

There are eight photographic collections with approximately 25,000 images.

Focus of the Collections

The photographs fall into three categories: 1) accessioned fine art photographs, which form part of the HMSG accessioned art works-on-paper holdings; 2) images of HMSG art objects; and 3) archival manuscript collections that contain longer series of images documenting the work of several artists, including Thomas Eakins, Samuel A. Murray, and Elie Nadelman.

Most of the images document 19th and 20th century American and European drawings, graphic prints, paintings, and sculptures including Armory Show (1913) art objects; HMSG art objects; and Joseph H. Hirshhorn's private art collection. There are also approximately 300 accessioned fine art photographs including allegorical works, animal studies, cityscapes, landscapes, portraits, and still lifes primarily by photographers Ralston Crawford, Thomas Eakins, Arnold Newman, and Lucas Samaras.

Photographic Processes and Formats Represented

There are albumen photoprints; color dye coupler photoprints, phototransparencies, and slides; cyanotypes; dye diffusion transfer photoprints (Polaroid SX-70); platinum photoprints; silver gelatin dry plate photonegatives; and silver gelatin photonegatives, photoprints, and phototransparencies.

Other Materials Represented

The department also contains curatorial records including accession forms, announcements, architectural drawings, bibliographies, biographies, birthday cards, correspondence, drawings, exhibit catalogs, exhibit histories, exhibit labels, government documents, graphic prints, index cards, inventories, invitations, magazine clippings, manuscripts, maps, newspaper clippings, notebooks, pamphlets, photomechanicals (collotypes), postcards, programs, reprints, scrapbooks, and xerographic copies.

Access and Usage Policies

Unrestricted collections are available by appointment only. Researchers should call or write two weeks in advance, describing their research topic, the type of material that interests them, and their research aim. Researchers must complete an application for examination of archival material and also are asked to provide the HMSG Library with a copy of any publication resulting from the research.

Publication Policies

Researchers must obtain permission from the Smithsonian Institution, particularly the HMSG Photographic Services Office, to reproduce a photograph and may also have to obtain permission from the copyright holder, which is not necessarily the Smithsonian Institution. The preferred credit line is "Courtesy of the [Collection Archives or Prints and Drawings Curator's Office], Hirshhorn Museum and Sculpture Garden, Smithsonian Institution." The photographer's name, if known, also should appear.

HM·11

HMSG Accessioned Photograph Collection

Dates of Photographs: 1880–1976

Collection Origins

Hirshhorn Museum and Sculpture Garden (HMSG) staff assembled the collection from photographs included in the donation of New York financier Joseph H. Hirshhorn (1899–1981), from other gifts, and from purchases. For Hirshhorn's biography, see the *Collection Origins* field of *HM·2*. While the HMSG's collecting mandate does not include photography, there are 280 fine art photographs within the collection, the largest group by Ralston Crawford, Thomas Eakins, and Arnold Newman. The Eakins photographs, originally part of the Samuel A. Murray Scrapbooks *(HM·17)*, have been conserved, arranged by subject, described, and accessioned into this collection.

Photographers represented include Berenice Abbott (2 photoprints), Vito Acconci (5), Ralston Crawford (98), Douglas Davis (1), Thomas Eakins (122), Arnold Genthe (1), Lewis W. Hine (2), Lotte Jacobi (1), Sally Mann (1), Samuel A. Murray (3), Arnold Newman (32), William Reeder (2), Lucas Samaras (6), Bert Stern (3), and Alfred Stieglitz (1). HMSG accessioned photographs have appeared in the following publications: 1) Abram Lerner, ed. *An Introduction to the Hirshhorn Museum and Sculpture Garden, Smithsonian Institution.* New York: H.N. Abrams, 1974. 2) Michael W. Panhorst. *Samuel Murray: The Hirshhorn Museum and Sculpture Garden Collection.* Washington, D.C.: Smithsonian Institution Press, 1982. 3) Phyllis D. Rosenzweig. *The Thomas Eakins Collection of the Hirshhorn Museum Collection.* Washington, D.C.: Smithsonian Institution Press, 1977.

Physical Description

There are 280 photographs including albumen photoprints, cyanotypes, dye diffusion transfer photoprints (Polaroid SX-70), platinum photoprints, silver gelatin dry plate photonegatives, and silver gelatin photoprints. Other materials include drawings, graphic prints, paintings, photomechanicals (including a collotype), and sculptures.

Subjects

Most of the photographs are portraits, although there are also allegorical works, animal studies, cityscapes, landscapes, and still lifes. People portrayed include Oscar F. Bluemner by Arnold Genthe and Alfred Stieglitz; Louis M. Eilshemius by Berenice Abbott; Abraham Walkowitz by Lotte Jacobi; Walt Whitman by Thomas Eakins, Samuel A. Murray, and William Reeder; and self-portraits (phototransformations) by Lucas Samaras. There are numerous portraits of artists by Arnold Newman. The collection also contains four photographs from Douglas Davis's *Questions New York Moscow New York Set—Why is the Line Between Us?* and two untitled historical cityscapes by Lewis W. Hine.

The largest group of photographs is by Thomas Eakins, including nude studies of models; portraits of his family, friends, and pets; studies for paintings and sculptures; and Marey-wheel images of motion, one of which has notations attributed to Thomas Eakins or Eadweard Muybridge. People shown in motion studies, nude studies, and portraits include Charles Bregler, Weda Cook, Ben Crowell, Frank H. Cushing, Benjamin Eakins, Jesse Godley, Ruth Harding, George W. Holmes, David W. Jordan, Anna Kershaw, Jane (Jennie Dean) Kershaw (Mrs. Samuel A. Murray), Frank B.A. Linton, Elizabeth Macdowell, Susan H. Macdowell (Mrs. Thomas Eakins), William H. Macdowell, Mrs. William H. Macdowell, Samuel A. Murray, William O'Donovan, George Reynolds, Franklin L. Schenck, J. Laurie Wallace, Walt Whitman, and Talcott Williams. Photographic studies for paintings include *Arcadia;* geese at the site of *Mending the Net;* a model with an antique cast (sculpture reproduction); models in Greek costumes; *Rock Thrower;* students at the site of *The Swimming Hole; Thorn Puller;* and wrestlers in Eakins's studio. Animals shown include cats, dogs, geese, and Eakins's horse with Samuel A. Murray astride.

Arranged: By artist, then by accession number.

Captioned: Some with accession number, date, or photographer.

Finding Aid: 1) HMSG Curatorial Index, arranged alphabetically by artist, lists the object's accession number, copyright, inscription, date, medium, size, and title; artist's country of origin, dates, and name; and date and source of acquisition. 2) HMSG Artist Frequency Data, arranged alphabetically by artist, lists the number of drawings, graphic prints, paintings, photographs, and sculptures by each artist. 3) Collection Archives, a further guide to the collection, includes accession records, bibliographical data, correspondence with the artist, exhibit history, provenance and authentication information, and reference history. The Curatorial Index and Artist Frequency Data are computer printouts for accessioned objects in the collections. Researchers interested in these two printouts should contact Registrar Douglas Robinson, Office of the Registrar, HMSG, Room G14, Smithsonian Institution, Washington, D.C., 20560, (202) 357-3281. For access to the Collection Archives, researchers should contact Judith K. Zilczer, Curator of Paintings, Department of Painting and Sculpture, HMSG, Room 436, Smithsonian Institution, Washington, D.C., 20560, (202) 357-3230.

Restrictions: No. Contact Curator of Prints and Drawings Frank Gettings, Department of Painting and Sculpture, HMSG, Room G26, Smithsonian Institution, Washington, D.C., 20560, (202) 357-3286.

HM·12

HMSG Collection Archives Curatorial Records

Dates of Photographs: 20th Century

Collection Origins

Hirshhorn Museum and Sculpture Garden (HMSG) curators assembled the collection from diverse sources to document HMSG accessioned drawings, graphic prints, paintings, and sculptures for administrative purposes. Photographers represented include Geoffrey Clements, Marianne B. Gurley, Bill Herz, Mattie Edwards Hewitt, O.E. Nelson, M. Lee Stalsworth, and John R. Tennant.

The photographs have appeared in the following publications: 1) Valerie J. Fletcher. *Alberto Giacometti, 1901–1906.* Washington, D.C.: Smithsonian Institution Press, 1988. 2) Edward F. Fry. *David Smith, Painter, Sculptor, Draftsman.* New York: G. Braziller, 1982. 3) Frank Gettings. *E.E. Cummings: The Poet as Artist.* Washington, D.C.: Smithsonian Institution Press, 1977. 4) Frank Gettings. *George Grosz: Hirshhorn Museum and Sculpture Garden Collection.* Washington, D.C.: Smithsonian Institution Press, 1978. 5) Frank Gettings. *Raphael Soyer: Sixty-five Years of Printmaking.* Washington, D.C.: Smithsonian Institution Press, 1982. 6) Abram Lerner, ed. *An Introduction to the Hirshhorn Museum and Sculpture Garden, Smithsonian Institution.* New York: H.N. Abrams, 1974. 7) Robert Moskowitz. *Robert Moskowitz.* Washington, D.C.: Smithsonian Institution, 1989. 8) Phyllis D. Rosenzweig. *Larry Rivers: The Hirshhorn Museum and Sculpture Garden Collection.* Washington, D.C.: Smithsonian Institution Press, 1981. 9) Judith Zilczer. *Oscar Bluemner: The Hirshhorn Museum and Sculp-ture Garden Collection.* Washington, D.C.: Smithsonian Institution Press, 1979. 10) Judith Zilczer. *Joseph Stella, the Hirshhorn Museum and Sculpture Garden Collection.* Washington, D.C.: Smithsonian Institution Press, 1983.

Physical Description

There are 23,155 photographs including color dye coupler photoprints, phototransparencies, and slides and silver gelatin photoprints. Other materials include accession forms, bibliographies, biographies, correspondence, exhibit catalogs, exhibit histories, index cards, inventories, lists of related work, reference histories, reprints, sketches, a videotape, and xerographic copies (including copies of wills).

Subjects

The photographs document drawings, graphic prints, paintings, and sculptures by American and European artists, primarily from the 19th and 20th centuries. Artists whose works are photograhically reproduced include Josef Albers, Milton Avery, Eugenie Baizerman, Oscar F. Bluemner, Alexander Stirling Calder, Honoré Daumier, Arthur B. Davies, Stuart Davis, Edgar Degas, Willem de Kooning, Jean Dubuffet, Thomas Eakins, Louis M. Eilshemius, Philip Evergood, Lyonel C.A. Feininger, Alberto Giacometti, Arshile Gorky, Chaim Gross, Winslow Homer, George B. Luks, André Masson, Henry Moore, Robert Motherwell, Elie Nadelman, Jules Pascin, Pablo Picasso, Maurice B. Prendergast, Pierre Auguste Renoir, Larry Rivers, Georges Rouault, John Singer Sargent, John Sloan, David Smith, Raphael Soyer, Joseph Stella, Abraham Walkowitz, and James Abbott McNeill Whistler.

Arranged: Alphabetically by artist.

Captioned: With artist's name.

Finding Aid: 1) HMSG Curatorial Index (computer printout), arranged alphabetically by artist, lists the artist's name, country of origin, and dates; accession number, date, inscriptions, process, size, support material, and subject or title of the work; and the source of the image. 2) HMSG Artist Frequency Data (computer printout), arranged alphabetically by artist, lists the number of drawings, paintings, photographs, sculptures, and other works in HMSG, as well as the total numbers of works by each artist represented in HMSG holdings.

Researchers interested in using the printouts should contact Registrar Douglas Robinson, Office of the Registrar, HMSG, Room G14, Smithsonian Institution, Washington, D.C., 20560, (202) 357-3281; or Curator of Prints and Drawings Frank Gettings, Department of

Painting and Sculpture, HMSG, Room G26, Smithsonian Institution, Washington, D.C., 20560, (202) 357-3286.

Restrictions: Available by appointment only. Contact Judith K. Zilczer, Curator of Paintings, Department of Painting and Sculpture, HMSG, Room 436, Smithsonian Institution, Washington, D.C., 20560, (202) 357-3230.

HM·13

HMSG Collection Archives Louis M. Eilshemius Paintings Photograph Album

Dates of Photographs: Circa 1940s–1950s

Collection Origins

Financier Joseph H. Hirshhorn (1899–1981) created the collection to document his private collection of paintings by Louis M. Eilshemius. For a biography of Hirshhorn, see the *Collection Origins* field of *HM·2*. Eilshemius (1864–1946), who described himself as "the transcendental eagle of the arts," was active in the late 19th and early 20th centuries. Working primarily with oils, he specialized in landscape paintings and portraits. In 1987, Olga Hirshhorn (Joseph Hirshhorn's widow) donated the album to the Hirshhorn Museum and Sculpture Garden. All photographs in the collection were taken by Colten Photos.

Physical Description

There are 50 silver gelatin photoprints, mounted in an album.

Subjects

The images are photographic reproductions of paintings by Louis M. Eilshemius, which were owned by Joseph H. Hirshhorn.

Arranged: Sequentially by assigned number.

Captioned: With assigned number, possibly the photographer's negative number.

Finding Aid: No.

Restrictions: Available by appointment only. Contact Judith K. Zilczer, Curator of Paintings, Department of Painting and Sculpture, HMSG, Room 436, Smithsonian Institution, Washington, D.C., 20560, (202) 357-3230.

HM·14

HMSG Collection Archives Hirshhorn Foundation Records *A.K.A.* Armory Show Papers

Dates of Photographs: Circa 1960s–1988

Collection Origins

Art historian and author Milton W. Brown (1911–   ) created the collection under the aegis of the Joseph H. Hirshhorn Foundation for his book, *The Story of the Armory Show*. The collection was later given to the Foundation.

Brown was a professor and later an executive officer of the Graduate Department of Art History at the Brooklyn College of the City University of New York. His book was published by the Foundation to coincide with the opening of "The Fiftieth Anniversary Exhibition (of the Armory Show)" at the Henry Street Settlement House in New York City. The original 1913 Armory Show, officially titled "The International Exhibition of Modern Art," was organized by the Association of American Painters and Sculptors for exhibition at the New York City Armory. The controversial show later traveled to the Chicago Art Institute and the Copley Society of Boston.

Photographers and studios represented include the Addison Gallery of American Art, Albright-Knox Art Gallery, Andover Art Studio, Art Institute of Chicago, Baltimore Museum of Art, Thomas H. Curley, Felix Landau Gallery, Leonard Hutton Galleries, Metropolitan Museum of Art, the Munson-Williams-Proctor Institute Museum of Art, National Gallery (London), New York Graphic Society, Peter A. Juley & Son, Pierre Matisse Gallery, Sanborn Studio, Soichi Sunami, and the Whitney Museum of American Art. The photographs appear in the following books by Milton W. Brown: 1) *American Painting from the Armory Show to the Depression*. Princeton: Princeton University Press,

1955. 2) *The Story of the Armory Show.* 2nd ed. New York: Abbeville Press, 1988.

There are several related collections: 1) the Elmer Livingston MacRae Papers, in the HMSG Collection Archives, which contains vintage photomechanical reproductions of many of the paintings exhibited in the Armory Show; 2) the Walt Kuhn Papers in the Smithsonian's Archives of American Art; and 3) the John Quinn Memorial Collection in the Manuscripts and Archives Division, New York Public Library.

Physical Description

There are 105 photographs including silver gelatin photonegatives and photoprints. Other materials include correspondence and photomechanicals.

Subjects

The photographs document art objects from the 1913 Armory Show including George W. Bellows's *Circus;* Constantin Brancusi's *The Kiss;* Marcel Duchamp's *Nude Descending a Staircase, No. 2;* Robert Henri's *The Spanish Gipsy;* Walt Kuhn's *Morning;* Henri Matisse's *The Blue Nude;* Pablo Picasso's *Female Nude;* Maurice B. Prendergast's *Landscape with Figures;* Albert Pinkham Ryder's *Moonlight Marine;* Charles Sheeler's *Chrysanthemums;* John Sloan's *Sunday, Girls Drying Their Hair;* and Maurice de Vlaminck's *Village.*

There also are exhibit installation views, as well as an image of the exterior of the Armory building with a banner announcing the show, a photographic reproduction of the front page of the exhibit catalog, and portraits of Arthur B. Davies, Walt Kuhn, Elmer Livingston MacRae, Walter Pach, and John Quinn.

Arranged: In three series. 1) Correspondence. 2) Records related to the Hirshhorn Foundation's acquisition of the MacRae Papers. 3) Photographs used in *The Story of the Armory Show.*

Captioned: With date, exhibit title, names of people shown, occasion, and the published source of the image.

Finding Aid: Yes.

Restrictions: Available by appointment only. No reproductions may be made. Contact Judith K. Zilczer, Curator of Paintings, Department of Painting and Sculpture, HMSG, Room 436, Smithsonian Institution, Washington, D.C., 20560, (202) 357-3230.

HM·15

HMSG Collection Archives Hirshhorn Oversize and Miscellaneous Records

Dates of Photographs: 1966–1970s

Collection Origins

Hirshhorn Museum and Sculpture Garden (HMSG) staff assembled the collection from the files of Charles Bregler, a pupil of Thomas Eakins; former HMSG director Abram Lerner; and other HMSG staff. Photographers and studios represented include Jan W. Faul and Waintrob. Some of the collection photographs have appeared in the following publications: 1) Abram Lerner, ed. *An Introduction to the Hirshhorn Museum and Sculpture Garden, Smithsonian Institution.* New York: H.N. Abrams, 1974. 2) Phyllis D. Rosenzweig. *The Thomas Eakins Collection of the Hirshhorn Museum and Sculpture Garden.* Washington, D.C.: Smithsonian Institution Press, 1977.

Physical Description

There are 75 photographs including color dye coupler photoprints (on a contact sheet) and silver gelatin photoprints. Other materials include architectural drawings and correspondence.

Subjects

The photographs document HMSG activities, donors, holdings, and staff, as well as artists whose work is represented in the HMSG holdings. The photographs illustrate art works being packed at donor Joseph H. Hirshhorn's New York City home, as well as sculptures by Giacomo Manzù. People portrayed include Hirshhorn (outside the HMSG) and artist Raphael Soyer.

Arranged: No.

Captioned: No.

Finding Aid: No.

Restrictions: Available by appointment only. Contact Judith K. Zilczer, Curator of Paintings, Department of Painting and Sculpture, HMSG, Room 436, Smithsonian Institution, Washington, D.C., 20560, (202) 357-3230.

HM·16

HMSG Collection Archives Joseph H. Hirshhorn's Art Holdings Documentation

Dates of Photographs: 1950s–1970s

Collection Origins

Hirshhorn Museum and Sculpture Garden (HMSG) curatorial staff, particularly former HMSG director Abram Lerner, assembled the collection from Joseph H. Hirshhorn's records to document objects from his private art holdings that were not donated to the museum. For a biography of Hirshhorn, see the *Collection Origins* field of *HM·2*. Photographers and studios represented include the André Emmerich Gallery, Bacci, R. Bonache, Geoffrey Clements, Richard Di Liberto, Gimpel Fils Gallery, Ltd., Hanover Square Gallery, Knoedler and Company, Marlborough-Gerson Gallery, Ugo Mulas, O.E. Nelson, Nathan Rabin, John D. Schiff, and John Webb.

Physical Description

There are 650 photographs including color dye coupler photoprints and phototransparencies and silver gelatin photonegatives, photoprints, and phototransparencies. Other materials include biographies, correspondence, inventories, and xerographic copies.

Subjects

The photographs document art objects from Joseph H. Hirshhorn's private collection that were not included in his donations to the HMSG. These include 19th and 20th century American and European drawings, graphic prints, paintings, and sculptures.

Arranged: Alphabetically by artist.

Captioned: With artist, dimensions, and title of work. Sleeves with accession number, artist, dimensions, medium, and title of work.

Finding Aid: No.

Restrictions: Available by appointment only. Write or call Judith K. Zilczer, Curator of Paintings, Department of Painting and Sculpture, HMSG, Room 436, Smithsonian Institution, Washington, D.C., 20560, (202) 357-3230.

HM·17

HMSG Collection Archives Samuel A. Murray Scrapbooks *A.K.A.* Thomas Eakins Collection

Dates of Photographs: Circa 1886–Circa 1965

Collection Origins

Philadelphia-born sculptor Samuel A. Murray (1870–1941) and his family assembled the collection to document Murray's art work and that of his teacher and friend Thomas Eakins. Murray, who studied anatomy, drawing, painting, and sculpture under Eakins in Philadelphia, also worked with Eakins in the formation and operation of the Art Students League of Philadelphia in 1886.

Philadelphia-born painter and photographer Thomas Eakins (1844–1916) studied at the Pennsylvania Academy of Fine Arts and under Léon Bonnât, Augustin Dumont, and Jean L. Gérôme at the École des Beaux-Arts in Paris. In 1870, Eakins returned to Philadelphia. He joined the faculty of the Pennsylvania Academy of Fine Arts in 1876, became a professor of drawing and painting in 1879, and served as director of the school from 1882 until 1886.

Eakins first purchased a camera around 1880. Initially photographing family, friends, and students, Eakins often used his photographs as sources for his paintings. When the University of Pennsylvania invited pioneering motion photographer Eadweard Muybridge to continue his photographic research at the school in 1884, Eakins was appointed to Muybridge's supervisory committee. Influenced by Muybridge's locomotion studies, Eakins designed and built his own stop-action cameras, which he demonstrated to the Photographic Society of Philadelphia in 1883.

In 1886—after disputes with the administration over his use of dissection and nude models in the classroom and disagreements over his salary—Eakins left the Pennsylvania Academy and founded the Art Students League of Philadelphia. Many of Eakins's students later joined him there. Until his death in 1916, Eakins continued to make photographic studies of his family, his students, his portrait subjects (including Walt Whitman) and the surrounding landscape.

Photographers represented include Susan H. Macdowell (Mrs. Thomas Eakins), Samuel A. Murray, William Reeder, and Carl Van Vechten, as well as unidentified students and associates. The original scrapbooks have been dismantled for conservation reasons, and portions of this collection have been added to the HMSG Accessioned Photograph Collection *(HM·11)*. The collection as originally mounted in the scrapbooks is available on microfilm, which, along with a calendar index to the scrapbooks, is available to researchers in the HMSG Library.

The photographs have appeared in the following publications: 1) Gordon Hendricks. *A Family Album: Photographs by Thomas Eakins, 1880–1890.* New York: Coe Kerr Gallery, 1976. 2) Gordon Hendricks. *The Photographs of Thomas Eakins.* New York: Grossman Publishers, 1972. 3) Gordon Hendricks. *Thomas Eakins: His Photographic Works.* Philadelphia: Pennsylvania Academy of the Fine Arts, 1969. 4) William Innes Homer. "Who Took Eakins' Photographs?" *Art News* 112 (May 1983): 112–119. 5) Michael W. Panhorst. *Samuel Murray: The Hirshhorn Museum and Sculpture Garden Collection.* Washington D.C.: Smithsonian Institution Press, 1982. 6) Phyllis D. Rosenzweig. *The Thomas Eakins Collection of the Hirshhorn Museum Collection.* Washington D.C.: Smithsonian Institution Press, 1977.

Physical Description

There are 465 photographs including albumen photoprints, color dye coupler photoprints, cyanotypes, platinum photoprints, silver gelatin dry plate photonegatives, and silver gelatin photoprints (some nonvintage prints made from original Eakins photonegatives). Some of the images are Marey-wheel motion-sequence photographs. The photographs originally were mounted in scrapbooks but have since been removed; a microfilm copy reproduces the scrapbooks in their original form. Other materials, also originally mounted in the scrapbooks, include announcements, birthday cards, correspondence, exhibit labels, government documents, invitations, lists, magazine clippings, manuscripts, maps, newspaper clippings, oil paintings, pamphlets, photomechanicals, postcards, programs, reprints, silhouettes, sketches, and watercolors.

Subjects

The photographs document Thomas Eakins and Samuel A. Murray, their art and photographic work, and their families, friends, pets, and students, primarily in Philadelphia between the 1870s and 1941.

Photographs attributed to Eakins include portraits of Samuel A. Murray and Walt Whitman. Photographs attributed to Murray include a portrait of Walt Whitman. Other photographs include informal portraits of Thomas Eakins and William O'Donovan sitting on the floor of a studio; Eakins, an unidentified man, and Murray bathing in the Cohansey River in New Jersey;

Eakins and Murray near a boat at Eakins's cottage; and Eakins painting. Formal portraits show Eakins as a young man seated in his studio (1909), at age 56, and in profile. Photographs of Murray show him as a youth, in Marey motion-sequence images, and modeling for paintings.

Eakins's paintings and sculptures photographically reproduced include *Portrait of Ruth Harding, Portrait of Walt Whitman, The Swimming Hole,* and *Woman Knitting.* There are photographic studies created as source material for Eakins's paintings such as *Arcadia, Mending the Net,* and *The Swimming Hole.* There is also a series of 23 photographic sequences of human motion made by Eakins with a Marey-wheel camera. These sequential stop-action photographs, which show the influence of Eadweard Muybridge's work, include one with notations by Muybridge or Eakins.

Photographic reproductions of Murray's paintings and sculptures include *The Boxer (Elwood McCloskey), Commodore John Barry, Dr. William Houston Green, Grief, Portrait Bust, Portrait Bust of Thomas Eakins, Ruth (Ruth Harding Thomson), Standing Figure,* and *Walt Whitman.* Other artists whose work is reproduced include Mrs. James Mapes Dodge and David W. Jordan.

Arranged: No.

Captioned: With artist, date, and description or title of the object; and page number, photographer, polarity, process, and size of the photograph.

Finding Aid: 1) HMSG Curatorial Index, which lists, alphabetically by photographer, the items removed from the collection for accessioning. For each photograph the Index lists the photographer and the photographer's country of origin and dates; the photograph's accession number, date, inscriptions, process, size, support material, and subject or title; and the source of the image. 2) Indexes to the microfilm reproduction of the scrapbooks as they originally existed, which list the date, page number, photographer, polarity, process, size, and subject of the images in the album. The indexes also describe all other types of materials such as correspondence, lists, newspaper clippings, and programs within the same sequence. 3) Index to the photographs in the collection.

Restrictions: Available by appointment only. Contact Phyllis Rosenzweig, Associate Curator, Department of Painting and Sculpture, HMSG, Room 436, Smithsonian Institution, Washington, D.C., 20560, (202) 357-3230.

HM·18

HMSG Collection Archives Sylvan Schendler Photograph File

Dates of Photographs: 1950s

Collection Origins

Author and professor Sylvan Schendler (1925–) assembled the collection as research material for his 1967 monograph on painter, photographer, and teacher Thomas Eakins (1844–1916). For a biography of Eakins, see the *Collection Origins* field in *HM·17*.

Schendler, who received a Ph.D. in English from Northwestern University in 1956, taught English at New Mexico State College (1948–1950), Wayne State University (1950–1954), Texas Western College (1955–1956), Smith College (1956–1957), and Point Park College (1967–1971), as well as American studies and literature in Finland (1960), Hong Kong (1966–1967), and India (1971–1974). While in India, Schendler served as the editor of both the *Indian Journal of American Studies* and *Reviews in American Studies*.

Photographers and studios represented include the Albright-Knox Art Gallery; Art Institute of Chicago; Lillian Bristol; Brooklyn Museum; Frick Art Reference Library; Hyde Collection; Joseph Klima, Jr.; Metropolitan Museum of Art; Montclair Art Museum; Pennsylvania Academy of Design; Philadelphia Museum of Art; Walter Rosenblum; Sheldon Art Gallery; and Yale University Art Gallery. The photographs were published in the following monograph: Sylvan Schendler. *Eakins*. Boston: Little, Brown and Company, 1967. Schendler donated the collection to HMSG in 1984.

Physical Description

There are 155 silver gelatin photoprints.

Subjects

The photographs reproduce paintings, primarily portraits, completed between 1860 and 1913 by American painter Thomas Eakins and reproduced in Sylvan Schendler's 1967 monograph *Eakins*.

Eakins's paintings reproduced include the following: *Addie, Woman in Black; The Agnew Clinic; Arcadia; The Artist and His Father Hunting Reed Birds; At the Piano; Becalmed; The Cello Player; The Chess Players; The Concert Singer; The Coral Necklace; The Crucifixion; The Dean's Roll Call; Drawing the Seine; Father of Mrs. Eakins; Home Scene; In the Studio; John Biglen in a Single Scull; A May Morning (Fairman Rogers Four-in-Hand); Mending the Net; Music; Oarsmen on the Schuylkill; The Oboe Player; The Old-Fashioned Dress; Portrait of Amelia Van Buren; Portrait of Architect John Joseph Borie; Portrait of Benjamin Eakins; Portrait of Charles E. Dana; Portrait of Girl in a Big Hat; Portrait of Henry F. Rowland; Portrait of Jacob Mendez da Costa; Portrait of Leslie W. Miller; Portrait of Maud Cook; Portrait of Mrs. Frank Hamilton Cushing; Portrait of Mrs. Samuel Murray; Portrait of Mrs. Thomas Eakins; Portrait of Philip R. McDevitt; Portrait of Professor Gross (The Gross Clinic); Portrait of Robert C. Ogden; Portrait of Samuel Murray; Portrait of Walt Whitman; Portrait of William D. Marks;* and *Portrait of William Thomson.*

Other artworks reproduced in the collection include *The Red Shawl; The Schreiber Brothers; Self Portrait; Shad Fishing at Gloucester on the Delaware; Sketch of Walt Whitman; Spinning; Street Scene in Seville; The Swimming Hole; The Thinker; The Veteran; Walter Macdowell; William H. Macdowell; William Rush and His Model; William Rush Carving His Allegorical Figure of the Schuylkill; Will Schuster and Black Man Going Shooting for Rail;* and *The Writing Master.*

Arranged: No.

Captioned: With the name of the museum holding the original painting and the painting's accession number, dimensions, and subject.

Finding Aid: Inventory listing the date, location, medium, size, and title of the painting, along with the plate number from Schendler's book *Eakins*.

Restrictions: Available by appointment only. Contact Judith K. Zilczer, Curator of Paintings, Department of Painting and Sculpture, HMSG, Room 436, Smithsonian Institution, Washington, D.C., 20560, (202) 357-3230.

HM

Conservation Laboratory

Conservation Laboratory
Hirshhorn Museum and Sculpture Garden
Smithsonian Institution
Washington, D.C. 20560
Laurence Hoffman, Chief Conservator
(202) 357-3268
Hours: By appointment.

Scope of the Collection

There is one photographic collection with approximately 6,400 images.

Focus of the Collection

The photographs document art objects in Hirshhorn Museum and Sculpture Garden (HMSG) holdings, including 19th and 20th century American and European drawings, graphic prints, paintings, and sculpture, shown before, during, and after preservation and restoration treatments.

Photographic Processes and Formats Represented

There are color dye coupler slides and silver gelatin photonegatives and photoprints.

Other Materials Represented

The laboratory also contains conservation treatment records.

Access and Usage Policies

The photograph collection is restricted. For further information, researchers should contact Laurence Hoffman, Chief Conservator.

Publication Policies

Researchers must obtain permission from the Smithsonian Institution, particularly the HMSG Photographic Services Office, to reproduce a photograph and may also have to obtain permission from the copyright holder, which is not necessarily the Smithsonian Institution. The preferred credit line is "Courtesy of the Conservation Laboratory, Hirshhorn Museum and Sculpture Garden, Smithsonian Institution." The photographer's name, if known, also should appear.

HM·19

HMSG Conservation Laboratory Photograph File

Dates of Photographs: 1975–Present

Collection Origins

Hirshhorn Museum and Sculpture Garden (HMSG) Conservation Laboratory staff created the collection to aid in the restoration of works of art from the HMSG's permanent collection. Photographers represented include the staff of the HMSG Conservation Laboratory and the Photographic Services Office.

Physical Description

There are 6,400 photographs including color dye coupler slides (Ektachrome, 3,500) and silver gelatin photonegatives (200) and photoprints (2,700). Other materials include correspondence and work requests.

Subjects

The photographs document HMSG accessioned art objects that have undergone restoration work. Images show 19th and 20th century American and European drawings, graphic prints, paintings, and sculpture before, during, and after conservation treatment.

Arranged: In two series. 1) Photonegatives, photoprints, and slides arranged first by medium, then alphabetically by artist, and then by accession number. 2) Photoprints and slides largely unarranged.

Captioned: Slides with accession number, artist, and title of the work and type of shot (detail or full view). Photonegatives and photoprints with accession number, artist, and, often, title of the work.

Finding Aid: A card index to series 1, which lists accession number, artist, and title of the work; conservator; and date, description, and stage of the conservation treatment (before, during, or after).

Restrictions: Available to HMSG staff on a "need-to-know" basis.

OFFICE OF HORTICULTURE

Kathryn R. Meehan, Acting Director

Created in 1972, the Smithsonian Institution's Office of Horticulture manages the 50-plus acres of Smithsonian gardens and grounds, cares for a horticultural artifact collection, and operates 11 greenhouses that provide plants for Smithsonian exhibits, grounds, interiors, and special events. Through its archival holdings, library, and tours, the office supports education and research in historical and practical horticulture. For 13 years beginning in 1977, the office sponsored an annual "Trees of Christmas" exhibit, which was displayed at the National Museum of American History. The office also helped design the Enid A. Haupt and Mary Livingston Ripley Gardens, which opened on the Mall in Washington, D.C., in 1987 and 1988. In 1991, as this volume was going to press, the office was renamed the Horticulture Services Division and became part of the Office of Plant Services.

The office's photographic holdings illustrate horticultural and landscape design, particularly historical American gardens; horticultural artifacts, mostly from the Victorian period; and many species of decorative plants. There also are images of horticultural publications, techniques, and tools. The 72,370 photographs in the division's three collections represent only part of its research resources. The office maintains living plant collections of many species and an artifact collection that includes Christmas tree ornaments, garden furniture, Victorian hand bouquet (posy) holders, and wire floral frames. Additionally, the library contains books, information files, periodicals, and trade catalogs.

HO

Office of Horticulture

Office of Horticulture
Smithsonian Institution
Washington, D.C. 20560
Kathryn R. Meehan, Acting Director
Sally Tomlinson, Museum Technician
(202) 357-1926
Hours: Tuesday–Thursday, 8:30 a.m.–5 p.m.

Scope of the Collections

There are three photographic collections with approximately 72,370 images.

Focus of the Collections

These photographs document historical and practical horticulture from the mid-19th century to the present, primarily in the United States. Most photographs illustrate the landscape architecture of cemeteries, churches, museums, parks, private gardens and homes, and public buildings and gardens. Images also show floral decorations, garden artifacts (such as furniture and statuary), gardeners, greenhouses, horticultural tools, plants, and plant holders. Note: In 1991, after this volume was completed, the office became part of the Office of Plant Services and changed its name to the Horticulture Services Division.

Photographic Processes and Formats Represented

There are albumen photoprints (some stereographs), collodion gelatin photoprints (POP), color dye coupler photoprints and slides, silver gelatin dry plate lantern slides (tinted), and silver gelatin photonegatives, photoprints (some stereographs), and slides.

Other Materials Represented

The office also contains correspondence; horticultural artifacts, especially Christmas tree ornaments, garden furniture, and hand bouquet (or posy) holders; identification forms; lists; memorabilia; and scripts. There is a library containing books, information files, periodicals, and trade catalogs.

Access and Usage Policies

The office is available to the public by appointment only. Scholarly researchers should write the director and describe their research topic, the type of material that interests them, and their research aim. As this book went to press, the Archives of American Gardens was scheduled to become accessible in June 1992. There are partial finding aids to each of the collections. Certain materials have copyright restrictions.

Publication Policies

Researchers must obtain permission from the Smithsonian Institution to reproduce a photograph and may also have to obtain permission from the copyright holder, which is not necessarily the Smithsonian Institution. The preferred credit line is "Courtesy of the Horticulture Services Division, Office of Plant Services, Smithsonian Institution." The photographer's name, if known, also should appear.

HO·1

Accessions File of the Office of Horticulture

Dates of Photographs: 1972–Present

Collection Origins

Staff at the Office of Horticulture created the collection to document its collection of horticultural artifacts. The Smithsonian Institution formed the office in 1972 to collect botanical specimens and related artifacts, create interior botanical displays, establish research facilities and educational programs in historical and practical horticulture, and manage the Smithsonian's grounds and gardens. As artifacts were added, they were photographed for the accession record. Photographers represented include James R. Buckler, Kathryn Meehan, Karen Miles, and OPPS staff. Note: In 1991, after this volume was completed, the office became part of the Office of Plant Services and changed its name to the Horticulture Services Division.

Physical Description

There are 1,920 photographs including color dye coupler photoprints and silver gelatin photoprints, mounted on index cards.

Subjects

The photographs document the artifacts collected by the office, including garden elements such as fountains, furniture, hitching posts, statuary, sundials, urns, and wellheads. Many different types of plant holders are shown, including aquariums, basins, vases, and wire frames. Also depicted is a large collection of ornate Victorian hand bouquet (or posy) holders.

Arranged: On index cards, alphabetically by subject, then by object's accession number.

Captioned: With object's accession information including description, location, and number.

Finding Aid: The collection functions as a card catalog to accessioned objects.

Restrictions: No.

HO·2

Archives of American Gardens *A.K.A.* Garden Club of America Slide Library of Notable American Parks and Gardens

Dates of Photographs: 1908–Present

Collection Origins

Garden Club of America (GCA) members created this collection to document their gardens and other examples of horticulture for lecture, publication, and research purposes. Founded in 1913, the GCA has documented gardens extensively since the 1920s. In the 1980s, the GCA established a "Slide Library of Notable American Parks and Gardens," containing images donated by GCA members from around the country. In 1987 the Smithsonian Institution's Office of Horticulture accepted the collection. The office agreed to catalog and store the collection while providing access to researchers. The collection will be opened to the public in 1992. Note: In 1991, after this volume was completed, the office became part of the Office of Plant Services and changed its name to the Horticulture Services Division.

Photographs from this collection appear in the following book: Mac K. Griswold and Eleanor C. Weller. *Gardens of a Gilded Age (1880–1940): The American South, the Antebellum Era.* New York: Harry N. Abrams, Inc., 1991. Photographers represented include M.E. Hewitt, Russ Marchand, O.H. Smith, George Stritikus, Edward Van Altena, and Eleanor Weller.

Physical Description

There are 15,450 photographs including color dye coupler slides, silver gelatin dry plate lantern slides (tinted), and silver gelatin slides. (The number of photographs will increase as more slides are received.) Other materials include correspondence, lists, identification forms, and slide scripts.

Subjects

The photographs document gardens in the United States from the colonial period to the present, with an emphasis on those with historical significance or with outstanding design or horticultural features. Gardens from almost every state are illustrated. Particularly well-represented are the gardens of California; Connecticut; New Jersey; and New York, especially Long Island. Types of gardens depicted include colonial Virginia gardens, desert gardens, Newport gardens, and Southern plantation gardens. In addition to private gardens, there are images of arboretums, botanical gardens, cemeteries, monuments, museums, orchards, and parks.

Individual public and private gardens illustrated include those at the Arkansas governor's mansion (Little Rock); Audubon Park (New Orleans); the Chicago Botanic Gardens (Glencoe, Illinois); Dumbarton Oaks (Washington, D.C.); Golden Gate Park (San Francisco); Monticello and Mount Vernon (Virginia); and the Van Rensselaer Estate (New York); as well as on the grounds of DuPont and Rockefeller family estates. Decorative garden artifacts depicted include bridges, fountains, furniture, garden houses, gates, hedges, ponds, rock gardens, statuary, steps, terraces, urns, and walls. There are also photographic reproductions of blueprints, lithographs, paintings, and plans.

Arranged: Alphabetically by state, then city, then subject; then by assigned slide number.

Captioned: With city and state, name, and slide number.

Finding Aid: 1) Documentation files for each slide, including the caption information and background material. 2) Scripts for several slide sets, including the GCA 75th anniversary project, "The History of American Gardens." 3) Caption lists for some slide groups, including specific garden elements in each image. 4) A database containing image date and garden designer, description, name, location, and owner, as well as photo caption and publication credit information, is in preparation. 5) A laser disk featuring the slides is planned.

Restrictions: As this book went to press, the collection was scheduled to open in 1992. For further information contact Kathryn R. Meehan, Horticultural Services Division, Office of Plant Services, Arts and Industries Building, Room 2282, Smithsonian Institution, Washington, D.C., 20560, (202) 357-1926.

HO·3

Office of Horticulture Photograph Collection

Dates of Photographs: 1860s–Present

Collection Origins

Office of Horticulture staff assembled this collection to provide information on historical and practical horticulture to staff and outside researchers. The images have appeared in exhibits such as "American Garden" at the 1983 Internationale Gartenbau Austellung (IGA 83) in Munich; "The Art of Gardening: Maryland Landscapes and the American Garden Aesthetic, 1730–1930" at the Historical Society of Talbot County, Maryland, in 1985; "A Victorian Horticultural Extravaganza" at the Smithsonian Institution from 1980 to 1987; and "Victorian Gardens: A Horticultural Extravaganza," a 1988 Smithsonian Institution Traveling Exhibition Service exhibit. The images have also been used in lectures and the following publications: 1) James R. Buckler. *The Smithsonian Gardener's Journal.* New York: Galison, 1987. 2) James R. Buckler and Kathryn Meehan. *Victorian Gardens: A Horticultural Extravaganza.* Washington, D.C.: Smithsonian Institution, 1988. 3) Kathryn Meehan. "Cast-Iron Ornaments of the 19th-Century Landscape." *Garden* (March-April 1987). Photographers and studios represented include James Buckler, James Esson, Griffith & Griffith, Susan Gurney, H. Ropes & Co., Keystone View Company, Kathryn Meehan, Karen Miles, OPPS, and Underwood and Underwood. Note: In 1991, after this volume was completed, the office became part of the Office of Plant Services and changed its name to the Horticulture Services Division.

Physical Description

There are 55,000 photographs including albumen photoprints (some stereographs), collodion gelatin photoprints (POP), color dye coupler slides, and silver gelatin photonegatives, photoprints (some stereographs), and slides.

Subjects

The photographs document the history and contemporary practice of of horticulture in America. Images depict decorations made with plants, equipment and tools used to tend plants, garden elements, landscape architecture on public and private grounds, people engaged in horticultural activities, people in gardens, and plants.

Decorations shown include artificial flowers, bouquets, cards, Christmas ornaments, floral frames, hair ornaments, and pins. Equipment depicted includes glass enclosures and seed boxes. Garden elements shown include arborettes, bathhouses, birdhouses, fencing, foot scrapers, fountains, furniture, gazebos, hitching posts, lighting, patios, paving, pedestals, pools, statues, sundials, trellises, and urns; as well as plant holders such as aquariums, baskets, cut-flower holders, plant stands, pots, and window boxes. Most of the plants shown are orchids; other types illustrated include annuals, aquatics, cacti and succulents, deciduous trees, evergreen trees, ferns, fruit trees and shrubs, house plants, miniature trees, ornamental grasses, perennials, tropical foliage, vegetables, vines, and wildflowers.

Landscape architecture and decorative plant displays are depicted in arboretums, botanical gardens, cemeteries, churches, conservatories, fields, greenhouses, museums, parks, public buildings, public gardens, shops, vineyards, and zoos. The collection includes images of gardens located throughout Europe, as well as in Canada, China, Colombia, Panama, and the United States. Several expositions are illustrated, such as the Centennial Exposition (Philadelphia, 1876); the Great Exhibition of the Works of Industry of All Nations (London, 1851); and the World's Columbian Exposition (Chicago, 1893). Views of the Smithsonian Institution include most of the museum buildings and grounds, especially the Enid A. Haupt Garden, Mary Livingston Ripley Garden, and Victorian Garden. Also illustrated are exhibits such as "American Garden" (1983); "Trees of Christmas" (1977–1989); "Victorian Gardens: A Horticultural Extravaganza" (1988); and "A Victorian Horticultural Extravaganza" (1980–1987). There are also images of flower shows, lectures, parties, seminars, and tours.

Horticultural occupations portrayed include designers, florists, growers, landscape architects, nurserymen, and seedmen. There are portraits of Office of Horticulture personnel and volunteers, as well as horticulturists such as Luther Burbank. Gardening activities (such as planting and pruning) are shown, as are outdoor sports (such as croquet, golf, and tennis) and celebrations (lawn parties, parades, and weddings). There are also photographic reproductions of graphic prints, maps, and paintings, especially trade literature such as seed advertisements and catalogs. Photographs from the collection are reproduced in the illustrations section of this volume.

Arranged: By subject.

Captioned: Most with subject.

Finding Aid: Slide storage cabinet directory, listing subjects in each slide tray.

Restrictions: No.

PG

NATIONAL PORTRAIT GALLERY

Alan Fern, Director

Established by an act of Congress in 1962, the National Portrait Gallery (NPG) was designed to serve as "a free public museum for the exhibition and study of portraiture and statuary depicting men and women who have made significant contributions to the history, development, and culture of the people of the United States, and the artists who created such portraiture and statuary." The NPG opened to the public in 1968. Today NPG staff study, preserve, and exhibit portraits of historic figures in all media. The museum's major accessions include the Auguste Edouart Collection of silhouettes; Jo Davidson portrait sculptures of early 20th century Americans; the Meserve Collection of Civil War and post-Civil War photographic portraits, primarily from Mathew Brady's studio; and the Saint-Mémin Collection of portrait engravings.

The NPG is located in the historic Patent Office Building, on the site that Pierre Charles L'Enfant specified for a pantheon to honor notable Americans. The NPG shares its building and facilities, including a conservation laboratory, library, and photography department, with the National Museum of American Art (NMAA). The NPG also operates the Catalog of American Portraits (CAP), a national reference center that surveys and maintains photographs of and documentation on more than 80,000 likenesses of historically important Americans. CAP also collects information about portraits by prominent American artists. CAP collections document one-of-a-kind portraits, including decorative art objects, drawings, paintings, sculpture, and silhouettes (but not graphic prints or photographs, except for one-of-a-kind images such as daguerreotypes).

As an ongoing project in conjunction with Yale University Press, the NPG's Peale Family Papers Project transcribes, researches, and annotates the personal papers of American artist and naturalist Charles Willson Peale and his sons Raphael, Rembrandt, and Rubens. Project staff also are identifying Rembrandt Peale's portraits for an upcoming *catalogue raisonne* and exhibit. The NPG conducts the following types of outreach activities: 1) temporary and permanent exhibits, including iconographic studies of life portraits by a single artist, surveys of portraits by significant American artists, and thematic exhibits on historical subjects; 2) lectures, including gallery tours, public interviews with prominent Americans, a slide-lecture series, and pre-packaged educational programs for teachers; and 3) public programs, such as the "Cultures in Motion: Portraits of American Diversity" series.

In addition to an 80,000-volume library it shares with NMAA, the NPG supports research through its fellowship and internship programs as well as by opening to scholars the extensive biographical files of the NPG Office of the Historian. The NPG Curatorial Department Office of Photographs also contains research files documenting photographic portraiture.

The NPG's 125,220 photographs, which are contained in nine photographic collections, portray people who have made significant contributions to American history, document the work of major American artists, and record the history of the Patent Office Building and the holdings of the NPG.

The following NPG departments or offices report they do not contain photographs: the Office of the Curator of Paintings and Sculpture; the Office of the Curator of Prints; the Department of Education; the Charles Willson Peale Papers; the Office of Public Affairs; and the Office of Publications.

PG

Catalog of American Portraits

Catalog of American Portraits
National Portrait Gallery
Smithsonian Institution
Washington, D.C. 20560
Linda Thrift, Keeper
(202) 357-2578
Hours: Monday–Friday, 8:45 a.m.–5:15 p.m.

Scope of the Collection

There is one photographic collection with approximately 70,000 photographs.

Focus of the Collection

The photographs are reproductions of decorative arts objects, drawings, paintings, sculptures, and silhouettes that either portray historically significant Americans or were created by prominent American artists. About 50,000 individuals are represented in over 70,000 distinct portraits.

Photographic Processes and Formats Represented

There are color dye coupler photoprints, color dye diffusion transfer photoprints, and silver gelatin photoprints.

Other Materials Represented

The Catalog also contains correspondence, a database with printouts, newspaper clippings, and xerographic copies of published information.

Access and Usage Policies

Researchers should call or write in advance for an appointment and describe their research topic, the type of material that interests them, and their research aim.

Publication Policies

No photographic copies may be made without the written permission of the owner of the object reproduced, who retains the copyright.

PG·1

Catalog of American Portraits

Dates of Photographs: Circa 1910s–Present

Collection Origins

Catalog of American Portrait (CAP) staff created the collection as a study file of American portraits. Established in 1966, CAP collects photographs that reproduce one-of-a-kind portraits of historically significant Americans and related documentation. Portraits documented must be unique art objects such as daguerreotypes, decorative-art items, drawings, miniatures, paintings, sculptures, or silhouettes; they may not be multiple works such as graphic prints or photographs produced from photonegatives.

CAP staff members photograph portraits in the NPG as well as in gallery, museum, and private collections nationwide. CAP also accepts donated photographs of portraits. In 1978 CAP staff began preparing a computer index to make the collection accessible to researchers. The staff also began assembling a separate series of copy photoprints that illustrate costume from the 17th century through World War I, primarily used to help date portraits. CAP currently is concentrating on adding portraits of American Indians and Hispanic Americans.

Physical Description

There are 70,000 photographs including color dye coupler photoprints, color dye diffusion transfer photoprints, and silver gelatin photoprints. Other materials include correspondence, newspaper clippings, and xerographic copies of published information.

Subjects

The photographs reproduce one-of-a-kind images—daguerreotypes, drawings, paintings, sculptures, and silhouettes—of nearly 50,000 historically significant Americans. There are also reproductions of images of less well-known people as portrayed by prominent American artists. Portrait subjects particularly well-represented in the collection include Benjamin Franklin, Andrew Jackson, Abraham Lincoln, George Washington, and Daniel Webster.

There are photographic reproductions of portraits of every U.S. president. Other political figures portrayed include Spiro T. Agnew, Bernard M. Baruch, John Brown, John C. Calhoun, Henry Clay, Jefferson Davis, Eugene V. Debs, Frederick Douglass, Geraldine Ferraro, John C. Frémont, Nathan Hale, Alexander Hamilton, William D. Haywood, and Harry Hopkins.

The collection contains portraits of actors (such as John Wilkes Booth, Marlon Brando, the Marx Brothers, and Gregory Peck); artists (such as Wanda Gag, Rembrandt Peale, Edward Weston, and Frank Lloyd Wright); musicians (such as Duke Ellington, George Gershwin, Woody Guthrie, Merle Haggard, and Sergei Rachmaninoff) and other entertainment and media figures (such as Isadora Duncan, Alfred Hitchcock, Harry Houdini, and Edward R. Murrow). Inventors and scientists portrayed include Thomas A. Edison, Albert Einstein, Charles Goodyear, Joseph Henry, J. Robert Oppenheimer, and Wilbur Wright. Writers portrayed include Conrad Aiken, Samuel Clemens (A.K.A. Mark Twain), E.E. Cummings, John Dewey, Theodore Dreiser, T.S. Eliot, Ralph Waldo Emerson, William Faulkner, Robert Frost, Horace Greeley, Bret Harte, Nathaniel Hawthorne, Ernest Hemingway, Aldous Huxley, Henry James, Herman Melville, Edgar Allan Poe, Noah Webster, and Richard Wright.

American Indians portrayed include Goyathlay (A.K.A. Geronimo), Hinmaton-Yalaktit (A.K.A. Chief Joseph), and Tashunka Witco (A.K.A. Crazy Horse). Other individuals portrayed include Davy Crockett, George A. Custer, Jack Dempsey, Amelia Earhart, Henry Ford, Jesse James, Helen Keller, and Charles Lindbergh.

Artists whose work is reproduced include Eldridge Ayer Burbank, George Catlin, Boris Chaliapin, William Merritt Chase, John Singleton Copley, Jo Davidson, Thomas Eakins, Daniel Chester French, Chester Harding, George P.A. Healy, Henry Inman, John W. Jarvis, Charles B. King, Roy Lichtenstein, Henry Major, Man Ray, Paul Manship, Henri Matisse, Gari Melchers, Samuel F.B. Morse, Charles Osgood, Charles Willson Peale, Rembrandt Peale, Pablo Picasso, Hiram Powers, Augustus Saint-Gaudens, John Singer Sargent, Ben Shahn, Gilbert Stuart, John Trumbull, Abraham Walkowitz, and Benjamin West.

Arranged: In two series. 1) CAP files, alphabetically by subject. 2) Costume study, chronologically by decade, then by age and sex: a) women; b) children; and c) men.

Captioned: With artist, date, owner, subject, and subject's life dates.

Finding Aid: Indexes arranged by artist; execution date; location; medium; object class (drawing, miniature, painting, sculpture, and silhouette); subject; and subject occupation (or principal distinction such as ethnic group). The indexes list accession number, artist, artist's life dates, execution date, location, object class, subject, and subject's life dates. There is also a master list that contains more background information.

Restrictions: The images may not be reproduced without the written permission of the owner of the art object illustrated, who retains the copyright.

PG

Conservation Laboratory

Conservation Laboratory
National Portrait Gallery
Smithsonian Institution
Washington, D.C. 20560
CindyLou Ockershausen, Chief Conservator
(202) 357-2685
Hours: Monday–Friday, 8:45 a.m.–5:15 p.m.

Scope of the Collection

There is one photographic collection with approximately 12,000 photographs.

Focus of the Collection

The photographs document the conservation treatment of National Portrait Gallery holdings, showing portraits before, during, and after treatment. Portraits reproduced include drawings, graphic prints, paintings, and sculptures.

Photographic Processes and Formats Represented

There are color dye coupler slides (Kodachrome Type A) and silver gelatin photonegatives and photoprints (Polaroid 55 Professional).

Other Materials Represented

The laboratory also maintains conservation reports.

Access and Usage Policies

Available to Smithsonian Institution staff and to outside scholars upon request.

Publication Policies

Smithsonian Institution staff members may obtain photographic and xerographic copies. The preferred credit line is "Courtesy of the Conservation Laboratory, National Portrait Gallery, Smithsonian Institution."

PG·2

NPG Conservation Reports

Dates of Photographs: Circa 1970–Present

Collection Origins

Conservation Laboratory staff created the collection to document the preservation and restoration of National Portrait Gallery (NPG) holdings. This documentation is used for collections management and to assist in planning future conservation treatments. Photographs of art objects are taken before, during, and after conservation.

Physical Description

There are 12,000 photographs including color dye coupler slides (Kodachrome Type A) and silver gelatin photonegatives and photoprints (Polaroid 55 Professional). Other materials include conservation reports.

Subjects

The photographs document NPG portraits, including drawings, graphic prints, paintings, and sculptures, which are shown before, during, and after conservation treatment.

Drawings reproduced include a portrait of Ludwig Mies Van Der Rohe by Hugo Weber and a self-portrait by Joseph Stella. Portrait graphic prints reproduced include Sergei V. Rachmaninoff by Alfred Bendiner, Carl C. Van Doren by Bertrand Zadig, and George Washington by Charles Willson Peale. Portrait paintings reproduced include John Adams by John Trumbull, Mary Cassatt by Edgar Degas, Stephen A. Douglas by Duncan Styles, Marsden Hartley by Richard Tweedy, Justus H.C. Helmuth by John Eckstein, William T. Hornaday by George R. Boynton, Charles S. Johnson by Betsy G. Reyneau, Alfred M. Landon by Vera Dvornikoff, Andrew W. Mellon by Oswald H.J. Birley, and Leonard Wood by Joseph C. Chase. Portrait sculptures reproduced include Helen Keller by Onorio Ruotolo, Abraham Lincoln by Leonard W. Volk, and a self-portrait by Paul Manship.

Other portraits shown before, during, and after conservation include Franklin P. Adams by William H. Cotton, John Dos Passos by Adolf Dehn, a self-portrait by Arshile Gorky, George W.F. Mellon by Winslow Homer, Dorie Miller by David Stone Martin, George W. Norris by Kathleen Wheele, Paul Robeson by Hugo Gellert, Will Rogers by Louis M. Glackens, John Sloan by Isabella Harland, Elizabeth Cady Stanton by Thomas Hovenden, and John Updike by Robert Vickrey.

Arranged: In three series by medium. 1) Drawings. 2) Paintings. 3) Sculptures. Then alphabetically by subject.

Captioned: On file folders with object's accession number, artist, and subject. Accompanied by the object's conservation report, which lists the object's accession number, artist, dimensions, execution date, medium, and sitter, along with conservator, date of treatment, and a description of the treatment.

Finding Aid: No.

Restrictions: Available by appointment only.

PG

Curatorial Department

Curatorial Department
Office of Photographs
National Portrait Gallery
Smithsonian Institution
Washington, D.C. 20560
Ann M. Shumard, Acting Curator
(202) 357-1637
Hours: Monday–Friday, 10 a.m.–5 p.m.

Scope of the Collection

There is one photographic collection with approximately 8,500 images.

Focus of the Collection

The curatorial department of the National Portrait Gallery (NPG) collects, exhibits, preserves, and studies portraits of individuals who have played significant roles in the cultural, political, social, or scientific history of America. The collection is particularly rich in portraits of American presidents and Civil War figures in addition to actors, artists, businessmen, explorers, musicians, politicians, social reformers, and writers.

Photographic Processes and Formats Represented

There are albumen photoprints; ambrotypes; calotype photonegatives; carbon photoprints; collodion wet plate photonegatives; cyanotypes; daguerreotypes; dye diffusion transfer photoprints; platinum photoprints; salted paper photoprints; silver gelatin dry plate lantern slides, photonegatives, and a phototransparency (Orotone); silver gelatin photoprints; and tintypes. Formats represented include cartes-de-visite, a daguerreotype in the form of a campaign pin, dye diffusion transfer images measuring up to 40″ × 80″, full-plate daguerreotypes, a full-plate tintype, half-plate daguerreotypes, and imperial photoprints.

Other Materials Represented

The collection also contains correspondence (on the the last days of Mathew Brady) and photogravures. Other offices in this curatorial division contain portraits in other forms such as drawings, graphic prints, paintings, and sculptures.

Access and Usage Policies

The collection is open to researchers by appointment only. Interested researchers should call or write the office and describe their research topic, the type of material that interests them, and their research aim. The NPG sells copy photoprints and transparencies of many of the portraits in its collection. Submit requests in writing to the Office of Rights and Reproductions, NPG, Room 185, Smithsonian Institution, Washington, D.C., 20560.

Publication Policies

Researchers must obtain permission from the National Portrait Gallery and may also have to obtain permission from the copyright holder, which may not necessarily be the Smithsonian Institution. The preferred credit line is "Courtesy of the National Portrait Gallery, Smithsonian Institution." The photographer's name, if known, also should appear. Publication inquiries should be made to the Office of Rights and Reproductions, NPG, Room 185, Smithsonian Institution, Washington, D.C., 20560, (202) 357-2791.

PG·3

NPG Curatorial Department Photography Collection

Dates of Photographs: 1843–Present

Collection Origins

Former curator William Stapp (1945–) and acting curator Ann Shumard (1954–) assembled this collection of primarily late 19th century to mid-20th century images of prominent Americans for purposes of exhibition, preservation, and scholarly studies in American history.

Stapp, who received an M.A. in South Asia regional studies from the University of Pennsylvania in 1970 and in the history of photography from Goddard College in 1976, taught the history of photography at Moore College of Art, the Philadelphia College of Art, the Community College of Philadelphia, and the Philadelphia Museum of Art. Stapp was a research assistant to the director of the Princeton University Art Museum before becoming the NPG's curator of photographs, where he served from 1976 until 1991.

Shumard received a B.A. in art history from Scripps College in 1976. She joined the staff of the NPG in 1979, having previously worked for the National Gallery of Art and the National Museum of American Art. She served as curatorial assistant in the NPG Office of Photographs from 1981 until 1991, when she was named acting curator. Shumard's NPG exhibit credits include "Through Light and Shadow: Photographs by Clara Sipprell" (1986) and "Lincoln and His Contemporaries: Photographs by Mathew Brady from the National Portrait Gallery's Frederick Hill Meserve Collection" (1991–1992), as well as the photographic section of the NPG's semi-annual "Recent Acquisitions" shows.

Most of the collection was acquired through various donations and purchases. Many images originally were acquired by the museum in eight accessions: 1) the Philippe Halsman accession, consisting of 127 Halsman photographs donated by George R. Rinhart; 2) the Harris & Ewing Studio accession, consisting of 55 photographs donated by Aileen Conkey, daughter of photographer George Harris; 3) the Alice Roosevelt Longworth accession of 71 photographs donated by Joanna Sturm, Longworth's granddaughter; 4) the Meade Brothers Studio accession, donated by Mr. and Mrs. Dudley Emerson Lyons; 5) the Meserve accession of approximately 5,400 collodion glass plate nega-

tives, taken by the Mathew Brady Studio and acquired from the descendents of Frederick Hill Meserve; 6) the Arnold Newman accession, consisting of 101 photographs by Newman; 7) the Irving Penn accession, consisting of 60 portrait photographs by Penn; and 8) the Clara Sipprell accession, consisting of images taken by Sipprell.

Some of the photographs have appeared in the following publications: 1) National Portrait Gallery. *National Portrait Gallery, Smithsonian Institution, Permanent Collection Illustrated Checklist.* Washington, D.C.: Smithsonian Institution Press, 1987. 2) National Portrait Gallery. *National Portrait Gallery, Smithsonian Institution, Permanent Collection of Notable Americans* [CD-ROM version of the *Permanent Collection Illustrated Checklist*]. Cambridge, Massachusetts: ABT Books, Inc., 1991. (This is an on-line catalog made up of approximately 3,100 paintings, photographs and other works of portraiture from the NPG holdings. The CD-ROM package includes individual portraits acquired by the NPG before 1985, as well as some group portrait images.) 3) Merry A. Foresta and William F. Stapp. *Irving Penn Master Images.* Washington, D.C.: Smithsonian Institution Press, 1990. The images also appear with photographs from other sources in the following: Dorothy Meserve Kunhardt and Philip B. Kunhardt, Jr. *Mathew Brady and His World: Produced by Time-Life Books from Pictures in the Meserve Collection.* Alexandria, Virginia: Time-Life Books, 1977.

The *Permanent Collection Illustrated Checklist* may be purchased from the NPG Museum Shop, Smithsonian Institution, Washington, D.C., 20560, or by mail from the Smithsonian Institution Press, Blue Ridge Summit, Pennsylvania, 17294-0900, (717) 794-2148. (Please mention the book's International Standard Book Number, ISBN 0-87474-373-7, when ordering.) The CD-ROM version can be ordered by contacting ABT Books, 146 Mount Auburn Street, Cambridge, Massachusetts, 02138, (617) 661-1300. (This product also may be available from the museum's bookshop.)

Photographers represented include Berenice Abbott, Ansel Adams, Robert Adamson, Lucien Aigner, Charles Aliskey, Alexander Alland, Sr., L. Allman, David H. Anderson, Rufus Anson, Richard Avedon, G.B. Ayres, David Bachrach, Louis Fabian Bachrach, George Grantham Bain, Balch, Russell Ball, George N. Barnard, Henry Walter Barnett, Herbert Barraud, Jessie Tarbox Beals, Arthur P. Bedou, C.M. Bell, Curtis Bell, David Bendann, Alexander Bender, Harry Benson, Zaida Ben-Yusuf, Anthony Berger, H.W. Berthrong, Edward Bierstadt, J.H. Bigelow, J.S. Black, James Wallace Black, A. Aubrey Bodine, Abraham Bogardus, J.A. Bostwick, Alice Boughton, H.W. Bradley, Mathew Brady, Josef Breitenbach, Francis Bruguière, Esther Bubley, Clarence Sinclair Bull, T.R. Burnham, N.H. Busey, Julia Margaret Cameron,

Charles Cann, Robert Capa, John Carbutt, Eric Carpenter, Carter-Bailey, Henri Cartier-Bresson, Charles W. Carter, J.G. Case, Henry L. Chase, Elmer Chickering, R.E. Churchill, Barnet M. Clinedinst, Jr., Alvin Langdon Coburn, George S. Cook, Mariana Cook, Harold Haliday Costain, Gordon Coster, Sidney Cowell, George C. Cox, Konrad Cramer, Imogen Cunningham, and Edward S. Curtis.

Other photographers whose work is found in the collection include Louise Dahl-Wolfe, Henri Dauman, Granville Davies, John W. Davies, P.H. Delamotte, De Young, Menzies Dickson, William Dinwiddie, André Adolphe Eugène Disderi, Robert Disraeli, Alexander W. Dreyfoos, Arthur Radyclyffe Dugmore, Arnold Eagle, Thomas Eakins, Asa B. Eaton, Hugo Erfurth, Walker Evans, G. Arthur Fairbanks, Benjamin J. Falk, Samuel M. Fassett, Benedict J. Fernandez, Fetter, Carl Fischer, George C. Fisher, J. Montgomery Flagg, Louis Fleckenstein, Trude Fleischmann, Robert Frank, Stephen Frank, Charles DeForest Fredricks, Davis Garber, Alexander Gardner, James Gardner, Arnold Genthe, W.L. Germon, J.G. Gessford, Laura Gilpin, Edwin Gledhill, George W. Godfrey, Timothy Greenfield-Sanders, Henry Groskinsky, Sid Grossman, Paul Grotz, W.H. Guild, Jr., Jeremiah Gurney, and Frederick Gutekunst.

Other photographers represented include Ernst Haas, Otto Hagel, E. Haines, Hall, Philippe Halsman, A.N. Hardy, Gilbert K. Harroun, Paul B. Haviland, J.J. Hawes, F. Jay Haynes, Sumner Heald, Alexander Hesler, David Octavius Hill, Ernest W. Histed, William M. Hollinger, Leo Holub, C.H. Hopkins, Emile Otto Hoppé, William R. Howell, H.B. Hull, Gustine L. Hurd, George Hurrell, David L. Iwerks, Lotte Jacobi, Edward Jacobs, Arthur Johnson, G.B. Johnson, Alfred C. Johnston, Frances Benjamin Johnston, W.D. Jones, Peter A. Juley, Yousuf Karsh, Gertrude Käsebier, Sy Kattelson, Joseph T. Keiley, William Keith, André Kertész, Dimitri Kessel, Lucien Swift Kirtland, Joseph G. Kitchell, E. Klauber, J. Lee Knight, Murray Korman, Heinrich Kühn, W. Kurtz, Ellen Land-Weber, F.L. Lay, Alphonse Liébert, J. Ludovici, George Platt Lynes, Isabel V. Lyon, Susan H. Macdowell (Mrs. Thomas Eakins), Pirie MacDonald, Man Ray, Theodore C. Marceau, Benjamin D. Maxham, John Jabez Edwin Mayall, J.E. McClees, Hallum B. McClellan, Duncan McCosker, Cornelius McGillacuddy, Hugh Daniel McLaughlin, Jr., Frances McLaughlin-Gill, Charles R. Meade, Lisette Model, László Moholy-Nagy, M.H. Monroe, José M. Mora, Barbara Morgan, E.R. Morgan, Helen B. Morrison, William M. Morrison, Charles D. Mosher, Columbus W. Motes, Nickolas Muray, Robert R. Murray, and Eadweard Muybridge.

The collection additionally contains photographs by Paul Nadar, Lusha Nelson, George Newbold, Arnold Newman, John Wesley Nichols, Sonya Noskowiak, James Notman, William Notman, V. Novak, Timothy H. O'Sullivan, G.W. Pach, Albert B. Paine, Charles Parker, Titian Ramsey Peale, G. Frank E. Pearsall, Irving Penn, George C. Phelps, Nata Piaskowski, H.H. Pierce, John Plumbe, Jr., Prentis H. Polk, W.H. Potter, P. Pougnet, Powelson, Longworth Powers, Jack Price, Ida Williams Prichett, James E. Purdy, Ben Magid Rabinovitch, Isaac A. Rehn, Charles Reutlinger, Paul Reutlinger, Kay Bell Reynal, Moses P. Rice, Frederick DeBourg Richards, George G. Rockwood, P.S. Rogers, Marcus Aurelius Root, Samuel Root, P.H. Rose, and D.J. Ryan.

Also included in the collection are photographs by Erich Salomon, Lucas Samaras, August Sander, Napoleon Sarony, Charles R. Savage, John D. Schiff, F. George Schreiber, Sarah C. Sears, Emily and Lilian Selby, Herbert J. Seligmann, William Shew, Clara E. Sipprell, Rosalind Solomon, Antoine Sonrel, A.S. Southworth, William Ireland Starr, Edward Steichen, Ralph Steiner, Grete Stern, Alfred Stieglitz, Dennis Stock, Paul Strand, Peter Strongwater, F. Stucken, John Swartz, I.W. Taber, Prentiss Taylor, Robert Templeton, John Thomson, William J. Thompson, Thwaites, George A. Tice, James W. Twitty, Henry Ulke, Doris Ulmann, B.F. Upton, Florence Vandamm, Carl Van Vechten, George K. Warren, H.F. Warren, William W. Washburn, Carleton E. Watkins, Todd Webb, E.G. Weld, F.A. Wenderoth, Edward Weston, Neil Weston, John Adams Whipple, Clarence H. White, Jesse H. Whitehurst, Joseph W. Whitesell, Roger B. Whitman, J.E. Whitney, James J. Williams, Garry Winogrand, Kelly Wise, Carl Wolf, Frank Wolfe, and L.S. Zumbuhl.

Studios represented include Allen & Horton; Allen & Rowell; Bradley & Rulofson; E. & H.T. Anthony, Co.; Bishop & Gray; Black & Batchelder; Black & Case; Bundy & Williams; Case & Gretchell; Davis and Sanford; Eaton & Weber; Edy Bros.; Elliott & Fry; Garrett Bros.; Ghemar Frères; Gilbert & Bacon; G.L. Manuel Frères; Harris & Ewing; Hill & Adamson; H.J. Whitlock & Sons; James Valentine & Sons; J. Gurney & Son; Keystone View Company; London Stereoscopic Company; Manchester & Brother Studio; Meade Brothers; M.P. & A.I. Rice; Notman Photographic Company; Pach Brothers; Peter A. Juley & Son; Quinby & Co.; Randall Studio; Wallin Gallery; Reed & Wallace; Richie Studio; Rintoul & Rockwood; Silsbee, Case & Company; Snyder Bros.; Southworth & Hawes; Strohmeyer & Wyman; Underwood & Underwood; Wenderoth & Taylor; and White Studio.

Physical Description

There are 8,500 photographs including albumen photoprints; ambrotypes; calotype photonegatives; carbon photoprints; collodion wet plate photonegatives; cyanotypes; daguerreotypes; dye diffusion transfer photoprints; platinum photoprints; salted paper photoprints; silver gelatin dry plate lantern slides, photonegatives, and a phototransparency (Orotone); silver gelatin photoprints; and tintypes. Formats represented include cartes-de-visite, a daguerreotype in the form of a campaign pin, double-sided cased images, dye diffusion transfer images measuring up to 40″ × 80″, full-plate daguerreotypes, a full-plate tintype, half-plate daguerreotypes, and imperial photoprints. Other materials include correspondence and photomechanicals (photogravures).

Subjects

The photographs document individuals who played a significant role in American cultural, political, social, or scientific life. The collection is particularly rich in portraits of American presidents including John Quincy Adams, Chester A. Arthur, James Buchanan, George Bush, Jimmy Carter, Grover Cleveland, Calvin Coolidge, Dwight D. Eisenhower, Millard Fillmore, Gerald Ford, James A. Garfield, Ulysses S. Grant, Warren G. Harding, Benjamin Harrison, Rutherford B. Hayes, Herbert Hoover, Andrew Johnson, Lyndon B. Johnson, John F. Kennedy, Abraham Lincoln, William McKinley, Richard M. Nixon, Franklin Pierce, Ronald Reagan, Franklin D. Roosevelt, Theodore Roosevelt, William Howard Taft, Harry S Truman, Martin Van Buren, and Woodrow Wilson.

There are images of other politicians including foreign leaders (such as Winston Churchill) and U.S. cabinet secretaries (such as William Jennings Bryan, John Foster Dulles, James V. Forrestal, Harold Ickes, Robert Lansing, Frances Perkins, and William H. Seward); congressmen (such as James G. Blaine, Joseph Cannon, Frank Church, Henry Clay, Roscoe Conkling, Henry Laurens Dawes, Stephen A. Douglas, Edward Everett, Hamilton Fish, J. William Fulbright, Barry Goldwater, Estes Kefauver, Robert F. Kennedy, Henry Cabot Lodge, Henry Cabot Lodge, Jr., Robert Dale Owen, Henry J. Raymond, Charles Sumner, William M. [A.K.A. Boss] Tweed, and Daniel Webster); diplomats and ambassadors (such as Charles F. Adams, Allen W. Dulles, Joseph C. Grew, Eleanor Roosevelt, and Adlai Stevenson); governors (such as Thomas Dewey, Samuel Houston, and Samuel Tilden); mayors (such as Richard J. Daley); presidential advisors (such as Edward Mandell House); and vice presidents (such as Alben W. Barkley, John C. Calhoun, Schuyler Colfax, Charles G. Dawes, John Nance Garner, Thomas A. Hendricks, Hubert H. Humphrey, Henry A. Wallace, and Henry Wilson).

There are photographs of judges and lawyers, such as Warren Burger, Salmon P. Chase, Stephen J. Field, Felix Frankfurter, Arthur Goldberg, Learned Hand, Oliver Wendell Holmes, Jr., Charles Evans Hughes, Robert Green Ingersoll, Potter Stewart, Roger B. Taney, Morrison R. Waite, Edward Bennett Williams, and Wendell Willkie.

The collection features images of many Civil War figures, including Confederate politicians (such as Jefferson Davis and William Lowndes Yancey); Confederate military officers (such as Pierre G.T. Beauregard, Braxton Bragg, Thomas [A.K.A. Stonewall] Jackson, Robert E. Lee, Matthew Fontaine Maury, John S. Mosby, and J.E.B. Stuart); and Union soldiers (such as Louis Blerker, Don Carlos Buell, Ambrose E. Burnside, Benjamin Butler, Silas Casey, George A. Custer, David G. Farragut, William B. Franklin, Willis A. Gorman, Samuel P. Heintzelman, James Lane, George A. McCall, George B. McClellan, Irvin McDowell, Andrew Porter, David Dixon Porter, Fitz John Porter, Carl Schurz, Winfield Scott, Philip Sheridan, William T. Sherman, George Henry Thomas, and Gouverneur Kemble Warren). Other military leaders portrayed include Tasker Howard Bliss, George Dewey, Curtis E. LeMay, Douglas MacArthur, Chester W. Nimitz, Matthew Perry, John J. Pershing, Winfield S. Schley, George Steers, Charles Wilkes, and Leonard Wood.

The collection includes photographs of Native Americans, including North American Indians, such as Goyathlay (A.K.A. Geronimo), Hinmaton-Yalaktit (A.K.A. Chief Joseph), Little Crow the Younger, Mahpina Luta (A.K.A. Red Cloud), Och-Lochta Micco (A.K.A. Billy Bowlegs), Tatanka Yotanka (A.K.A. Sitting Bull), and Sarah Winnemucca, as well as Hawaiian rulers, such as Emma, David Kalakaua, Jonah Kuhio Kalanianaole, King Kamehameha IV, King Kamehameha V, Kapiolani, Liliuokalani, and William C. Lunalilo.

There are also images of American explorers (such as John C. Frémont, Robert E. Peary, John Wesley Powell, and Henry Stanley) and figures from the Old West (such as Bill Carver, William F. [A.K.A. Buffalo Bill] Cody, James B. [A.K.A. Wild Bill] Hickok, Jesse James, Ben Kilpatrick [A.K.A. The Tall Texan], Harvey Logan [A.K.A. Kid Curry], Harry Longbaugh [A.K.A. the Sundance Kid], and Robert L. Parker [A.K.A. Butch Cassidy]).

Economists, historians, university founders, and other educators shown include Felix Adler, George Bancroft, James H. Breasted, Ralph Bunche, John W. Draper, John Kenneth Galbraith, Edward M. Gallaudet, Alain L. Locke, Francis Parkman, Booker T. Washington, Andrew D. White, and Emma Hart Willard. Religious leaders pictured include Henry Ward Beecher, John McCloskey, Aimee Semple McPherson, Billy Sunday, and Brigham Young.

Scientists represented include astronomers (such as Henry Draper and Asaph Hall); biologists (such as Min Chueh Chang); botanists (such as George Washington Carver and Asa Gray); chemists (such as Linus C. Pauling and Benjamin Silliman); engineers (such as Werner Von Braun); geologists (such as Ferdinand V. Hayden); medical illustrators (such as Max Broedel); naturalists (such as Luther Burbank, John Burroughs, George Bird Grinnell, and Joseph Leidy); physicians (such as Abraham Jacobi, Jonas E. Salk, and Benjamin Spock); physicists (such as Herbert L. Anderson, Albert Einstein, Robert H. Goddard, and J. Robert Oppenheimer); and zoologists (such as Jean L.R. Agassiz). Also shown are inventors such as George Eastman, Thomas A. Edison, Richard J. Gatling, and Samuel F.B. Morse, as well as scientists who served as Secretary of the Smithsonian including Spencer F. Baird, Joseph Henry, Samuel P. Langley, and S. Dillon Ripley.

Portraits of artists make up a significant part of the collection. Artists shown include cartoonists (such as Walt Disney, Jules Feiffer, and Thomas Nast); painters (such as Romare Bearden, George W. Bellows, Albert Bierstadt, William Merritt Chase, Thomas C. Cole, Willem de Kooning, Arthur G. Dove, Marcel Duchamp, Asher Brown Durand, Thomas Eakins, Jacob Epstein, Childe Hassam, Edward Hopper, George Inness, Jasper Johns, Franz Kline, Jacob A. Lawrence, Morris Louis, John Marin, Anna Mary Robertson [A.K.A. Grandma] Moses, Georgia O'Keeffe, Maxfield Parrish, Rembrandt Peale, Titian Ramsey Peale, Horace Pippin, Thomas B. Read, Katharine Nash Rhoades, Norman Rockwell, Albert Pinkham Ryder, John Singer Sargent, John F. Sloan, Thomas Sully, Andy Warhol, Max Weber, and James Abbott McNeill Whistler); photographers (such as Diane Arbus, Abraham Bogardus, Mathew Brady, Imogen Cunningham, Edward S. Curtis, Walker Evans, Arnold Genthe, Lewis Hine, Dorothea Lange, Man Ray, the Meade Brothers, Eadweard Muybridge, Napolean Sarony, Edward Steichen, Alfred Stieglitz, Paul Strand, Carl Van Vechten, Alfred R. Waud, and Edward Weston); and sculptors (such as Frédéric A. Bartholdi, Alexander Calder, Jo Davidson, Malvina Hoffman, Harriet Goodhue Hosmer, Gaston Lachaise, Isamu Noguchi and Hiram Powers).

The collection includes portraits of prominent architects, such as Walter Gropius, Philip Johnson, Ludwig Mies van der Rohe, Robert Mills, Edward Durrell Stone, and Frank Lloyd Wright. Art collectors, such as Peggy Guggenheim, Joseph H. Hirshhorn, and Duncan Phillips, also are shown.

There are many portraits of actors such as Woody Allen, George Arliss, John Barrymore, Humphrey Bogart, Edwin Thomas Booth, John Wilkes Booth, James Cagney, Charles Chaplin, Katharine Cornell, Ossie Davis, James Dean, Ruby Dee, Clint Eastwood, Edwin Forrest, Clark Gable, Lillian Gish, Jean Harlow, William S. Hart, Helen Hayes, Oscar Homolka, Laura Keene, Gertrude Lawrence, Peter Lorre, Julia Marlowe, Raymond Massey, Adah I. Menken, Marilyn Monroe, Paul Robeson, Norma Shearer, Gloria Swanson, Rudolph Valentino, and Loretta Young.

The collection contains images of other show business figures, including circus personalities (such as P.T. Barnum, Emmett Kelly, and Dan Rice); costume and stage designers (such as Remo Bufano); film, record,

and theatrical producers (such as David Belasco, Charles Frohman, Berry Gordy, Jr., D.W. Griffith, Oscar Hammerstein, John Hammond, John Huston, David Merrick, and Antonio Pastor); and radio and television performers (such as Fred Allen, Steve Allen, Lucille Ball, Sid Caeser, Dave Garroway, Bob Hope, and Dinah Shore).

Dancers and choreographers portrayed include Josephine Baker, George Balanchine, Isadora Duncan, Katherine Dunham, Michel Fokine, Martha Graham, Doris Humphrey, Luther (A.K.A. Bill "Bojangles") Robinson, Ruth St. Denis, and Ted Shawn. There are also images of composers (such as George Anthiel, Aaron Copland, Oscar Ham-merstein II, W.C. Handy, Paul Hindemith, Charles Ives, Cole Porter, and Sergei V. Rachmaninoff); musicians (such as Louis Armstrong, Ole Bull, Dizzy Gillespie, the Grateful Dead, Vladimir Horowitz, and Charlie Parker); and singers (such as Marian Anderson, Ella Fitzgerald, Judy Garland, Roland Hayes, Billie Holiday, Lena Horne, Mahalia Jackson, Janis Joplin, Clara Louise Kellogg, Eartha Kitt, Huddie Ledbetter [A.K.A. Leadbelly], John McCormack, Lauritz Melchior, Jessye Norman, Adelina Patti, Leontyne Price, Lillian Russell, Bessie Smith, Ethel Waters, and Josh White).

There are also images of astronauts and aviators (such as Amelia Earhart, Carl Eielson, Charles Lindbergh, Alan B. Shepard, Jr., and Chuck Yeager); athletes (such as Muhammad Ali, James John Corbett, Jack Dempsey, Althea Gibson, Red Grange, Joe Louis, Christy Mathewson, Arnold Palmer, Jackie Robinson, Babe Ruth, Casey Stengal, Jim Thorpe, Bill Tilden, and Gene Tunney); business leaders and executives (such as Philip D. Armour, Bernard M. Baruch, Andrew Carnegie, Peter Cooper, Cyrus W. Field, James Fisk, Collis P. Huntington, Henry J. Kaiser, J. Pierpont Morgan, George Peabody, George M. Pullman, Eliphalet Remington, David Sarnoff, and Cornelius Vanderbilt); and labor leaders (including Cesar Chavez, Samuel Gompers, John Mitchell, A. Philip Randolph, and Walter Reuther).

Also shown are social reformers, including abolitionists (such as John Brown, Cassius M. Clay, Frederick Douglass, and Sojourner Truth); civil rights activists (such as W.E.B. Du Bois, Jesse Jackson, James Weldon Johnson, Martin Luther King, Jr., and Walter F. White); prohibitionists (such as Carrie A. Nation); radicals (such as Emma Goldman); and suffragists (such as Susan B. Anthony, Carrie Chapman Catt, Mary A.R. Livermore, Lucretia C. Mott, Anna H. Shaw, Elizabeth Cady Stanton, and Lucy Stone).

Writers shown in the collection include critics (such as Van Wyck Brooks, Granville Hicks, George J. Nathan, and Alexander Woollcott); editors and publishers (such as James T. Fields, Philip L. Graham, Henry R. Luce, and Samuel S. McClure); essayists (such as Arna Bontemps, William F. Buckley, Jr., Will Durant,

Ralph Waldo Emerson, Betty Friedan, John Gunther, Oliver Wendell Holmes, Gertrude Stein, and Henry David Thoreau); and humorists (such as Charles F. Browne [A.K.A. Artemus Ward], David R. Locke [A.K.A. Petroleum V. Nasby], Dorothy Parker, S.J. Perelman, and James Thurber).

Other writers portrayed include journalists (such as Samuel Bowles, Richard H. Dana, Janet Flanner, Edward Godkin, Horace Greeley, H.L. Mencken, John Reed, Whitelaw Reid, Ida Tarbell, Henry Watterson, Thurlow Weed, Gideon Welles, and Nathaniel P. Willis); novelists (such as James Agee, Sherwood Anderson, James Baldwin, Djuna Barnes, Kay Boyle, Pearl S. Buck, Frances Hodgson Burnett, Samuel Clemens [A.K.A. Mark Twain], James Fenimore Cooper, John Dos Passos, Theodore Dreiser, William Faulkner, Edna Ferber, Erle Stanley Gardner, Hamlin Garland, Bret Harte, Nathaniel Hawthorne, Ernest Hemingway, William Dean Howells, Zora Neale Hurston, Henry James, Edward Z.C. Judson [A.K.A. Ned Buntline], Sinclair Lewis, Clare Boothe Luce, Norman Mailer, Mary Roberts Rinehart, Mari Sandoz, John Steinbeck, Harriet Beecher Stowe, Bayard Taylor, Margaret Walker, Robert Penn Warren, Tom Wolfe, and Richard Wright); playwrights (such as Bertold Brecht, Ben Hecht, Lillian Hellman, Eugene O'Neill, Thornton Wilder, and Ten-nessee Williams); and poets (such as William Cullen Bryant, Hart Crane, Countee Cullen, T.S. Eliot, Robert Frost, Langston Hughes, Robinson Jeffers, Henry Wadsworth Longfellow, Edwin Markham, Claude McKay, Edna St. Vincent Millay, Cincinnatus H. Miller [A.K.A. Joaquin], Marianne Moore, Ezra Pound, James Whitcomb Riley, Carl Sandburg, Walt Whitman, and John Greenleaf Whittier).

In addition to the portraits, there are photographs of the former Patent Office Building, which now houses the National Museum of American Art and the National Portrait Gallery.

Arranged: By subject.

Finding Aid: 1) An item-level computer index listing the inventory number and subject's name and occupation. 2) A fact sheet about how to access the resources of the NPG, a copy of which may be obtained by writing the Curatorial Department, NPG, Room 316, Smithsonian Institution, Washington, D.C., 20560.

Restrictions: For conservation purposes, some images, such as those in the Meserve accession may not be accessible to researchers.

PG

Department of Design and Production

Department of Design and Production
National Portrait Gallery
Smithsonian Institution
Washington, D.C. 20560
Nello R. Marconi, Design Chief
(202) 357-2980
Hours: Monday–Friday, 8:45 a.m.–5:15 p.m.

Scope of the Collection

There is one photographic collection with approximately 40 photographs.

Focus of the Collection

The photographs document the renovation of the NPG's third floor in 1975.

Photographic Processes and Formats Represented

There are silver gelatin photoprints.

Other Materials Represented

None.

Access and Usage Policies

Open by appointment with the permission of the department chief. Researchers should call or write in advance and describe their research topic, the type of material that interests them, and their research aim.

Publication Policies

Researchers must obtain permission from the Smithsonian Institution. The preferred credit line is "Courtesy of the Department of Design and Production, National Portrait Gallery, Smithsonian Institution." The photographer's name, if known, also should appear.

PG·4

NPG Department of Design and Production Renovation Photographs

Dates of Photographs: 1975

Collection Origins

National Portrait Gallery (NPG) Department of Design and Production staff created the collection to document the renovation work done on the NPG's third floor in 1975. Chief of exhibits Mike Carrigan asked NPG staff photographers to take the pictures in the presence of Carrigan and another witness. The photographs were used as evidence of the contracting renovation company's poor workmanship.

Physical Description

There are 40 silver gelatin photoprints.

Subjects

The photographs document poor workmanship in the 1975 renovation of the NPG's third floor in the former Patent Office Building. Areas shown include corridors, doors, moldings, panels, and walls. Problems depicted include absence of fixtures, glass, panels, and refinishing work; cracked plaster; and the incorrect installation of hardware.

Arranged: By assigned number, roughly by location of area shown.

Captioned: With date and signatures of witnesses.

Finding Aid: 1) List of photographs describing location and problem. 2) Diagram showing location of each photograph on the third floor.

Restrictions: No.

PG

Department of History

Department of History
National Portrait Gallery
Smithsonian Institution
Washington, D.C. 20560
Frederick Voss, Historian/Curator
(202) 357-1673
Hours: By appointment.

Scope of the Collection

There is one photographic collection with approximately 250 photographs.

Focus of the Collection

These original photographs have been reproduced on the covers of *Time* magazine since the 1930s. The images show people and events in the news. People portrayed include politicians and other leaders, as well as arts, media, science, and sports figures from around the world.

Photographic Processes and Formats Represented

There are color dye bleach photoprints (Cibachrome), color dye coupler photoprints, and silver gelatin photoprints, some in collage or mixed-media format.

Other Materials Represented

The department also contains drawings, paintings, and sculptures.

Access and Usage Policies

Researchers should call or write in advance for an appointment, describing their research topic, the type of material that interests them, and their research aim.

Publication Policies

Except for NPG staff use, no photographic or xerographic copies may be made unless arranged through Time, Inc., which holds the copyright. Contact the Office of Rights and Reproductions, Time-Life Building, New York, New York, 10020.

PG·5

Time Collection

Dates of Photographs: 1931–Present

Collection Origins

Time, Inc., created the collection from commissioned work by many artists and photographers for the covers of *Time* magazine. Founded in 1923 by Henry Luce, *Time* publishes reports on international news and often features portraits of contemporary figures on its cover. The covers reproduce original drawings, paintings, and sculptures, as well as photographs. In 1978, Time, Inc., presented the National Portrait Gallery (NPG) with over 800 pieces of original art work that had been used to produce *Time* magazine covers from the early 1930s to 1978. With additional gifts from *Time* and other parties, the collection has since more than doubled in size.

In addition to their publication in *Time* magazine, the images have appeared in the following: National Portrait Gallery. *National Portrait Gallery, Smithsonian Institution, Permanent Collection Illustrated Checklist.* Washington, D.C.: Smithsonian Institution Press, 1987. (This publication is available for purchase at the NPG Museum Shop, Smithsonian Institution, Washington, D.C., 20560, or by mail from the Smithsonian Institution Press, Blue Ridge Summit, Pennsylvania, 17294-0400. Mention the book's International Standard Book Number, ISBN 0-87474-373-7, when ordering.)

Photographers represented include Abbas, Michael Abramson, Eddie Adams, Severo Antonelli, Ollie Atkins, Richard Avedon, Mario Bellini, Chris Ogden Bennett, Walter Bennett, Dennis Brack, Lou Brook, Roberto Brosan, David Bryne, John Bryson, Fred Burrell, David Burnett, Jack Cheetham, Michael Chesney, Rich Clarkson, Gianfranco Corgoni, William Coupon, Frank Cowan, Robert S. Crandall, Giorgia Cualco, Robert A. Cummins, Charles Cuttner, Alain Dejean, Michael Dressler, Kenn Duncan, Alfred Eisenstaedt, Robert Ellison, Michael Evans, Enrico Ferorelli, Carl Fischer, Chuck Fishman, Frank Fournier, Jean-Claude Francolon, Rudy Frey, Stanley Glaubach, Mark Godfrey, Norman Gorbaty, Susan Greenwood, Philippe Halsman, Dirck Halstead, Dimitrios Harissiadis, Gregory Heisler, Hiro, Andy Hoyt, and Robert Huntzinger.

Other photographers whose work is represented include Shyla Irving, Pana Jiji, Fred Kaplan, Robert W. Kelley, David Hume Kennerly, Mike Kerr, Douglas Kirkland, Tony Korody, Bob Krieger, J. Alex Langley, Larry Lee, David Lees, Neil Leifer, Michael Leonard,

Philippe Lerdu, George Platt Lynes, Phil Marco, Arturo Mari, Mary Ellen Mark, Dan McCoy, Richard Meek, Eric Meola, Reid Miles, Charles Moore, Gordon Munro, Carl Mydans, Arnold A. Newman, Nguyen Cong Phuc, Steve Northrup, Alan Pappe, Irving Penn, Bill Pierce, Lou L.A. Prade, Julien Quideau, Vittoriano Rastelli, Ken Regan, and David Rubinger.

Additional photographers represented in the collection include Salhani-Sygma, Gerald Scarfe, Francesco Scavullo, Steve Schapiro, Arthur Schatz, George Segal, Arthur Siegel, Art Shay, Rick Smolan, Allan Tannenbaum, T. Tanuma, J. Rudolph Tesa, Ted Thai, Alwyn Scott Turner, Gilbert Uzan, William Vandivert, Raul Vega, Christian Viojard, Roman Vishniac, Emily B. Waite, Diana Walker, Julian Wasser, Albert MacKenzie Watson, Stan Wayman, Bruce Weaver, Norman Webster, Roger Werth, Theo Westenberger, Edward Weston, Dennis Wheeler, Henry Wolf, Dan Wynn, and John Zimmerman.

Studios represented include Action Press, Associated Press, International Photo Agency, Kahn & Turner, NASA, Oliphant & Waite, United Press International, Vandamm Studio, Walt Disney Studios, and Wide World.

Physical Description

There are 250 photographs including color dye bleach photoprints (Cibachrome), color dye coupler photoprints, and silver gelatin photoprints. Formats include collages and mixed-media images. Other materials represented include cover portrait drawings, paintings, and sculptures.

Subjects

The photographs are primarily full-face or three-quarter-profile portraits of contemporary people in the news including artists, entertainers, military figures, politicians, world leaders, and writers. There are also images illustrating current events, such as protests, riots, strikes, and wars.

Actors portrayed include Isabelle Adjani, Woody Allen, Warren Beatty, Marisa Berenson, Cher, Clint Eastwood, Margaux Hemingway, Katharine Hepburn, Diane Keaton, Nastassja Kinski, Diane Lane, Shirley MacLaine, Robert Mitchum, Paul Newman, Jack Nicholson, Burt Reynolds, Diana Rigg, Molly Ringwald, Brooke Shields, Jaclyn Smith, Sylvester Stallone, Meryl Streep, John Travolta, Liv Ullmann, Sigourney Weaver, and Robin Williams.

The photographs portray artists (such as Ansel Adams and Robert Rauschenberg); dancers (such as Gelsey Kirkland); designers (such as Georgio Armani and Pierre Cardin); fashion models (such as Cheryl Tiegs); media figures (such as Dan Rather and Ted Turner); motion-picture and theatrical directors (such as Cecil

B. DeMille and Steven Spielberg); and conductors, musicians, and singers (such as Sarah Caldwell, Merle Haggard, Madonna, Liza Minnelli, Luciano Pavarotti, Beverly Sills, and Leopold Stokowski).

There are portraits of military figures (such as William Calley, Jr., Alexander M. Haig, Jr., Oliver North, and William C. Westmoreland) and politicians (such as Wendell R. Anderson, Edmund G. Brown, Jr., Richard J. Daley, Michael Deaver, Thomas F. Eagleton, Geraldine Ferraro, Edward M. Kennedy, Henry Kissinger, Edward I. Koch, Alfred M. Landon, John Lindsay, Walter Mondale, and Claude Pepper).

World leaders portrayed include Yasser Arafat, Willy Brandt, Leonid I. Brezhnev, George Bush, Constantine Caramanlis, Jimmy Carter, Chiang Kai-Shek, Deng Xiaoping, Valery Giscard D'Estaing, Gerald Ford, Hua Kuo Feng, Wojciech W. Jaruzelski, Pierre Mendès-France, François Mitterrand, Richard M. Nixon, George Papadopoulos, Chung Hee Park, Helmut H.W. Schmidt, and Kakuei Tanaka. Members of royalty, including Princess Caroline of Monaco and Prince Charles of England, also are shown.

Other individuals depicted include inventors and scientists (such as Edwin Land, Richard Leakey, Carl Sagan, and Andrei Sakharov); religious leaders (such as Cardinal Dougherty, Pope John Paul I, Pope John Paul II, and Pat Robertson); sports figures (such as Paul "Bear" Bryant, Rod Carew, Steve Cauthen, Charles O. Finley, Dwight Gooden, Dorothy Hamill, Beth Heiden, Eric Heiden, Carl Lewis, Arnold Palmer, Pete Rose, and Mark Spitz); and writers (such as Maxwell Anderson, Russell Baker, Erma Bombeck, John Kenneth Galbraith, John Irving, Robinson Jeffers, Neil Simon, Alexander I. Solzhenitsyn, and Gertrude Stein).

Events documented include the 1981 air controllers' strike; the 1981 Grand Prix; the Los Angeles riots of the 1960s; massacres in the Mideast in 1974; and a 1970 student protest in the United States. Places shown include Beirut, Lebanon; China; Hanoi, Vietnam; Indochina; Italy; Japan; the Sahara Desert; and Saigon (now Ho Chi Minh City), Vietnam. There are also images of American fashions, birth control pills, computers, ice cream, a satanic mask, the planet Saturn from *Voyager I,* and the Space Shuttles *Challenger* and *Columbia.*

Arranged: By accession number.

Captioned: Some with notes.

Finding Aid: 1) Indexes arranged by artist, medium, and subject, listing accession number, artist, date, medium, and subject. 2) The curator's files, with the same information. 3) The museum's published checklist: National Portrait Gallery. *National Portrait Gallery, Smithsonian Institution, Permanent Collection Illustrated Checklist.* Washington, D.C.: Smithsonian Institution Press, 1987.

Restrictions: Researchers must contact the curator in advance. Except for use in museum exhibits, all reproductions must be arranged through Time, Inc., Office of Rights and Reproductions, Time-Life Building, New York, New York, 10020.

PG

National Museum of American Art and National Portrait Gallery Library

National Museum of American Art and National Portrait Gallery
 Library
National Portrait Gallery
Smithsonian Institution
Washington, D.C. 20560
Cecilia Chin, Librarian
(202) 357-1886
Hours: Monday–Friday, 10 a.m.–5 p.m.

Scope of the Collection

There is one photographic collection with 330 images.

Focus of the Collection

The photographs primarily document the Patent Office Building, which houses the National Portrait Gallery (NPG) and National Museum of American Art (NMAA). The NMAA/NPG Library also contains 80,000 volumes, receives 800 serials, and houses extensive clipping and pamphlet files (450 drawers) documenting American art and art institutions. Note: Another collection from this library is listed in the NMAA section as collection *AA·11.*

Photographic Processes and Formats Represented

There are color dye coupler photoprints and silver gelatin photonegatives and photoprints.

Other Materials Represented

The collection also contains architectural plans, blueprints, caption lists, correspondence, drawings, exhibit labels, legislative records, magazine clippings, manuscripts, newspaper clippings, photomechanicals, photostats, press releases, programs, and xerographic copies.

Access and Usage Policies

The collection is open to researchers during regular library hours.

Publication Policies

Researchers must obtain permission from the National Portrait Gallery to reproduce a photograph and may also have to obtain permission from the copyright holder, which is not necessarily the Smithsonian Institution. The preferred credit line is "Courtesy of the National Museum of American Art and National Portrait Gallery Library, Smithsonian Institution." The photographer's name, if known, also should appear.

PG·6

Patent Office Building Photograph Collection

Dates of Photographs: 1880s–1980s

Collection Origins

National Portrait Gallery (NPG) and National Museum of American Art (NMAA) staff assembled the collection to document the history of the Patent Office Building, which now houses the NMAA and NPG, and the major renovations the building has undergone. The building was designed in 1836 by Robert Mills (1781–1855), who was then the D.C. Architect of Public Buildings. Mills, who studied under Thomas Jefferson, planned and designed many prominent buildings including the Bank of Philadelphia; Brockenbrough House (later referred to as "The White House of the South") in Richmond, Virginia; the State Hospital for the Insane in Columbia, South Carolina; and the Washington Monument and Treasury and Post Office buildings in Washington, D.C. His design for the Patent Office Building featured a portico, with eight Doric columns, based on the proportions of the Parthenon.

Construction of the Patent Office Building lasted from 1836 until 1867, with additions by several architects. Between 1840 and 1932, the building housed the U.S. Patent Office. The building also was home to the National Institute for the Promotion of Science (whose art collection is now part of the NMAA holdings), from 1842 to 1862, and to the Department of the Interior, from 1849 to 1917. During the Civil War the building served as a barracks, hospital, and morgue for the Union forces. The Civil Service Commission occupied the facility between 1932 and 1963.

In 1958 Congress transferred the building to the Smithsonian Institution to house the National Collection of Fine Arts (NCFA) and the separate NPG, which Congress established in 1962. The museums moved into the facility in 1968. Renovations during the 1960s, 1970s, and 1980s fitted the building more closely to the needs of NMAA and NPG staff. In 1980 the NCFA became the NMAA.

Gary Edwards, Peter Fink, and Lawrence E. Gichner donated parts of the collection. Photographers and studios represented include Brown Bros.; Davis Dunlop; National Archives and Records Administration (Brady Collection); N. Peters Photo-Lithographer; OPPS; T.H. McAllister Co.; and Colin Varga.

Physical Description

There are 330 photographs including color dye coupler photoprints and silver gelatin photonegatives and photoprints. Other materials include architectural drawings and plans, blueprints, caption lists, correspondence, drawings, exhibit labels, legal documents, magazine clippings, manuscripts, newspaper clippings, photomechanicals, photostats, press releases, programs, and xerographic copies.

Subjects

The photographs primarily show exteriors and interiors of the Patent Office Building from the 1840s to the present. Major renovations after an 1877 fire in the Patent Office Building are illustrated, as is the movement of the NMAA and NPG to the facility in 1968. There are also images of the Smithsonian Institution Building (the Castle) and the Mall in the early 20th century, as well as some of the NMAA holdings.

Arranged: No.

Captioned: Some with subject.

Finding Aid: Caption list to part of the collection.

Restrictions: No. Contact Cecilia H. Chin, Librarian, NMAA/NPG Library, Room 331, Smithsonian Institution, Washington, D.C., 20560, (202) 357-1886.

Office of Exhibitions

Office of Exhibitions
National Portrait Gallery
Smithsonian Institution
Washington, D.C. 20560
Beverly Cox, Curator of Exhibitions
(202) 357-2688
Hours: By appointment

Scope of the Collection

There is one photographic collection with approximately 10,000 photographs.

Focus of the Collections

The photographs document National Portrait Gallery (NPG) exhibit installations and objects borrowed by the NPG for exhibits. Objects shown include drawings, graphic prints, paintings, photographs, sculptures, and other types of art work portraying people significant to U.S. history, as well as some related artifacts.

Photographic Processes and Formats Represented

There are color dye coupler phototransparencies and slides and silver gelatin photonegatives and photoprints.

Other Materials Represented

The office also contains exhibit and loan records.

Access and Usage Policies

Qualified researchers interested in further information on this collection should call or write in advance for an appointment, describing their research topic, the type of material that interests them, and their research aim.

Publication Policies

Images of objects lent to the NPG by museums outside of the Smithsonian should be obtained directly from those museums. Individuals wishing to reproduce images of objects owned by private collectors should write the Office of Exhibitions, NPG, Room 185, Smithsonian Institution, Washington, D.C., 20560. The request will be forwarded to the object's owner, as necessary.

PG·7

NPG Office of Exhibitions Borrowed Objects Photograph Collection

Dates of Photographs: 1968–Present

Collection Origins

Office of Exhibitions staff created this admininstrative collection to document items lent to the National Portrait Gallery (NPG) for exhibits, as well as the exhibits themselves. Most borrowed items, if not restricted by the owner, are photographed when they arrive at the museum. Photographers represented include K.B. Basseches, Eugene Mantie, and Rolland White.

Physical Description

There are 10,000 photographs including color dye coupler phototransparencies and slides and silver gelatin photonegatives and photoprints. Other materials include exhibit and loan records.

Subjects

The photographs document items lent to the NPG for special exhibits, viewed individually and in installations. Objects shown are primarily portraits, consisting of drawings, graphic prints, paintings, photographs, sculptures, and other types of art work, along with some related artifacts.

Exhibits documented include "Aaron Burr Acquitted"; "Abraham Lincoln: The White House Years"; "Abroad in America: Visitors to the New Nation 1776–1914"; "Adalbert Volck: Fifth Column Artist"; "Adventurous Pursuits: Americans and the China Trade 1784–1844"; "The Algonquin Round Table"; "Alice Stalknecht: Portrait of a New England Town"; "American Authors"; "American Colonial Portraits"; "American Icon: The Eighteenth Century Image of George Washington in Prints and Illustrations"; "American Portrait Drawings"; "American Portrait Prints: A Survey"; "American Portraiture in the Grand Manner: 1720–1920"; "The American Presidency in Political Cartoons"; "American Self-Portraits 1670–1973"; "The Americans: The Democratic Experience"; "Arnold Genthe: The Celebrity Portraits"; "Artists and Illustrators of the Civil War: Conrad Wise Chapman and Winslow Homer"; "Artists and Models"; "Artists by

Themselves: Artists' Portraits from the National Academy of Design"; "The Artist's Mother: Portraits and Homages"; "Artists on Paper: Prints, Photos, and Drawings from the National Portrait Gallery Collection"; "The Art of Henry Inman"; "Auguste Edouart Silhouettes"; and "Augustus Saint-Gaudens."

Other exhibits illustrated include "Baseball Immortals: The Photos of Charles Martin Conlan"; "Benjamin West and His American Students"; "Bishop Neumann"; "Black Hawk and Keokuk: Prairie Rebels"; "The Black Presence in the Era of the American Revolution 1770–1800"; "Blessed Are the Peacemakers"; "Booth Tarkington: The Gentleman from Indiana"; "Bret Harte"; "The Call: The Early Years of the NAACP"; "Carl Schurz: America's Teutonic Reformer"; "Champions of American Sport"; "Charles Lindbergh"; "Charles Willson Peale"; "Charles Willson Peale and His World"; "Charles Willson Peale and the Challenge of Mezzotint Portraiture"; "Chester Alan Arthur: From Spoilsman to Statesman 1871–1885"; "Christian Gullager: Portrait Painter to Federal America"; "The Code Duello in America"; "The Coming of Age of American Music: Ives, Gershwin, and Copland"; "Conflict at Dayton: The Scopes Trial"; "Davy Crockett: Gentleman from the Cane"; "A Decade of Print Collecting: The Highlights"; "The Dye is Now Cast: The Road to American Independence"; "The Eight"; "Elisha Kent Kane"; "Erastus Salisbury Field 1805–1900"; "Facing the Light: Historic American Portrait Daguerreotypes"; "FDR: The Early Years"; "First Federal Congress 1789–1791"; "The Frederick Hill Meserve Collection"; and "From Reliable Sources."

Additional exhibits documented include "Gallant Harry of the West"; "Gaston Lachaise, Portrait Sculpture"; "Gertrude Vanderbilt Whitney"; "A Glimmer of Their Own Beauty: Black Sounds of the Twenties"; "The Godlike Black Dan: Daniel Webster"; "The Great Crash"; "The Great War"; "Guardianship of Memory"; "The Haptic Gallery"; "Helen Keller and Anne Sullivan Macy"; "Henry Benbridge: American Portrait Painter"; "Heroes, Martyrs and Villains: Printed Portraits from the Civil War"; "The Hollywood Portrait Photographer 1921–1941"; "Howard Chandler Christy"; "Howard University: Sixtieth Anniversary"; and "How Fleeting is Fame."

Other exhibits illustrated include "If Elected. . . . Unsuccessful Candidates for the Presidency 1797–1968"; "Instrument of the Lord: Harriet Beecher Stowe"; "In the Minds and Hearts of the People: Prologue to Revolution"; "Irving Penn: Master Images"; "Isamu Noguchi: Portrait Sculpture"; "Is This Portrait of Thomas Sully?"; "James Barton Longacre"; "James Weldon Johnson"; "Jay Gould: Mesphistopheles of Wall Street"; "Jo Davidson Portrait Sculpture"; "John Brown: Mad Man or Martyr"; "John Frazee, Sculptor"; "John Muir"; "John Stevens and Sons: A Family of Inventors"; "Joseph Wright, American Artist"; "Keep the Last Bullet for Yourself: The Battle of Little Big Horn"; and "A Knot of Dreamers: The Brook Farm Community 1841–1847."

Additional exhibits documented include "The Lazzaroni: Science & Scientists in Mid-19th Century America"; "The Life Portraits of John Quincy Adams"; "Look Homeward Angel: Thomas Wolfe"; "Mary McLeod Bethune"; "Masterpieces from Gripsholm Castle: The Swedish National Portrait Collection"; "Masterpieces from Versailles: Three Centuries of French Portraiture"; "Matthew C. Perry and the Japan Expedition of 1852–1855"; "Miguel Covarrubias Caricatures"; "Mr. Sully: Portrait Painter 1783–1872"; "A 19th Century Gallery of Distinguished Americans"; "Notable Women"; "Not the Model Boy: Mark Twain"; "Official Photographs of the Carter Administration"; "Old Hickory: A Life Sketch of Andrew Jackson"; "Oliphant's Presidents"; "On the Air"; "One Hundred Years of the Metropolitan Opera"; and "O, Write My Name: Photographs by Carl Van Vechten."

There are also photographs of the following exhibits: "Peace and Friendship: Indian Peace Medals in American History"; "Peggy Bacon—Drawings"; "Photographs of Theodore and Alice Roosevelt"; "Portrait Prints: The 20th Century Approach"; "Portraits by Brady: Imperial Photographs from the Harvard College Library"; "Portraits by George Bellows"; "Portraits from the New Deal"; "Portraits of American Newsmakers"; "Portraits of the American Law"; "Portraits of the American Stage 1771–1971"; "Presidential Highlights (Coolidge, Pierce, Eisenhower, TR, Van Buren)"; "Presidential Highlights (Jackson, Grant, FDR, Tyler, Wilson)"; "President Monroe's Message"; "The President's Medal 1789–1977"; and "Private Lives of Public Figures: The 19th Century Family Print."

Other exhibits shown include "Recent Acquisitions"; "Return to Albion: Americans in England 1776–1940"; "Robert Cornelius: Portraits from the Dawn of Photography"; "Robert Edge Pine: A British Portrait Painter in America"; "Saint-Mémin"; "Selections from the Frederick Hill Meserve Collection"; "Selections from the National Portrait Gallery Photography Collection"; and "The Spirit of Fact: The Daguerreotypes of Southworth and Hawes."

Other exhibits illustrated include "They Have Made a Nation"; "This New Man: A Discourse in Portraits"; "Thomas Paine: A Hero Scorned"; "Three Centuries of Education: Noah Webster, William H. McGuffey, John Dewey"; "Through Light and Shadow: Photographs by Clara Sipprell"; "Time and the Presidency"; "Time: Art and Entertainment"; "The Time of Our Lives"; "Time Room"; "To Color America: Portraits by Winold Reiss"; "A Touch of the Poet: Portraits from the Permanent Collection"; "Translations: Lithographs after Daguerreotypes"; "A Truthful Likeness: Chester Harding and His Portraits"; and "U.S. Grant: The Man and the Image."

Other exhibits documented include "Variations: Musicians in Caricature"; "Waiting for the Hour: The Emancipation Proclamation"; "Washington in the 1840s"; "Washington in the New Era 1870–1970"; "Washington Irving Commemorative"; "Wedgewood Portraits and the American Revolution"; "We Never Sleep: The First 50 Years of the Pinkertons"; "We Were But a Handful"; "The Whiskey Rebellion"; "White House Families: Portraits from Life"; "Why Not a Woman: Belva Ann Lockwood"; "William Cullen Bryant"; "William Edward West, Kentucky Painter"; "Winston Churchill"; "Women on Time"; and "Zelda and Scott: The Beautiful and Damned."

Non-portrait objects depicted include books, cartoons, documents, furniture, maps, medals, and political memorabilia.

Arranged: By format in three series, then alphabetically by sitter. 1) 4″ × 5″ photonegatives and phototransparencies. 2) 8″ × 10″ photoprints. 3) Slides.

Captioned: With artist, credit line, date, exhibit date, exhibit title, lender, medium, size, and subject.

Finding Aid: Exhibit history database (in progress, currently incomplete) lists the exhibit title and dates, lender documentation, object documentation, and whether the object was photographed.

Restrictions: Restricted to qualified researchers, by appointment only. Images of objects in other museums should be obtained directly from that museum; images of private collection objects may be copied with the owner's written permission. Contact Claire Kelly, Assistant Curator of Exhibitions, NPG, Room 187, Smithsonian Institution, Washington, D.C., 20560, (202) 357-2688.

PG

Office of the Registrar

Office of the Registrar
National Portrait Gallery
Smithsonian Institution
Washington, D.C. 20560
Suzanne Jenkins, Registrar
(202) 357-2690
Hours: Monday–Friday, 8:45 a.m.–5:15 p.m.

Scope of the Collection

There is one photographic collection with approximately 15,000 photographs.

Focus of the Collection

The photographs document accessioned objects at the National Portrait Gallery (NPG), including drawings, graphic prints, paintings, photographs, sculptures, and other types of art work portraying people significant to U.S. history.

Photographic Processes and Formats Represented

There are color dye coupler slides, dye diffusion transfer photoprints, and silver gelatin photonegatives and photoprints.

Other Materials Represented

The office also contains accession records, correspondence, newspaper clippings, and xerographic copies of photographs.

Access and Usage Policies

Images of NPG holdings are more easily accessible in the Office of Rights and Reproductions. To use the Registrar's files, researchers must be accompanied by a staff member and should call or write in advance for an appointment and describe their research topic, the type of material that interests them, and their research aim.

Publication Policies

Copies of images of NPG accessioned objects must be obtained from the Office of Rights and Reproductions, NPG, Room 185, Smithsonian Institution, Washington, D.C., 20560, (202) 357-2791. To reproduce these images, researchers must obtain permission from the National Portrait Gallery and may also have to obtain permission from the copyright holder, which is not necessarily the Smithsonian Institution. The preferred credit line is "Courtesy of the National Portrait Gallery, Smithsonian Institution." A specific donor credit and the photographer's name, if known, also should appear.

PG·8

NPG Registrar's Accession Files

Dates of Photographs: 1962–Present

Collection Origins

The Registrar's Office created the collection to document all accessioned objects in the holdings of the National Portrait Gallery (NPG) for collections management purposes. Photographers represented include Lowell Kenyon, Eugene Mantie, and Rolland White.

The photographs have appeared in the following: National Portrait Gallery. *National Portrait Gallery, Smithsonian Institution, Permanent Collection Illustrated Checklist.* Washington, D.C.: Smithsonian Institution Press, 1987. 2) National Portrait Gallery. *National Portrait Gallery, Smithsonian Institution, Permanent Collection of Notable Americans* [CD-ROM version]. Cambridge, Massachusetts: ABT Books, Inc., 1991. See the *Collection Origins* section of *PG·3* for information on where to purchase these items and a description of the CD-ROM database.

Physical Description

There are 15,000 photographs including color dye coupler slides, dye diffusion transfer photoprints, and silver gelatin photonegatives and photoprints. Other materials include accession records, correspondence, newspaper clippings, and xerographic copies of photographs.

Subjects

The photographs reproduce NPG accessioned art objects in many media including drawings, graphic prints, paintings, photographs, and sculptures portraying men and women significant to the history of the United States.

The photographs portray presidents of the United States and other political figures including Dean G. Acheson, Samuel Adams, William Jennings Bryan, Ralph Bunche, John C. Calhoun, Henry Clay, DeWitt Clinton, Jefferson Davis, Stephen A. Douglas, Edward Everett, Benjamin Franklin, Alexander Hamilton, John Hancock, Alger Hiss, Samuel Houston, Harold Ickes, Robert M. La Follette, Fiorello La Guardia, Liliuokalani, Henry Cabot Lodge, Thomas Paine, Adlai Stevenson, Charles Sumner, William M. (*A.K.A.* Boss) Tweed, and Daniel Webster. Chief Justices of the Supreme Court and other jurists portrayed include Louis D. Brandeis, Clarence Darrow, Learned Hand, Oliver Wendell Holmes, Jr., Thurgood Marshall, and Levi Woodbury.

Actors portrayed include Ethel Barrymore, Humphrey Bogart, Edwin Thomas Booth, Charles Chaplin, James Dean, Edwin Forrest, Paul Robeson, Gloria Swanson, and Rudolph Valentino. Dancers portrayed include Isadora Duncan, Katherine Dunham, Michio Ito, and Ruth St. Denis. Other entertainers portrayed include William F. (*A.K.A.* Buffalo Bill) Cody, Al Jolson, Emmett Kelly, and Bill Pickett. Artists portrayed include Alexander Calder, George Catlin, Aaron Douglas, Arshile Gorky, Childe Hassam, Edward Hopper, George Inness, Yasuo Kuniyoshi, Jacob A. Lawrence, Morris Louis, Man Ray, Georgia O'Keeffe, Horace Pippin, Hiram Powers, Raphael Soyer, Edward Steichen, Alfred Stieglitz, Andy Warhol, Benjamin West, Edward Weston, James Abbott McNeill Whistler, and William Zorach.

Musicians and singers portrayed include Marian Anderson, Louis Armstrong, Irving Berlin, Duke Ellington, Stephen C. Foster, Woody Guthrie, W.C. Handy, Roland Hayes, Mahalia Jackson, Fritz Kreisler, Huddie Ledbetter (*A.K.A.* Leadbelly), Jenny Lind, Charlie Parker, Lillian Russell, Arnold Schoenberg, Bessie Smith, John Philip Sousa, Leopold Stokowski, and Igor Stravinsky.

Activists, reformers, and revolutionaries portrayed include Jane Addams, Susan B. Anthony, Mary McLeod Bethune, John Brown, Carrie Chapman Catt, Eugene V. Debs, Frederick Douglass, W.E.B. Du Bois, William Lloyd Garrison, Emma Goldman, Samuel Gompers, James Weldon Johnson, Martin Luther King, Jr., John L. Lewis, Lucretia C. Mott, Robert Dale Owen, Rosa Parks, A. Philip Randolph, Elizabeth Cady Stanton, Lincoln Steffens, Sojourner Truth, and Harriet Tubman.

Writers portrayed include James Agee, Sherwood Anderson, W.H. Auden, James Baldwin, Joel Barlow, William Cullen Bryant, Pearl S. Buck, Samuel Clemens (*A.K.A.* Mark Twain), James Fenimore Cooper, Countee Cullen, E.E. Cummings, John Dos Passos, Max Eastman, Ralph Waldo Emerson, F. Scott Fitzgerald, Horace Greeley, Zane Grey, Ernest Hemingway, Langston Hughes, Zora Neale Hurston, Aldous Huxley, Washington Irving, Robinson Jeffers, Henry Wadsworth Longfellow, Edna St. Vincent Millay, Eugene O'Neill, Edgar Allan Poe, Ezra Pound, Will Rogers, Carl Sandburg, Isaac Bashevis Singer, Gertrude Stein, John Steinbeck, Harriet Beecher Stowe, Bayard Taylor, Henry David Thoreau, James Thurber, Jean Toomer, Margaret Walker, Walt Whitman, and Tennessee Williams. Historians and philosophers portrayed include George Bancroft, Van Wyck Brooks, and John Dewey.

American Indians portrayed include Goyathlay (*A.K.A.* Geronimo), Hinmaton-Yalaktit (*A.K.A.* Chief

Joseph), Little Crow the Younger, Mahpina Luta *(A.K.A.* Red Cloud), Pocahontas, Se-Quo-Yah, Tatanka Yotanka *(A.K.A.* Sitting Bull), and Tecumseh.

Other portraits include businessmen such as Andrew Carnegie, James Fisk, Henry Ford, Andrew W. Mellon, J. Pierpont Morgan, Julius Rosenwald, and Cornelius Vanderbilt; criminals such as John Wilkes Booth, Jesse James, and Harry Longbaugh *(A.K.A.* The Sundance Kid); explorers such as Davy Crockett, John C. Frémont, Meriwether Lewis, and Zebulon Pike; inventors and scientists such as Jean L.R. Agassiz, Alexander Graham Bell, George Washington Carver, Thomas A. Edison, Albert Einstein, Robert H. Goddard, Joseph Henry, Samuel F.B. Morse, and J. Robert Oppenheimer; military figures such as Pierre G.T. Beauregard, Benjamin F. Butler, George A. Custer, George Dewey, Nathaniel Green, Robert E. Lee, Douglas MacArthur, Robert E. Peary, Matthew C. Perry, John J. Pershing, Winfield Scott, William T. Sherman, and Anthony Wayne; religious figures such as Henry Ward Beecher, Joseph Smith, and Brigham Young; and sports figures such as Joe Louis, Jackie Robinson, and Babe Ruth.

There are also photographs of accessioned art works in the NPG's holdings being created or viewed. Images include Aaron Copland sitting for his portrait with artist Marcos Blahove, Lyndon B. Johnson sitting for his portrait with artist Jimilu Mason, and an unidentified woman standing with a self-portrait of Thomas Hart Benton.

Arranged: Alphabetically by subject.

Captioned: Files with accession number, artist, and sitter.

Finding Aid: 1) National Portrait Gallery. *National Portrait Gallery, Smithsonian Institution, Permanent Collection Illustrated Checklist.* Washington, D.C.: Smithsonian Institution Press, 1987. 2) National Portrait Gallery. *National Portrait Gallery, Smithsonian Institution, Permanent Collection of Notable Americans* [CD-ROM version]. Cambridge, Massachusetts: ABT Books, Inc., 1991. (Information on where to purchase these items and a description of the CD-ROM database are given in the *Collection Origins* section of *PG.3.*) 3) Computer-generated indexes arranged by accession number; artist; execution date; location; medium or object class (drawing, miniature, painting, sculpture, and silhouette); subject; and subject's occupation. The indexes list accession number, artist, execution date, object class, and subject. There are also additional indexes for African Americans and the Meserve Collection.

Restrictions: Researchers must make an appointment in advance and be accompanied by a staff member. Duplicates of these photographs can be viewed more easily at the Office of Rights and Reproductions, where prints may also be ordered. Contact Pamela Kirschner, Manager, the Office of Rights and Reproductions, NPG, Room 185, Smithsonian Institution, Washington, D.C., 20560, (202) 357-2791.

PG

Office of Rights and Reproductions

Office of Rights and Reproductions
National Portrait Gallery
Smithsonian Institution
Washington, D.C. 20560
Pamela Kirschner, Manager
(202) 357-2791
Hours: Monday–Friday, 10 a.m.–5 p.m.

Scope of the Collection

There is one photographic collection with approximately 9,100 photographs.

Focus of the Collection

The photographs document National Portrait Gallery (NPG) holdings including accessioned and study objects. Objects shown include drawings, graphic prints, paintings, photographs, sculptures, and other types of art work portraying significant people in U.S. history, as well as some related artifacts.

Photographic Processes and Formats Represented

There are color dye coupler photonegatives, phototransparencies, and slides and silver gelatin photonegatives and photoprints.

Other Materials Represented

None.

Access and Usage Policies

To locate images of objects in the NPG collections, researchers should first consult the following guides: 1) National Portrait Gallery. *National Portrait Gallery, Smithsonian Institution, Permanent Collection Illustrated Checklist.* Washington, D.C.: Smithsonian Institution Press, 1987. 2) National Portrait Gallery. *National Portrait Gallery, Smithsonian Institution, Permanent Collection of Notable Americans* [CD-ROM version]. Cambridge, Massachusetts: ABT Books, Inc., 1991. Information on where to purchase these items and a description of the CD-ROM database are given in the *Collection Origins* section of *PG·3*. Photoprints of images listed may be ordered from the Office of Rights and Reproductions, National Portrait Gallery, Smithsonian Institution, Washington, D.C., 20560.

Publication Policies

Researchers must obtain written permission from the National Portrait Gallery and may also have to obtain permission from the copyright holder, which is not necessarily the Smithsonian Institution. For further information, write to the Office of Rights and Reproductions, NPG, Smithsonian Institution, Washington, D.C., 20560. The preferred credit line is "Courtesy of the National Portrait Gallery, Smithsonian Institution." The artist's name should appear, as well as any required copyright notices.

PG·9

NPG Office of Rights and Reproductions Holdings Photograph Files

Dates of Photographs: 1968–Present

Collection Origins

Office of Rights and Reproductions staff created the collection to document National Portrait Gallery (NPG) holdings, including permanent and study collection objects. Museum objects are photographed when they are acquired and after they have received conservation treatment. Photographers represented include K.B. Basseches, Eugene Mantie, and Rolland White. Photographs of permanent accessions appear in the NPG checklist and CD-ROM database, described in the *Collection Origins* field of *PG·3*.

Physical Description

There are 9,100 photographs including color dye coupler photonegatives, phototransparencies, and slides and silver gelatin photonegatives and photoprints.

Subjects

The images are photographic reproductions of art objects, such as drawings, graphic prints, paintings, photographs, and sculpture, in the NPG's holdings including permanent objects, study collection objects, and *Time* Collection portraits (see *PG·5*).

People portrayed include Dean G. Acheson, Jane Addams, James Agee, Louis Armstrong, Alexander Graham Bell, Louis D. Brandeis, William Jennings Bryan, Ralph Bunche, John C. Calhoun, Andrew Carnegie, George Washington Carver, Henry Clay, Clarence Darrow, Jefferson Davis, Eugene V. Debs, John Dewey, Stephen A. Douglas, Duke Ellington, Ralph Waldo Emerson, Henry Ford, Arshile Gorky, Zane Grey, Childe Hassam, Hinmaton-Yalaktit *(A.K.A. Chief Joseph)*, Oliver Wendell Holmes, Jr., Samuel Houston, Zora Neale Hurston, Harold Ickes, Jesse James, Al Jolson, Martin Luther King, Jr., Robert M.

La Follette, Fiorello La Guardia, Robert E. Lee, Jenny Lind, Man Ray, Thurgood Marshall, Eugene O'Neill, Robert Dale Owen, Thomas Paine, Rosa Parks, Edgar Allan Poe, Paul Robeson, Jackie Robinson, Will Rogers, Joseph Smith, Edward Steichen, Adlai Stevenson, Leopold Stokowski, Charles Sumner, Sojourner Truth, Walt Whitman, and Tennessee Williams.

Artists whose work is reproduced include Ansel Adams, Peggy Bacon, Richmond Barthe, Mathew Brady, Alexander Calder, Miguel Covarrubias, Currier and Ives, Jo Davidson, Charles Fenderich, Aline Fruhauf, Philippe Halsman, Russell Hoban, Roy Lichtenstein, Man Ray, Soss Melik, Charles Willson Peale, Winold Reiss, Augustus Saint-Gaudens, Napolean Sarony, Gilbert Stuart, Carl Van Vechten, and Samuel Johnson Woolf. Non-portrait objects depicted include books, cartoons, documents, furniture, maps, medals, and political memorabilia.

Arranged: In two series by type of collection, then by format, then alphabetically by sitter. 1) Permanent and study collections. 2) *Time* collection.

Captioned: With the art object's accession number, date, medium, and size; artist's name and life dates; credit line; and sitter's name and life dates.

Finding Aid: 1) National Portrait Gallery. *National Portrait Gallery, Smithsonian Institution, Permanent Collection Illustrated Checklist.* Washington, D.C.: Smithsonian Institution Press, 1987. 2) National Portrait Gallery. *National Portrait Gallery, Smithsonian Institution, Permanent Collection of Notable Americans* [CD-ROM version]. Cambridge, Massachusetts: ABT Books, Inc., 1991. (Information on where to purchase these items and a description of the CD-ROM database are given in the *Collection Origins* section of *PG·3*.) 3) Computer-generated indexes arranged by accession number; artist; medium or object class (drawing, miniature, painting, sculpture, and silhouette); subject; and subject occupation. The indexes list accession number, artist, execution date, object class, and subject.

Restrictions: Researchers should first consult the National Portrait Gallery, Smithsonian Institution, Permanent Collection Illustrated Checklist or the CD-ROM database. Photoprints of images listed may be ordered by writing Pamela Kirschner, Manager, Office of Rights and Reproductions, NPG, Smithsonian Institution, Washington, D.C., 20560, (202) 357-2791.

SG

ARTHUR M. SACKLER GALLERY

Milo C. Beach, Director

The Arthur M. Sackler Gallery (ASG) collects, exhibits, publicizes, and researches the arts of China, Japan, the Near East, and southern Asia. ASG collections feature art works made of bronze, ceramics, gold, ink, jade, lacquer, paper, silk, silver, and stone, in such forms as books (including bindings, calligraphy, and illuminations), graphic prints, manuscripts (including calligraphy and illuminations), paintings (including screens, scrolls, and wall paintings), and sculptures.

The core collection was acquired by Brooklyn-born publisher, philanthropist, and pioneering biological psychiatrist Arthur M. Sackler (1913–1987) over 32 years of collecting Asian art. In 1982 Sackler gave the Smithsonian Institution 1,000 masterworks of Asian and Near Eastern art, as well as $4 million for the construction of a new museum. Opened to the public in September 1987, the ASG forms part of the Quadrangle, an underground educational, museum, and research complex on the Mall composed of the ASG, Freer Gallery of Art, National Museum of African Art, and S. Dillon Ripley International Center.

Dedicated to the advancement of the scholarly understanding and public knowledge of the arts, cultures, religions, and societies of Asia, the Arthur M. Sackler Gallery sponsors international exhibits, publications (including the journal *Asian Art*), public lectures, scholarly seminars, and research programs.

The ASG library, shared with the Freer Gallery of Art, includes 55,000 volumes of monographs and serials, 800 rare books, and a 53,000-image slide collection. The library also administers an archives, which contains manuscript collections, personal papers, photographic collections, and expeditionary records of archaeologists, art historians, and scholars of Asia and the Near East.

In addition to the library and archives, the ASG shares its administration, staff, and other research facilities with the Freer Gallery of Art (see separate section). Many of the photograph collections contained in the Freer Gallery of Art were created jointly with ASG staff.

SG

Photography Laboratory

Photography Laboratory
Arthur M. Sackler Gallery and Freer Gallery of Art
Smithsonian Institution
Washington, D.C. 20560
John G. Tsantes, Photography Department
(202) 357-2029
Hours: Monday–Friday, 10 a.m.–5 p.m.

Scope of the Collections

There are two collections with approximately 22,550 images. Note: Six related collections housed in the Photography Laboratory, containing 77,400 images, are described in the Freer Gallery of Art. See *FG·58* through *FG·63* for more information.

Focus of the Collections

The photographs document Arthur M. Sackler Gallery Art holdings, both accessioned and unaccessioned. Objects illustrated include items from the Far East including China, Japan, Korea, and Tibet (now Xizang); India and Indo-China; and the Near East including Asia Minor, Byzantium (now Istanbul, Turkey), Egypt, Iraq, Persia (now Iran), and Syria, dating from prehistory to the present. Objects depicted include calligraphy, graphic prints, manuscripts, metalwork, paintings, pottery, and sculptures.

Photographic Processes and Formats Represented

There are color dye coupler photonegatives, photoprints, phototransparencies, and slides and silver gelatin photonegatives and photoprints.

Other Materials Represented

The Photography Laboratory also contains videotapes.

Access and Usage Policies

The collections are open to the public for research by appointment only. The registrar's database serves as a finding aid to the accessioned objects collections. Photographic copies of unrestricted images must be arranged through the Museum Shop, which determines the charge.

Publication Policies

Researchers must obtain permission from the appropriate Arthur M. Sackler Gallery staff member to reproduce a photograph and may also have to obtain permission from the copyright holder, which is not necessarily the Smithsonian Institution. Each reproduction must bear the credit line "Courtesy of the Arthur M. Sackler Gallery, Smithsonian Institution," as well as the accession number and any additional information required by the Gallery.

Copies of photographs may be ordered by contacting Laveta Emory, Supervisor, Mail Order Department, Gallery Shop, ASG, Smithsonian Institution, Washington, D.C., 20560. Those wishing to publish an image must complete a Permission Request Form, obtained from the Rights and Reproductions Office, ASG, Smithsonian Institution, Washington, D.C., 20560, (202) 786-2088. All permissions to publish are for one-time use, only for the publication specified, and may not be sold or transferred. A copy of the publication must be sent gratis to the ASG library. No ASG images may be cropped, overprinted with type, or altered in any way without prior written approval from the Gallery.

SG·1

ASG Accessioned Objects Photograph Collection

Dates of Photographs: 1982–Present

Collection Origins

The Photography Laboratory staff of the Arthur M. Sackler Gallery (ASG) created the collection to document all accessioned objects in the Sackler's holdings. Staff photographers represented include Jeffrey Crespi, James T. Hayden, Kim Nielsen, Ray Schwartz, Bernard Shoper, and John G. Tsantes.

Some of the photographs have appeared in the museum's journal, *Asian Art,* and the following books: 1) Thomas Lawton. *Asian Art in the Arthur M. Sackler Gallery: The Inaugural Gift.* Washington, D.C.: The Gallery, 1987. 2) Thomas W. Lentz. *Timur and the Princely Vision: Persian Art and Culture in the Fifteenth Century.* Washington, D.C.: Smithsonian Institution Press, 1989. 3) Glenn D. Lowry and Susan Nemazee. *A Jeweler's Eye: Islamic Arts of the Book from the Vever Collection.* Washington, D.C.: Smithsonian Institution Press, 1987.

Physical Description

There are 16,300 photographs including color dye coupler photonegatives, photoprints, phototransparencies, and slides and silver gelatin photonegatives and photoprints.

Subjects

The photographs document accessioned objects in the Arthur M. Sackler Gallery. Objects shown include Chinese bronzes, calligraphy, jade items, lacquerware, and paintings; Indian and Persian bookbindings, calligraphy, illuminations, manuscripts, and paintings; Japanese ceramics and graphic prints; ancient Near Eastern ceramics and metalwork; and south Asian ceramics, stonework, and wood sculpture.

Arranged: By object's accession number.

Captioned: With object's accession number.

Finding Aid: Registrar's database, listing object's accession number, country of origin, date, and medium.

Restrictions: No.

SG·2

ASG Loans Photograph Collection

Dates of Photographs: 1982–Present

Collection Origins

Arthur M. Sackler Gallery (ASG) Photography Laboratory staff created the collection to document unaccessioned Asian art objects that form part of the Sackler holdings or that are on loan to the Sackler for exhibit or study purposes. Unaccessioned items include Gallery holdings of unknown origins, as well as objects belonging to Arthur M. Sackler that were not donated to the ASG. Staff photographers represented include Jeffrey Crespi, James T. Hayden, Kim Nielsen, Ray Schwartz, Bernard Shoper, and John G. Tsantes.

Physical Description

There are 6,250 photographs including color dye coupler phototransparencies and slides and silver gelatin photonegatives and photoprints.

Subjects

The photographs document unaccessioned Asian art objects that have been loaned to the Arthur M. Sackler Gallery or are held there for other reasons. Objects documented include Chinese calligraphy, paintings, and sculptures, as well as ceramics, graphic prints, manuscripts, metalwork, and sculpture from Japan, the Near East, and south Asia, dating from prehistory to the present.

Arranged: In five series according to purpose, then chronologically. 1) Sackler Study Collection (objects owned by the Gallery, but not accessioned). 2) Sackler Long-Term Loan Collection. 3) Sackler Exhibition Loan Collection. 4) Sackler Research Loan Collection (objects sent for research). 5) Sackler Master Loan Collection (objects owned by Arthur M. Sackler but not donated to the museum).

Captioned: With date and series.

Finding Aid: No.

Restrictions: Available for research only. No reproductions may be made.

Creators Index

The Creators Index lists individuals and groups who produced or assembled images in Smithsonian Institution photographic collections. Creators include photographers, studios, distributors, manufacturers, researchers, donors, artists, and collectors. Collection names or titles also are listed in this index because they sometimes provide the only existing clues to the collection's origins.

All creators' names appearing in the *Collection Origins* field of this volume are listed in this index. Since this book is not an item-level survey, some photographers and studios whose work is represented in the Smithsonian art museums may not appear in the text. The names of the photographers who are listed were checked against the following authorities:

William L. Broecker, ed. *International Center of Photography Encyclopedia of Photography.* New York: Crown Publishers, Inc., 1984.

Turner Browne and Elaine Partnow. *Macmillan Biographical Encyclopedia of Photographic Artists and Innovators.* New York: Macmillan Publishing Company, 1983.

Gary Edwards. *International Guide to Nineteenth-Century Photographers and Their Works.* Boston, Massachusetts: G.K. Hall & Co., 1988.

James Enyeart, ed. *Decade by Decade: Twentieth-Century American Photography.* Boston: Bullfinch Press, Little Brown and Company, 1988.

Andrew H. Eskind and Greg Drake, eds. *Index to American Photographic Collections.* Boston, Massachusetts: G.K. Hall & Co., 1990.

William S. Johnson. *Nineteenth-Century Photography: An Annotated Bibliography, 1839–1979.* Boston, Massachusetts: G.K. Hall & Co., 1990.

Ross J. Kelbaugh. *Directory of Maryland Photographers: 1839–1900.* Baltimore, Maryland: Historic Graphics, 1988.

Carl Mautz. *Checklist of Western Photographers: A Reference Workbook.* Brownsville, California: Folk Image Publishing, 1986.

Colin Naylor. *Contemporary Photographers.* Chicago, Illinois: St. James Press, 1988.

Oregon Historical Society. *Union Guide to Photograph Collections in the Pacific Northwest.* Portland: Oregon Historical Society, 1978.

Christopher Seifried, ed. *Guide to Canadian Photographic Archives.* Ottawa, Canada: Public Archives of Canada, 1984.

Photographers are listed alphabetically by surname. Photographers associated with a studio may be listed under both the studio name and their personal name. Corporate creators are listed in strict alphabetical order. For example, "A. Leimgruber and Company" is listed under "A" rather than under "L," although there is a cross-reference from "Leimgruber" to "A. Leimgruber and Company."

Information in parentheses following a name is generally a fuller form of the same name. Cross-references beginning with the instruction *See* indicate alternate forms of the same name that are used for indexing. *See also* references indicate additional names under which related information may be found.

Individuals shown in a photograph are listed in the subject index, as are the names of the artists whose work is reproduced in the photographs. If photographer Ron Mom took a photograph of an Ansel Adams exhibit, "Mom, Ron" would appear in the creator's index, while "Adams, Ansel: exhibits" would appear in the subject index.

Researchers unable to find a creator's name should check for possible pseudonyms or alternative spellings. (These are provided when known.) Next, check the names of related studios, employers, or organizations.

The collection codes indicate the location of the collection entry within the volume. For example, *CH·2* indicates that the reader should check the second collection report within the section on the Cooper-Hewitt Museum (*CH*). Other collection codes are *AF* for the National Museum of African Art, *AM* for the National Museum of American Art, *FG* for the Freer Gallery of Art, *HM* for the Hirshhorn Museum and Sculpture Garden, *HO* for the Office of Horticulture, *PG* for the National Portrait Gallery, and *SG* for the Arthur M. Sackler Gallery.

Forms and Processes Index

The Forms and Processes Index lists examples of physically distinct types of photographic formats (size, shape, and configuration of an image); processes (final image material, binder, base, and production process); techniques (specific manipulative procedures for obtaining visual effects in a variety of processes); and modifiers (additional information on format, process or technique, when available). The index also includes other audio-visual formats, such as audiotapes, microfilm, motion-picture film, videodiscs, and videotapes, when they form part of a Smithsonian photographic collection.

The index contains cross-references to assist researchers with minimal knowledge of photographic processes and formats. For example, all photoprint processes and formats discovered in Smithsonian art bureaus are listed under their individual process and format names as well as under "photoprints." Major headings are off-set to the left, with subheadings placed alphabetically beneath them in outline format.

Describing photographic processes is a challenge, since thousands of process variants exist. In this volume, processes are described with as much of the following information as possible: 1) final image material; 2) binder; 3) image format or configuration; 4) base (not noted if a photoprint is on paper or if a photonegative or phototransparency is on film, as these are the routine or default values); 5) DOP or POP (developing-out-print or printing-out-print); 6) chemical process variant; 7) trade name; and 8) other descriptive or technical details. Descriptive elements 4 through 8 are enclosed within parentheses, for example, "silver gelatin photoprint (DOP chloride Velox gaslight paper)."

On occasion, vernacular or generic descriptive process terms (such as tintypes and ambrotypes) are used if they provide an adequate description. Use of the phrases "photoprints," "photonegative," and "phototransparencies" is based on the descriptive standards found in the following publication: Elisabeth Betz Parker and Helena Zinkham. *Descriptive Terms for Graphic Materials: Genre and Physical Characteristic Headings.* Washington, D.C.: Library of Congress, 1986. In addition, project staff generated an in-house glossary of photographic terms culled from 28 source publications. Limited quantities of this glossary are available to researchers who write the Smithsonian Institution Archives, Photographic Survey Project, A&I 2135, 900 Jefferson Drive, S.W., Washington, D.C., 20560. Many of the terms in this glossary have since appeared in the following publication: *Art and Architecture Thesaurus.* New York: Oxford University Press, 1990.

Researchers unable to find a process, format, or other physical description term should check alternative spellings and both broader and narrower variant terms.

Collection codes indicate the location of the collection entry within the volume. For example, *CH·2* indicates that the reader should check the second collection report within the section on the Cooper-Hewitt Museum *(CH).* Other collection codes are *AF* for the National Museum of African Art, *AM* for the National Museum of American Art, *FG* for the Freer Gallery of Art, *HM* for the Hirshhorn Museum and Sculpture Garden, *HO* for the Office of Horticulture, *PG* for the National Portrait Gallery, and *SG* for the Arthur M. Sackler Gallery.

Subject Index

The Subject Index provides topical access to the Smithsonian photographic collections, which include documentation of decorative and fine arts in many media (architecture, drawings, furniture, graphic prints, paintings, photomechanical prints, photography, sculpture, and textiles) and other forms of material culture (buildings, cave temples, commercial products, lighting devices, markets, museums, ships, and tools); geographical places (continents, cities, countries, and regions both contemporary and historical); peoples (associations, castes, corporations, culture groups, nationalities, and organizations); occupations (actors, architects, artists, farmers, labor leaders, politicians, and soldiers); activities (dancing, eating, farming, painting, and sculpting); and events (ceremonies, exhibits, parades, and visits). Index terms also include photographic genres (cityscapes, landscapes, narrative works, portraits, still lifes, and waterscapes) and topics (agriculture, education, and music).

Many of the collections include accessioned "fine arts" and historical photographs, archaeological research and travel photographs, advertising and fashion imagery, artists' source images used to create paintings, and files documenting the museums' holdings.

The source terminology for the index came both from the photographic documentation itself and from a series of published sources. Broad terms used for index entries and cross-references were taken from the following publications: Elizabeth Betz Parker and Helena Zinkham. *L.C. Thesaurus for Graphic Materials: Topical Terms for Subject Access.* Washington, D.C.: Library of Congress, 1987. *Art and Architecture Thesaurus.* New York: Oxford University Press, 1990. Specific or technical language was standardized using the following sources:

African Art

African Arts 1967–1977. Index. Los Angeles: African Studies Center, University of California, 1977.

African Arts 1977–1982. Index. Los Angeles: African Studies Center, University of California, 1982.

Historical Atlas of Africa. Cambridge: Cambridge University Press, 1985.

Marshall Ward Mount. *African Art: The Years since 1920.* Bloomington: Indiana University Press, 1973.

Museums in Africa: A Directory. Munich: German Africa Society, 1970.

Warren M. Robbins and Nancy Ingram Nooter. *African Art in American Collections: Survey 1989.* Washington, D.C.: Smithsonian Institution Press, 1989.

Frank Willet. *African Art.* New York: Praeger Publishers, 1973.

The World of Learning 1988. 38th Edition. London: Europa Publications Limited, 1987.

American and European Art

Matthew Baigell. *A History of American Painting.* New York: Praeger Publishers, 1971.

Peter Hastings Falk, editor. *Who Was Who in American Art.* Sound View Press, 1985.

Dorothy B. Gilbert, editor. *Who's Who in American Art.* New York: R.R. Bowker Company, 1970.

International Directory of Arts. Frankfurt: Art Address Verlag Muller GmbH & Co., 1988.

Bernard Karpel, editor. *Arts in America: A Bibliography.* Washington, D.C.: Smithsonian Institution Press, 1979.

William Kloss. *Treasures from the National Museum of American Art*. Washington, D.C.: Smithsonian Institution Press, 1985.

Russell Lynes. *More Than Meets the Eye: The History and Collections of Cooper-Hewitt Museum, the Smithsonian Institution's National Museum of Design*. Washington, D.C.: Smithsonian Institution Press, 1981.

Cynthia Jaffe McCabe. *The Golden Door: Artist-Immigrants of America, 1876–1976*. Washington, D.C.: Smithsonian Institution Press, 1976.

Barbara McNeil, editor. *Artist Biographies Master Index*. Detroit: Gale Research Company, 1986.

Glenn B. Opitz, editor. *Mantle Fielding's Dictionary of American Painters, Sculptors and Engravers*. 2nd edition. Poughkeepsie: Apollo, 1987.

Phyllis D. Rosenzweig. *The Thomas Eakins Collection of the Hirshhorn Museum and Sculpture Garden*. Washington, D.C.: Smithsonian Institution Press, 1977.

Smithsonian Year. 1974–1989. Washington, D.C.: Smithsonian Institution Press, 1975–1990.

Who's Who in American Art, 1989–1990. New York: Bowker, 1989.

Who Was Who In American Art. Madison, Connecticut: Soundview Press, 1985.

Asian Art

Jeannine Auboyer et al. *Oriental Art: A Handbook of Styles and Forms*. New York: Rizzoli International Publications, Inc., 1980.

Biographical Dictionary of Japanese Art. Tokyo: International Society for Educational Information, 1981.

Richard Bird. *General Index. The Heibonsha Survey of Japanese Art*, vol. 31. New York: John Weatherhill, Inc., 1980.

John D. Hoag. *Islamic Architecture*. New York: Harry N. Abrams, Inc., Publishers, 1977.

Margaret Medley. *A Handbook of Chinese Art*. New York: Harper & Row, Publishers, 1964.

Hugo Munsterberg. *Dictionary of Chinese and Japanese Art*. New York: Hacker Art Books, 1981.

Jagdish Saran Sharma. *Encyclopaedia Indica*. 2 vols. New Delhi: S. Chand & Company Ltd., 1981.

Margaret and James Stutley. *A Dictionary of Hinduism*. London and Henley: Routledge & Kegan Paul, 1977.

A Survey of Persian Art from Prehistoric Times to the Present. London: Oxford University Press, 1958.

Peter Swann. *Art of China, Korea, and Japan*. New York: Frederick A. Praeger, Inc., Publishers, 1963.

Photography

Turner Browne and Elaine Partnow, editors. *Macmillan Biographical Encyclopedia of Photographic Artists and Innovators*. New York: Macmillan Publishing Company, 1983.

Gary Edwards. *International Guide to Nineteenth-Century Photographers and Their Works*. Boston: G.K. Hall & Co., 1988.

James Enyeart, editor. *Decade by Decade: Twentieth-Century American Photography*. Boston: Bullfinch Press, Little Brown and Company, 1988.

George Walsh, Colin Naylor, and Michael Held, editors. *Contemporary Photographers*. New York: St. Martin's Press, 1982.

Culture Group Names

Art and Architecture Thesaurus. New York: Oxford University Press, 1990.

George Peter Murdock. *Outline of World Cultures*. New Haven, Connecticut: Human Relations Area Files, Inc., 1983.

Other Names

The American Heritage Dictionary. 2nd College Edition. Boston: Houghton Mifflin Company, 1982.

Guide to the Smithsonian Archives, 1983. Washington, D.C.: Smithsonian Institution Press. 1983.

National Portrait Gallery. National Portrait Gallery, Smithsonian Institution, Permanent Collection Illustrated Checklist. Washington, D.C.: Smithsonian Institution Press, 1987.

Who's Who in America. 41st ed., 1980–1981. Chicago: Marquis Who's Who, Inc., 1980.

Who Was Who in America. Vol. 1, 1897–1942. Chicago: A.N. Marquis Company 1943.

Who Was Who in America with World Notables. Index 1607–1981. Chicago: Marquis Who's Who, Inc., 1981.

Geographic Names

The Times Atlas of the World. 7th Comprehensive Edition. New York: Times Books, 1988.

Index entries followed by *See* refer the reader from an indexing term which is not used to a term that is used, for example, "Authors. *See* Writers." Index entries followed by *See also* refer the reader to another indexing term such as a synonym, antonym, related term, or narrower term, for example, "Executives. *See also* Businessmen."

To pull together all information on a single area, regardless of time period, geographical references are listed under the current country name and cross-referenced from non-current versions of the name used in the text, for example, "Persia. *See* Iran.

Information in parentheses after an index entry modifies or clarifies ambiguous or technical terms, for example, "Drawnwork (fabric)"; "Models (artists')";

"trenches (WW I)"; "*Country Road* (photograph)"; or "Smith (craft)." Author's names; exhibit sponsors; geographical locations of culture groups, cities, parks, and islands; common names of esoteric art objects; and other types of explanatory information appear in parentheses following the index term. Publication and art work titles are in italics. Titles of exhibits and slide sets are in quotes.

Researchers unable to find a particular term should check the cross-references. Variant terms, including broader and narrower terms, technical and popular terminology, and alternative spellings, should also be checked.

The collection codes indicate the location of the collection entry within the volume, for example, CH·2 indicates that the reader should check the second collection report within the section on the Cooper-Hewitt Museum *(CH)*. Other collection codes are *AM* for the National Museum of American Art, *FG* for the Freer Gallery of Art, *AS* for the Arthur M. Sackler Gallery, *HM* for the Hirshhorn Museum and Sculpture Garden, *HO* for the Horticulture Services Divsion, *AF* for the National Museum of African Art, and *PG* for the National Portrait Gallery.

Russia *(cont.)*
cityscapes, AF63; empress of, CH9; exhibits, AM10, HM6, HM7, HM9, HM10; landscapes, AF63; museums, AF63. *See also* U.S.S.R.; Uzbekistan.
"Russia, the Land, the People" (NMAA exhibit), AM10
Ruth, Babe, PG3, PG8
Ruth (Ruth Harding Thomson) (Samuel A. Murray painting), HM17
Rwanda (ancient African kingdom), AF51, AF56, AF74; art objects, AF8; mission, AF56. *See also* Burundi; Ruanda; Ruanda-Urundi.
Ryan, Anne: art works by, HM1
Ryder, Albert Pinkham: art works by, AM2–AM4, AM12, AM14, FG16, FG58, FG65, FG69, HM14; exhibits, AM10; portraits of, AM7, PG3
Ryūei, Momoda: art works by, FG1

S.A. Maxwell & Co.: art works by, CH18
Sable antelopes, AF67. *See also* Gazelles.
Sackler, Arthur M., FG59. *See also* Arthur M. Sackler Gallery.
Saddle accessories, FG23
"Safe and Secure: A World of Design in Locks and Keys" (CH exhibit), CH20
Safes, CH27. *See also* Keys; Locks; Toy banks.
Sagan, Carl, PG5
Sages (Japanese motif), FG57. *See also* Elders; Philosophers.
Sahara Desert, PG5
Said, Port (Egypt). *See* Port Said (Egypt).
Saigon (Vietnam), PG5
St. Bartholomew's Church, AM1
St. Denis, Ruth, PG3, PG8
St. Joseph (Missouri), AM1
St. Louis (Senegal), AF64
St. Mark's Church, AM1
St. Peter's Square (Vatican City), AM14. *See also* Vatican City.
Saint-Gaudens, Augustus: art works by, AM6, AM7, PG1, PG9; exhibit, PG7; portraits of, AM7, FG19
"Saint-Mémin" (NPG exhibit), PG7
Saints (iconography), CH10, CH22. *See also* Angels; Icons; Madonnas; Reliquaries.
Saitō Sharaku. *See* Sharaku, Saitō.
Sakharov, Andrei, PG5
Salampasu (African people): art objects, AF19
Sales. *See* Bazaars; Buying and selling; Market scenes; Merchants; specific products; specific vendors (Ice vendors).
Salesmen, AF5, AF33, AM1, CH22, FG30, FG37, FG45, HO3. *See also* Bazaars; Buying and selling; Cloth sellers; Coconut vendors; Fish vendors; Horse dealers; Ice vendors; Ivory trade; Market scenes; Merchants; Shoppers.
Salisbury, Frank: art works by, AM7
Salk, Jonas E., PG3
Sallah (Islamic festival), AF14

Salon des Refusés. *See* specific artists (Edouard Manet, Claude Monet, James Abbott McNeil Whistler).
Salt Lake City (Utah): Hopi mesas, AM13
Samaras, Lucas: art works by, HM1, HM8, HM11, PG8; portraits of, HM11
Samarkand (Uzbekistan, U.S.S.R.), FG22, FG23
Sāmarrā (Iraq), FG23
Samburu (African people), AF17, AF50
Samplers (embroidery), CH14, CH15; exhibits, CH20. *See also* Embroidered pictures; Mourning pictures.
"Samuel Murray: The Hirshhorn Museum and Sculpture Garden Collection" (HMSG exhibit), HM7
San (African people), AF54
San Francisco (California), AM1; De Young Memorial Museum, FG27; Golden Gate Bridge, AM1; Golden Gate Park, HO2
Sand, George, CH9
Sand paintings, AF27
Sandals, AF25. *See also* Accessories; Costume.
Sandburg, Carl, PG3, PG8
Sandcastings. *See* Casting.
Sande (women's secret society), AF4, AF21, AF24, AF71
Sandoz, Gustav: art works by, CH24
Sandoz, Mari, PG3
Sangha (Mali), AF4
Sangu (African people): art objects, AF32
Sansō Collection (Japanese paintings), FG9
Santa Clara, Church of. *See* Church of Santa Clara (Assisi, Italy).
Santa Cruz (California), AM1
Santa Fe (New Mexico), AM1
Santa Monica (California): J. Paul Getty Museum, HM3
"Santos" (NMAA exhibit), AM10. *See also* Ceremonial objects; Reliquaries.
Sao (African people): art objects, AF21
São Paulo biennial exhibits, AM12
Saora (culture group of India), FG37
"Sara Roby Collection" (NMAA exhibit), AM10
Sardinia (Italy), CH9
Sargent, John Singer: art works by, AM2–AM5, AM12, FG58, FG65, FG69, HM1, HM3, HM8, HM12, PG1; portraits of, PG3
Sarnoff, David, PG3
Sarony, Napolean: art works by, PG9; portraits of, PG3
Satanic masks, PG5. *See also* Demons; Devils.
Saturn (planet), PG5
"Saul Steinberg" (HMSG exhibit), HM7
Savage, W. Lee: art works by, HM8
Savannahs (Zaire), AF29. *See also* Grassfields (Cameroon).
Saw mills, AF58. *See also* Forests; Wood objects.

Scandinavia, CH15, CH20. *See also* Denmark; Finland; Norway; Sweden.
"Scandinavian Modern 1880–1980" (CH exhibit), CH20
Scarabs (talisman), FG23
Scarification, AF15, AF26, AF38, AF51, AF59, AF60, AF74. *See also* Body adornment; Body painting; Tattoos.
Scarves, CH15. *See also* Hats.
Schattenstein, Nikol: art works by, AM7
Schenck, Franklin L., HM11
Schley, Winfield S., PG3
Schmidt, Helmut H.W., PG5
Schoenberg, Arnold, PG8
Scholars, AF41, FG45. *See also* Classes (education); Lectures; Reading; Seminars; Students; Writers; specific individuals (George Bancroft, Myron Bement Smith).
Scholar's inkscreens, FG27. *See also* Writing, implements.
Schongauer, Martin: art works by, CH10
School of Paris. *See* specific art schools.
School of Visual Arts: posters, CH20
Schoolchildren, AF54, HM11, HM17, PG5. *See also* Classes (education); Education; Lectures; Reading; Scholars; Schools; Seminars; Studying.
Schools, AF26, AF36, AF37, AF56, AF58, AF60, AF71, FG30. *See also* Classes (education); Colleges; Education; Lectures; Schoolchildren; Seminars; Universities; specific schools (Art Students League, Cooper Union, School of Visual Arts); specific universities.
Schooners, AM1
The Schreiber Brothers (Thomas Eakins painting), HM18
Schulenberg, Friedrich von der. *See* Von der Schulenberg, Friedrich.
Schurz, Carl: exhibits, PG7; portraits of, PG3
Schwachheim, Baroness (Russia), CH5
Schweitzer, Gertrude: art works by, AM7
Schwob, Guy: art works by, CH24
Scientific equipment. *See* Scientific instruments.
Scientific instruments, CH22. *See also* Tools.
Scientists, PG1, PG3, PG5, PG7–PG9. *See also* Anthropologists; Archaeologists; Astronomers; Biologists; Botanists; Chemists; Engineers; Geologists; Inventors; Midwives; Naturalists; Nurses; Physicians; Physicists; Zoologists; specific individuals.
Sconces, CH1. *See also* Lighting devices.
Scopes Monkey Trial: exhibits, PG7.
Scotland, CH7; Hunterian Art Gallery (University of Glasgow), FG51. *See also* Great Britain.
Scott, Winfield, PG3, PG8
Scrapbooks. *See* Albums.

Selected Photographs from the
Collections at the National Museum
of African Art, National Museum of
American Art, Cooper Hewitt
Museum, Freer Gallery of Art and
Arthur M. Sackler Gallery, Hirshhorn
Museum and Sculpture Garden,
Office of Horticulture, and National
Portrait Gallery

*Note: Captions in quotations appear on the
photograph or were provided by Smithsonian
Institution collection custodians.*

Wilhelm Schneider. "Funeral of Nzong Nzüe in Weh, Cameroon." 1935. Silver gelatin photoprint. Wilhelm Schneider Collection (AF·60). NMAfA photoprint #137.

Keystone View Company. "Kikuyu women with water vessels (gourds) beside village store houses, East Africa; Kenya; 10551." Ca. 1910. Silver gelatin stereograph. Keystone-Underwood Stereograph Collection (AF·33). Keystone View Company #62.

Anon. "Vanniers (basket weavers), Kibira Forest, Burundi." Ca. 1910. Collodion gelatin photoprint (POP). Pères Blancs (White Fathers) Mission Photograph Collection (AF·56). NMAfA photoprint #53.

Casimir d'Ostoja Zagourski. "Ruanda, the King's Mother; the Tutsi Queen Mother Radegonde, Nyaramvuga, Kigali, Rwanda. Series 2, L'Afrique qui disparait!" 1926. Silver gelatin postcard. Casimir d'Ostoja Zagourski Photograph Collection (AF·74). NMAfA photoprint #100.

Augustus Browning. "Kaduna, Nigeria, West Africa." 1965. Silver gelatin photoprint. Augustus Browning Photograph Collection (AF·14). Unnumbered.

Anon. "Mwambutzu; Mwami Mwambutsa, the grandson of Mwezi (king) Gisabo and Ririkumutima. Born in 1912, he ruled Burundi from December 16, 1915, to July 7, 1966. Burundi." Ca. 1920. Collodion gelatin photoprint (POP). Pères Blancs (White Fathers) Mission Photograph Collection (AF·56). NMAfA photoprint #11.

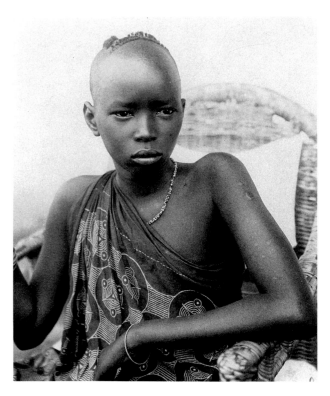

Bonnevide Photographic Studio. "Portrait of a young Wolof man with gold and bead jewelry, Senegal." Ca. 1890. Albumen carte-de-visite. NMAfA Cartes-de-Visite Collection (AF·46). Unnumbered.

*Agbenyega Adedze.
"Cloth market in
Agbozume, Ghana."
1989. Color dye
coupler slide.
Agbenyega Adedze
Slide Collection (AF·5).
NMAfA photoprint
#93.*

*Anon. "Two Zulu war-
riors photographed in a
studio setting, South Af-
rica." Ca. 1880. Albu-
men photoprint.
NMAfA Miscellaneous
Vintage Photograph
Collection (AF·49).
Unnumbered.*

Eliot Elisofon. "Kente cloth weaver; two pairs of heddles used to construct the ground weave and decorative patterns; Asante peoples; Kumasi area, Ghana." 1971. Silver gelatin photoprint. Eliot Elisofon Field Photograph Collection (AF·20). NMAfA photoprint #VIII-45, 31.

Eliot Elisofon. "Kuba King Mbop Mabiinc maKyen, who ruled 1939–1969, flanked by royal drums; Mushenge, Zaire." 1947. Silver gelatin photoprint. Eliot Elisofon Field Photograph Collection (AF·20). NMAfA photoprint #22923, P-6, 2.

Eliot Elisofon. "Tundandi, dance of boys after circumcision, led by masked dancer; Lulua peoples; Bashila Kasonge, Zaire." 1947. Silver gelatin photoprint. Eliot Elisofon Field Photograph Collection (AF·20). NMAfA photoprint #22923, C-4, 23.

Eliot Elisofon. "Ntore elite dance performed by Tutsi warriors; Goma, Zaire." 1972. Color dye coupler slide. Eliot Elisofon Field Photograph Collection (AF·20). NMAfA photoprint #F4 Tts, 28 EE 72.0.

Edward Weston. "Pepper." 1930. Silver gelatin photoprint. American Art Photograph Collection (AM·1). Accession #1985.56. Copyright 1981, Center for Creative Photography, Arizona Board of Regents.

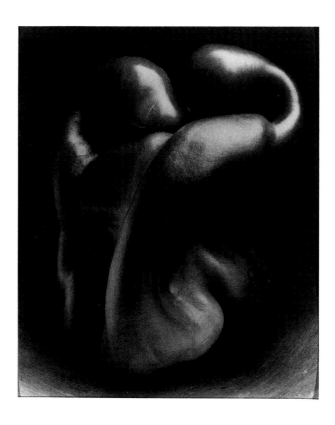

Andrea Modica. "Treadwell, New York." 1987. Palladium photoprint. American Art Photograph Collection (AM·1). Accession #1989.42.3.

Danny Lyon. "Llanito, New Mexico." 1971. Silver gelatin photoprint. American Art Photograph Collection (AM·1). Accession #1983.63.916.

Lois Conner. "Covered Bridge." 1982. Platinum photoprint. American Art Photograph Collection (AM·1). Accession #1984.18.2.

Jerry Uelsmann. "Untitled." 1982. Silver gelatin photoprint. American Art Photograph Collection (AM·1). Accession #1984.10.3.

Todd Webb. "On the Portal at the Ghost Ranch, New Mexico." 1959. Silver gelatin photoprint. American Art Photograph Collection (AM·1). Gift of Todd Webb. Copyright 1959, Todd Webb.

Lee Friedlander. "Peter Exline, Spokane." 1970. Silver gelatin photoprint. American Art Photograph Collection (AM·1). Accession #1984.97.3. Copyright 1970, Lee Friedlander.

Berenice Abbott. "Normandie, North River, Manhattan, from Pier 88." 1938. Silver gelatin photoprint. American Art Photograph Collection (AM·1). Accession #1983.16.7. Gift of George McNeil.

Weegee. "Untitled (In the Movie House Watching Haunting of Hill House*)." 1950. Silver gelatin photoprint. American Art Photograph Collection (AM·1). Accession #1988.45.*

Ansel Adams. "Spanish-American Woman." 1937. Silver gelatin photoprint. American Art Photograph Collection (AM·1). Accession #1977.74.5. Courtesy of the Trustees of the Ansel Adams Publishing Rights Trust.

Peter A. Juley or Paul P. Juley. "From left to right: Lucile Blanch, Diego Rivera, Arnold Blanch, Frida Kahlo." Ca. 1930s. Copy silver gelatin photonegative from original Juley silver gelatin photonegative on nitrate. Peter A. Juley & Son Collection (AM·7). Negative #J0033257.

Peter A. Juley or Paul P. Juley. "Thomas Hart Benton." Ca. 1930s–1940s. Copy silver gelatin photonegative from original Juley silver gelatin photonegative on nitrate. Peter A. Juley & Son Collection (AM·7). Negative #J0001255.

Peter A. Juley or Paul P. Juley. "William Robinson Leigh." Ca. 1920s–1930s. Copy silver gelatin photonegative from original Juley silver gelatin photonegative on nitrate. Peter A. Juley & Son Collection (AM·7). Negative #J0010849.

Peter A. Juley or Paul P. Juley. "José de Creeft" Ca. 1930s. Copy silver gelatin photonegative from original Juley silver gelatin photonegative on nitrate. Peter A. Juley & Son Collection (AM·7). Negative #J0001461.

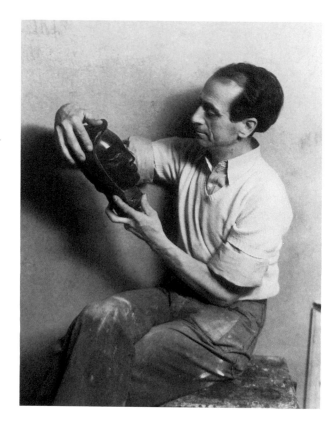

Attributed to Paul P. Juley. "Grant Wood." Ca. 1940s. Silver gelatin photoprint from original Juley silver gelatin photonegative on acetate. Peter A. Juley & Son Collection (AM·7). Negative #J0002303.

Peter A. Juley or Paul P. Juley. "Paul Manship." Ca. 1930s–1940s. Silver gelatin photoprint from original Juley silver gelatin photonegative on acetate. Peter A. Juley & Son Collection (AM·7). Negative #J0085168.

Myra Albert (Wiggins). "Augustus Saint-Gauden's Class at Art Students League." 1892–1893. Silver gelatin photoprint from silver gelatin photonegative on nitrate. Peter A. Juley & Son Collection (AM·7). Negative #J0107741.

Carleton Eugene Watkins. "Nevada Fall, Yosemite, California." 1861–1866. Albumen photoprint. Drawings and Prints Carleton Eugene Watkins Yosemite Photograph Collection (CH·13). Accession #1976-23-16.

E. & H.T. Anthony & Co. "War Views, the 5th Penn. Cavalry on the Battle Field of Oct. 29th, 1864, near Richmond, Virginia." 1864. Albumen stereograph. Drawings and Prints Stereograph Collection (CH·11). Accession #1950-75-15. Gift of Mrs. George Linzboth.

Anon. "George Sand." Ca. 1870. Albumen carte-de-visite. Drawings and Prints Photograph Albums Collection (CH·9). Accession #1956-38-10(23).

Aimé DuPont. "Sarah Bernhardt as L'Aiglon." N.D. Platinum photoprint. Drawings and Prints Fine Arts Photograph Collection (CH·5). Accession #1953-187-2. Gift of W.E. Dyer.

James H. Hyde and Mr. and Mrs. Byne. "Abydos. A Good Cold Luncheon—December 5, 1924." 1924. Silver gelatin photoprint. Drawings and Prints Photograph Albums Collection (CH·9). Accession #1948-125-2(5)R.

Dornac. "Whistler in
his studio." Ca. 1893.
Albumen photoprint.
Charles Lang Freer
Papers (FG·19).
Unnumbered.

Alfred Stieglitz. Katha-
rine Nash Rhoades. Ca.
1915. Platinum photo-
print. Charles Lang
Freer Papers (FG·19).
Unnumbered.

Leon Colson. Henri Vever painting. Ca. 1890s. Albumen photoprint. Henri Vever Papers (FG·54). Unnumbered.

Hsün-ling. "Tz'u-hsi with ladies in snow-filled garden." 1903–1905. Silver gelatin copy photoprint from silver gelatin dry plate photonegative. Tz'u-hsi, Empress Dowager of China, 1835–1908, Photographs (FG·50). Negative #SC-GR-259.

Hsün-ling. "Tz'u-hsi standing before throne." 1903–1905. Silver gelatin copy photoprint from silver gelatin dry plate photonegative. Tz'u-hsi, Empress Dowager of China, 1835–1908, Photographs (FG·50). Negative #SC-GR-251.

Carl Whiting Bishop. "Longwang Cave Temple, Hubei Province." 1923. Silver gelatin photoprint. Carl Whiting Bishop Papers (FG·4). Negative #722.2-6.

Utai. "Caves at Lung-men." 1910. Silver gelatin photoprint. Charles Lang Freer Papers (FG·19). Negative #2.

Anon. "Exterior of the Hōmyōin Temple at the time of the memorial service for Ernst Fenollosa." 1909. Silver gelatin photoprint. Charles Lang Freer Papers (FG·19). Unnumbered.

T. Morita. "Interior of the the Hōmyōin Temple during the Fenellosa memorial." 1909. Silver gelatin photoprint. Charles Lang Freer Papers (FG·19). Unnumbered.

Anon. "Kandarya Temple from southwest, Khajuraho." Ca. early 20th century. Silver gelatin photoprint. Milton S. Eisenhower South Asian Architecture Photograph Collection (FG·11). Unnumbered.

Ernst Herzfeld. "Samarra shrine and mosque." Ca. 1911– 1920. Silver gelatin photoprint. Ernst Herzfeld Papers (FG·23). Unnumbered.

Anon. "Herzfeld and main gate to Persepolis." Ca. 1932–1935. Silver gelatin copy photoprint from silver gelatin dry plate photonegative. Ernst Herzfeld Papers (FG·23). Negative #406.

Antoin Sevruguin. "Baghi Shah bridge." Ca. 1880s–1920s. Silver gelatin copy photoprint from silver gelatin dry plate photonegative. Myron Bement Smith Collection (FG·45). Negative #46.11.

Antoin Sevruguin. "Train station on gas street, Tehrān." Ca. 1890–1910. Silver gelatin photoprint. Myron Bement Smith Collection (FG·45). Unnumbered.

Anon. *"The Maude Bridge, Baghdad." Ca. 1920s–1940s. Silver gelatin photoprint. Ernst Herzfeld Papers (FG·23). Unnumbered.*

Antoin Sevruguin. *"Nur Mahmud and his family." Ca. 1890–1910. Silver gelatin photoprint. Myron Bement Smith Collection (FG·45). Unnumbered.*

Antoin Sevruguin. *"Ice vendor." Ca. 1880s–1920s. Silver gelatin photoprint. Myron Bement Smith Collection (FG·45). Unnumbered.*

Antoin Sevruguin. "Carpet makers." Ca. 1880s–1920s. Silver gelatin photoprint. Myron Bement Smith Collection (FG·45). Unnumbered.

Antoin Sevruguin. "Dervish." Ca. 1890–1910. Silver gelatin photoprint. Myron Bement Smith Collection (FG·45). Unnumbered.

Antoin Sevruguin. "Naser al-Din Shah on Peacock Throne." Ca. 1885–1890. Silver gelatin copy photoprint from collodion wet plate photonegative. Myron Bement Smith Collection (FG·45). Negative #31.1.

Antoin Sevruguin. "Wrestlers of the traditional Zurkhana, or House of Power." Ca. 1880s–1920s. Silver gelatin copy photoprint from silver gelatin dry plate photonegative. Myron Bement Smith Collection (FG·45). Negative #26.6.

Antoin Sevruguin. "Abi Garm of Damawand: tents in landscape." Ca. 1880s–1920s. Silver gelatin copy photoprint from silver gelatin dry plate photonegative. Myron Bement Smith Collection (FG·45). Negative #50.4.

Antoin Sevruguin. "Maneuvers." Silver gelatin copy photoprint from silver gelatin dry plate photonegative. Myron Bement Smith Collection (FG·45). Negative #52.11.

Thomas Eakins. "Samuel Murray." Ca. 1890. Platinum photoprint. HMSG Collection Archives Samuel A. Murray Scrapbooks A.K.A. Thomas Eakins Collection (HM·14). Negative #83.73.

Thomas Eakins. "Walt Whitman in Camden, New Jersey." Ca. 1891. Silver gelatin photoprint. HMSG Collection Archives Samuel A. Murray Scrapbooks A.K.A. Thomas Eakins Collection (HM·14). Negative #83.75.

*Thomas Eakins.
"Eakins's students at
the site of* The Swim-
ming Hole.*" 1883. Al-
bumen photoprint.
HMSG Collection
Archives Samuel A.
Murray Scrapbooks
A.K.A. Thomas Eakins
Collection (HM·14).
Negative #83.17.*

*Thomas Eakins.
"Marey Wheel photo-
graphs of unidentified
model, with notations."
1884. Albumen photo-
print. HMSG Collec-
tion Archives Samuel A.
Murray Scrapbooks
A.K.A. Thomas Eakins
Collection (HM·14).
Negative #83.59.*

Thomas Eakins. "Frank Hamilton Cushing." 1895. Cyanotype. HMSG Collection Archives Samuel A. Murray Scrapbooks A.K.A. Thomas Eakins Collection (HM·14). Negative #83.86.

Thomas Eakins. "Unidentified models in Greek costumes." Ca. 1883. Platinum photoprint. HMSG Collection Archives Samuel A. Murray Scrapbooks A.K.A. Thomas Eakins Collection (HM·14). Negative #83.103.

Thomas Eakins. "Mrs. Anna Kershaw." Ca. 1903. Platinum photoprint. HMSG Collection Archives Samuel A. Murray Scrapbooks A.K.A. Thomas Eakins Collection (HM·14). Negative #83.98.

Anon. "Luther Burbank." N.D. Silver gelatin slide. Office of Horticulture Photograph Collection (HO·3). Negative #91-7271.

Griffith & Griffith. "Children around Christmas tree." 1897. Albumen stereograph. Office of Horticulture Photograph Collection (HO·3). Negative #87-11092.

Underwood and Under-wood. "Little Alice, White Mountain Flower Girl." 1890s. Albumen stereograph. Office of Horticulture Photograph Collection (HO·3). Negative #87-905.

1543   Little Alice, White Mt. Flower Girl.

Susan Gurney. "Greenwood Cemetery, Brooklyn, New York." 1985. Color dye coupler slide. Office of Horticulture Photograph Collection (HO·3). Negative #91-7268.

George Clyde Fisher. "John Burroughs, 1837–1921, naturalist." 1918. Silver gelatin photoprint. NPG Curatorial Department Photography Collection (PG·3). Accession #NPG.78.100.

Isabel V. Lyon. "Mark Twain (Samuel Langhorne Clemens), 1835–1910, and Helen Adams Keller, 1880–1968." 1908. Silver gelatin photoprint from silver gelatin photonegative. NPG Curatorial Department Photography Collection (PG·3). Accession #NPG.79.163.

Anon. "Winfield Scott Hancock, 1824–1886 (center left), David Bell Birney, 1825–1864 (center right), and their staffs." 1862. Albumen photoprint. NPG Curatorial Department Photography Collection (PG·3). Accession #NPG.78.96

Lisette Model. "Louis Armstrong, 1900–1971, musician." 1950. Silver gelatin photoprint. NPG Curatorial Department Photography Collection (PG·3). Accession #NPG.82.138.

Garry Winogrand. "Diane Arbus, 1923–1971, photographer." 1969. Silver gelatin photoprint. NPG Curatorial Department Photography Collection (PG·3). Accession #NPG.84.74. Copyright 1984, the Estate of Garry Winogrand.

Sid Grossman. "Billie Holiday, 1915–1959, singer." Ca. 1948. Silver gelatin photoprint. NPG Curatorial Department Photography Collection (PG·3). Accession #NPG.87.44.

Berenice Abbott. "Frank Lloyd Wright, 1869–1959, architect." Ca. 1950. Silver gelatin photoprint. NPG Curatorial Department Photography Collection (PG·3). Accession #NPG.76.99. Copyright Commerce Graphics Ltd., Inc.

Paul Strand. "John Marin, 1870–1953, artist." 1930. Silver gelatin photoprint. NPG Curatorial Department Photography Collection (PG·3). Accession #NPG.82.99. Copyright 1971, Aperture Foundation Inc., Paul Strand Archive.

Benedict J. Fernandez. "Martin Luther King, Jr., 1929–1968, civil rights statesman." 1967. Silver gelatin photoprint. NPG Curatorial Department Photography Collection (PG·3). Accession #NPG.80.173. Copyright 1967, Benedict J. Fernandez.

Kay Bell Reynal. "Thomas Stearns Eliot, 1888–1965, poet." 1955. Silver gelatin photoprint. NPG Curatorial Department Photography Collection (PG·3). Accession #NPG.77.52.

André Kertész. "Alexander Calder, 1898–1976, artist." 1929. Silver gelatin photoprint. NPG Curatorial Department Photography Collection (PG·3). Accession #NPG.83.212. Copyright the Estate of André Kertész.

Henri Cartier-Bresson. "William Cuthbert Faulkner, 1897–1962, author." 1947. Silver gelatin photoprint. NPG Curatorial Department Photography Collection (PG·3). Accession #NPG.89.196. Copyright Henri Cartier-Bresson/Magnum Photos Inc.

Garry Winogrand. "John Fitzgerald Kennedy, 1917–1963, 35th president of the United States." 1960–1963. Silver gelatin photoprint. NPG Curatorial Department Photography Collection (PG·3). Accession #NPG.84.18. Copyright 1984, the Estate of Garry Winogrand.

Man Ray. "Gertrude Stein, 1874–1946, with Alice B. Toklas, 1877–1967." Silver gelatin photoprint. NPG Curatorial Department Photography Collection (PG.3). Accession #NPG.88.209. Copyright Gregory Browner, Man Ray Trust.

Edward S. Curtis. "Self portrait." 1899. Silver gelatin photoprint. NPG Curatorial Department Photography Collection (PG.3). Accession #NPG.77.49.

Anon. "Frederick Douglass, 1818–1895, abolitionist, statesman." Ca. 1850. Daguerreotype. NPG Curatorial Department Photography Collection (PG·3). Accession #NPG.80.21.

Alexander Gardner. "Abraham Lincoln, 1809–1865, 16th president of the United States [last portrait]." 1865. Albumen photoprint. NPG Curatorial Department Photography Collection (PG·3). Accession #NPG.81.M1.

Underwood and Underwood. "Christopher (Christy) Mathewson, 1880–1925, athlete." Ca. 1915. Silver gelatin photoprint. NPG Curatorial Department Photography Collection (PG·3). Accession #NPG.80.232.

Randall Studio. "Soujourner Truth, ca. 1797–1883, abolitionist." Ca. 1870. Silver gelatin photoprint from albumen photoprint. NPG Curatorial Department Photography Collection (PG·3). Accession #NPG.79.220.

José Maria Mora. "William Frederick Cody (Buffalo Bill), 1846–1917, showman." Ca. 1889. Albumen photoprint. NPG Curatorial Department Photography Collection (PG·3). Accession #NPG.77.155.

707 BROADWAY. N. Y.

John Swartz. "The Wild Bunch; seated, left to right: Harry Longbaugh (The Sundance Kid), ca. 1862–1909; Ben Kilpatrick (The Tall Texan), ?–1912; Robert LeRoy Parker (Butch Cassidy), ca. 1865–1909; standing, left to right: William Todd Carver (Bill), ?–1901; Harvey Logan (Kid Curry), ca. 1865–1903." 1900. Silver gelatin photoprint. NPG Curatorial Department Photography Collection (PG·3). Accession #NPG.82.66.

*Mathew Brady Studio.
"William Tecumseh
Sherman, 1820–1891,
Union general." Ca.
1865. Silver gelatin
copy photoprint from
collodion wet plate
photonegative. NPG
Curatorial Department
Photography Collection
(PG·3). Accession
#NPG.81.M177.*

*Clara E. Sipprell.
"Anna Eleanor Roose-
velt, 1884–1962, first
lady, stateswoman."
1949. Silver gelatin
photoprint. NPG Cura-
torial Department
Photography Collection
(PG·3). Accession
#NPG.82.158.*

Mathew Brady Studio. "Mathew Brady, 1823–1896, with Juliette Handy Brady and Mrs. Haggerty Brady." Ca. 1850. Daguerreotype. NPG Curatorial Department Photography Collection (PG-3). Accession #NPG.85.78.

Lusha Nelson. "Peter Lorre, 1904–1964, Actor." 1935. Silver gelatin photoprint. NPG Curatorial Department Photography Collection (PG-3). Accession #NPG.88.14.

*David Hume Kennerly.
"Ansel Adams, 1902–
1984, photographer,
conservationist." 1979.
Color dye bleach photo-
print (Cibachrome).
Time Collection (PG·5).
Accession #NPG.82.
TC58.*

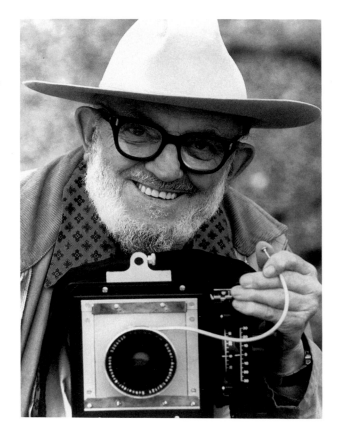

*Frank Cowan. "Hey-
wood (Woody) Allen,
1935–   , film director,
writer, actor." 1972.
Color dye bleach photo-
print (Cibachrome).
Time Collection (PG·5).
Accession #NPG.78.
TC200.*